F
Cape Coa

Candice Gianetti

Bran & Chris Gooding
July 1991

Fodor's Travel Publications, Inc
New York and London

Fodor's Cape Cod

Editor: Larry Peterson
Editorial Contributors: Suzanne Brown, Phil Joseph, Malcolm Wilson
Art Director: Fabrizio LaRocca
Cartographer: David Lindroth
Illustrator: Karl Tanner
Cover Photograph: David Lawrence/Stock Photos

Design: Vignelli Associates

About the Author

Candice Gianetti is a freelance writer and editor who lives in Martha's Vineyard.

Special Sales

MANUFACTURED IN THE UNITED STATES
OF AMERICA

10 9 8 7 6 5 4 3 2 1

Contents

Maps

Foreword

The author wishes to thank Nancy Wurlitzer of the Cape Cod Chamber of Commerce, Randi Vega of the Martha's Vineyard Chamber of Commerce, and Elizabeth Oldham of the Nantucket Chamber of Commerce for all of their help in putting together this guide.

While every care has been taken to ensure the accuracy of the information in this guide, the pasage of time will always bring change, and consequently the publisher cannot accept responsibility for errors that may occur.

All prices and opening times quoted here are based on information supplied to us at press time. Hours and admission fees may change, however, and the prudent traveler will avoid inconvenience by calling ahead.

Fodor's wants to hear about your travel experiences, both pleasant and unpleasant. When a hotel or restaurant fails to live up to its billing, let us know and we will investigate the complaint and revise our entries where the facts warrant it.

Send your letters to the editors of Fodor's Travel Publications, 201 E. 50th Street, New York, NY 10022.

Highlights'91 and Fodor's Choice

Highlights '91

Tourism is a $1 billion-a-year industry on Cape Cod, accounting for about 60% of the region's income; on Martha's Vineyard and Nantucket, three months of tourism sustain the economy throughout the rest of the year. Thus, the downturn in the state and national economies, which has forced many people to cut back on vacation spending, has been sorely felt here. In response, 1990 prices were kept pretty much at 1989 levels, and little rise for 1991 is predicted. On Nantucket, where the cost of eating out was a sore point with many tourists, restaurants began offering lower-priced prix-fixe or café menus.

Both Martha's Vineyard and Nantucket took steps to address a problem voiced by some visitors: an unfriendly attitude or downright resentment toward tourists on the part of some locals. Efforts to raise islanders' consciousness about the dynamics of a service economy, along with week-long workshops at the beginning of the summer for shop workers, police, and seasonal workers from off-island, are aimed at creating a more positive image of the islands.

The **Cape Cod Commission Act,** passed in 1990, has a more long-term goal: to control future development so that the Cape's special appeal—its natural setting—is not further eroded by unregulated and unthinking building and destruction of the environment.

The **Steamship Authority,** which runs ferries to the islands, has made its Woods Hole and Hyannis terminals totally accessible to the disabled and has equipped many of its vessels with elevators. It has also added more parking lots in Falmouth. On the Vineyard, **shuttle service** between the main towns has been extended (weekends only from fall through Christmas) in response to increased off-season tourism, to make getting around easier for visitors without cars.

Several Cape Cod museums have undergone changes over the past year or two. The **Cape Museum of Fine Arts,** which moved to new quarters in the Cape Playhouse complex in Dennis in summer 1990, now has much more space for both exhibitions and classes, as well as a 91-seat auditorium for films, lectures, and performance art. The **Donald G. Trayser Museum** in Barnstable reopened in 1990 after two years of renovation, bringing it back to its 1856 customhouse origins. **Brooks Academy,** Harwich's historical society museum, reopened in late 1990 after a year of renovation, having acquired an additional floor of display space when the town hall was moved out of the building. In Eastham, the **Salt Pond Visitor Center** of the Cape Cod National Seashore was revamped in 1989, including the addition of new exhibits.

More Cape changes: **Buzzards Bay** has revitalized its Main Street, with a new park and marina and renovated shops and restaurants. **Sealand** in Brewster was bought in 1989 by an educational organization and now, as the **Cape Cod Aquarium,** offers classes and lectures, along with marine mammal shows. The **Melody Tent** in Hyannis, which for 40 years has been bringing top-name entertainment to the Cape, changed owners in 1990 and has shifted its focus more toward music and comedy concerts and away from theater. Also new on the Cape are a **dinner train** offered by the Cape Cod Scenic Railroad and a **mystery dinner theater** at the Tara Hyannis Hotel.

In the arena of bed and board, Cape Cod got a new sports-theme restaurant, **Champions,** where the old Stromboli's used to be in Hyannis, and a very fine new bed-and-breakfast, the **Bacon Barn Inn** in Barnstable. The **Iyannough Hills Motor Lodge** in Hyannis was renovated in 1990 and is now a **Hampton Inn.**

The most dramatic news in accommodations, however, is the feverish activity on the part of the First Winthrop Corporation. Having acquired two long-established but run-down hotels on Martha's Vineyard at auction in 1989, as well as two hotels and wharfside cottages on Nantucket in 1987 (along with 158 other commercial properties on Nantucket Town's waterfront), the real-estate firm set about making major renovations. On the Vineyard, a multimillion-dollar renovation of the century-old **Harbor View Hotel** in Edgartown was completed in 1990. The interior was stripped down to the studs and most everything is new, including a Victorian gazebo and turrets. Further work, including new landscaping, will be completed for the 1991 season, as will a thorough redo of the **Kelley House,** the less-upscale sister property nearby. Both will be open year-round. On Nantucket, First Winthrop's **White Elephant** hotel and its luxury arm, **The Breakers,** received similar down-to-the-studs renovation. The **Harbor House** got a major face-lift, with all new furnishings and a redesigned restaurant, and the **Wharf Cottages** got a crisp new nautical look.

From other quarters, Martha's Vineyard got a welcome new bed-and-breakfast, the **Outermost Inn,** surrounded by moorland adjacent to the Gay Head Cliffs and the lighthouse. A longtime favorite B&B, the **Thorncroft Inn,** has complemented its antiques with a very modern touch: hookups for computers in every room. (Also acknowledging the modern age is the Harbor View, which has included fax machines in its suites and laptop connections in all rooms.)

The **Dukes County Historical Society** acquired a Greek Revival building adjacent to its complex in Edgartown and now has much more exhibit space; displayed for the first time in 1990 was its Wampanoag Indian artifact collection, including tools and arrowheads. **Lawry's** seafood restaurant in Edgartown has become self-service, to lower costs, and added an ice cream bar. The **Wharf Restaurant** now becomes a small dance club (with DJ music) when it closes for the season in fall, bringing dancing to off-season Edgartown.

On Nantucket, the old **Peter Foulger Museum** was dissolved in 1990 to give additional space to the Nantucket Historical Association Research Center for its extensive collection of marine and island research materials. The artifacts were distributed among the historical society's other properties on the island, including the **Museum of Nantucket History**, created in 1989 in the old Macy Warehouse. Meanwhile, the **Oldest House**—a 1686 saltbox that was severely damaged by lightning in 1987—reopened for the 1990 season after $1 million in renovations.

Also, the Nantucket high school got a big **new indoor pool,** which is open to the public.

Fodor's Choice

No two people will agree on what makes a perfect vacation, but it's fun and helpful to know what others think. We hope you'll have a chance to experience some of Fodor's Choices yourself in Cape Cod. For detailed information about each entry, refer to the appropriate chapter.

Festivals and Events

Daffodil Festival, Nantucket (April)

Blessing of the Fleet, Provincetown (June)

Barnstable County Fair, Hatchville (July)

Martha's Vineyard Agricultural Fair, West Tisbury (August)

Cranberry Festival, Harwich (September)

Christmas (or Shopper's) Stroll, Nantucket (December)

Special Moments

Sunset rides through the Provincetown dunes by Jeep or horseback

Watching fireworks from the Oak Bluffs green, Martha's Vineyard

A community sing at the Oak Bluffs Camp Ground, Martha's Vineyard

Glimpsing Nantucket town as you approach by ferry

Lunch in the rose garden of Chanticleer, Nantucket

Stargazing from Nantucket's Loines Observatory

Sights

Bright purple cranberries floating on the flooded bogs just before harvest, Cape Cod and Nantucket

The old New England scene of the waterwheel-powered Dexter Gristmill on Shawme Pond in Sandwich

Hallet's Store, a century-old drugstore in Yarmouth Port

The marsh life at Bass Hole Boardwalk, Yarmouth Port

Harbor seals off Race Point in winter, Provincetown

Whales breaching alongside your whale-watch boat

The candy-colored Victorian cottages of the Oak Bluffs Camp Ground, Martha's Vineyard

The sea captains' homes and tidy gardens of Edgartown, Martha's Vineyard

Nantucket's cobblestone streets and historic architecture

The moors of Nantucket in fall

"Three Bricks," Nantucket

Museums

Heritage Plantation, Sandwich

Cape Cod Museum of Natural History, Brewster

Julia Wood House, Falmouth

Old Atwood House and Museums, Chatham

Dukes County Historical Society, Edgartown, Martha's Vineyard

Whaling Museum, Nantucket

Viewpoints

From the Pilgrim Monument, Provincetown, of the town and surrounding waters

From Province Lands Visitor Center observation deck, for a 360-degree panorama of dunelands and ocean

From Nobska Light, Woods Hole, of the Elizabeth Islands and Martha's Vineyard across the sound

From Chatham Light, of the "Chatham Break"

From Scargo Hill, Dennis, of the lake and town below and of ocean and bay beyond

From Gay Head Cliffs, Martha's Vineyard, of the cliff striations and the Elizabeth Islands across the sound

From First Congregational Church, Nantucket, for the best view of Nantucket's moors, ponds, streets, and lighthouses

Nature Areas

Cape Cod National Seashore

Nickerson State Park, Brewster

Wellfleet Bay Wildlife Sanctuary, South Wellfleet

Felix Neck, Martha's Vineyard

Eel Point, Nantucket

Coatue-Coskata-Great Point, Nantucket

Gardens

Ashumet Holly Reservation, Falmouth

Heritage Plantation, Sandwich

Green Briar Nature Center, Sandwich

Beaches

Nauset Light, Coast Guard, and Race Point beaches on the Cape Cod National Seashore

Sandy Neck Beach, West Barnstable

Lucy Vincent Beach, Chilmark, Martha's Vineyard

South Beach, Martha's Vineyard

Surfside Beach, Nantucket

Eel Point, Nantucket

Shopping

The weekly flea market at the Wellfleet Drive-In Theatre

Farmer's markets on Martha's Vineyard

Farm stands everywhere

Route 6A on Cape Cod for crafts and antiques

Wellfleet, Provincetown, and Nantucket for art

Cape Cod Mall, Hyannis

Eldred's auction house, East Dennis

Rafael Osona auction house, Nantucket

Tree's Place, Orleans, for crafts and art

Scargo Pottery, Dennis

Impulse, Provincetown, for crafts

Lightship baskets on Nantucket

Nantucket-theme rugs by Claire Murray, Nantucket

Janis Aldridge on Nantucket for beautifully framed antique prints

Art Galleries

Long Point, Provincetown

Sweetgrass Gallery, Provincetown

Provincetown Art Association and Museum

Blue Heron Gallery, Wellfleet

Granary Gallery, Martha's Vineyard

Sherburne Gallery, Nantucket

Main Street Gallery, Nantucket

Taste Treats

Clam chowder at The Flume, Mashpee

Fried clams at Baxter's, Hyannis

Ice cream at Four Seas, Centerville

Cioppino at Roadhouse Cafe, Hyannis

Portuguese kale soup at Land Ho!, Orleans,
or The Moors, Provincetown

Fresh, sweet bay scallops in fall and winter

Dining

Chillingsworth, Brewster (*Very Expensive*)

Regatta of Falmouth (*Very Expensive*)

The Paddock, Hyannis (*Expensive*)

Dan'l Webster Inn, Sandwich (*Expensive–Moderate*)

The Flume, Mashpee (*Moderate*)

Up the Creek, Hyannis (*Moderate*)

Andrea's, Edgartown, Martha's Vineyard (*Expensive*)

Home Port, Menemsha, Martha's Vineyard (*Expensive*)

Lambert's Cove Country Inn, Martha's Vineyard
(*Expensive*)

Giordano's, Oak Bluffs, Martha's Vineyard (*Inexpensive*)

Chanticleer, Nantucket (*Very Expensive*)

Boarding House, Nantucket (*Expensive*)

American Seasons, Nantucket (*Expensive*)

Le Languedoc, Nantucket (*Expensive*)

Beach Plum Cafe and Bakery, Nantucket (*Moderate*)

The Brotherhood of Thieves, Nantucket (*Inexpensive*)

Quaker House, Nantucket (*Inexpensive*)

Lodging

Chatham Bars Inn, Chatham (*Very Expensive*)

Beechwood, Barnstable (*Expensive*)

Captain's House Inn, Chatham (*Expensive*)

Coonamessett Inn, Falmouth (*Expensive*)

Mostly Hall, Falmouth (*Moderate*)

Old Sea Pines Inn, Brewster *(Moderate–Inexpensive)*

Charlotte Inn, Edgartown, Martha's Vineyard
(Very Expensive)

Lambert's Cove Country Inn, West Tisbury,
Martha's Vineyard *(Expensive)*

Oak House, Oak Bluffs, Martha's Vineyard *(Expensive)*

Cliffside Beach Club, Nantucket *(Very Expensive)*

Wauwinet, Nantucket *(Very Expensive)*

Harbor House, Nantucket *(Expensive)*

Jared Coffin House, Nantucket *(Moderate–Expensive)*

76 Main Street, Nantucket *(Moderate)*

Ten Lyon Street Inn, Nantucket *(Moderate)*

Corner House, Nantucket *(Inexpensive–Moderate)*

Hawthorn House, Nantucket *(Inexpensive)*

Theater

Cape Playhouse, Dennis

Falmouth Playhouse

Monomoy Theater, Chatham

Barnstable Comedy Club

Vineyard Playhouse, Martha's Vineyard

Actors Theatre of Nantucket

Children's Activities

Pirate's Cove minigolf, South Yarmouth

Cape Cod Aquarium, West Brewster

Aqua Circus of Cape Cod, West Yarmouth

Water Wizz Water Park, Wareham

Windfarm Museum, Martha's Vineyard

Vineyard Playhouse children's events, Martha's Vineyard

Cape Cod, Martha's Vineyard, and Nantucket

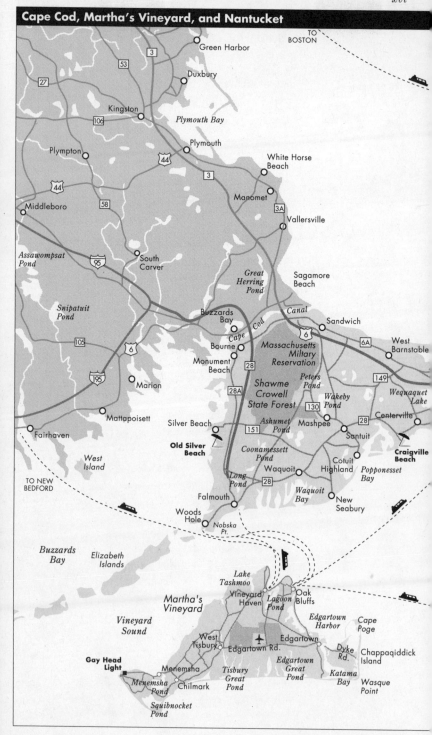

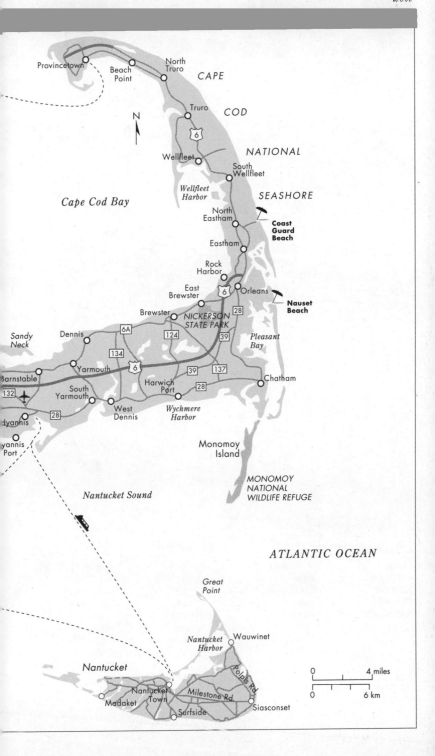

World Time Zones

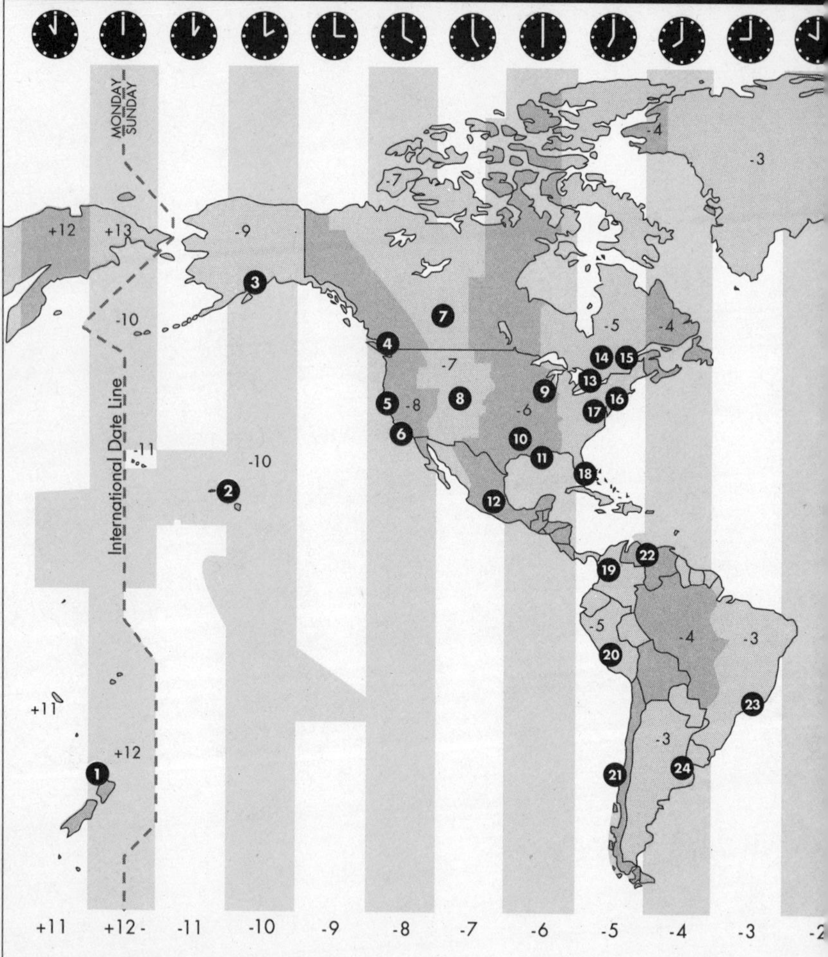

MONDAY
SUNDAY

International Date Line

+12 +13   -9

-10

-7

-11

-10

-5   -4

-3

-4

-7

-8

-6

+11

+12

3 Anchorage

7

4

5 **8**

6

14 **15**
13
9
17 **16**
10
11
18

2

12

19 **22**

20

23

1

21 **24**

-5

-4

-3

-3

+11   +12 -   -11   -10   -9   -8   -7   -6   -5   -4   -3   -2

Numbers below vertical bands relate each zone to Greenwich Mean Time (0 hrs.).
Local times frequently differ from these general indications,
as indicated by light-face numbers on map.

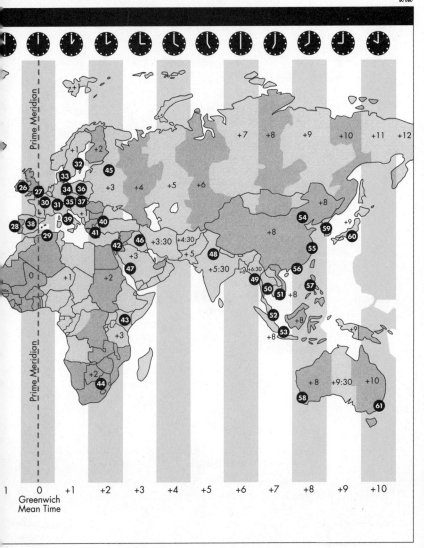

Introduction

The world to-day is sick to its thin blood for lack of elemental things," wrote Henry Beston in his 1928 Cape Cod classic *The Outermost House*, "for fire before the hands, for water welling from the earth, for air, for the dear earth itself underfoot." It is this that the Cape and its neighboring islands most have to offer an increasingly complex and artificial world: the chance to reconnect with elemental things. Walking along the shore, poking among the washed-up sea life or watching birds fish in the surf, listening to the rhythm of the waves, experiencing the mystery and tranquillity of night on the beach or the power of a storm on water—all this is somehow strengthening and life-affirming and utterly, satisfyingly real.

Cape Cod—a craggy arm of a peninsula 50 miles southeast of Boston—and its neighboring islands of Martha's Vineyard and Nantucket share their geologic origins as debris deposited by a retreating glacier in the last ice age. They also share a moderate coastal climate and a diversity of terrain that foster an equally diverse assortment of plant and animal life, some of which exist nowhere else in northern climes.

Barrier beaches (sandbars that protect an inner harbor from the battering of the ocean), such as Monomoy on the Cape and Coatue on Nantucket, are breeding and resting grounds for a stunning variety of shore and sea birds, and the marshes and ponds are rich in waterfowl. Georges Bank, just north of Provincetown, is a prime feeding grounds for whales and dolphins, and shallow sandbars are favorite playgrounds for harbor seals.

Among the flotsam and jetsam along the shores beachcombers find horseshoe crabs, starfish, sea urchins, sponges, jellyfish, coral, and a plethora of shells: white quahogs, elegant scallops, blue mussels, long straight razor clams, spiraling periwinkles, pointy turret shells, smooth round moon snails, conical whelks, rough-ridged oysters. (The best time to collect, by the way, is at low tide or after storms. Also check tidal pools and around jetties and wharf pilings.)

Much of the land, including a third of Nantucket's acreage and a quarter of the Vineyard's, is protected from development. Nature preserves encompassing pine forests, marshes, swamps, cranberry bogs, and many other varieties of terrain are laced with well-marked walking and bicycling trails. On Nantucket, acres of moorland are spread with a rough tapestry of gnarled scrub oaks, low-lying blueberry bushes, fragrant bayberry, bearberry, and heather (the last originally brought to Nantucket from Scotland by accident in a shipment of pine trees).

Thanks to the establishment of the Cape Cod National Seashore in 1961, one can walk for almost 30 miles along the Atlantic beach virtually without seeing a trace of human habitation—besides a few historic shacks in the dunes of Provincetown, or the lighthouses that stand watch over the Cape's dangerous shoals. Across dunes anchored by hearty poverty grass sprawl beach plums, pink salt-spray roses, and purple beach peas.

Through the creation of many National Historic Districts— in which change is kept to a minimum to preserve the historical integrity of the area—similar protection has been extended to the Cape and islands' oldest and loveliest manmade landscapes. One of the most important, as well as most visually harmonious, is along the Old King's Highway, where the Cape's first towns—Sandwich, Barnstable, and Yarmouth—were incorporated in 1639. Lining this treeshaded country road are simple saltboxes from the earliest days, fancier houses built later by prosperous sea captains, and the traditional Cape cottages, shingles weathered to a silvery gray, with soft pink roses spilling across them or massed over low split-rail fences. Here, too, are the whitesteepled churches, taverns, and village greens that savor of old New England, as well as some of the Cape's many windmills.

Practically the entire island of Nantucket is part of its historic district. A rigid enforcement of district guidelines has created a town architecturally almost frozen in time, and one of the world's great treasures. Among the neat clapboard and weathered-shingle houses that line its cobblestone streets and narrow lanes are former warehouses, factories, and mansions dating back to the golden age of whaling.

Most recently, Provincetown was designated a historic district, preserving for posterity its cheerful mix of tiny waterfront shops (former fish shacks) and everything from a 1746 Cape to a mansarded French Second Empire to an octagonal house.

Besides the districts, the Cape and islands preserve their past in a wealth of small museums—nearly every town has one—that document local history, often back to Indian days. (In 1620, when the Pilgrims first anchored at Provincetown, exploring the Cape before heading on to Plymouth, an estimated 30,000 Wampanoags lived on Cape Cod, as they had for thousands of years.) Often set in houses that are themselves historic, these museums provide a visual history of the lives of the English settlers and their descendants, including their economic pursuits: from farming, to the harvesting of salt, salt hay, and cranberries (still an important local crop), to fishing and whaling, to early tourism, which began as far back as the late 19th century.

The importance of whaling to the area—Nantucket was the world's premier whaling port in the early to mid-19th century, and it was a Yarmouth man who taught Nantucketers how—is reflected in the historical museums. The travels of the area's whaling and packet-schooner seamen and captains are illustrated with such items as antique nautical equipment, harpoons, charts, maps, journals, scrimshaw created during the often years-long whaling voyages, and gifts brought back from exotic ports for wives who had waited so patiently (those who *had* waited, that is—some women chose to go along with their husbands for the ride).

A number of museums have a specific historical focus—for example, Nantucket has a wonderful one dedicated to whaling. The area's first documented trading post has been re-created in Bourne on its original site. Provincetown and Nantucket have museums on the U.S. Life Saving Service. Brewster has a whole complex of exhibits on firefighting. Chatham has a train museum, Sandwich doll and car museums, Mashpee an Indian museum.

The economies of the Cape and the islands are extremely dependent on tourism, and most options in tourist facilities can be found. Lodgings range from no-frills guest houses and motels to antiques-and-lace bed-and-breakfasts to full-service resort hotels on the beach. Restaurants include rustic, nautical-motif fish houses as well as elegant gourmet restaurants (a specialty of Nantucket) and everything in between. Dining can be a romantic experience, with views of dramatic sunsets over water, or a gathering of family and friends at wharfside picnic tables to devour fried clams.

All three areas are noted for interesting shopping (for crafts, art, and antiques especially); for lots of theater, both small community groups and professional summer stock; and for plenty of recreational offerings that take advantage of the marine environment, including water sports, fishing charters, and even Jeep safaris to isolated beaches for surfcasting. All are also family oriented—especially the Cape, which has endless amusements to offer children beyond the ever-beckoning beach. There are also such typically New England entertainments as chowder suppers and clambakes.

Cape Cod is the area most suffering from overdevelopment. Massive growth in tourism in years past led to construction of tacky roadside motels, nightmare stretches of wall-to-wall tourist magnets along Route 28, and the megabuildup of Hyannis. Also, getting over the bridges that join the Cape to the mainland can be misery at peak weekend times in summer. But wise planners can avoid that problem, as they can avoid the built-up areas and stick to the many still-charming areas if they choose. Within its 70-mile span, the Cape offers a broad spectrum of vacation experiences: picturesque old New England towns, an extraordinary scientific community at Woods Hole, the frenetic shopping and people-watching former art colony of Provincetown, the tamer art-gallery town of Wellfleet, and quiet cottage communities with little more than a clam shack and a general store to divert one's attention from the beach.

Nantucket, about 12 miles by 3, is reached by plane or a two-hour ferry ride, and its remoteness appeals to those seeking escape. It has just the one town, plus a small beachside village of rose-covered cottages that once housed an actors' colony. Large tracts of undeveloped moorland and nature preserves give the island an open, breezy feel. It has long been a summer bastion of the quietly wealthy, who are likely to be seen dressed down to the hilt and tooling around on beat-up bicycles.

Martha's Vineyard, on the other hand, is known as the celebrity island, for its star summer residents in the arts and entertainment who participate in the annual Celebrity Hat Auction and other worthy and visible causes. Nantucketers tend to think of their sister island as glitzy, which it could be called only in comparison. About 20 miles by 10, the Vineyard offers more variety than Nantucket: its six towns range from a young and rowdy town of Victorian cottages to a rural New England village to an elegant, well-manicured town of sea captains' homes and flower gardens. The landscape, too, is more varied, including a 4,000-acre pine forest, rolling farmland, and dramatic clay cliffs.

Both islands are ringed with beautiful wide, sandy beaches, some backed with high or low dunes, others with moorland, others bordering marshes. Either can be profitably visited in a day trip from a Cape Cod base but will well repay a longer stay.

"The season" used to be strictly from Memorial Day to Labor Day, but the boundaries have blurred; many places now open in April or earlier and close as late as November, and a core remain open year-round. Unfortunately, most of the historic sites and museums, largely staffed by volunteers, still adhere to the traditional dates and so are inaccessible in the off-season.

Each of the seasons invites a different kind of visit. In summer, you have your choice of plunking down somewhere near a beach and never moving, filling your schedule with museums and activities, or combining the two in whatever mix suits you. In fall, the water may be warm enough for swimming as late as October, crowds are gone, and prices are lower. Turning foliage, though nothing like the dramatic displays found elsewhere in New England, is still an enjoyable addition to a fall visit; it reaches its peak around the end of October. Moors turn purple and gold and rust; burning bush along roadsides flames a brilliant red. Cranberries ripen to a bright burgundy color and are harvested by a method fascinating to watch. Trees around freshwater marshes, ponds, and swamps tend to color earlier and brighter; the red maple swamps, Beech Forest in Provincetown, and Route 6A from Sandwich to Orleans are particularly colorful spots.

Fall and winter are oyster and scallop season, and the restaurants that remain open feature a wide selection of dishes made with the freshly caught delicacies. Winter is a quiet time, when many tourist-oriented activities and facilities shut down, but prices are low and you can walk the beaches in often total solitude. For a quiet or romantic weekend getaway, country inns offer cozy rooms with canopy beds, where you can curl up before the fireplace after returning from a leisurely, candlelit dinner. The Chatham Bars Inn in Chatham offers theme weekends, such as wine tasting or swing dancing, that can make for a festive winter break. On Martha's Vineyard, the Harbor View Hotel also offers winter mystery and other theme weekends in attractive transportation-plus packages.

As for spring, it gets a bit wet, and on Nantucket expect a good dose of fog. Still, the daffodils come bursting up from roadsides, especially on Nantucket, and everything begins to turn green. By April, seasonal shops and restaurants begin to open, and locals again prepare for another summer.

1 Essential Information

Before You Go

Visitor Information

Cape Cod Chamber of Commerce (junction of Rtes. 6 and 132, Hyannis 02601, tel. 508/362–3225) will send free general information and a directory of accommodations. Let them know if you're interested in a particular town or activity; they will provide more detailed information or pass your request on to the local chambers, which also provide brochures.

Martha's Vineyard Chamber of Commerce (Box 1698, Vineyard Haven 02568, tel. 508/693–0085, telex 928 111) publishes an excellent free guidebook. The **Nantucket Chamber of Commerce** (Main St., Nantucket 02554, tel. 508/228–1700) puts out a thick directory of member services, as well as listings of events and lots of ads; for a copy, send $3.

In New York City, the **New England Vacation Center** (630 5th Ave., Concourse Shop, New York, NY 10111, tel. 212/307–5780) also provides information on Cape Cod and the islands.

The following offer free information on all of Massachusetts, including the Cape and islands:

Department of Environmental Management (Division of Forests and Parks, 100 Cambridge St., Boston 02202) has brochures and maps on state forests and parks.
Department of Food and Agriculture (100 Cambridge St., Boston 02202) has information on agricultural fairs and pick-your-own apple and strawberry farms.
Division of Fisheries and Wildlife (Field Headquarters, Westborough 01581) will send a freshwater fishing guide and information on fish and wildlife laws if you supply a stamped, self-addressed business-size envelope.
Massachusetts Office of Travel & Tourism (100 Cambridge St., 13th floor, Boston 02202, tel. 617/727–3201) puts out a guidebook, a calendar of events, a skiing brochure, a bed-and-breakfast guide, and a road map.

Tour Groups

If you want to see as much of Cape Cod as possible in a short time, then you might want to consider an escorted motorcoach tour. Group tours generally pack a lot of sightseeing into a relatively short time span, traversing the entire Cape in less than a week. This way, you're sure to hit all the traditional tourist spots and perhaps a few out-of-the-way places you might not be able to get to on your own. Keep in mind, though, that you can only spend as much time in one place as the tour itinerary allows. If freedom and flexibility are more important to you, pick up a map, decide where you want to go, plot a route, and experience Cape Cod on your own at a leisurely pace. Most major rental-car companies offer weekly rates.

When evaluating a tour, be sure to find out exactly what expenses are included (particularly tips, taxes, service charges, side trips, additional meals, and entertainment); ratings of all hotels on the itinerary and the facilities they offer; cancellation policies for both you and the tour operator; and, if you are traveling alone, the cost for a single supplement.

Listed below is a sampling of operators and packages to give you an idea of what is available. For additional resources, contact your travel agent or the Cape Cod Chamber of Commerce. Most tour operators request that bookings be made through a travel agent—there is no additional charge for doing so.

Brush Hill Tours (109 Norfolk St., Dorchester, MA 02124, tel. 617/287–1900 or, in MA, 800/343–1328) runs day trips to the Cape from Boston, Memorial Day–October, with stops in Provincetown, Sandwich, and Hyannis.

Casser Tours (46 W. 43rd St., New York, NY 10036, tel. 212/840–6500 or, outside NY, 800/251–1411) offers three- and four-day tours to the Cape and Newport, Rhode Island or New Bedford, Memorial Day–Columbus Day. Highlights are a Hyannis harbor cruise, Provincetown, a clambake, and an optional Boston excursion.

Cosmos Tourama, the budget affiliate of **Globus Gateway** (150 S. Los Robles Ave., Pasadena, CA 91101, tel. 818/449–0919 or 800/556–5454), combines Boston and Cape Cod, with stops in New York, New Haven, Plymouth, and Newport.

Country Squire Tours (668 Main St., Hyannis, MA 02601, tel. 508/771–6441 or 800/225–8051) offers three- to six-day tours to the Cape and islands, and longer packages including other New England destinations year-round.

Domenico Tours (751 Broadway, Bayonne, NJ 07002, tel. 800/554–8687) offers three- to five-day escorted tours April–October, including visits to Falmouth, Hyannis, the National Seashore, and Provincetown. Different packages add Plymouth, a whale watch, Boston, Nantucket, Martha's Vineyard, and/or Newport.

Gadabout Tours (700 E. Tahquitz Way, Palm Springs, CA 92262, tel. 619/325–5556) has an 11-day tour of New England that includes several days at the Cape.

Maupintour (Box 807, Lawrence, KA 66044, tel. 800/255–4266 or 913/843–1211) begins its tour in Boston, with stops in Lexington and Concord. On the Cape, sightseeing includes Sandwich, Brewster, and Nantucket.

Mayflower Tours (1225 Warren Ave., Downers Grove, IL 60515, tel. 312/960–3430) offers an eight-day tour of New England that includes several days on the Cape.

Talmage Tours (1223 Walnut St., Philadelphia, PA 19107, tel. 215/923–7100) gives you four days in Cape Cod and Martha's Vineyard during the spring and fall.

Tauk Tours (11 Wilton Rd., Westport, CT 06881, tel. 203/226–6911 or 800/468–2825) gives you six nights on the Cape, Martha's Vineyard, and Nantucket.

Package Deals for Independent Travelers

Amtrak (tel. 800/USA–RAIL; ask for Tour Desk) offers three-day "Cape Escape" packages that include hotels and transfers.

Tips for British Travelers

Visitor Information   The **U.S. Travel and Tourism Administration** (22 Sackville St., London W1X 2EA, tel. 071/439–7433) has information and brochures.

Passports and Visas   You need a valid 10-year passport to enter the United States (cost: £15 for a standard 32-page passport, £30 for a 94-page passport). Application forms are available from most travel agents and major post offices and from the Passport Office (Clive House, 70 Petty France, London SW1H 9HD, tel. 071/ 279–3434 for recorded information or 071/279–4000). You do not need a visa if you are visiting on either business or pleasure, are staying less than 90 days, have a return ticket, are traveling with a major airline (in effect, any airline that flies from the United Kingdom to the United States), and complete visa waiver form I791, which is supplied either at the airport of departure or on the plane. If you fail to comply with any one of these requirements or are entering the United States by land, you will need a visa. Apply to a travel agent or the **United States Embassy** (Visa and Immigration Department, 5 Upper Grosvenor St., London W1A 2JB, tel. 071/499–3443 for a recorded message or 071/499–7010). Visa applications to the U.S. Embassy must be made by mail, not in person. Visas can be given only to holders of 10-year passports, although visas in expired passports remain valid.

Customs Entering the United States, a visitor age 21 or older can bring in 200 cigarettes or 50 cigars or three pounds of tobacco; one U.S. quart of alcohol; and duty-free gifts to a value of $100. You may not bring in meat or meat products, seeds, plants, or fruit.

Returning to the United Kingdom, a traveler age 17 or older can take home: (1) 200 cigarettes or 100 cigarillos or 50 cigars or 250 grams of tobacco (if you live outside Europe these allowances are doubled); (2) one liter of alcoholic drink over 22% volume *or* two liters of alcoholic drink under 22% volume *or* two liters of fortified or sparkling wine; (3) two liters of still table wine; (4) 60 ml of perfume and 250 ml of toilet water; and (5) other goods to the value of £32.

Airports and Airlines There are no transatlantic flights directly to Cape Cod. Boston is the nearest city with an airport that handles international flights. To get from Boston to Cape Cod, *see* Arriving and Departing, below.

Flying time from all British airports is more than six hours on most flights, about four hours on the Concorde.

Three airlines fly to Boston from London Heathrow: **British Airways** (tel. 071/897–400), **Northwest** (tel. 0293/576955), and **TWA** (tel. 071/439–0707). Northwest also has four flights a week to Boston from Prestwick, near Glasgow in Scotland. There are no flights to Boston from London's Gatwick airport.

British travelers combining a trip to New England with a visit to New York should consider flying into New York's JFK airport or the Newark airport, both of which offer more flights from Britain than Boston does. Five airlines fly to New York from London Heathrow: **British Airways, TWA, Air India** (tel. 071/491–7979), **El Al** (tel. 071/437–9255), and **Pan Am** (tel. 071/ 935–5400). British Airways has as many as six flights a day, two on the Concorde. Three airlines fly to New York from London Gatwick: **British Airways, Continental** (tel. 0293/567–955), and **Virgin Atlantic** (tel. 0293/567–711); British Airways also flies to New York from Manchester, England.

Airfares vary enormously, depending on the type of ticket you buy and the time of year you travel. Full-fare prices start at £700 round-trip for economy (coach class); £1,760 round-trip for business class; and £3,270 round-trip for first class. Concorde to New York costs £2,125 one way. Round-trip tourist tickets in peak season start at around £360, however, and fares are even lower mid-January to mid-March, starting at as little as £150 round-trip, though £250 is an average price. Ticket agencies such as Trail Finders, STA, and Travel Cuts offer good deals.

Insurance We recommend that you take out insurance to guard against health problems, motoring mishaps, theft, flight cancellation, and loss of luggage. Most major tour operators offer holiday insurance, and details are given in brochures. For free general advice on all aspects of holiday insurance, contact the **Association of British Insurers** (Aldermary House, Queen St., London EC4N 1TT, tel. 071/248–4477). A proven leader in the holiday insurance field is **Europ Assistance** (252 High St., Croyden, Surrey CRO 1NF, tel. 081/680–1234).

Tour Operators The following is a selection of companies that offer tour packages to Cape Cod. For details of these and other resources, consult a travel agent.

Bales Worldwide Tours (Bales House, Barrington Rd., Dorking, Surrey RH4 3EJ, tel. 0306/76881) and **Kuoni Travel** (Kuoni House, Dorking, Surrey RH5 4AZ, tel. 0306/76711), in conjunction with the American company Tauk Tours, can arrange seven-day tours of Cape Cod that include a night on Martha's Vineyard. Prices start at about £1,275. In summer there are two cruise programs: one eight days long with five days spent on a boat in the waters around the Cape, and one 10-day trip with eight days afloat.

Jetlife Holidays (33 Swanley Centre, Swanley, Kent BRS 7TL, tel. 0322/614801) has an 11-night "Grand New England Coach Tour" that visits Boston, Portland, Mount Canon, Springfield, and Cape Cod; prices range from £989 to £1,089. The "Complete New England Fly Drive" package gives you 14 nights at prices from £799 to £1,139. Jetlife will also help you plan your own driving holiday in New England.

When to Go

Memorial Day through Labor Day (in some cases, Columbus Day) is high season on Cape Cod, Martha's Vineyard, and Nantucket; then you'll find good beach weather (swimming from about mid-June sometimes into October) and everything open, but also high prices, crowds, and traffic.

Spring and fall are the times to enjoy more peaceful bird walks, nature hikes, and country drives, along with lower inn and restaurant prices. Evergreens and scrub make up a good part of the area's ground cover, so the display of autumn colors is not like that in other parts of New England; still, under crisp blue skies in the clear autumn light, the Lower Cape and islands' cover of heather, gorse, blueberry, bayberry, boxberry, and beach plum resembles, in Thoreau's words, "the richest rug imaginable spread over an uneven surface." Spring, too, is beautiful, bursting with wildflowers and greening grasses, though it does arrive late and is unpredictable—on Nantucket especially, spring is often damp and foggy.

In winter, many museums, shops, restaurants, and lodging places close, especially on the islands. Many golf courses, however, remain open year-round, except when it snows (some then open their courses to cross-country skiers), and the Cape's strong community theater network continues throughout the year, as do a core of other activities. A number of intimate bed-and-breakfasts and inns—some with fireplaces, canopy beds, and well-stocked libraries and board-game collections—also remain open, and for as much as 50% off high-season rates, they make romantic retreats after a day of ice fishing, pond skating, or otherwise enjoying winter in the country. On the islands especially, though, don't come in winter looking for action.

Many towns on the Cape and islands celebrate Christmas in an old-fashioned way, with wandering carolers and bands, theatrical performances, crafts sales, and holiday house tours. Nantucket's Christmas (or Shoppers) Stroll is the best-known event; Martha's Vineyard has a special celebration in Edgartown (*see* Festivals and Seasonal Events, below).

Lodging reservations are extremely tight in summer in the whole area. The most intense tourist time is the last two weeks in July and most of August; if you come then without a hotel or inn reservation, you'll still find accommodations, but be prepared to settle for whatever is available. Also book well in advance (several months) for a visit to Nantucket during the Daffodil Festival, in late April, or the Christmas Stroll, on the first weekend in December; many people return every year for these events, which are worth planning a trip around.

Climate Remember that though its beaches rival the best the Caribbean has to offer, the Cape is not the Caribbean and does not come with its near-guarantee of sun-filled days. Certainly there are plenty of idyllic beach days to go around, but rain or fog is not an uncommon part of even an August vacation on the Cape. Visitors who do not learn to appreciate the beauty of the land and sea in mist and downright rain may find themselves mighty cranky (remember, there's always the Cape Cod Mall).

Temperatures in winter and summer are milder on the Cape and islands than on the mainland, due in part to the warming influence of the Gulf Stream and the moderating ocean breezes. As a rule (and there have been dramatically anomalous years), the Cape gets much less snow than the mainland, and what falls generally does not last. Still, winter can bring bone-chilling dampness, especially on the windswept islands.

What follows are the average daily maximum and minimum temperatures for Hyannis.

Jan.	40F	4C	May	62F	17C	Sept.	70F	21C
	25	−4		48	9		56	13
Feb.	41F	5C	June	71F	22C	Oct.	59F	15C
	26	−3		56	13		47	8
Mar.	42F	6C	July	78F	26C	Nov.	49F	9C
	28	−2		63	17		37	3
Apr.	53F	12C	Aug.	76F	24C	Dec.	40F	4C
	40	4		61	16		26	−3

Rainfall is heaviest November through March, averaging 3.7 to 4.7 inches per month. For tide information and weather and coastal marine forecasts, call 508/771–5522 or 508/255–8500.

Festivals and Seasonal Events

The Massachusetts Office of Travel & Tourism (*see* Visitor Information, above) offers a complete "Spring/Summer Calendar of Events and Whale Watch Guide" for the entire state.

Late Apr.: Nantucket's five-day **Daffodil Festival** (tel. 508/228–1700) celebrates spring with a flower show, shop-window displays, and a procession of antique cars adorned with daffodils that ends in tailgate picnics at Siasconset. For about five weeks from mid-April to mid-May, 2 million daffodils bloom along Nantucket roadsides and in private gardens. **Brewster in Bloom** (tel. 508/896–5766) is this Cape town's own daffodil celebration, marked with a golf tournament, a crafts show, a parade, and children's events over three days.

Mid-May–mid-June: Rhododendrons bloom profusely at Sandwich's **Heritage Plantation** (tel. 508/888–3300).

Summer: From June through August, the area is busy with **summer theater, town band concerts,** and **arts and crafts fairs.**

Early June: Hyannis Harbor Festival (tel. 508/775–2201) is a two-day celebration that includes the blessing of the fleet, boat races, entertainment, and food. **Cape Cod Antique Dealers Association Annual Antiques Show** at the Heritage Plantation (tel. 508/888–3300) is attended by dealers in fine 18th- and 19th-century English and American furniture, folk art, Sandwich glass, clocks, jewelry, and more.

Mid- to late June: More than 50 dealers participate in the **Antiques and Collectibles Show** at the Pilgrim Monument in Provincetown (tel. 508/487–1310). In Edgartown's **Taste of the Vineyard** (tel. 508/627–4440), a benefit for the Historical Preservation Society, ticket holders wander among tents set up downtown as they sample treats provided by many local restaurants, caterers, and wine sellers; there is dancing in the streets and a small auction.

Last Sun. in June: The Blessing of the Fleet (tel. 508/487–3424) in Provincetown is the culmination of a weekend of festivities, including a quahog feed, a public dance, and a crafts show. On Sunday, a parade ends at the wharf, where fishermen and their families and friends pile onto their boats and form a procession. The bishop stands on the dock and blesses the boats with holy water as they pass by.

July: Falmouth Festival (tel. 508/385–8689) displays the work of 200 artists and craftsmen and features live music, jugglers, and food. The **Summertime Fair** (tel. 508/845–0677) in Chatham features quilts and other handicrafts.

Fourth of July weekend: The Mashpee Powwow (tel. 508/477–0792) brings together Wampanoag Indians from North and South America—and welcomes visitors—for three days of dance contests, drumming, a fireball game, and a clambake, plus the crowning of the Mashpee Wampanoag Indian princess on the final night. Native American foods and crafts are sold, and many tribe members dress in traditional or ceremonial garb. **Fireworks displays** are still a part of Fourth of July celebrations in Falmouth, Hyannis, Orleans, Provincetown, and Yarmouth, and on Nantucket.

Mid-July: Edgartown Regatta (tel. 508/627–4361) is three days of yacht racing around Martha's Vineyard. In East Sandwich, an **Antiquarian Book Fair** (tel. 508/888–6870) features the offerings of more than 50 dealers in old and rare books.

Late July: The Barnstable County Fair (tel. 508/563–3200) in Hatchville, begun in 1844, is Cape Cod's biggest event. The six-day affair features livestock and food judgings, horse and pony pulls and shows, arts and crafts demonstrations, musical and stage entertainment, carnival rides, and lots of food. The traffic is horrendous, but the fair is worth the trip.

Aug.: On Nantucket, an **Annual House Tour** is held by the garden club (tel. 508/228–0340), and a **Sandcastle Contest** at Jetties Beach (tel. 508/228–1700) results in some amazing sculptures. On Martha's Vineyard, a superior **fireworks display** (tel. 508/693–0085) takes place over the ocean while the town watches from the Oak Bluffs village green and the town band plays on the gazebo.

Early Aug.: The Hyannis Street Festival (tel. 508/775–2201) is a weekend of Main Street shopping, food, and fun. Merchants display sale items on the sidewalk; clowns, jugglers, and other street entertainers stroll the street, and up to 20 bands perform.

Mid-Aug.: Martha's Vineyard Agricultural Fair (tel. 508/693–0085) is pure Americana, with livestock and food judging, log-cutting contests, animal shows, a carnival, and food galore, plus evening musical entertainment, over three days. The **Falmouth Road Race** (Box 732, Falmouth 02541 [send SASE], tel. 508/540–7000) is a world-class race covering 7.1 miles of coast from Woods Hole to Falmouth Heights. In Hyannis, a **Dollhouse & Miniature Show** (Cape Cod Miniature Society, Box 1541, Sandwich 02563 [send SASE], tel. 508/477–5121 or 508/255–3216) has been held each year since 1980.

Sept.: The Bourne Scallopfest (tel. 508/888–6202), the weekend after Labor Day, attracts thousands of people to Buzzards Bay for three days of fried scallops (and barbecued chicken, hot dogs, and burgers) served under a tent, plus 85 crafts and food booths and entertainment. Planned for 1991 is a one-day **Nantucket County Fair and Seafest** (tel. 508/228–1700), to be held at Children's Beach, which will combine the former Seafest and Heritage Days celebrations and include a scallop-shucking contest, a rowing contest, a food festival, entertainment, and a celebration of island crafts. **The Harwich Cranberry Harvest Festival** (tel. 508/543–0100) is 10 days of festivities, including a country-western jamboree, an arts and crafts show, a parade, fireworks, pancake breakfasts, an antique car show, a regatta, and much more.

Early Sept.: Tivoli Day (tel. 508/693–0085), an end-of-summer celebration in Oak Bluffs on Martha's Vineyard, features a fishing derby for kids, a world-class 60-mile bike race (**Tour of Martha's Vineyard**), a street fair, and a blessing of the fleet. Tour racing on the Vineyard is a tradition that can be traced back to 1887; the race on Tivoli Day (named for the town's onetime dance hall) has been going strong since 1977.

Mid-Sept.–mid-Oct.: The month-long **Martha's Vineyard Striped Bass and Bluefish Derby** (tel. 508/693–1881) is one of the East Coast's premier fishing contests, offering $100,000 in prizes.

Thanksgiving Eve: Provincetown Festival of Lights (tel. 508/487–3424) begins on this night with the lighting of 5,000 colored bulbs draped over the Pilgrim Monument. The lights are lit nightly thereafter until the New Year and can be seen as far away as the canal. A performance of the "Hallelujah Chorus" accompanies the lighting; the monument museum offers an open house and tours, and local establishments add to the festivities.

Early Dec.: Many Cape and island towns do up the Christmas season in grand style. The best-known celebration is the Nantucket **Christmas (or Shoppers) Stroll** (tel. 508/228–1700), which takes place the first weekend of the month. Costumed carolers and other musicians entertain hordes of strollers as they walk the festively decorated cobblestone streets and dip into stores to shop and sample the seasonal refreshments offered. Activities include theatrical performances, art exhibitions, crafts sales, and a tour of historic homes. In this most historic town, the old-time celebration is magical. To avoid the throngs, shop and enjoy the decorations on one of the following weekends.

On Martha's Vineyard, **Christmas in Edgartown** (tel. 508/693–0085), the second weekend of the month, includes walking tours of historic homes, old-fashioned teas, carriage rides, a parade, caroling, and other entertainment.

Falmouth's **Christmas by the Sea** (tel. 508/548–8500), the first weekend of December, includes lighting ceremonies at the Village Green and at Nobska Light in Woods Hole, plus caroling, an antiques show, tours of B&Bs, concerts, plays, cruises, and a parade.

Chatham's **Main Street Open House** (tel. 508/945–0342) takes place the following weekend, with street entertainment, hayrides, caroling, hand-bell ringing, and more, culminating in a dinner dance at the grand Chatham Bars Inn. The open house is part of a monthlong celebration beginning just after Thanksgiving.

What to Pack

A few restaurants on Cape Cod, Martha's Vineyard, and Nantucket require formal dress; the area prides itself on informality. Do pack a sweater or jacket, even in summer, for the nights can be cool. Also, see clothing suggestions in Staying Healthy, below, regarding Lyme disease.

Of course, protective sunscreens, sunglasses with UV screen, hats, and insect repellent are important in summer; all are readily available throughout the Cape and islands. And don't forget your raingear. . . .

Carry-on Luggage Passengers aboard major U.S. carriers are usually limited to two carry-on bags. Bags stored under the seat must not exceed 9″ x 14″ x 22″. Bags hung in a closet can be no larger than 4″ x 23″ x 45″. The maximum dimensions for bags stored in an overhead bin are 10″ x 14″ x 36″. Any item that exceeds the specified dimensions will generally be rejected as a carryon and handled as checked baggage. Keep in mind that an airline can adapt these rules to circumstances; on a crowded flight, you may be allowed to take only one carry-on bag aboard.

In addition to the two carryons, passengers may bring aboard: a handbag, an overcoat or wrap, an umbrella, a camera, a reasonable amount of reading material, an infant bag, and crutches, braces, a cane, or other prosthetic device upon which the passenger is dependent. Infant/child safety seats can also be brought aboard if parents have purchased a ticket for the child or if there is space in the cabin.

Checked Luggage   Luggage allowances vary slightly among airlines. Many carriers allow three checked pieces; some allow only two. It is best to consult with the airline before you go. In all cases, checked luggage cannot weigh more than 70 pounds per piece or be larger than 62 inches (length + width + height).

Staying Healthy

A problem that affects coastal areas from Virginia to Massachusetts is Lyme disease (named after Lyme, Connecticut, where it was first diagnosed). This bacterial infection is transmitted by deer ticks and can be very serious, leading to chronic arthritis and worse if left untreated, which it often is because it is difficult to diagnose. Pregnant women are advised to avoid areas of possible infestation; the disease can harm a fetus if contracted during early pregnancy.

Deer ticks are most prevalent April through October but can be found year-round. They are about the size of a pinhead; wearing light-colored clothing makes it easier to spot any ticks that might have attached themselves to you. Anyone planning to explore wooded areas or places with tall grasses (including dunes) should wear long pants, socks drawn up over pant cuffs, and a long-sleeve shirt with a close-fitting collar; boots are also recommended. The National Centers for Disease Control recommends DEET repellent applied to clothing directly before entering infested areas but warns that it should be used very carefully and conservatively with small children.

Avoid walking in pathless brush areas and dune grasses, or brushing against low foliage. On returning from an outing, check your clothes and body for ticks (they also attach themselves to pets). To remove a tick, apply a tweezers to where it is attached to the skin and pull without squeezing the body of the tick—if squeezed, the body fluids containing the bacteria will be released and spread. Afterward, disinfect the bite with alcohol and save the tick in a closed jar in case symptoms of the disease develop.

The first symptom may be a ringlike rash, or you may experience flulike symptoms, such as malaise, fever, chills, and joint or facial pains. If diagnosed early, Lyme disease can be treated with antibiotics. If you suspect your symptoms may be due to a tick bite, inform your doctor and ask to be tested for the disease. For more information, contact the Lyme Borreliosis Foundation (Tolland, CT 06084, tel. 203/871–2900). Brochures on the disease are also available at many tourist information areas.

Other health risks of a visit to Cape Cod and the islands are sunburn, poison ivy, and swimming in areas with dangerous currents.

Cash Machines

Virtually all U.S. banks belong to a network of ATMs (automatic teller machines) that dispense cash 24 hours a day in cities throughout the country. There are some eight major networks in the United States, the largest of which are Cirrus, owned by MasterCard, and Plus, affiliated with Visa. Some banks belong to more than one network. To receive a card for one of these systems, you must apply for it. Cards issued by Visa and MasterCard also may be used in the ATMs, but the fees are usually higher than the fees on bank cards. There is also a daily interest charge on credit card "loans," even if monthly bills are paid on time. Each network has a toll-free number you can call to locate machines in a given city. The Cirrus number is 800/424–7787; the Plus number is 800/843–7587. Check with your bank for information on fees and on the amount of cash you can withdraw on any given day.

Traveling with Film

If your camera is new, shoot and develop a few rolls of film before you leave home. Pack some lens tissue and an extra battery for your built-in light meter. Invest about $10 in a skylight filter: It will protect the lens and reduce haze.

Film doesn't like hot weather, so if you're driving in summer, don't store film in the glove compartment or on the shelf under the rear window. Put it behind the front seat on the floor, on the side opposite the exhaust pipe.

On a plane trip, never pack unprocessed film in checked luggage; if your bags get X-rayed, say goodbye to your pictures. Always carry undeveloped film with you through security and ask to have it inspected by hand. (It helps to keep your film in a plastic bag, ready for quick inspection.) Inspectors at American airports are required by law to honor requests for hand inspection. The newer airport scanning machines used in all U.S. airports are safe for anything from five to 500 scans, depending on the speed of your film. The effects are cumulative; you can put the same roll of film through several scans without worry. After five scans, though, you're asking for trouble.

If your film gets fogged and you want an explanation, send it to the **National Association of Photographic Manufacturers** (550 Mamaroneck Ave., Harrison, NY 10528), which will try to determine what went wrong. The service is free.

Traveling with Children

Cape Cod is very much family oriented and provides every imaginable diversion for kids, plus plenty of lodgings and restaurants that cater to them and are affordable for families on a budget. Cottages and condominiums are increasingly popular with families, offering privacy, room, kitchens, and sometimes laundry facilities; often cottage or condo communities have play yards and pools, sometimes even full children's programs.

Publications The Bristol County Development Council (Box BR–976, New Bedford, MA 02741, tel. 508/997–1250) has a calendar of events for children along south coastal New England, called "Happenings Especially for Kids."

Just for Kids: The New England Guide and Activity Book for Young Travelers, by Ed and Roon Frost (Glove Compartment Books, Box 1602, Fort Smith, NH 03801), is available by mail for $7.95 plus $3 shipping and handling.

Family Travel Times is a newsletter published 10 times a year by Travel With Your Children (TWYCH, 80 8th Ave., New York, NY 10011, tel. 212/206–0668). A one-year subscription for $35 includes access to back issues and twice-weekly opportunities to call for specific advice.

Getting There On domestic flights, children under age 2 not occupying a seat travel free. Various discounts apply to children age 2–12. If possible, reserve a seat behind the bulkhead of the plane; these offer more legroom and usually enough space to fit a bassinet (supplied by the airlines). At the same time, inquire about special children's meals or snacks, which are also offered by most airlines. (See "TWYCH's Airline Guide," in the February 1990 issue of *Family Travel Times,* for a rundown on children's services offered by 46 airlines.) Ask the airline if you can bring aboard your child's car seat. For the booklet "Child/Infant Safety Seats Acceptable for Use in Aircraft," write the Community and Consumer Liaison Division (APA-400 Federal Aviation Administration, Washington, DC 20591, tel. 202/267–3479).

Hotels The **Sheraton Ocean Park Inn** in Eastham, the **Quality Inn** in Falmouth, and the **Hampton Inn Hotel** in Hyannis allow children under age 18 to share their parents' room for free. The **Tara Hyannis Hotel** in Hyannis has a full children's program (some fees are involved), including all-night pajama parties; supper parties; swimming, game, and crafts programs; tennis and golf clinics; and swimming lessons. *See* Lodging in Chapter 3.

On Martha's Vineyard (*see* Lodging in Chapter 4), the **Mattakesett** condominium community has a full children's program and plenty of amenities for kids (pool, tennis clinics, and so forth).

On Nantucket (*see* Lodging in Chapter 5), the First Winthrop properties—**White Elephant, Harbor House,** and **Wharf Cottages**—have a full children's program Memorial Day–Labor Day.

Hints for Disabled Travelers

Lift-van service is available on the Cape and on Martha's Vineyard through *Elder Services of Cape Cod* (*see* Hints for Older Travelers, below).**Cape Organization for Rights of the Disabled** (CORD; tel. 508/775–8300) will supply information on accessibility of restaurants, hotels, and other tourist facilities on Cape Cod.

The **Cape Cod National Seashore** has made many facilities, services, and programs accessible to disabled visitors. For information on what is available, write to Cape Cod National Seashore (Wellfleet 02663), or ask at any Seashore visitor center (Eastham, tel. 508/255–3421; Provincetown, tel. 508/487–1256; South Wellfleet, tel. 508/349–3785).

The Information Center for Individuals with Disabilities (Fort Point Pl., 27-43 Wormwood St., Boston, MA 02210, tel. 617/727–

5540) offers useful problem-solving assistance, including lists of travel agents who specialize in tours for the disabled.

Moss Rehabilitation Hospital Travel Information Service (12th St. and Tabor Rd., Philadelphia, PA 19141, tel. 215/329–5715) provides information on tourist sites, transportation, and accommodations on destinations around the world for a small fee.

Travel Industry and Disabled Exchange (TIDE; 5435 Donna Ave., Tarzana, CA 91356, tel. 818/368–5648), for a $15-per-person annual membership fee, provides a quarterly newsletter and a directory of travel agencies that specialize in service to the disabled.

Mobility International USA (Box 3551, Eugene, OR 97403, tel. 503/343–1284) is an internationally affiliated organization with 500 members. For a $20 annual fee, it coordinates exchange programs for disabled people in the United States and around the world and offers information on accommodations and organized study programs.

Amtrak (tel. 800/872–7245) advises that you request redcap service, special seats, or wheelchair assistance when you make reservations. (Not all stations are equipped to provide these services.) All disabled passengers are entitled to a 25% discount on regular coach fares. A special children's disabled fare, which offers qualified kids age 2–12 a 50% discount on already discounted children's fares, is also available. Check with Amtrak to be sure discounts are available when you plan to travel. For a free copy of Amtrak's Travel Planner, which outlines all its services for the elderly and disabled, contact Amtrak (National Railroad Corp., 400 N. Capitol St., NW, Washington, DC 20001, tel. 800/872–7245).

Greyhound Lines will carry a disabled person and companion for the price of a single fare. Contact any Greyhound ticket office for details.

Publications Three useful resources—*Travel for the Disabled* ($9.95), *Directory of Travel Agencies for the Disabled* ($12.95), and *Wheelchair Vagabond* ($9.95)—can be ordered through bookstores or from the publisher, Twin Peaks Press (Box 129, Vancouver, WA 98666, tel. 206/694–2462). When ordering by mail, add $2 postage for one book, $1 for each additional book.

Access to the World: A Travel Guide for the Handicapped, by Louise Weiss, offers tips on travel and accessibility around the world. It is available from Henry Holt & Co. for $12.95 (tel. 800/247–3912; order number 0805001417).

Access America: An Atlas and Guide to the National Parks for Visitors with Disabilities, published by Northern Cartographic (Box 133, Burlington, VT 05402, tel. 802/655–4321), contains detailed information on access for the 37 largest and most visited national parks in the United States. Available directly from the publisher, the award-winning book costs $44.95 plus $5 shipping.

"Fly Rights," a free brochure available on request from the U.S. Department of Transportation (tel. 202/366–2220), gives airline access information for the disabled.

Hints for Older Travelers

More than half of Cape Cod's year-round population is made up of retirees, so the area caters to older people in many ways: for example, senior discounts are widely available, many restaurants offer early-bird specials from around 4 to 7 PM, and wheelchair-access ramps are common.

Elder Services of Cape Cod and the Islands (68 Rte. 134, South Dennis 02660, tel. 508/394–4630 or 800/352–7178; on Martha's Vineyard, tel. 508/693–4393) has limited information of use to tourists but may make referrals in response to specific problems or questions.

Many country inns will accommodate requests for rooms on the ground floor if innkeepers are notified when reservations are made. Older travelers may want to request a room with a shower or ask that they not be put in a room with a Victorian clawfoot tub that requires one's climbing in and out.

The **American Association of Retired Persons** (AARP; 1909 K St., NW, Washington, DC 20049, tel. 202/662–4850) has two programs for independent travelers: (1) the **Purchase Privilege Program,** which offers discounts on hotels, airfare, car rentals, RV rentals, and sightseeing; and (2) the **AARP Motoring Plan,** which furnishes emergency aid (road service) and trip-routing information for an annual fee of $33.95 per person or couple. (Both programs include the member and member's spouse or the member and another person who shares the household.) The AARP also arranges group tours at reduced rates through **Olson-Travelworld** (100 N. Sepulveda Blvd., El Segundo, CA 90245, tel. 213/323–7323). As of January 1991, tours will be arranged by **American Express Vacations**. AARP members must be age 50 or older; annual dues are $5 per person or per couple.

Elderhostel (80 Boylston St., Suite 400, Boston, MA 02116, tel. 617/426–7788) is an innovative 17-year-old educational program for people age 60 and older. Participants live in dorms on some 1,200 campuses around the world. Mornings are devoted to lectures and seminars, afternoons to sightseeing and field trips. Fees for two- to three-week trips, including room, board, tuition, and round-trip transportation, range from $1,700 to $3,200. The catalog is free for the first 18 months, and $15 after that (or free if you participate in a program).

National Council of Senior Citizens (925 15th St., NW, Washington, DC 20005, tel. 202/347–8800) is a nonprofit advocacy group with some 5,000 local clubs across the country. Annual membership ($12 per person or per couple) brings you a monthly newspaper with travel information and an ID card for reduced-rate hotels and car rentals.

Mature Outlook (6001 N. Clark St., Chicago, IL 60660, tel. 800/336–6330), a subsidiary of Sears Roebuck & Co., is a travel club for people over age 50, with hotel and motel discounts and a bimonthly newsletter. Annual membership is $9.95; there are 800,000 members currently. Instant membership is available at participating Holiday Inns.

Golden Age Passport is a free lifetime pass to all parks, monuments, and recreation areas run by the federal government.

People over age 62 can pick one up at any national park that charges admission. The passport also provides a 50% discount on camping, boat launching, and parking (lodging is not included). A driver's license or other proof of age is required.

Saga International Holidays (120 Boylston St., Boston, MA 02116, tel. 800/343–0273), which specializes in group travel for people over age 60, offers a variety of tour packages at various prices.

September Days Club (tel. 800/241–5050) is run by the moderately priced Days Inns of America. The $12 annual membership fee for individuals or couples over age 50 entitles them to reduced car-rental rates and reductions of 15%–50% at most of the chain's 350 motels.

Amtrak (tel. 800/872–7245) offers a 25% discount on regular coach fares for elderly passengers. Also, *see* Hints for Disabled Travelers, above.

Greyhound Lines has special fares for senior citizens, subject to date and destination restrictions. Contact any Greyhound ticket office for details.

When using an AARP or other discount identification card, ask for reduced hotel rates when you make your reservation, not when you check out. At restaurants, show your card to the maître d' before you're seated, because discounts may be limited to certain set menus, days, or hours. When renting a car, remember that economy cars, priced at promotional rates, may cost less than cars available with your discount ID card.

Publications   *The International Health Guide for Senior Citizen Travelers*, by W. Robert Lange, MD, is available for $4.95 plus $1 shipping, and *The Senior Citizens Guide to Budget Travel in the United States and Canada*, by Paige Palmer, is available for $4.95 plus $1 shipping, both from Pilot Books (103 Cooper St. Babylon, NY 11702, tel. 516/422–2225). *The Discount Guide for Travelers Over 55*, by Caroline and Walter Weintz, lists helpful addresses, package tours, and reduced-rate car rentals in the United States and abroad. To order, send $7.95 plus $1.50 shipping to Penguin USA/NAL (120 Woodbine St., Bergenfield, NJ 07621, tel. 800/526–0275; order number ISBN 0-525-483-58-6).

Further Reading

General   The classic works on Cape Cod are Henry David Thoreau's
Cape Cod   *Cape Cod*, an account of his walking tours in the mid-1800s, and Henry Beston's 1928 *The Outermost House*, which chronicles the seasons during a solitary year in a cabin at ocean's edge. Both reveal the character of Cape Codders and are rich in tales and local lore, as well as observations on nature and its processes. *Cape Cod: Henry David Thoreau's Complete Text with the Journey Recreated in Pictures*, by William F. Robinson, is a handsome edition, illustrated with prints from the period and current photographs.

Paul Theroux's 1985 collection of short nonfiction, *Sunrise with Seamonsters*, contains an account of the author's circumnavigation of the Cape by rowboat. *Cape Cod Pilot*, by Josef Berger (alias Jeremiah Digges), is a WPA guidebook from 1937 filled with "whacking good yarns" about everything from religion to fishing, as well as a lot of still useful information.

Martha's Vineyard *On the Vineyard II*, including 38 essays by island authors and more than 200 photographs by islander Peter Simon, captures the Vineyard's many moods.

Nantucket *Nantucket Style*, by Leslie Linsley and Jon Aron (published by Rizzoli), is a look at 25 houses, from 18th-century mansions to rustic seaside cottages, with 300 illustrations. *Old Houses on Nantucket*, by Kenneth Duprey, is a thick volume with 352 interior and some exterior black-and-white photographs and drawings with accompanying (minimal) text.

Nature *A Vanishing Heritage: Wildflowers of Cape Cod* is a field guide with full-color plates. *Wading and Shore Birds*, by Roger S. Everett, contains color photos and short descriptions of birds seen on the Eastern seaboard. *Martha's Vineyard Nature Guide*, by Sylvia Mader, is a useful pocket guidebook that will help hikers find bayberry and beach plum but steer clear of poison ivy.

History *Cape Cod, Its People & Their History*, by Henry C. Kittredge
Cape Cod (first published in 1930; 1968 "post-epilogue" by John Hay), is the standard history of the area, told with anecdotes and style as well as scholarship. *Sand in Their Shoes*, compiled by Edith and Frank Shay, is a compendium of writings on facets of Cape Cod life throughout history. *Of Plimoth Plantation* is Governor William Bradford's description of the Pilgrims' voyage to and early years in the New World. *The Wampanoags of Mashpee*, by Russell Peters, provides a Native American perspective on American history.

Shipwrecks Around Cape Cod, by William P. Quinn, and a sequel, *Book II*, describe in text and photos of some of the scores of shipwrecks in this most hazardous area. *The Cape Cod Canal*, by Robert H. Farson, gives the history of the canal, accompanied by black-and-white photos. *Art in Narrow Streets*, by Ross Moffett, is a history of the Provincetown Art Association in its early years, 1914–1947, and of the artists who worked there at that time.

Martha's Vineyard The many books written by Henry Beetle Hough, the Pulitzer Prize–winning editor of the *Vineyard Gazette* for 60 years, include his 1970 *Martha's Vineyard* and his 1936 *Martha's Vineyard, Summer Resort*. Ellen Weiss's *City in the Woods: The Life and Design of an American Camp Meeting on Martha's Vineyard* tells the story of the Oak Bluffs Camp Ground through words and pictures.

Nantucket Alexander Starbuck's 1924 *History of Nantucket* is the most comprehensive on early Nantucket. *Nantucket: The Life of an Island*, by Edwin P. Hoyt, is a lively and fascinating history. *Captain's Best Mate*, edited by Stanton Garner, is a journal kept by a woman who accompanied her husband on a whaling ship for four years.

Fiction Herman Melville's novel *Moby-Dick*, set on a 19th-century Nantucket whaling ship, captures the spirit of the whaling era. *Murder on Martha's Vineyard*, by David Osborn, and *A Beautiful Place to Die*, by Philip R. Craig, are mystery novels set on the island. *Nantucket Slayrides, Three Short Novels*, by Lucius Shepard and Robert Frazier, is a collection of thrillers set in Nantucket. *Sweet Anarchy* is Nantucketer Nathaniel

Benchley's satirical novel of an island that tries (as Nantucket did in the late 1970s) to secede from the state. *Nantucket Daybreak* is set in off-season Nantucket and portrays the life of the scallopers in a story of love and betrayal. *East of America*, edited by John V. Hinshaw, is a selection of poems influenced by or about Cape Cod.

Photography   *A Summer's Day* (winner of the 1985 Ansel Adams Award for Best Photography Book) and *Cape Light* present color landscapes, still lifes, and portraits by Provincetown-associated photographer Joel Meyerowitz. *Remembrance and Light: Images of Martha's Vineyard* is a collection of the nature photography of Alison Shaw, with text by Henry Beetle Hough. *Martha's Vineyard* and *Eisenstaedt: Martha's Vineyard* are explorations of the island by *Life* magazine photographer Alfred Eisenstaedt, a summer resident for decades. *Nantucket Island*, by Robert Gambee, has more than 430 color photographs plus text.

Miscellaneous   *Short Bike Rides on Cape Cod, Nantucket & the Vineyard*, by Edwin Mullen and Jane Griffith, and *Short Nature Walks on Cape Cod & the Vineyard*, by Hugh and Heather Sadlier, are useful touring guides with maps. *Names of the Land*, by Eugene Green and William Sachse, is a compendium of Cape and island proper names with their derivations. *Cape Cod Architecture*, by Clair Baisly, is a study of all the architectural styles of the area from the beginning—a slim, useful book with lists of identifying characteristics of each style and discussions of how they evolved. *Nantucket Lightship Baskets*, by Katherine and Edgar Seeler, is the definitive work on this craft.

Periodicals   Glossy magazines on the area include *Cape Cod Life* (Box 222, Osterville 02655, tel. 508/428–5706), *Cape Cod Home & Garden* (60 Munson Meeting, Chatham 02633, tel. 508/945–3542), *Martha's Vineyard Magazine* (Box 66 Edgartown 02539, tel. 508/627–4311), and *Nantucket Journal* (7 Sea St., Nantucket 02554, tel. 508/228–8700).

Sources   **The Butterworth Company** (476 Main St., Harwich Port 02646, tel. 508/432–8200) sells street and road maps covering all of Cape Cod and the islands, plus a Cape Cod Rail Trail map. To anyone spending a couple weeks or more touring, its *Cape Cod & Islands Atlas* is indispensable—it gives virtually every street and describes points of interest.

Parnassus Imprints (Box 335, Orleans 02653, tel. 508/255–2932) carries a number of Cape-related and marine titles and will send a list. **Mitchell's Book Corner** (54 Main St., Nantucket 02554, tel. 508/228–1080) puts out a brochure on Nantucket-related books. Also try contacting any of the bookstores listed in the shopping sections throughout this book.

Arriving and Departing

By Plane

Most flights to Cape Cod land in Hyannis; regular flights are also scheduled year-round between Boston and Provincetown. Service to Martha's Vineyard and Nantucket is available out of Hyannis, Chatham, and New Bedford airports, as well as through nationwide connections; air service also connects the islands. For details, *see* individual chapters.

Smoking The Federal Aviation Administration has banned smoking on all scheduled flights within the 48 contiguous states; to and from the U.S. Virgin Islands and Puerto Rico; and on flights of under six hours to and from Alaska and Hawaii. The rules apply to both domestic and foreign carriers. A request for a seat in a nonsmoking section should be made at the time you make your reservation.

Lost Luggage On domestic flights, airlines are responsible for up to $1,250 per passenger in lost or damaged property. If you're carrying valuables, either take them with you on the plane or purchase additional insurance for lost luggage. Some airlines will issue luggage insurance when you check in, but many do not. Insurance for lost, damaged, or stolen luggage is available through travel agents or directly through insurance companies. Luggage-loss coverage is usually part of a comprehensive travel-insurance package that includes insurance against personal accident, trip cancellation, and sometimes default and bankruptcy. Two companies that issue luggage insurance are **Tele-Trip** ((Box 31685, 3201 Farnam St., Omaha, NE 68131, tel. 800/228–9792), a subsidiary of Mutual of Omaha, and the **Travelers Insurance Co.** (Ticket and Travel Dept., 1 Tower Sq., Hartford, CT 06183, tel. 203/277–0111 or 800/243–3174). TeleTrip operates sales booths at airports and issues insurance through travel agents. Tele-Trip will insure checked luggage with a valuation of $500–$3,000 for up to 180 days. Rates for $500 valuation are $8.25 for one–three days, $100 for 180 days. The Travelers Insurance Co. will insure checked or hand luggage with a valuation of $500–$2,000 per person for up to 180 days. Rates for $500 valuation are $10 for one–five days, $85 for 180 days. Other companies with comprehensive policies include **Access America**, a subsidiary of Blue Cross–Blue Shield (Box 807, New York, NY 10163, tel. 212/490–5345 or 800/284–8300) and **Near Services** (450 Prairie Ave., Calumet City, IL 60409, tel. 708/868–6700 or 800/654–6700).

By Car

The speed limit in Massachusetts is 55 mph. Except on Cape Cod's Route 6, you'll find little opportunity to reach the limit on the Cape and islands. For driving routes to Cape Cod, *see* Arriving and Departing by Car in Chapter 3. To get to Martha's Vineyard by car, you'll have to take a ferry from Woods Hole; to Nantucket, a ferry from Hyannis (*see* Arriving and Departing by Ferry in Chapters 4 and 5, respectively).

Car Rentals

Avis (tel. 800/331–1212), **Budget** (tel. 800/527–0700), **Dollar** (tel. 800/421–6868), **Hertz** (tel. 800/654–3131), **National** (tel. 800/328–4567), and **Thrifty** (tel. 800/367–2277) maintain airport and city locations throughout New England.

For local rental agencies, *see* the relevant chapters, below.

By Train

Amtrak (tel. 800/USA–RAIL) has limited service to Cape Cod in season; in the off-season, trains to Boston connect with bus service to the Cape. For more details, *see* Arriving and Departing by Train in Chapter 3.

By Bus

A number of bus companies serve Cape Cod, with stops at many towns and some connecting service to the islands by ferry; express buses run from Logan Airport in Boston to Hyannis (*see* Arriving and Departing by Bus in Chapter 3).

By Boat

Provincetown is reached by ferry from Boston in season; Martha's Vineyard, from Woods Hole year-round and from Falmouth, Hyannis, and New Bedford in season; Nantucket, from Hyannis year-round. *See* Arriving and Departing by Ferry in Chapters 3–5.

Staying in Cape Cod and the Islands

Shopping

Art galleries and crafts shops abound on Cape Cod, Martha's Vineyard, and Nantucket, a reflection of the long attraction the area has held for artists and craftsmen. The region is also a popular antiquing spot. For a directory of area antiques dealers and auctions, contact the Cape Cod Antique Dealers Association (Box 1223, Brewster 02631, tel. 508/896–7198). On the Cape, Provincetown and Wellfleet are the main centers for art. For the "Provincetown Gallery Guide," a detailed listing and map, write Provincetown Gallery Guild (Box 242, Provincetown 02657). For "Wellfleet, the Art Gallery Town," a similar listing and map of galleries and restaurants, write Wellfleet Art Galleries Association (Box 916, Wellfleet 02667). For a listing of crafts shops on the Cape, write to the Society of Cape Cod Craftsmen (Box 2381, Orleans 02653). For a list of potters, write Cape Cod Potters (Box 76, Chatham 02633).

Coastal environments and a shared seafaring past account for the proliferation of sea-related crafts on the Cape and the islands (as well as of marine antiques dealers). A craft form that originated as a time passer on the years-long voyages to faraway whaling grounds is scrimshaw, the art of etching finely detailed designs of sailing ships and sea creatures onto a hard surface. In the beginning, the bones or teeth of whales were used; today's ecologically minded (and legally constrained) scrimshanders use a synthetic substitute like Corian, a DuPont material for countertops.

Another whalers' pastime was the sailor's valentine: a glass-enclosed wood box, often in an octagonal shape (derived from the shape of the compass boxes that were originally used) containing an intricate arrangement of seashells. The shells were collected on stopovers in the West Indies and elsewhere, sorted by color, size, and shape, and then glued into elaborate patterns during the long hours aboard ship. Exquisite examples can be seen at a Nantucket gallery, the Sailor's Valentine (*see* Chapter 5).

Yet another invention of bored guys on boats is the Nantucket lightship basket, though this one was developed just off the island's coast. In the mid-19th century a lightship was placed 24 miles out to aid in navigation during foggy spells; in good weather there was little to do, and so (the story goes) crew members began weaving intricately patterned baskets of cane, a trade some continued onshore and passed on. Later a woven lid and decoration were added, and the utilitarian baskets were on their way to becoming the handbags that today fetch prices in excess of $1,000. While Nantucket is still the locus of the craft, with a dozen active basket makers, the baskets have made their way off the island, both antiques and new ones.

Throughout the Cape and islands, remember that shop owners respond to the flow of tourists as well as to their own inclinations (escape from big-city pressure is one reason many people move here in the first place) and may stay open later in the year or close earlier than planned. In the off-season especially, it's best to phone a shop before going out of your way to visit it.

Shop hours are generally 9 or 10 to 5, though in high season many tourist-oriented stores stay open until 10 PM or later. Except in the main tourist areas, shops are often closed on Sunday. The Massachusetts sales tax is 5%.

Sports and Outdoor Activities

The Cape and the islands are top spots for swimming, surfing, windsurfing, sailing, and virtually all water sports. Shipwrecks make for interesting dive sites, but don't expect a tropical underwater landscape. Golfers have many excellent courses to choose from, including championship layouts, and most remain open nearly year-round. Bicycling is a joy on the mostly level roads, along paved and scenic bike paths, and through the many nature preserves. Bird-watchers have an endless variety of habitats to choose from, often in a single nature preserve.

Fishing is extremely popular, especially for bluefish and striped bass. A license is required for persons age 15 or over to fish in inland waters (apply to the Dept. of Fisheries, Wildlife and Recreational Vehicles, 100 Cambridge St., Boston 02202, tel. 617/727–3151). The Cape Cod Chamber of Commerce (*see* Visitor Information, above) puts out a "Sportsman's Guide to Cape Cod," with a map pinpointing boat-launching facilities, surf-fishing access locations, and pond and stream fishing. The guide also contains information on charter, party, and whale-watch boats; game, bottom, and freshwater fishing (which fish to look for and where); and hunting and fishing regulations and licenses.

Bicyclists should know that Massachusetts law requires a headlight after dark, a red rear reflector, and reflectors visible from either side of the bike. Spectators can choose from a plethora of bike and running races, golf competitions (including the New England PGA championships at Ocean Edge in Brewster), horse shows, sailboat races around the islands, and the well-patronized games of the Cape Cod Baseball League, breeding ground of champions (*see* Chapter 3).

Beaches

Cape Cod, Martha's Vineyard, and Nantucket are known for long, dune-backed sand beaches, both surf and calm. Swimming season is approximately mid-June–September (sometimes into October). The Cape Cod National Seashore has the best beaches, with high dunes, wide strands of sand, and no development on the shores. The islands have miles of beautiful, protected coastline as well.

National and State Parks

The Cape and islands are very outdoors-oriented and have set aside many areas for the enjoyment of nature. For further information on the parks mentioned here, as well as on nature and wildlife preserves, *see* the relevant chapters.

National Parks The **Cape Cod National Seashore** is a 40-mile stretch of the Cape between Eastham and Provincetown that is protected from development. It includes spectacular beaches, dunes, and many other habitats, making for excellent swimming, fishing, bike riding, bird-watching, and nature walks.

State Parks **Manuel F. Correllus State Forest** is 4,000 acres on Martha's Vineyard, laced with hiking, biking, and horse trails.

Nickerson State Park, more than 1,700 acres of forest in Brewster, is a popular camping, biking, boating, fishing, hiking, freshwater swimming, and cross-country skiing area.

Scusset Beach State Reservation in Sandwich is 380 acres with camping, biking, ocean swimming, fishing, and walking trails.

Shawme-Crowell State Forest in Sandwich is more than 2,700 acres with camping and walking trails.

Dining

Cape Cod, Martha's Vineyard, and Nantucket restaurants offer an endless variety of fresh fish and shellfish. Each restaurant has its version of New England clam chowder, a rich milk- (and sometimes cream-) based dish usually made with the large clams called quahogs (pronounced "KO-hawgs"), chunks of potato, and salt pork. Clams are served in a variety of other ways as well—on the half shell, fried, or baked into a splendid concoction of clams, butter, and bread crumbs called seaclam pie. Clam shacks everywhere serve tasty fried fish and shellfish, accompanied by crisp onion rings—a nice, greasy meal to be savored when you're in a hurry or just on strike against sensible eating.

Other area specialties are the much-prized Wellfleet oysters and the tiny, delicate, buttery-sweet bay scallops, available fresh from the sea in late fall and winter and too often faked by cutting large sea scallops into small pieces. Visitors are often surprised at the many Portuguese dishes—such as kale soup or *linguiça* (a spicy sausage)—available on Cape and islands menus; the reason is a long history of Portuguese immigration. Since whaling days, Portuguese have made their living from these seas, particularly around Provincetown.

Most Cape restaurants feature traditional New England family fare—pot roast, baked scrod (codfish), chicken pot pie, mashed potatoes and gravy—though a few offer haute cuisine that rivals the best anywhere. Nantucket has spawned a number of first-rate gourmet restaurants (with price tags to match). Consistency from year to year is a problem, because there is a high turnover among chefs. Because of the short high season and the generally conservative year-round population largely made up of senior citizens on fixed incomes, in the off-season even the adventurous restaurants must retreat to more traditional fare, early-bird specials, and buffets in order to survive.

At establishments where "come as you are" does not always apply, the most that is usually expected is "smart casual," meaning just a neat, minimally dressy look—no shorts, T-shirts, or ripped jeans. The drinking age in Massachusetts is 21; a few towns on Martha's Vineyard are dry. The going rate for tipping in restaurants is 15% of the bill before tax.

Throughout this book, restaurant price ranges are based on one appetizer, one entrée, and one dessert, without wine, tax, or service. Highly recommended restaurants in each price category are indicated by a star ★.

Lodging

Bed-and-breakfasts are especially popular on Cape Cod, Martha's Vineyard, and Nantucket. Many are housed in old sea captains' homes and other 17th- through 19th-century buildings, which are often decorated with antiques and lace and sometimes furnished with feather beds. In most cases, B&Bs are not appropriate for families, because noise travels easily, rooms are often small, and the furnishings are too fragile to withstand normal children's abuse. Usually a B&B will not offer a phone or TV in guest rooms; also, more and more B&Bs no longer allow smoking. The Massachusetts Office of Travel and Tourism (*see* Visitor Information, above) offers a free guide to 300 B&Bs and 62 reservation services in Massachusetts.

Besides B&Bs, this highly developed tourist region has all the other lodging options. Luxurious self-contained resorts, beachfront and otherwise, offer all kinds of sporting facilities, restaurants, entertainment, services (including business services and children's programs), and all the assistance one could most likely ever need in making vacation arrangements. Single-night lodgings for those just passing through can be found at countless tacky but cheap and conveniently located little roadside motels, as well as at others that are spotless and cheery yet still inexpensive, or at chain hotels at all price levels; these places often have a pool, TVs, or other amenities to keep children entertained in the evening. Families may want to consider condominiums, cottages, and efficiencies, which offer more space, living areas, kitchens (important if keeping food expenses down is an issue), and sometimes laundry facilities, children's play areas, or children's programs.

There are AYH hostels on Martha's Vineyard and Nantucket, as well as in Eastham, Hyannis, and Truro on Cape Cod (for information and reservations—which are strongly recommended—write to AYH Hostel Dept., Reservations, Box 37613, Washington, DC 20013). Accommodations are simple, dormitories are segregated for men and women, common rooms and kitchens are shared, and everyone helps with the cleanup. Usually it's lights out at 11 PM. The price can't be beat—about $10 a night.

Camping is not allowed on Nantucket, but there are many private and state-park camping areas on Cape Cod and Martha's Vineyard. For a directory of private campgrounds in the state, with maps and lots of ads, write to the Massachusetts Association of Campgrounds (MACO Spirit, RR –1, Box 179Z, Brookfield 01506, tel. 508/248–6373). For state-park campgrounds, see the relevant chapters.

Regarding peak season and the necessity for reservations at various times, *see* When to Go, above.

Throughout this book, lodging price ranges are based on a standard double room (double occupancy) in high season. Unless otherwise noted, a listed establishment's rooms have private baths. Also, one should be aware that "Continental breakfast" can mean anything from coffee and muffins to elaborate spreads with various fresh-squeezed juices, fruit plate, homemade granola, and many breads and muffins. Highly recommended lodgings in each price category are indicated by a star ★.

Credit Cards

The following credit-card abbreviations are used in this book: AE, American Express; CB, Carte Blanche; D, Discover; DC, Diners Club; MC, MasterCard; V, Visa.

2 Portraits of Cape Cod and the Islands

A Brief History

The fortunes of Cape Cod have always been linked to the sea. For centuries, fishermen in search of a livelihood, explorers in search of new worlds, and pilgrims of one sort or another in search of a new life—down to the beach-bound tourists of today—all have turned to the waters around this narrow peninsula arcing into the Atlantic to fulfill their needs and ambitions.

European exploration of Cape Cod dates back at least as far as 1602, when Bartholomew Gosnold sailed from Falmouth, England, to investigate the American coast for trade opportunities. He first anchored off what is now Provincetown and named the cape for the great quantities of cod his crew managed to catch. He then moved on to Cuttyhunk in the Elizabeth Islands (which he named for the queen); on leaving after a few weeks, he noted that the crew were "much fatter and in better health than when we went out of England." Samuel de Champlain, explorer and geographer for the king of France, visited in 1605 and 1606; his encounter with the resident Wampanoag tribe in the Chatham area resulted in deaths on both sides. One theory holds that the Viking Thorwald from Iceland broke his keel on the shoals here in 1004.

None of these visits, however, led to settlement; that began only with the chance landing of the Pilgrims, some of whom were Separatists rebelling from enforced membership in the Church of England, others merchants looking for economic opportunity. On September 16, 1620, the *Mayflower*, with a crew of about 25 men, and 101 passengers, set out from Plymouth, England, for an area of land granted them by the Virginia Company (Jamestown had been settled in 1607). After more than two months at sea in the crowded boat they saw land; it was far north of their intended destination, but after the stormy passage and considering the approach of winter, they put in at Provincetown Harbor on November 21. Before going ashore they drew up the Mayflower Compact, America's first document establishing self-governance, because they were in an area under no official jurisdiction and dissension had already begun to surface.

Setting off in a small boat, a party led by Captain Myles Standish made a number of expeditions over several weeks, seeking a suitable site for a settlement in the wilderness of woods and scrub. Finally they chose Plymouth, and there they established the colony, governed by William Bradford, that is today re-created at Plimoth Plantation.

Over the next 20 years, settlers spread north and south of Plymouth. The first parts of Cape Cod to be settled were the bay-side sections of Sandwich, Barnstable, and Yar-mouth (all incorporated in 1639), along an old Indian trail that is now Route 6A. (Martha's Vineyard was first settled in 1642, and Nantucket in 1659.) Most of the newcomers hunted, farmed, and fished; salt hay from the marshes was used to feed cattle and roof houses.

The first homes built by the English settlers on Cape Cod were wigwams built of twigs, bark, hides, cornstalks, and grasses, which they copied from those of the local Wampanoag Indians who had lived here for thousands of years before the Europeans arrived. Eventually, the set-tlers stripped the land of its forests to make farmland, graze sheep, and build more European-style homes, though with a New World look all their own. The steep-roofed saltbox and the Cape Cod cottage—still the most popular style of house on the Cape, and copied all over the country—were designed to accommodate growing fami-lies.

A newly married couple might begin by building a one- or two-room half-Cape, a rather lopsided 1½-story building with a door on one side of the facade and two windows on the other; a single chimney rose up on the wall behind the door. As the family grew, they might build an addition on the windowless side large enough for a single window, turning the half-Cape into a three-quarter-Cape; a two-window addition would make it a symmetrical full Cape. Additions built onto the sides and back were called warts. An interesting feature of some Cape houses is the graceful bowed roof, slightly curved as the bottom of a boat is (not surprising, since ship's carpenters did much of the house-building as well). More noticeable, often in the older houses, is a profusion of small, irregularly shaped and located windows in the gable ends (Thoreau wrote of one such house that it looked as if each of the various occupants "had punched a hole where his necessities required it").

Many historic houses have been turned into historical mu-seums, such as Sandwich's Hoxie House, a saltbox built in 1637 that is believed to be the oldest house extant on the Cape and islands. In some, docents can take you on a tour of the times as you pass from the keeping room—the heart of the house, where meals were cooked at a great hearth be-fore which the family gathered for warmth—to the nearby borning room, in whose warmth babies were born and the sick were tended, to the "showy" front parlors where com-pany was entertained. Summer and winter kitchens, back-yard pumps, beehive ovens, elaborate raised wall paneling, wide-board pine flooring, wainscoting, a doll made of corn husks, a spinning wheel, a stereopticon, a hand-stitched sampler or glove—each of these historic remnants gives a glimpse into the daily life of another age.

The Wampanoags taught the settlers what they knew of the land and how to live off it. Early on they showed them how

to strip and process blubber from whales that became
stranded on the beaches. To coax more whales onto the
beach, farmers would sometimes surround them in small
boats and make a commotion in the water with their oars
until the whales swam to their doom in the only direction
left open to them. By the mid-18th century, as the supply of
near-shore whales thinned out, the hunt for the far-flung
sperm whale began, growing into a major New England industry and making many a sea captain's fortune. Wellfleet,
Truro, and Provincetown were the only ports on the Cape
that could support deep-water distance whaling (and these
were overtaken by Nantucket and New Bedford), but ports
along the bay conducted active trade with packet ships carrying goods and passengers to and from Boston. Cape seamen were in great demand for ships sailing from Boston,
New York, and other deep-water ports. In the mid-19th
century, the Cape saw its most prosperous days, thanks
largely to the whaling industry.

Whereas previously people traveled from Boston to and
along the Cape only by stagecoach or packet boat, in 1848
the first train service from Boston began, reaching to Sandwich; by 1873 it had been extended little by little to Provincetown.

The decline in whaling hit the economies of Martha's
Vineyard and Nantucket first and hardest, and both
islands began cultivating tourism in the 19th century.
Martha's Vineyard had played host to annual Methodist
Camp Meetings since 1835, and 'Sconset, in Nantucket, became a summer haven for New York theater folk when train
service reached that remote end of the island in 1884. At the
turn of the century, Cape Cod began to actively court visitors. Creative people, in particular, were lured by the
Cape's increasingly Bohemian reputation as artists from
New York's Greenwich Village and from Europe discovered
the unspoiled beauty, special light, and lively community of
Provincetown; by 1916 five schools of art flourished here.

In 1914, several successful writers joined the artists for the
summer, and the following year, some of these writers, including John Reed (*Ten Days That Shook the World*) and
Mary Heaton Vorse (*Footnote to Folly*), began the Cape's
first significant theater group, the Provincetown Players,
producing plays at a fish house on Lewis Wharf (the theater—where 571 Commercial Street now is—was lost to fire
and storm). A young, unknown playwright named Eugene
O'Neill joined them in 1916, when his *Bound East for Cardiff* premiered at the fish house theater, and several other
O'Neill plays had Provincetown debuts. Though this was to
be their last Cape season (they moved on to New York), the
Provincetown Players were the germ of Cape community
theater and professional summer-stock companies.

The Barnstable Comedy Club, founded in 1922 and still going strong, is the most notable of the area's many amateur

groups; novelist Kurt Vonnegut acted in its productions in the 1950s and 1960s, and had some of his early plays produced by the group. Professional summer stock began with the Cape Playhouse in Dennis in 1927, and its early years featured such stars as Bette Davis (who was first an usher there), Henry Fonda, Ruth Gordon, Humphrey Bogart, and Gertrude Lawrence. In 1928, the University Players Guild (which today is called Falmouth Playhouse) opened in Falmouth, attracting such stars as James Cagney, Orson Welles, Josh Logan, Tallulah Bankhead, and James Stewart (who, while on summer vacation from Princeton, had his first bit part during Falmouth's first season).

The idea of a Cape Cod canal, linking the bay to the sound, was studied as early as the 17th century, but not until 1914 did the privately built canal merge the waters of the two bays. It was not, however, a crashing success; too narrow and winding, the canal allowed only one-way traffic and created dangerous currents. The federal government bought it in 1928 and had the U.S. Army Corps of Engineers rebuild it. In the 1930s three bridges—two traffic and one railroad—went up, and the rest is the latter-day history of tourism on Cape Cod.

The building of the Mid-Cape Highway in the 1950s marked the great boom in the Cape's growth, and the presidency of John F. Kennedy, who summered in Hyannis Port, certainly added to the area's allure. Today the Cape's summer population is about 500,000, triple the year-round population.

Though tourism, construction, and light industry are the mainstays of the Cape's economy these days, the earliest inhabitants' occupations have not disappeared. There are still more than 100 farms on the Cape, and fishing—including lobstering, scalloping, and oyster aquaculture, as well as the fruits of fishing fleets such as those in Provincetown and Chatham—is an industry that brings in $2 million a month.

Visitors are still drawn here by the sea: scientists come to delve into the mysteries of the deep, artists come for the light, and everyone comes for the charm of the beach towns, the beauty of the white sand, the soft breezes, and the roaring surf.

The Outermost House

by Henry Beston

The sand bar of Eastham is the sea wall of the inlet. Its crest overhangs the beach, and from the high, wind-trampled rim, a long slope well overgrown with dune grass descends to the meadows on the west. Seen from the tower at Nauset, the land has an air of geographical simplicity; as a matter of fact, it is full of hollows, blind passages, and amphitheatres in which the roaring of the sea changes into the far roar of a cataract. I often wander into these curious pits. On their floors of sand, on their slopes, I find patterns made by the feet of visiting birds. Here, in a little disturbed and claw-marked space of sand, a flock of larks has alighted; here one of the birds has wandered off by himself; here are the deeper tracks of hungry crows; here the webbed impressions of a gull. There is always something poetic and mysterious to me about these tracks in the pits of the dunes; they begin at nowhere, sometimes with the faint impression of an alighting wing, and vanish as suddenly into the trackless nowhere of the sky.

Below the eastern rim the dunes fall in steeps of sand to the beach. Walking the beach close in along these steeps, one walks in the afternoon shade of a kind of sand escarpment, now seven or eight feet high and reasonably level, now 15 or 20 feet high to the top of a dome or mound. In four or five places storms have washed gullies or "cuts" clean through the wall. Dune plants grow in these dry beds, rooting themselves in under old, half-buried wreckage, clumps of dusty miller, *Artemisia stelleriana*, being the most familiar green. The plant flourishes in the most exposed situations, it jumps from the dune rim to the naked slopes, it even tries to find a permanent station on the beach. Silvery gray-green all summer long, in autumn it puts on gold and russet-golden colourings of singular delicacy and beauty.

The grass grows thickest on the slopes and shoulders of the mounds, its tall leaves inclosing intrusive heads and clumps of the thick-fleshed dune goldenrod. Still lower down the slope, where the sands open and the spears rise thin, the beach pea catches the eye with its familiar leaf and faded topmost bloom; lower still, on desert-like floors, are tussock mats of poverty grass and the flat green stars of innumerable spurges. The only real bushes of the region are beach plum thickets, and these are few and far between.

All these plants have enormously long taproots which bury themselves deep in the moist core of the sands. The greater part of the year I have two beaches, one above, one below.

This essay is excerpted from Henry Beston's 1928 book The Outermost House, *which chronicles a year spent in a solitary cottage on the Great Beach on Cape Cod.*

The lower or tidal beach begins at mean low water and climbs a clean slope to the high-water mark of the average low-course tide; the upper beach, more of a plateau in form, occupies the space between high water and the dunes. The width of these beaches changes with every storm and every tide, but I shall not be far out if I call them both an average 75 feet wide. Unseasonable storm tides and high-course tides make of the beach one vast new floor. Winter tides narrow the winter's upper beach and often sweep across it to the dunes. The whole beach builds up in summer as if each tide pushed more and more sand against it out of the sea. Perhaps currents wash in sand from the outer bars.

It is no easy task to find a name or a phrase for the color of Eastham sand. Its tone, moreover, varies with the hour and the seasons. One friend says yellow on its way to brown, another speaks of the colour of raw silk. Whatever color images these hints may offer to a reader's mind, the color of the sand here on a June day is as warm and rich a tone as one may find. Late in the afternoon, there descends upon the beach and the bordering sea a delicate overtone of faintest violet. There is no harshness here in the landscape line, no hard northern brightness or brusque revelation; there is always reserve and mystery, always something beyond, on earth and sea something which nature, honouring, conceals.

The sand here has a life of its own, even if it is only a life borrowed from the wind. One pleasant summer afternoon, while a high, gusty westerly was blowing, I saw a little "wind devil," a miniature tornado six feet high, rush at full speed out of a cut, whirl itself full of sand upon the beach, and spin off breakerward. As it crossed the beach, the "devil" caught the sun, and there burst out of the sand smoke a brownish prism of burning, spinning, and fantastic color. South of me, the dune I call "big dune" now and then goes through a curious performance. Seen lengthwise, the giant has the shape of a wave, its slope to the beach being a magnificent fan of purest wind-blown sand, its westward slope a descent to a sandy amphitheatre. During a recent winter, a coast guard key post was erected on the peak of the dune; the feet of the night patrols trod down and nicked the crest, and presently this insignificant notch began to "work" and deepen. It is now eight or nine feet wide and as many deep. From across the marshes, it might be a kind of great, roundish bite out of the crest. On windy autumn days, when the sand is still dry and alive, and westerly gusts and currents take on a genuine violence, the loose sand behind the dune is whirled up by the wind and poured eastward through this funnel. At such times the peak "smokes" like a volcano. The smoke is now a streaming blackish plume, now a thin old-ivory wraith, and it billows, eddies, and pours out as from a sea Vesuvius.

Between the dunes and the marshes, an irregular width of salt-hay land extends from the sand slopes to the marshier widths of tidal land along the creeks. Each region has its own grasses, the meadows being almost a patchwork of competing growths. In the late summer and the autumn the marsh lavender, thin-strewn but straying everywhere, lifts its cloud of tiny sun-faded flowers above the tawny, almost deer-coloured grasses. The marsh islands beyond are but great masses of thatch grass rising from floors of sodded mud and sand; there are hidden pools in these unvisited acres which only sunset reveals. The wild ducks know them well and take refuge in them when stalked by gunners.

How singular it is that so little has been written about the birds of Cape Cod! The peninsula, from an ornithologist's point of view, is one of the most interesting in the world. The interest does not centre on the resident birds, for they are no more numerous here than they are in various other pleasant places; it lies in the fact that living here, one may see more kinds and varieties of birds than it would seem possible to discover in any one small region. At Eastham, for instance, among visitors and migrants, residents and casuals, I had land birds and moor birds, marsh birds and beach birds, sea birds and coastal birds, even birds of the outer ocean. West Indian hurricanes, moreover, often catch up and fling ashore here curious tropical and semitropical forms, a glossy ibis in one storm, a frigate bird in another. When living on the beach, I kept a particularly careful lookout during gales.

Eastham bar is only 3 miles long and scarce a quarter of a mile wide across its sands. Yet in this little world nature has already given her humbler creatures a protective coloration. Stop at the coast guard station and catch a locust on the station lawn—we have the maritime locust here, *Trimerotropsis maritima harris*—and, having caught him, study him well; you will find him tinted with green. Go 50 feet into the dunes and catch another, and you shall see an insect made of sand. The spiders, too, are made of sand—the phrase is none too strong—and so are the toads that go beach combing on moonlit summer nights. One may stand at the breakers' edge and study a whole world in one's hand.

* * *

They say here that great waves reach this coast in threes. Three great waves, then an indeterminate run of lesser rhythms, then three great waves again. On Celtic coasts it is the seventh wave that is seen coming like a king out of the grey, cold sea. The Cape tradition, however, is no half-real, half-mystical fancy, but the truth itself. Great waves do indeed approach this beach by threes. Again and again have I watched three giants roll in one after the other out of the Atlantic, cross the outer bar, break, form again, and follow each other in to fulfillment and destruction on this solitary beach. Coast guard crews are all well aware of this triple rhythm and take advantage of the lull that follows the last wave to launch their boats.

It is true that there are single giants as well. I have been roused by them in the night. Waked by their tremendous and unexpected crash, I have sometimes heard the last of the heavy overspill, sometimes only the loud, withdrawing roar. After the roar came a briefest pause, and after the pause the return of ocean to the night's long cadences. Such solitary titans, flinging their green tons down upon a quiet world, shake beach and dune. Late one September night, as I sat reading, the very father of all waves must have flung himself down before the house, for the quiet of the night was suddenly overturned by a gigantic, tumbling crash and an earthquake rumbling; the beach trembled beneath the avalanche, the dune shook, and my house so shook in its dune that the flame of a lamp quivered and pictures jarred on the wall.

The three great elemental sounds in nature are the sound of rain, the sound of wind in a primeval wood, and the sound of outer ocean on a beach. I have heard them all, and of the three elemental voices, that of ocean is the most awesome, beautiful, and varied. For it is a mistake to talk of the monotone of ocean or of the monotonous nature of its sound. The sea has many voices. Listen to the surf, really lend it your ears, and you will hear in it a world of sounds: hollow boomings and heavy roarings, great watery tumblings and tramplings, long hissing seethes, sharp, rifle-shot reports, splashes, whispers, the grinding undertone of stones, and sometimes vocal sounds that might be the half-heard talk of people in the sea. And not only is the great sound varied in the manner of its making, it is also constantly changing its tempo, its pitch, its accent, and its rhythm, being now loud and thundering, now almost placid, now furious, now grave and solemn-slow, now a simple measure, now a rhythm monstrous with a sense of purpose and elemental will.

Every mood of the wind, every change in the day's weather, every phase of the tide—all these have subtle sea musics all their own. Surf of the ebb, for instance, is one music, surf of the flood another, the change in the two musics being most clearly marked during the first hour of a rising tide. With the renewal of the tidal energy, the sound of the surf grows louder, the fury of battle returns to it as it turns again on the land, and beat and sound change with the renewal of the war.

Sound of surf in these autumnal dunes—the continuousness of it, sound of endless charging, endless incoming and gathering, endless fulfillment and dissolution, endless fecundity, and endless death. I have been trying to study out the mechanics of that mighty resonance. The dominant note is the great spilling crash made by each arriving wave. It may be hollow and booming, it may be heavy and churning, it may be a tumbling roar. The second fundamental sound is the wild seething cataract roar of the wave's dissolution and the rush of its foaming waters up the beach—this second sound *diminuendo*. The third fundamental sound is the endless dissolving hiss of the inmost slides of foam. The first two sounds reach the ear as a unisonance—the booming impact of the tons of water and the wild roar of the up-rush blending—and this mingled sound dissolves into the foambubble hissing of the third. Above the tumult, like birds, fly wisps of watery noise, splashes and counter splashes, whispers, seething, slaps, and chucklings. An overtone sound of other breakers, mingled with a general rumbling, fells earth and sea and air.

Here do I pause to warn my reader that although I have recounted the history of a breaker—an ideal breaker—the surf process must be understood as mingled and continuous, waves hurrying after waves, interrupting waves, washing back on waves, overwhelming waves. Moreover, I have described the sound of a high surf in fair weather. A storm surf is mechanically the same thing, but it *grinds*, and this same long, sepulchral grinding—sound of utter terror to all mariners—is a development of the second fundamental sound; it is the cry of the breaker water roaring its way ashore and dragging at the sand. A strange underbody of sound when heard through the high, wild screaming of a gale.

Breaking waves that have to run up a steep tilt of the beach are often followed by a dragging, grinding sound—the note of the baffled water running downhill again to the sea. It is loudest when the tide is low and breakers are rolling beach stones up and down a slope of the lower beach.

I am, perhaps, most conscious of the sound of surf just after I have gone to bed. Even here I read myself to drowsiness, and, reading, I hear the cadenced trampling roar filling all the dark. So close is the Fo'castle to the ocean's edge that the rhythm of sound I hear oftenest in fair weather is not so much a general tumult as an endless arrival, overspill, and dissolution of separate great seas. Through the dark, mathematic square of the screened half window, I listen to the rushes and the bursts, the tramplings, and the long, intermingled thunderings, never wearying of the sonorous and universal sound.

Away from the beach, the various sounds of the surf melt into one great thundering symphonic roar. Autumnal nights in Eastham village are full of this ocean sound. The "summer people" have gone, the village rests and prepares for winter, lamps shine from kitchen windows, and from across the moors, the great levels of the marsh, and the bulwark of the dunes resounds the long wintry roaring of the sea. Listen to it a while, and it will seem but one remote and formidable sound; listen still longer and you will discern in it a symphony of breaker thunderings, an endless, distant,

elemental cannonade. There is beauty in it, and ancient terror. I heard it last as I walked through the village on a star-
ry October night; there was no wind, the leafless trees were
still, all the village was abed, and the whole sombre world
was awesome with the sound.

* * *

One reason for my love of this great beach is that, living
here, I dwell in a world that has a good natural smell, that is
full of keen, vivid, and interesting savours and fragrances.
I have them at their best, perhaps, when hot days are
dulled with a warm rain. So well do I know them, indeed,
that were I blindfolded and led about the summer beach, I
think I could tell on what part of it I was at any moment
standing. At the ocean's very edge the air is almost always
cool—cold even—and delicately moist with surf spray and
the endless dissolution of the innumerable bubbles of the
foam slides; the wet sand slope beneath exhales a cool savour of mingling beach and sea, and the innermost breakers
push ahead of them puffs of this fragrant air. It is a singular
experience to walk this brim of ocean when the wind is
blowing almost directly down the beach, but now veering a
point toward the dunes, now a point toward the sea. For 20
feet a humid and tropical exhalation of hot, wet sand encir-
cles one, and from this one steps, as through a door, into as
many yards of mid-September. In a point of time, one goes
from Central America to Maine.

Atop the broad eight-foot back of the summer bar, inland 40 feet or so from the edge of low tide, other
odors wait. Here have the tides strewn a moist ta-
bleland with lumpy tangles, wisps, and matted festoons of
ocean vegetation—with common sea grass, with rockweed
olive-green and rockweed olive-brown, with the crushed
and wrinkled green leaves of sea lettuce, with edible, pur-
ple-red dulse and bleached sea moss, with slimy and gelati-
nous cords seven and eight feet long. In the hot noontide
they lie, slowly, slowly withering—for their very sub-
stance is water—and sending an odor of ocean and vegetation into the burning air. I like this good natural savor.
Sometimes a dead, surf-trapped fish, perhaps a dead skate
curling up in the heat, adds to this odor of vegetation a faint
fishy rankness, but the smell is not earth corruption, and
the scavengers of the beach soon enough remove the cause.

Beyond the bar and the tidal runnel farther in, the flat region I call the upper beach runs back to the shadeless bastion of the dunes. In summer this beach is rarely covered by
the tides. Here lies a hot and pleasant odor of sand. I find
myself an angle of shade slanting off from a mass of wreckage still embedded in a dune, take up a handful of the dry,
bright sand, sift it slowly through my fingers, and note how
the heat brings out the fine, sharp, stony smell of it. There
is weed here, too, well buried in the dry sand—flotsam of
last month's high, full-moon tides. In the shadowless glare,

the topmost fronds and heart-shaped air sacs have ripened to an odd iodine orange and a blackish iodine brown. Overwhelmed thus by sand and heat, the aroma of this foliage has dissolved; only a shower will summon it again from these crisping, strangely colored leaves.

Cool breath of eastern ocean, the aroma of beach vegetation in the sun, the hot, pungent exhalation of fine sand—these mingled are the midsummer savour of the beach.

3 Cape Cod

Introduction

Hear the name Cape Cod, and what word springs to mind? If it's not *quaint*, you don't know your Patti Page, and you probably don't get out enough. Traditionally associated with weathered-shingle cottages, long dune-backed beaches, fog-enshrouded lighthouses, and clam chowder, the Cape has become so popular that it risks losing the charm that brought everyone here in the first place. More and more open land so restful to eyes wearied by concrete has been lost to housing developments, condominium complexes, and strip malls, built to service the expanding year-round and summer population. In summer, the large crowds mean having to seek out the tranquillity that once met one at every turn.

Yet, for those who *do* seek it out, it will be found, for much of the Cape remains compellingly beautiful and unspoiled. Even at the height of the season, there will be no crowds at the less-traveled nature preserves and beaches and in well-preserved old villages off the beaten path. In the off-season, still-beautiful beaches welcome solitary walkers, and life everywhere returns to a small-town hum.

In 1961, the Cape Cod National Seashore was established to preserve virtually the entire eastern shoreline in its natural state for all time, and in 1990 the Cape Cod Commission was created to put a stop to the unplanned development of years past. For the sake of its economy, which is based on the area's continued appeal to tourists, and for the sake of preserving a landscape just as dear to most of the people who live here, Cape Cod has seen the light and has taken its first steps toward it.

Separated from the Massachusetts mainland by the 17.4-mile Cape Cod Canal, the Cape is always likened in shape to an outstretched arm bent at the elbow, with fist turned back toward the mainland at Provincetown. Within the arm's embrace is Cape Cod Bay; to the east is the open Atlantic; to the south, Nantucket Sound. Being surrounded by all this water has its cost: Tides regularly eat away at the land, sometimes at an alarming rate. In his book *Cape Cod*, Henry David Thoreau described the Atlantic-side beach—which he walked from end to end on several trips to the Cape in the mid-19th century—as "the edge of a continent wasting before the assaults of the ocean." Through the years, many lighthouses—some built hundreds of feet from water's edge—have fallen into the sea, and others are now in danger of being lost. Billingsgate Island off Wellfleet, which once held a number of cottages and a lighthouse, today is a bare sandbar occupied only by resting birds. The U.S. Geological Survey estimates that "at some distant time—not for many generations, however—Cape Cod will be nothing more than a few low sandy islands surrounded by shoals."

The Cape's Atlantic coast is notorious for its shoals, which have accounted for more than 3,000 shipwrecks in 300 years of recorded history. Nicknamed "the graveyard of ships," the area once had 13 life saving stations from Monomoy to Wood End, at the tip of Provincetown. They were manned by a crew of surfmen who drilled in life saving techniques during the day and took turns walking the beach at night in all kinds of weather, watching for ships in distress.

Thoreau's book and Henry Beston's *The Outermost House* contain stories of shipwrecks, which are riveting in their revelation of the awesome power of the sea, of the tragedy of lives lost in icy waters, and of the bravery of the men of the Life Saving Service, whose motto was "You have to go out, but you don't have to come back." (In the service's history, hundreds of victims were rescued; only twice were surfmen's lives lost.) When the tide is low, you can sometimes see the skeletons of wrecked ships emerge briefly from the sand in which they lie buried.

During the early 20th century, sturdier ships with improved navigational aids (such as Loran, radar, radio, computers, and weather-forecasting equipment) greatly reduced the dangers of shipping in the area. The opening of the Cape Cod Canal in 1914 meant that the great number of ships traveling between Boston and New York and New Haven no longer had to skirt the treacherous coast. In 1915, the life saving service was absorbed into the new U.S. Coast Guard.

The Cape consists of 15 towns, each broken up into villages (for example, the town of Dennis comprises the villages of Dennis and East Dennis on the north shore, Dennis Port and West Dennis on the south, and South Dennis midway between, much to the dismay of precisionists). The term *Upper Cape* (think "upper arm," relating to the Cape's shape) refers to the towns of Bourne, Falmouth, Mashpee, and Sandwich; *Mid-Cape*, to Barnstable, Yarmouth, and Dennis; and *Lower Cape* ("lower arm"), to Harwich, Chatham, Brewster, Orleans, Eastham, Truro, Wellfleet, and Provincetown. The term *Outer Cape* ("outer reaches") refers to Wellfleet, Truro, and Provincetown, and sometimes is used synonymously with *Lower Cape*.

The Upper Cape, like each of the areas embraced by these designations, contains enough diversity to make generalizations about its character rife with exceptions. The area just before and after the canal and bridges, it encompasses a vast military complex and air base, the Massachusetts Military Reservation; a major training school for seamen, the Massachusetts Maritime Academy, the Cape's second-largest town (in population), Falmouth, still green and historic yet active with shopping and culture; the Cape's oldest town, Sandwich, whose center is picture-postcard old New England; an international center of marine and biological scientific research, Woods Hole; and the Cape's only Indian township, Mashpee. Along the west coast are wooded areas ending in secluded coves; along the south coast, long-established seaside communities.

The central section of the region, aptly called the Mid-Cape, includes the largest town, Barnstable; the Cape's main commercial hub, Hyannis, which is a village in Barnstable; Hyannis Port, a well-groomed enclave of wealth and site of the Kennedy Compound; and a number of historic districts and well-preserved back roads.

From the elbow to the fist of the Cape arm is the Lower Cape, the least developed Cape segment, which encompasses Chatham, a traditional and very Capey yet sophisticated town with good shopping and strolling; the Monomoy National Wildlife Refuge, a two-island Audubon bird sanctuary; Nickerson State Park, offering the Cape's prime camping in a forest setting; the beaches, woods, swamps, historic sites, and visitor centers of the Cape Cod National Seashore; the small fishing town of

Cape Cod Exploring *(Boxes Refer to Detail Maps)*

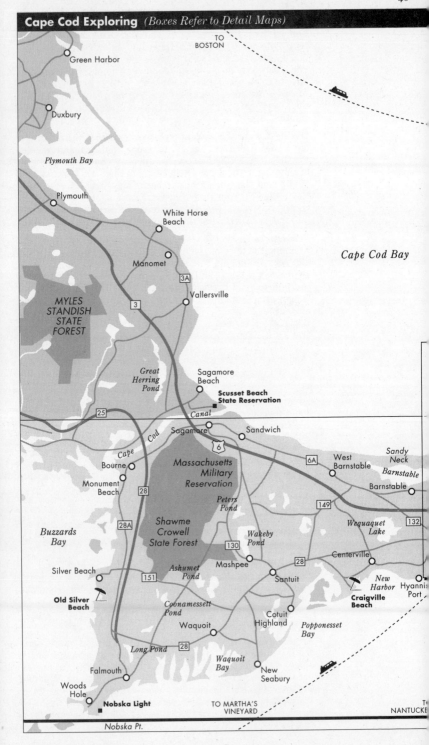

TO BOSTON

Green Harbor

Duxbury

Plymouth Bay

Plymouth

White Horse Beach

Manomet

Cape Cod Bay

3A

Vallersville

3

MYLES STANDISH STATE FOREST

Great Herring Pond

Sagamore Beach

Scusset Beach State Reservation

25

Cape Cod Canal

Sagamore

6

Sandwich

6A

West Barnstable

Sandy Neck

Barnstable

Barnstable

Bourne

Massachusetts Military Reservation

28

Monument Beach

Buzzards Bay

28A

Shawme Crowell State Forest

Peters Pond

149

132

Wequaquet Lake

Centerville

Silver Beach

151

Ashumet Pond

130

Wakeby Pond

Mashpee

28

Santuit

New Harbor

Hyannis Port

Old Silver Beach

Craigville Beach

Coonamessett Pond

Cotuit Highland

Popponesset Bay

Waquoit

28

Long Pond

Waquoit Bay

New Seabury

Falmouth

Woods Hole

Nobska Light

TO MARTHA'S VINEYARD

To NANTUCKE

Nobska Pt.

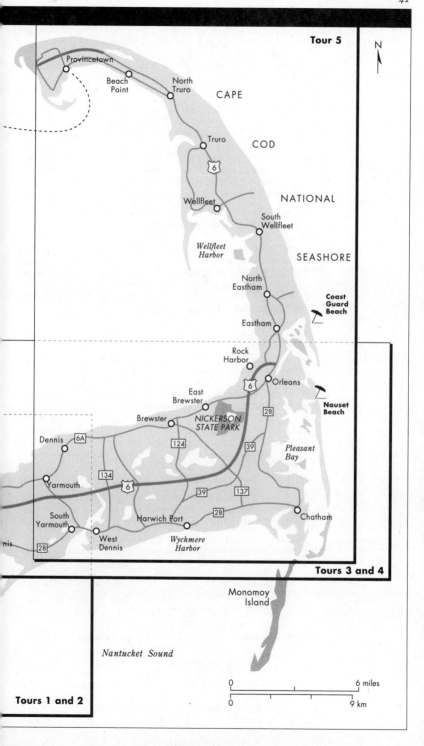

Tour 5

N

Provincetown

Beach
Point

North
Truro

CAPE

Truro

6

COD

Wellfleet

South
Wellfleet

NATIONAL

Wellfleet
Harbor

North
Eastham

SEASHORE

Coast
Guard
Beach

Eastham

Rock
Harbor

Orleans

6

Nauset
Beach

East
Brewster

Brewster

28

NICKERSON
STATE PARK

124

Dennis

6A

39

Pleasant
Bay

134

Yarmouth

6

39

137

South
Yarmouth

Harwich Port

28

Chatham

West
Dennis

nis

28

Wychmere
Harbor

Tours 3 and 4

Monomoy
Island

Nantucket Sound

0   6 miles

0   9 km

Tours 1 and 2

Wellfleet, with a number of art and crafts galleries; the high, sweeping dunes of Truro and the Province Lands; and, last but not least, Provincetown, in winter a quiet fishing village, in summer a wild and crazy place with important art galleries, wonderful crafts shops, whale-watch excursion boats, good restaurants and people-watching, and lots of nightlife, including drag shows.

Crossing these boundaries on the north is Route 6A, the Old King's Highway, preserved for miles as a National Historic District, and true to its 17th- to 19th-century origins. On the south, Route 28 is a busy, mostly commercial highway that includes the most overdeveloped areas on the Cape. And everywhere there are bay and sound beaches, calm or wild, dune- or forest-backed, blanket-paved or secluded, which continue to offer just about every option for seekers of summer sun and sea.

Cape Cod is only about 70 miles from end to end, and you can make a cursory circuit of it in about two days. But it is really a place for relaxing—for swimming and sunning; for fishing, boating, and playing golf or tennis; for attending the theater, hunting for antiques, and making the rounds of the art galleries; for lobsters and fish fresh from the boat; or for leisurely walks, bike rides, or drives along pretty country roads that continue to hold out against modernity.

Essential Information

Important Addresses and Numbers

Tourist Information The main source of information on the Cape is the **Cape Cod Chamber of Commerce** (junction of Rtes. 6 and 132, Hyannis, tel. 508/362–3225), open year-round, weekdays 8:30–5; July–Labor Day, also weekends 9–4. It has information booths in Bourne at the Sagamore Rotary (tel. 508/888–2438) and on MacArthur Boulevard (tel. 508/759–3814) heading toward Falmouth; like most town chamber booths, these are open from Memorial Day to Labor Day.

Each year the June/July issue of *Cape Cod Life* magazine (Box 222, Osterville 02655, tel. 508/428–5706) includes a Summer Leisure Guide, with a calendar of activities.

Emergencies For **police** emergencies, dial 911. For **fire and ambulance** emergencies anywhere on the Cape, call 800/352–7141.

For rescues at sea, call the **Coast Guard** (Woods Hole, tel. 508/548–1700; Sandwich, tel. 508/888–0020; Chatham, tel. 508/945–3830; Provincetown, tel. 508/487–0077).

Hospitals **Cape Cod Hospital** (27 Park St., Hyannis, tel. 508/771–1800, for emergencies ask for ext. 2235).
Falmouth Hospital (100 Ter Heun Dr., Falmouth, tel. 508/548–5300).

Walk-in Clinics The many Cape clinics include:

Dennis Medical Center (434 Rte. 134, South Dennis, tel. 508/394–7113).
Falmouth Walk-in Medical Center (309 Main St., Teaticket, tel. 508/540–6790).

HealthMaster Medical Clinic (Rte. 6A, Sandwich, tel. 508/833–1663).

Mashpee Family Medicine (Rte. 28, Deer Crossing, Mashpee, tel. 508/477–4282).

Medi-Center Five (525 Long Pond Dr., Harwich, tel. 508/432–4100).

Mid-Cape Medical Center (Rte. 28 at Bearse's Way, Hyannis, tel. 508/771–4092; Rte. 28, South Yarmouth, tel. 508/394–2151).

Outer Cape Health Services (Rte. 6, Wellfleet, tel. 508/349–3131; Harry Kemp Way, Provincetown, tel. 508/487–9395).

Dentists **Omni Dentix** (Cape Cod Mall, Hyannis, tel. 508/778–1200) is a dental clinic that accepts emergency walk-ins.

Late-Night Pharmacies Most of the Cape's 10 **CVS** stores (in the Cape Cod Mall, tel. 508/771–1774) are open Monday–Saturday until 9 PM, Sunday until 6. They usually accept out-of-town prescription refills with the prescribing doctor's phone verification. Most pharmacies post emergency numbers on their doors.

Other Information **Army Corps of Engineers 24-hour hot line** for events, tide, and fishing information on the canal area: tel. 508/759–5991.

Tide, marine, and weather forecast: tel. 508/255–8500 or 771–5522.

Arriving and Departing by Plane

Airports **Barnstable Municipal Airport** (Rte. 28 rotary, Hyannis, tel. 508/775–2020) is the region's main air gateway. **Provincetown Municipal Airport** (Race Point Rd., tel. 508/487–0241) offers year-round scheduled flights to Boston, plus charters anywhere. **Chatham Municipal Airport** (George Ryder Rd., West Chatham, tel. 508/945–9000) offers scheduled flights to and from the islands; charters are readily available. None of these airports is more than a few minutes from the town center.

Airlines Airline service is extremely unpredictable because of the seasonal nature of Cape travel—carriers come and go, others juggle their routes. The Barnstable airport will always know which carriers fly in, should you encounter difficulty in making reservations. **Continental Express** (tel. 800/525–0280) flies year-round between Hyannis and Boston, Newark, and New York, with connections from elsewhere. **Business Express/Delta Connection** (tel. 800/345–3400) flies into Hyannis nonstop from Boston (where connections are made with other routes) and New York April–September; in summer, it may offer weekend nonstops from Newark; Philadelphia; Washington, DC; and/or White Plains, NY (check for current availability). **Northwest Airlink** (tel. 800/225–2525) flies between Hyannis and Boston year-round, with connections to the Northwest routes. Provincetown is served by **Cape Air** (tel. 800/352–0714) year-round, with flights to and from Boston.

Cape Cod Air (tel. 508/945–9000 or 800/553–2376) has charter flights out of Chatham.

Arriving and Departing by Car

From Boston, take Route 3, the Southeast Expressway, south to the Sagamore Bridge—60 miles. From New York, take I–95 north to Providence; change to I–195 and follow signs for the

Cape to the Bourne Bridge—a total of 220 miles. At the Sagamore Bridge, take Route 6 east to reach the Lower Cape and
central towns quickly. At the Bourne Bridge, you can also get
onto Route 6, or take Route 28 south to Falmouth and Woods
Hole (about 15 miles). On summer weekends, when more than
100,000 cars a day cross each bridge, make every effort to avoid
arriving at the bridges in late afternoon, especially on holidays. The major routes—6, 6A, and 28—are heavily congested
eastbound on Friday evening and westbound on Sunday afternoon.

Arriving and Departing by Train, Bus, and Boat

By Train **Amtrak** (tel. 800/USA–RAIL) offers limited service to the
Cape, with stops at Buzzards Bay, Sandwich, West Barnstable, and Hyannis; each year the company reevaluates the
routes, so don't be surprised if you find changes. The *Cape
Codder*, on weekends from late June through Labor Day, travels between Hyannis and Washington, DC, with stops at Philadelphia, New York, and other points; first-class service is
available. Also in summer, the *Clamdigger* makes weekend
runs between Providence and Hyannis. Connections with
trains on other routes can of course be made at any point along
these trains' routes. The rest of the year, you can travel to Boston by train and connect with buses there for Hyannis; Amtrak
makes the arrangements, and connections are guaranteed.

By Bus **Bonanza Bus Lines** (tel. 508/548–7588 or 800/556–3815) offers
direct service to Bourne, Falmouth, the Woods Hole steamship
terminal, and Hyannis from Boston, Providence, Fall River,
and New Bedford, and connecting service from New York and
Connecticut. **Greyhound** (tel. 800/531–5332) serves the Cape
from Boston, Rhode Island, New York, and Connecticut; **Peter
Pan** (tel. 800/328–9997), from western Massachusetts; **Plymouth & Brockton Street Railway** (tel. 508/775–5524 or 800/328–
9997 in MA), from Boston and Logan Airport.

By Boat **Bay State Cruise Company** (tel. 617/723–7800 in Boston, 508/
487–1741 in Provincetown) runs ferries between Common-
wealth Pier in Boston and MacMillan Wharf in Provincetown
from Memorial Day to Columbus Day. *Cost one way/same-day
round-trip: $15/$25 adults, $12/$18 children and senior citizens, $5/$10 bicycles.*

Getting Around

By Car Traffic on Cape Cod in summer can be maddening, especially on
Route 28, which traces the populous south shore. Route 6 is the
main artery, a limited-access (mostly divided) highway running the entire length of the Cape. The Old King's Highway, or
Route 6A, parallels Route 6 and is a scenic country road lined
with crafts and antiques shops. When you're in no hurry, use
the back roads—they're less frustrating and much more re-
warding.

Rental cars are available at the airport in Hyannis—**Avis** (tel.
508/775–2888), **Hertz** (tel. 508/775–5825), and **National** (tel.
508/771–4353)—or through town branches of the other major
chains (*see* Chapter 1, Essential Information).

By Bus The **Cape Cod Regional Transit Authority** (tel. 800/352–7155)
provides bus service between Hyannis and Woods Hole; its

many stops include Cape Cod Community College, Cape Cod Mall, Mashpee Commons, and Falmouth center. **Plymouth & Brockton** (tel. 508/775–5524, or 800/328–9997 in MA) has service between Sagamore and Provincetown, with stops at many towns in between. **Bonanza** (tel. 508/548–7588) plies between Bourne, Falmouth, Woods Hole, and Hyannis. All service is year-round.

By Bicycle Bicycling is a satisfying way of getting around the Cape. There are many flat back roads, as well as a number of well-developed and scenic bike trails (*see* Bicycling in Sports and Outdoor Activities, below). The 14-mile Cape Cod Rail Trail is a scenic way to travel between Dennis and Eastham. The following is just a sampling of the many bike-rental shops available.

Upper Cape **Bill's Bike Shop** (847 E. Main St., Falmouth, tel. 508/548–7979).

Full Cycle (7 Merchant Sq., Sandwich, tel. 508/888–8445).

Holiday Cycles (465 Grand Ave., Falmouth Heights, tel. 508/540–3549).

P&M Cycles (29 Main St., Buzzards Bay, tel. 508/759–2830).

Summit Ski and Bike Shop (Rte. 28, Falmouth, tel. 508/540–2263), mountain bike specialists.

Mid-Cape **All Cape Sales** (627 Main St., West Yarmouth, tel. 508/771–8100).

Cascade Motor Lodge (201 Main St., Hyannis, tel. 508/775–9717).

Outdoor Shop (50 Long Pond Dr., South Yarmouth, tel. 508/394–3819).

Summit Ski and Bike Shop (269 Barnstable Rd., Hyannis, tel. 508/775–3301).

Lower Cape **Arnold's** (329 Commercial St., Provincetown, tel. 508/487–0844).

Bert & Carol's Lawnmower & Bicycle Shop (347 Orleans Rd., Rte. 28, North Chatham, tel. 508/945–0137).

Black Duck Sports Shop (Main St., Wellfleet, tel. 508/349–9801).

Idle Times (Rte. 6A, Brewster, tel. 508/896–9242).

Rail Trail Bike Rentals (302 Underpass Rd., Brewster, tel. 508/896–2361), just off the trail.

Summit Ski and Bike Shop (Rte. 6A, Orleans, tel. 508/255–7547).

The Little Capistrano (Rte. 6, across from Salt Pond Visitor Center, Eastham, tel. 508/255–6515).

By Moped **Outdoor Shop, All Cape Sales,** and **Bert & Carol's** also rent mopeds (*see* By Bicycle, above).

By Limousine **Great Escapes Tour & Limousine Co.** in Hyannis (tel. 508/790–3711), **Windsor Limousine Service** in Sandwich (tel. 508/888–3929 or 800/902–6319), **John's Taxi & Limousine** in Dennisport (tel. 508/394–3209), and **East Coast Limousine & Transportation** in Harwich (tel. 508/398–5466 or 430–0440) provide 24-hour Cape-wide limo service.

By Taxi A sampling of taxi companies: **All Village Taxi** (Falmouth, tel. 508/540–7200), **Brewster Taxi** (Orleans, tel. 508/255–3277), **Chatham Taxi** (tel. 508/945–0068), **Falmouth Taxi** (tel. 508/548–4100 or 3100), **Hyannis Taxi** (tel. 508/775–0400), **Martin's Taxi** (Provincetown, tel. 508/487–0243), **Orleans Town Taxi** (tel. 508/487–1827), and **Town Taxi** (Hyannis, tel. 508/771–5555).

By Horse-Drawn Carriage **Rambling Rose Carriage Co.** (tel. 508/487–4246) offers carriage rides in season through Provincetown. The carriage stand is on Commercial Street in front of the town hall. Sleigh bells are provided on request.

Guided Tours

Orientation **Croll Travel** (Box 2070, Orleans 02653, tel. 508/240–1317) offers guided day tours of the Cape, with Martha's Vineyard or Nantucket segments available, in a nine-passenger luxury van (June–Oct.). Owner Jeff Croll also arranges customized tours.

Special-Interest Cruises **Hy-Line** offers one-hour narrated tours of Hyannis Port Harbor, including a view of the Kennedy Compound; evening cocktail cruises are also available. *Ocean St. Dock, Pier 1, tel. 508/778–2600. Cost: $7 adults, $2 children 2–12 with adult.*

Cape Cod Canal Cruises (two or three hours, narrated) leave from Onset, just before the bridges onto the Cape. A Sunday jazz cruise, sunset cocktail cruises, and evening dance cruises are available. *Onset Bay Town Pier, tel. 508/295–3883. Cost: $6–$8 adults, $3–$4 children 6–12; $1 senior citizen discount Mon. and Fri.*

Patriot Party Boats offer two- to three-hour cruises between Falmouth and Woods Hole, past the Nobska Light and mansions. In winter and spring, the company runs trips to see harbor seals in the Elizabeth Islands; charters are available. *227 Clinton Ave., Falmouth, tel. 508/548–2626. Cost: $8 adults, $4 children 6–12.*

Water Safaris Ltd. offers 1½-hour tours of Bass River, past windmills, wilderness areas, and old captains' homes, on a 32-foot aluminum boat with an awning. *Bass River Marina, Rte. 28, West Dennis, tel. 508/362–5555. Cost: $7.50 adults, $4.50 children.*

The 30-foot sailing yacht *Wind Gypsy* sails out of Wellfleet Harbor, anchoring off Great Island; you get the use of a dinghy to explore, plus lunch and soft drinks. Minicruises, sunset cruises, and charters are available. *Tel. 508/240–1704 or 255–9640. Cost: $30 adults, $15 children under 13.*

The 68-foot gaff-rigged schooner *Bay Lady II* makes two-hour sails, including a sunset cruise, across Provincetown Harbor and into Cape Cod Bay. *MacMillan Pier, Provincetown, tel. 508/487–9308. Cost: $10 adults, $5 children under 12 ($2 discount on 9:30 AM sailings).*

All the above operate from May into October. For information on boats and ferries to the islands, *see* Chapter 4, Martha's Vineyard, and Chapter 5, Nantucket.

Train Tours **Cape Cod Railroad** runs 1¾-hour excursions between Sagamore and Hyannis with stops at Sandwich and the canal. The train passes ponds, cranberry bogs, and marshes. A new Dinner Train begins and ends in Hyannis (3 hours) and includes a full meal, with hors d'oeuvres and a champagne cocktail. Floodlights along the train light up the passing scenery. *Main and Center Sts., Hyannis, tel. 508/866–4526. Several departures per day (no service Mon. or Fri.) in each direction mid-June–Oct. Cost: $10.50 adults, $6.50 children 3–12, $9.50 senior citizens. Dinner train: mid-June–early Dec., departs Wed., Fri.,* *and Sat. at 6:30 PM (reservations required 24 hrs in advance). Cost: $37.50.*

Limo Tours **Great Escapes** (*see* Getting Around by Limousine, above) will plan half- or full-day tours of the Cape. **East Coast Limousine** offers twilight drives; from $99 for up to six people.

Nature Tours From June to mid-December, the **Massachusetts Audubon Society** (contact Wellfleet Bay Wildlife Sanctuary, Box 236, South Wellfleet 02663, tel. 508/349–2615) sponsors naturalist-led wildlife tours, including a tour of Nauset Marsh and Coast Guard Beach, with a walk on the tidal flats and a stop at the tern nesting colony; half- to full-day trips to the bird sanctuary of Monomoy Island, with 2–4 miles of walking in sand (not recommended for children); and a program of canoe trips, bay cruises, bird and insect walks, hikes, and more.

The Audubon Society's **Ashumet Holly Reservation** in East Falmouth (Ashumet Rd., tel. 508/563–6390) offers nature day trips and cruises to Cuttyhunk Island, with guided birding walks in season. Phone reservations are required.

The **Cape Cod National Seashore** (Salt Pond, tel. 508/255–3421; Wellfleet, tel. 508/349–3785; Province Lands, tel. 508/487–1256; also *see* Tour 5: Provincetown, below) has guided walks, canoe trips, and more, from Memorial Day to Columbus Day, plus seven self-guided trails with accompanying leaflets.

Cape Cod Museum of Natural History (*see* Tour 3: Route 6A, Hyannis to Orleans, below) offers tours to Monomoy, including overnights at the lighthouse.

Plane Tours Sightseeing by air is offered by **Cape Cod Airport** (1000 Race Lane, Marstons Mills, tel. 508/428–8732), **Cape Cod Air** (tel. 508/945–9000, or 800/553–2376 in MA; out of the Chatham and Provincetown airports), and **Ocean Air** (tel. 508/771–1231; seaplanes). **Hyannis Air Service** (tel. 508/775–8171 or 800/321–9912 in MA) and **Cape Air** (tel. 508/487–0240) offer helicopter sightseeing rides out of Hyannis and Provincetown, respectively.

Dune Tours **Art's Dune Tours** (tel. 508/487–1950 or 487–1050) has been offering narrated tours through the National Seashore and dunes around Provincetown, including sunset rides, since 1946. **Mitch's Dune Tours** (tel. 508/487–9500) leave from the Provincetown Inn.

Trolley Tours May through October in Provincetown, the **P-town Trolley** leaves from the Town Hall, with pickups at other locations, hourly from 10 to 8 (also half-hourly 11:30–5:30) for 40-minute narrated tours. Points of interest on the route include the downtown area and the Province Lands Visitor Center of the Cape Cod National Seashore. Riders can get on and off at will. *Tel. 508/487–9483. Cost: $6 adults, $4 children under 13, $5 senior citizens.*

Whale-watching One of the joys of Cape Cod is the opportunity it affords for making trips to the whale feeding grounds at Stellwagen Bank, about 6 miles off the tip of Provincetown. On a sunny day especially, the boat ride out into open ocean is part of the pleasure, but the thrill, of course, is the sightings. You may spot minke, humpback, or finback whales, or the most endangered great-whale species, the right whale; just as welcome are dolphins, which in fact are toothed whales, and the seabirds that tag along for the ride.

Several operators offer whale-watch tours from April through October, with morning, afternoon, or sunset sailings lasting three to four hours. Provincetown is the main center. All boats have food service, but remember to bring sunscreen and a sweater or jacket—the breeze makes it chilly. Some boats stock seasickness pills, but if you're susceptible, come prepared!

The **Dolphin Fleet** (tel. 508/255–3857, or 800/826–9300 in MA) tours are accompanied by scientists who provide commentary while collecting data on the whale population they've been monitoring for years. They know the whales by name and tell you about their habits and histories. *Ticket office in Chamber of Commerce building at MacMillan Wharf, tel. 508/255–3857, or 800/826–9300 in MA outside Lower Cape. Cost: $15–$16 adults (seasonal variation), $13–$14 children 7–12 and senior citizens.*

The ***Portuguese Princess*** sails with a naturalist on board to narrate, plus a folk singer or other entertainer on some trips; the snack bar offers Portuguese specialties. *Tickets available at Whale Watchers General Store, 309 Commercial St., tel. 508/487–1900, or at MacMillan Wharf ticket booth, tel. 508/487–2651, or 800/442–3188 in MA. Cost: $14–$16 adults, $12–$14 children 7–12 and senior citizens.*

The ***Ranger V*** also has a naturalist on board. *Ticket office on Bradford St. just east of Standish St., tel. 508/487–3322, 508/487–1582, or 800/992–9333 in MA. Cost: $14–$17 adults, $10–$12 children 7–12, $12–$14 senior citizens.*

Out of Barnstable Harbor, there's **Hyannis Whale Watcher Cruises.** A naturalist narrates and gives commentary on Cape Cod Bay. The boat ride is often longer than the others, since it's 21 miles to Stellwagen Bank. *Mill Way, Barnstable, tel. 508/775–1622 or 362–6088. Cost: $14–$20 adults, $9–$14 children 7–15, $12–$16 senior citizens. Tours Apr.–Nov.*

Video and Audio Tours **Video Marketing Associates** (Box 723, South Yarmouth 02664, tel. 508/760–1424, or 800/635–5220 in MA) has a range of Cape offerings, including a video on B&Bs and an audio tour.

Exploring Cape Cod

Orientation

The bridges over the canal are welcome sights to those approaching the Cape by land—signs every return vacationer eagerly awaits and never takes for granted. They're a bit magical, glistening silver arcs in the air, with boats small and large gliding smoothly below. The **Bourne Bridge** is the longest, at 2,384 feet; the **Sagamore Bridge** is 1,408 feet long. Each is supported by 44 steel cables suspended from the arch; these cables, all of which were replaced in 1979, support 100,000 cars each day in summer. The railroad bridge has a movable span that lowers on the approach of a train; it takes about 2½ minutes.

Beyond the bridges, Cape Cod is traversed by three main highways. Route 6, the Mid-Cape Highway, passes through the relatively unpopulated center of the Cape, characterized by a landscape of scrub pine and oak. This is the fastest route east-west, and to Provincetown.

Paralleling Route 6 but following the north coast is Route 6A (also known as the Old King's Highway, the Cranberry Highway, and the Grand Army of the Republic Highway), in most sections a winding country road that passes through some of the Cape's best-preserved old New England towns. Here are main streets lined with stately sea captains' mansions and shaded by ancient, leafy trees. The bay side, as the north coast is called, tends to be marshy, and the water in the protected bay is calmer than that of Nantucket Sound and the Atlantic.

The south shore of the Cape, traced by Route 28 and encompassing Falmouth, Hyannis, and Chatham, is heavily populated and is the major center for tourism. Its growth as a resort area has been abetted by its abundance of scenic harbors overlooking Nantucket Sound and its beaches with white sand and gentle surf. Route 28 itself is a busy highway, in summer densely packed with cars. Between about Hyannis and Harwich Port, it is flanked by strip malls, restaurants, motels, and kiddie attractions.

At Orleans, Routes 6A and 28 join with Route 6, which then continues alone through the sparsely populated Outer Cape, also called the back side, to the tip of Cape Cod.

More is included in each of the tours that follow than can be comfortably covered in one day, on the assumption that visitors will select the stops that are of most interest to them. Hyannis and Orleans are used as convenient beginning and end points; Hyannis itself is covered in Tour 1, Orleans in Tour 3.

Highlights for First-time Visitors

Cape Cod Museum of Natural History, Brewster (*see* Tour 3)
Cape Cod National Seashore (*see* Tour 5)
Heritage Plantation, Sandwich (*see* Tour 1)
Julia Wood House, Falmouth (*see* Tour 2)
Kennedy Memorial, Hyannis (*see* Tour 1)
Pilgrim Monument, Provincetown (*see* Tour 6)
Sandy Neck, Sandwich (*see* Tour 1)
Whale watching (*see* Guided Tours, above)

Tour 1: Route 6A, Sagamore Bridge to Hyannis

This tour traverses a quiet section of the north shore, on a country road lined with small shops. All of Route 6A from Sandwich east—encompassing the oldest settlements on the Cape—is part of the Old King's Highway historic district and therefore protected from development. In fall, the foliage along the road is bright because of the many ponds and marshes, and along 6A in Sandwich you can stop to watch the berries being harvested in flooded bogs. The whole tour covers about 25 miles.

Numbers in the margin correspond with points of interest on the Tours 1 and 2: The Canal to Hyannis map.

Take the first exit after crossing the Sagamore Bridge. Past the Cape Cod Factory Outlet Mall (*see* Shopping, below) and across the street from the Christmas Tree Shop entrance is **Pairpont Glass,** where you can watch richly colored lead crystal being hand-blown in the factory, as it has been for 150 years. The shop sells finished wares, including ornamental cup plates (used to hold the cup in the days when tea was poured into the saucer to drink). *Rte. 6A, Sagamore, tel. 508/888–2344. Open daily 9–6; demonstrations weekdays 10–4.*

❶ Continuing along Route 6A, you enter **Sandwich,** the oldest town on the Cape (founded in 1637). Signs direct you to Sandwich center, a perfect old New England village and a place where you'll probably want to walk around a bit (the following is an easy walking tour).

Across from two small greens is the **Sandwich Glass Museum.** Unlike other Cape towns, whose deep-water ports opened the doors to prosperity in the whaling days, Sandwich was an industrial town for much of the 19th century. The main industry was the production of colored glass, called Sandwich glass, which is today a collectors' item. The glass was made in the Boston & Sandwich Glass Company's factory here from 1825 until 1888, when competition with glassmakers in the Midwest—and finally a union strike—closed it. The museum contains relics of the town's early history, a diorama showing how the factory looked in its heyday, and an outstanding collection of pressed and lacy glass. *129 Main St., tel. 508/888–0251. Admission: $2.50 adults, 50¢ children over 6. Open Apr.–Oct., daily 9:30–4:30; Nov., Dec., Feb., and Mar., Wed.–Sun. 9:30–4; closed Jan.*

Farther down Main Street, across River Street on the left, is the **Yesteryears Doll Museum.** Housed in the unfortunately rundown 1833 First Parish Meetinghouse, the enormous collection includes dolls depicting famous people, such as Charlie Chaplin and Shirley Temple; lacquer-and-gold miniatures of a Chinese emperor and empress and their court; Henry VIII and his wives, elegantly clothed in velvets and brocades; samurai warriors; and Balinese shadow puppets. The museum also has some wonderful miniature sets, such as a toy millinery shop with display cases, hatboxes, even ladies trying hats on; three period German kitchens, complete with pewter, brass, copper, and tin implements; and an elaborately detailed four-story late Victorian dollhouse with wedding feast going on. *Corner of Main and River Sts., tel. 508/888–1711. Admission: $2.50 adults, $2 senior citizens, $1.50 children under 12. Open Mon.–Sat. 10–4. Closed Nov.–mid-May.*

Just beyond is the **Dan'l Webster Inn,** a reconstruction of a historic inn, and on both sides of the street are antiques and gift shops and art galleries. At School Street, turn right; across Water Street (Route 130) is the **Hoxie House,** a restored 1637 shingled saltbox that is the Cape's oldest house. Overlooking Shawme Pond, it has been furnished authentically to reflect daily life in the Colonial period; some pieces are on loan from the Museum of Fine Arts in Boston. A highlight is a collection of small antique textile machines (spinning wheels, yarn winders, a 17th-century harness loom). *Rte. 130, tel. 508/888–1173. Admission: $1.50 adults, 75¢ children 12–16. Open Mon.–Sat. 10–5, Sun. 1–5. Closed mid-Oct.–May.*

Turn left as you leave the Hoxie House and follow Water Street to the **Thornton W. Burgess Museum,** dedicated to this Sandwich native who created Peter Rabbit, Reddy Fox, and a host of other creatures of the Old Briar Patch who have been part of children's bedtimes for decades. Burgess, an avid conservationist, made his characters behave true to their species in order to educate children as he entertained them. A storytelling

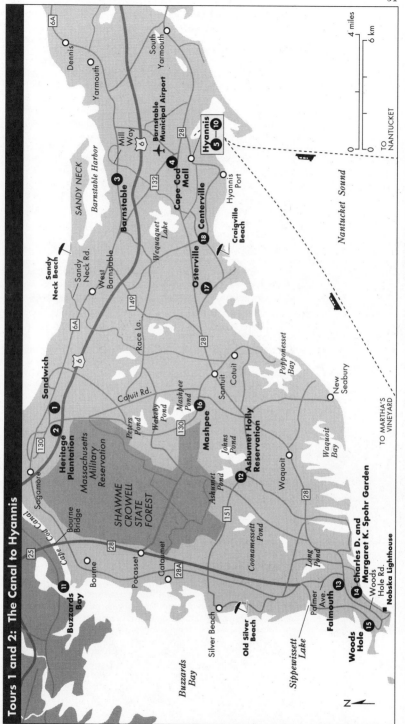

Tours 1 and 2: The Canal to Hyannis

TO NANTUCKET

4 miles

6 km

Nantucket Sound

Dennis

6A

South Yarmouth

Yarmouth

Mill Way

6

Barnstable Municipal Airport

Hyannis
5 10

28

Cape Cod Mall 4

SANDY NECK

Barnstable Harbor

Barnstable 3

132

Centerville 18

Hyannis Port

Sandy Neck Beach

Sandy Neck Rd.

West Barnstable

149

Wequaquet Lake

Osterville 17

Craigville Beach

6A

Sandwich 1

Race La.

28

Cotuit Rd.

Peters Pond

Wakeby Pond

Mashpee Pond

Mashpee 16

Sanfuit

Cotuit

Poppnesset Bay

Heritage Plantation 2

130

Massachusetts Military Reservation

130

Johns Pond

Ashumet Holly Reservation 12

Waquoit

New Seabury

Sagamore

SHAWME CROWELL STATE FOREST

Ashumet Pond

151

Waquoit Bay

Bourne Bridge

Cod Canal

28

Coonamessett Pond

TO MARTHA'S VINEYARD

25

Cape

Cataumet

28A

Long Pond

Bourne

Pocasset

Buzzards Bay 11

Silver Beach

Palmer Ave.

Charles D. and Margaret K. Spohr Garden 14

Buzzards Bay

Sippewissett Lake

Old Silver Beach

Falmouth 13

Woods Hole Rd.

Nobska Lighthouse

Woods Hole 15

N

session, featuring the live animal that the Burgess story is about, is held Monday–Saturday at 1:30 in July and August. The museum is best for small children or nostalgic adults; the many displays crowded into the small old house include stuffed birds, miniature woodland scenes with animals made from pussy willows, some of Burgess's 170 books (and information about him), and changing exhibits on nature. The small gift shop carries inexpensive items, including stuffed animals and Pairpont Glass cup plates decorated with Burgess characters. Out back is a small touch-and-smell herb garden and a labeled herb garden in the shape of a tussie-mussie (a Victorian nosegay); the lavender lends a subtle scent to the air. Benches overlook the lovely **Shawme Pond** as ducks and geese bathe along the shore and wander the grounds. *4 Water St. (Rte. 130), tel. 508/888–4668. Donations accepted. Open Mon.–Sat. 10–4, Sun. 1–4; Jan.–Mar., may close Sun. and/or Mon.*

Just beyond is the waterwheel-operated **Dexter Gristmill**, restored in 17th-century style and still grinding corn in season (you can buy the meal). Approach it via a covered wooden bridge over a watercourse in a picturesque park at the pond, where children seem always to be fishing and the ducks love to be fed. Where Main Street joins Water you'll notice the tall, white spire of the **First Church of Christ**, built in 1848, and inspired by a design of London architect Christopher Wren.

② Leaving the village (by car), take Grove Street to **Heritage Plantation**, an extraordinary complex of museum buildings and gardens on 76 beautifully landscaped acres overlooking Shawme Pond. The grounds, crisscrossed by paths, include daylily, herb, fruit-tree, and other gardens, as well as an extensive dell of rhododendrons begun by onetime estate owner Charles O. Dexter, an expert in hybridization. (In 1967, pharmaceuticals magnate Josiah K. Lilly III purchased the estate and turned it into a nonprofit museum.) In summer, evening concerts are held in the gardens. The Shaker Round Barn showcases classic and historic cars, including a 1931 yellow-and-green Duesenberg built for Gary Cooper, a 1919 Pierce-Arrow, and a 1911 Stanley Steamer. The Military Museum houses antique firearms, a collection of 2,000 hand-painted miniature soldiers, and military uniforms. The Art Museum exhibits Colonial tools, an extensive Currier & Ives collection, Americana (including a mechanical-bank collection), antique toys such as a 1920 Hubley Royal Circus, and a working 1912 carousel. *Grove and Pine Sts., tel. 508/888–3300. Admission: $7 adults, $6 senior citizens, $3 children 6–12. Open mid-May–Oct., daily 10–5. Closed Nov.–mid-May.*

Return to Sandwich center and from there to Route 6A, then head east. Before you get to Exit 3 you will come to the **Green Briar Nature Center and Jam Kitchen,** owned by the Thornton Burgess Society, which runs the Burgess museum as well. The nature center offers changing exhibits on natural history, such as live frogs or turtles, aquariums, Indian artifacts, and seashells, as well as nature classes, walks, lectures, and films for adults and children. Great smells waft from the vintage stoves in the Jam Kitchen, and you can watch as jams, cranberry dishes, sun-dried fruits, and pickles are made according to the recipes used here since 1903. *6 Discovery Hill Rd., off Rte. 6A, East Sandwich, tel. 508/888–6870. Donations accepted.*

*Open Mon.–Sat. 10–4, Sun. 1–4; Jan.–Mar., may close Sun.
and/or Mon.*

The center is set on 4 acres of gardens (labeled herb garden,
bee garden, wildflower garden) that adjoin 57 acres of town
conservation land laced with easy nature trails, dubbed the **Old
Briar Patch.** The many varieties of plants and trees include
black locust, white oak, red maple, tupelo, highbush blueberry, American beech and holly, swamp honeysuckle, gray birch,
and spice bush; a brochure (with map) of the trails, available at
the nature center, helps you identify them.

Sandy Neck Road (on the left, opposite Michael's at Sandy
Neck restaurant) leads to **Sandy Neck Beach.** The approach,
through duneland, is beautiful, and because it's a peninsula,
this is a good beach for walking; all you see is dunes and sand
and sea in both directions. The **Sandy Neck Light,** nonopera-
tional since 1952 and now privately owned, stands just a few
feet from the eroding shoreline. It was built in 1857 (to replace
an 1827 light) of steel painted white, and it ran on acetylene
gas.

3 As you continue east on 6A, past fine views of meadows and the
bay, you enter the town of **Barnstable,** the Cape's largest, with
more than 36,000 year-round residents, and the second oldest,
having been founded in 1639, two years after Sandwich. You've
just left the cozy Upper Cape for the busier Mid-Cape, but here
in the historic district you won't notice the difference.

Soon after the junction of Route 132 (which leads to the **Cape
Cod Community College,** set on 120 wooded acres, and opposite
it, the **Cape Cod Conservatory of Music and Arts**), a left at either Scudder Lane or one of the other small roads will bring you
to Barnstable Harbor, and a peaceful view of Sandy Neck
across the water. A bit farther on 6A and you're in **Barnstable
Village,** a lovely area of large old homes and the county seat.
The **Olde Colonial Courthouse,** on the left, built in 1772, is the
home of the historical society Tales of Cape Cod (tel. 508/362–
8927), which is restoring it to serve as a museum. The collection
includes paintings illustrating each Cape town's history and
many old photographs; a lecture series is held in summer.

Time Out **Piccadilly Deli** (Post Office Sq., Rte. 6A, tel. 508/362–2994) is a
cheery, bright spot for breakfast and lunch, with sandwiches,
deli items like bagels and lox, and great homemade pastries.
It's open daily year-round.

Just past the county courthouse, on the left, is the **Sturgis Library,** the oldest in the United States, built in 1644. Its hold-
ings include maps, land charts, and other historical and
genealogical material on Barnstable County dating back to the
17th century, plus an extensive maritime history collection.
*Rte. 6A, tel. 508/362–6636. Day use: $5. Open Mon. and Wed.
10–5, Tues. and Thurs. 1–5 and 7–9, Fri. 1–5.*

Beyond the library is the Barnstable Village Hall, home of the
Barnstable Comedy Club, one of the oldest community theater
groups in the country. A left onto Mill Way at the traffic light
leads to **Barnstable Harbor,** with a fleet of fishing, charter, and
whale-watch boats. Beyond the light, on the right, is the **Donald G. Trayser Memorial Museum,** reopened in 1990 after two
years of renovation. The downstairs re-creates the way it

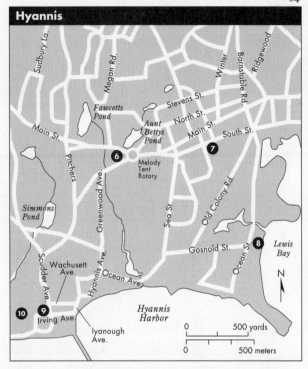

looked in 1856, when it was a customs house (don't miss the gilt capitals on the pillars). Listed on the National Register of Historic Places, the red-painted brick building now houses a small collection of maritime exhibits (telescopes, captains' shaving boxes, items brought back from voyages, ship paintings), plus ivory, Sandwich glass, and Indian arrowheads. *Rte. 6A, Barnstable, tel. 508/362–2092. Donations accepted. Open Tues.– Sat. 1–4:30. Closed mid-Oct–May.*

If you return to the traffic light, a left there will take you into Hyannis (about 2 miles) along a favorite local traffic-avoiding route. Beyond the intersection with Route 6, a left onto Route **4** 132 leads past the **Cape Cod Mall** to what's called the Airport rotary, with the **Barnstable Municipal Airport** just beyond, on Route 28. Signs at the rotary will lead you to downtown **5** **Hyannis,** the Cape's year-round commercial hub, and a visibly different scene from what you've just left. Now you're well and truly in the Mid-Cape.

Numbers in the margin correspond with points of interest on the Hyannis map.

A right turn onto Main Street will take you through the downtown. Three parallel streets run through the heart of Hyannis. The busy, shop-filled Main Street is one-way, from east to west; South Street runs from west to east; and North Street is open to two-way traffic. Following Main Street will take you to another rotary at the west end of town, referred to as the West **6** End or Melody Tent rotary for the famous **Melody Tent,** where top artists perform music and comedy during the summer (*see*

The Arts, below), just beyond the intersection on West Main Street. The tent was opened in 1950 by the actress Gertrude Lawrence and her husband, producer/manager Richard Aldrich, to showcase Broadway musicals and concerts; today the focus has shifted away from theater—for which the Cape has many other venues—to music and stand-up comedy.

7 Return to the rotary and Main Street; turn right onto South Street and on your right you'll pass **St. Francis Xavier Church,** the little church where Rose Kennedy and her family worshiped during their summers on the Cape. The pew that John F. Kennedy used regularly is marked by a plaque. A few doors down is the **Octagonal House,** a private home built in 1850 by a clipper ship master. At Ocean Street, turn right. Past the bustling docks—with boats for deep-sea fishing, harbor tours, and ferries to the islands, as well as seafood restaurants with great water views—is **Veterans Park,** with a beach and a tree-shaded **8** picnic area and playground. Adjacent to it and overlooking boat-filled Lewis Bay is the **John F. Kennedy Memorial,** a quiet esplanade with a plaque and fountain pool, erected in 1966 by the people of Barnstable in memory of the president who loved to sail these waters.

9 **Hyannis Port** was a mecca for Americans during the Kennedy presidency, when the **Kennedy family compound** became the summer White House. The days of hordes of Secret Service men and swarms of tourists trampling down the bushes are gone, and the area is once again a community of quietly posh estates, though the Kennedy mystique is such that tourists still seek it out. To get a glimpse of the compound, less than 2 miles from the memorial, continue down Ocean Street and take a right onto Gosnold Street. At the stop sign, turn left onto Sea Street; at the next stop sign, turn left onto Hyannis Avenue. If you stop a minute by the stone tower here, you'll get a good view of the long, narrow dock of the **Hyannis Port Yacht Club,** on Irving Avenue, stretching out into the harbor. Take the next left onto Iyanough Avenue, and then right onto Wachusett Avenue. The compound is one block over on the left, bounded by Scudder and Irving avenues. A walk to the end of Irving takes **10** you to **Sunset Hill,** another viewpoint, which overlooks Kennedy homes as well as the harbor.

Joseph P. and Rose Kennedy bought their house here—the largest one, closest to Nantucket Sound—in 1929, as a healthful place to summer with their soon-to-be-nine children. Sons Jack and Bobby bought neighboring homes in the 1950s. Jack's (now Jacqueline Onassis's) is the one at the corner of Scudder and Irving, with the six-foot-high stockade fence on two sides. Bobby's (now Ethel's) is next to it, with the white fieldstone chimney. Teddy bought a home on Squaw Island, a private island connected to the area by a causeway at the end of Scudder Avenue; it now belongs to his ex-wife, Joan. And Eunice (Kennedy) and Sargent Shriver have a house near Squaw Island, on Atlantic Avenue.

The compound is relatively self-sufficient in terms of entertainment: Rose Kennedy's home (with 14 rooms and nine baths) has a movie theater, and there's a private beach, a boat dock, a swimming pool, a tennis court, and a sports field, scene of the famous Kennedy touch-football matches. The Hy-Line harbor boat tour (*see* Guided Tours, above) passes in front of the compound, at a respectful distance, but close enough for a good view.

Scudder Avenue leads back to the Melody Tent rotary and from there to town.

Tour 2: Route 28, Buzzards Bay to Hyannis

Route 28 from the Bourne Bridge south to Falmouth is commercial in many areas, so this tour uses the scenic alternate Route 28A between Pocasset and North Falmouth. Side roads lead to attractive beaches and small harbors. The Falmouth–Hyannis segment traverses some little-developed south-coastal areas, a situation that quickly changes at Hyannis. The tour covers about 50 miles.

Numbers in the margin correspond with points of interest on the Tours 1 and 2: The Canal to Hyannis map.

Travelers heading for the Cape via Route 6 usually take the bypass through **Buzzards Bay,** part of Bourne, but taking the downtown route when traffic is light offers a terrific view of the shipping going on this little village's backyard. The Main Street—once decrepit but recently revitalized with a new park and marina, and renovated restaurants and shops—is practically on the bank of the canal, where giant ships and tankers pass continually between the Bourne Bridge and the turreted Railroad Bridge. In the **Train Depot,** a Spanish-style structure built in 1914, is a town information center. A right turn at the rotary before heading into the village leads to the **Massachusetts Maritime Academy,** founded in 1891 and the oldest such academy in the United States. Its library and training ship are open for tours (*see* Off the Beaten Track, below).

Leaving Buzzards Bay, head for the Bourne Bridge. Once over, take a right at the rotary onto Trowbridge Road to Trading Post Corners and follow signs to the **Aptucxet Trading Post Museum,** a monument to the birth of commerce in the New World. Here in 1627, Plimoth Plantation leaders established a way station between the Indian encampment at Great Herring Pond, 3 miles to the northeast; the Dutch colonists in New Amsterdam (New York) to the south, beyond Buzzards Bay; and the English colonists on Cape Cod Bay. Before the canal was built, the Manomet River connected Buzzards Bay with the pond, and a short portage connected the pond to Scusset River, which met Cape Cod Bay. The Indians traded furs; the Dutch, linen cloth, metal tools, glass beads, and sugar and other staples; the Pilgrims, wool cloth, clay beads, sassafras, and tobacco (which they imported from Virginia). Wampum was the medium of exchange.

A replica of the post, including the original brick hearth, was erected on the original's foundations; inside are 17th-century cooking utensils, firearms, furniture, and other artifacts, plus Indian arrowheads, tools, and tomahawks found on the site. Also on the grounds are a Dutch-style windmill, now a gift shop; a small Victorian railroad station built for the sole use of President Grover Cleveland, who had a summer home in Bourne; a saltworks; herb and wildflower gardens; and a picnic area overlooking the canal. *Aptucxet Rd., tel. 508/759-9487. Admission: $1.50 adults, 50¢ schoolchildren, $1.25 senior citi-*

zens. Open May–Columbus Day, Tues.–Sat. 10–5, Sun. 2–5 (also July–Aug., Mon. 10–5). Closed Columbus Day–Apr.

Return to Route 28 and head south. On your left is the 10,500-acre **Massachusetts Military Reservation,** consisting of the Camp Edwards Army National Guard and Reserve Training Site, the Coast Guard Air Station Cape Cod, the Otis Air Force Base (with the PAVE PAWS radar station, a sophisticated system designed to track military satellites and—if it's ever necessary—nuclear missiles), and the Massachusetts Air National Guard. The main entrance is at the rotary on Route 28; others are on Route 130 in Forestdale and on Route 151 in Falmouth. Tours can be arranged (*see* Off the Beaten Track, below).

The reservation, more often referred to as Otis Air Base, holds a free two-day open house each summer with exhibitions that include precision flying by teams of the Air Force's Thunderbirds or the Navy's Blue Angels (though the Cape's unpredictable weather has more than once grounded the flyers). Other highlights may be performances by the Air Force Band, the Air Force honor guard and drill team, the Massachusetts National Guard Equestrian Unit, or the Army's Golden Knights Parachute Team. Military planes are on display, and concession stands serve the large crowds. The open house lasts all day, but on flying days the gates close at around 2:30 to shut down traffic before the planes take off. For dates and other information, call 508/968–4090 or 508/968–4003.

Leave Route 28 at the Otis rotary for scenic Route 28A, which winds past the little villages of Pocasset and Cataumet, with their old houses, pretty streets, and ocean views. At the intersection of Route 151, a left leads to the renowned **Falmouth Playhouse,** one of the Cape's top theater venues.

⑫ Beyond the playhouse, before the fairgrounds, is the **Ashumet Holly Reservation,** a 45-acre tract of woods, shady groves, meadows, and hiking trails (self-guided maps are available). Founded in 1925 and operated by the Massachusetts Audubon Society, the reservation features more than 1,000 holly trees, including 65 American, Oriental, and European varieties. Like the Heritage Plantation in Sandwich, it was purchased and donated by Josiah K. Lilly III for preservation purposes. Grassy Pond is home to many turtles and frogs, and in summer, the pond is covered with pink and white Oriental lotus blossoms that stand 3 feet above the water. Also in summer, 35 nesting pairs of barn swallows live in the barn (they can be viewed Tues.–Sat. 9–4); downstairs, there's a gift shop with handcrafted items. In spring, there's an open house when the dogwoods and rhododendrons are in bloom; in September, a festival tied in with the flowering of the Franklinia shrub; in December, a three-day holly sale. Fall through spring, craft- and nature-related classes are given. *286 Ashumet Rd., East Falmouth, tel. 508/563–6390. Admission: $3 adults, $2 senior citizens and children under 13. Trails open daily sunrise–sunset; office open Tues.–Sat. 9–4.*

Retrace your route back to 28A and continue south. A right onto Curley Boulevard will take you to **Old Silver Beach,** one of the Cape's prettiest. Shortly after Route 28A merges into Route 28, a right onto Palmer Avenue will take you on another scenic drive past **Sippewissett Lake.** Route 28 brings you into **⑬** the center of **Falmouth.**

The Cape's second-largest town, Falmouth was settled in 1660 by Congregationalists from Barnstable who had been ostracized from their church and deprived of voting privileges and other civil rights for being sympathizers with the Quakers, then the objects of severe repression. The **Village Green**—a spare triangle of grass with a few trees, a flagpole ringed by flowers, and a low white fence—was used as a militia training field in the 18th century and a grazing ground for horses in the early 19th. Today it is flanked by attractive old homes, some built by sea captains, and the 1856 **Congregational Church** (built on the timbers of its 1796 predecessor), with a bell made by Paul Revere. The cheery inscription reads: "The living to the church I call, and to the grave I summon all."

Opposite the green, on Palmer Avenue, are the two museums maintained by the Falmouth Historical Society. The 1790 **Julia Wood House** retains wonderful architectural details (a widow's walk, wide-board floors, leaded-glass windows, a Colonial kitchen with wide hearth), plus antique embroideries, baby shoes and clothes, toys and dolls, portraits, furniture, and an authentically equipped doctor's office (from its onetime owner). Out back is a barn museum with antique farm implements, a 19th-century horse-drawn sleigh, and more. The smaller **Conant House** next door, a 1794 half-Cape, has military memorabilia, whaling items, scrimshaw, sailors' valentines, silver, glass, china, handmade quilts, and a genealogical and historical research library. There's also a collection of books, portraits, and other memorabilia relating to Katharine Lee Bates, the native daughter who wrote "America the Beautiful." Docents lead you through the museums; free walking tours of town are also available in season (Mon. at 5 in July and Aug., Sat. at 4 in Sept.; call for meeting place). *Palmer Ave., tel. 508/548–4857. Admission: $2 adults, 50¢ children. Open mid-June–mid-Sept., weekdays 2–5; other times possible by appointment.*

Adjacent to the museums is a pretty formal **garden,** with gazebo, statuary, flagstone paths, rosebushes, sculptured boxwood hedges, and labeled plantings.

On the other side of the green, a right onto Main Street will take you to the white Cape house (at No. 16) that is the **birthplace of Katharine Lee Bates.** Owned by the historical society, the 1812 house is no longer open to the public; a plaque on a rock out front commemorates Bates's birth, in 1859.

Leave town by way of Locust Street, which turns into Woods Hole Road, and a left onto Oyster Pond Road and another onto **⓮** Fells Road takes you to the **Charles D. and Margaret K. Spohr Garden**, a private garden of 3 planted acres on Oyster Pond that the generous owner invites the public to enjoy. In spring, there are glorious displays of more than 700,000 daffodils, plus lilies, tulips, azaleas, magnolias, flowering crabs, rhododendrons, climbing hydrangeas, and more. A collection of old millstones, bronze church bells, and ship's anchors are woven into the landscaping. Specimen trees and shrubs are tagged for identification.

At the Cape's southwest tip, about 4 miles from Falmouth, is **⓯** **Woods Hole,** a center for international marine research and home to several major scientific institutions. The National Marine Fisheries Service was here first, established in 1871 to study fish management and conservation. In 1888, the Marine

Biological Laboratories (MBL), a center for research and education in biology, moved in across the street. In 1930, the Woods Hole Oceanographic Institute (WHOI) joined the group, and in the 1960s the U.S. Geological Survey's Branch of Marine Geology set up shop.

The Oceanographic Institute is the largest of the institutions, with several buildings in the village and a 190-acre campus nearby. During World War II its research focused on underwater explosives and submarine detection. Today it is the largest independent oceanography research laboratory in the country, as well as the Cape's largest private-sector employer, with 800 year-round employees (MBL has 150) and a $50 million annual operating budget. A graduate program is offered jointly with MIT, in addition to postdoctoral studies. WHOI's five research vessels range throughout the world's waters conducting research; its staff led the successful U.S.-French search for the *Titanic* (found about 500 miles off Newfoundland) in 1986.

Most of the year, Woods Hole is a peaceful community of intellectuals, who quietly go about their work. In summer, however, the basically one-street village teems with the 1,000 or more scientists and graduate students from all over the world who come either to participate in the MBL's summer courses or in summer studies at WHOI, or to work on research projects. A handful of waterside cafés and shops along Water Street compete for most bicycles stacked up at the door.

What accounts for this incredible concentration of scientific minds is, first, the variety and abundance of marine life in Woods Hole's unpolluted waters. Second is the opportunity for easy interchange of ideas and information and the stimulation of daily lectures and discussions (many open to the public) by important scientists. Third, the pooling of resources among the various institutions makes for economies that benefit each while allowing all access to highly sophisticated equipment.

A good example of this pooling of resources is the **MBL-WHOI Library,** possessor of one of the best collections of biological, ecological, and oceanographic literature in the world, including access to over 200 computer data bases and subscriptions to more than 3,000 scientific journals in 40 languages (with complete collections of most from their first issue). During World War II, the librarian arranged with a German subscription agency to have German periodicals sent to neutral Switzerland, to be stored until the end of the war; thus the library's German collections are uninterrupted when even many German institutions' are not. All journals are always accessible, because they cannot be checked out and because the library is open 24 hours a day. The Rare Books Room contains photographs, monographs, and prints, as well as journal collections dating back to 1665.

Unless you are a scientific researcher, the only way you'll get to see the library is by taking the **Marine Biological Laboratory tour** (tel. 508/548–3705, ext. 423; call for reservations and meeting instructions). The 1½-hour tours are led by retired scientists (mid-June–Aug., weekdays at 1 PM; reserve well in advance, if possible) and include an introductory slide show, as well as stops at the library, the marine resources center (where live sea creatures collected each day are kept), and one of the many research labs, where scientists will demonstrate the project they are working on.

The Oceanographic Institute is not open to the public, but you can learn about it at the small **WHOI Exhibit Center,** which shows a video on the institute and has exhibits on its research projects. *15 School St., tel. 508/548–1400, ext. 2663. Admission free. Open early June–late Sept., Mon.–Sat. 10–4. Closed late Sept.–early June.*

The Fisheries Service's **Aquarium** displays 16 tanks of regional fish and shellfish, plus microscopes for kids to examine marine life with and several hands-on pools with banded lobsters, crabs, snails, starfish, and other creatures. The star attractions are two harbor seals, who can be seen in the outdoor pool near the entrance in summer (they winter in Connecticut). *Corner of Albatross and Water Sts., tel. 508/548–7684. Admission free. Open late June–mid-Sept., daily 10–4 late; mid-Sept.–late June, weekdays 9–4.*

On the way out of town via Woods Hole Road, you might stop in at the **Bradley House Museum,** which is devoted to the history of the town and its scientific institutions. Here you'll find old ships' logs, postcards, newspaper articles, maps, diaries, photographs; more than 200 tapes of oral history provided by local residents; a 100-volume library on maritime history; plus paintings, tools, a restored Woods Hole Spritsail boat, and a model of the town as it looked in the 1890s. Free guided walking tours of the village are available on Tuesdays in July and August. *573 Woods Hole Rd., tel. 508/548–7270. Donations accepted. Open mid-June–mid-Sept., Tues.–Sat. 10–4. Closed mid-Sept.–mid-June.*

Outside the Bradley House Museum is a fence covered in rambling roses. The fence is dedicated to the memory of Welshman Michael Walsh, who was a gardener to Woods Hole's first summer resident and developed the rambling rose.

Turn right onto Church Street, which takes you past some beautiful estates. On the left is the 1888 **Episcopal Church of the Messiah,** a stone church with a conical steeple and a 10- by 30-foot medicinal herb garden in the shape of a Celtic cross. The garden is enclosed by an ilex hedge and provided with benches for meditation. Inscriptions on either side of the intricately carved gate read "Enter in hope" and "Depart in peace."

Turning into a shore road, Church Street leads to **Nobska Light,** from which the views of the nearby Elizabeth Islands and of Martha's Vineyard, across Vineyard Sound, are spectacular. The 42-foot cast-iron tower lined with brick was built in 1876 with a stationary light; depending on a ship's position, it shows red (indicating dangerous waters) or white. The adjacent keeper's quarters have, since the light was automated in 1985, been the headquarters of the Coast Guard group commander—a fitting passing of the torch from one safeguarder of ships to another.

Follow the road around, and it will lead you back to the Woods Hole Road, which rejoins Route 28 in Falmouth; from here continue north. At the intersection of Route 130, take a left toward ⓖ **Mashpee,** one of two Massachusetts towns (the other is Gay Head, Martha's Vineyard) that have been governed continuously by Native Americans for more than 100 years. More than

600 residents are descended from the original Wampanoags. On the left is the **Wampanoag Indian Museum,** a small and somewhat disappointing museum on the history and culture of the tribe, set in a 1793 half-Cape. Exhibits include baskets, weapons, hunting and fishing tools, clothing, arrowheads, and a small diorama depicting a scene from an early settlement. *Rte. 130, tel. 508/477–1536. Donations accepted. Open Mon., Wed., Fri. 10–2; other times by chance.*

Across the way, a town landing gives a view of the **Mashpee-Wakeby Ponds,** two interconnecting ponds that form the Cape's largest freshwater lake—popular for swimming, fishing, and boating.

Return to Route 28; just past the junction is the **Cahoon Museum of American Art,** in a big Georgian Colonial home. Its several rooms display 30 or so of the primitive paintings of Ralph and Martha Cahoon, as well as other 19th- and early 20th-century art, including a number of pieces from the Hudson River School. A gift shop offers books, cards, prints, and so forth. *4676 Falmouth Rd. (Rte. 28), Cotuit, tel. 508/428–7581. Donations accepted. Open Apr.–Dec., Wed.–Sat. 10–4, Sun. 1–4. Closed Jan.–Mar.*

⑰ Two miles farther you'll see signs to **Osterville,** a wealthy Barnstable enclave, with upscale shopping in its downtown. In its Wianno area, on Nantucket Sound, Seaview Avenue is lined with elegant houses, including a few of the large "cottages" built beginning in the 19th century, when the area became popular with a monied set.

⑱ The next village along Route 28 is **Centerville.** Once a busy seafaring town, it still boasts 50 or so shipbuilders' and sea captains' homes along its quiet, tree-shaded streets. A right onto Main Street takes you to the **Centerville Historical Society Museum.** Set in a 19th-century house, the museum features furnished period rooms, Sandwich glass, miniature carvings of birds by Anthony Elmer Crowell, models of ships, marine artifacts, perfume bottles dating from 1760 to 1920, and 300 quilts and costumes dating from 1650 to 1950. Guided tours are given (last tour at 3:30). *513 Main St., tel. 508/775–0331. Admission: $1 adults, 50¢ children under 12. Open mid-June–mid-Sept., Wed.–Sun. 1:30–4:30. Closed mid-Sept.–mid-June.*

Time Out You must not leave Centerville (in summer) without stopping to sample the homemade offerings at **Four Seas Ice Cream** (360 S. Main St., tel. 508/775–1384), a tradition with generations of summer visitors.

Around the corner is the **1856 Country Store** (555 Main St., tel. 508/775–1856)—what used to be called the penny-candy store, today stocked with nickel and dime candy. It's not the place it once was, there's no longer a pickle barrel or huge slabs of cheddar cheese, but it does have old movie machines and all kinds of gadgets and toys.

Follow Main Street to **Craigville Beach,** a busy beach area with a community of weathered-shingle cottages community. Main Street continues to rejoin Route 28, which takes you to Hyannis, 3 miles away.

Tour 3: Route 6A, Hyannis to Orleans

For this tour, we return to the Old King's Highway and the north shore for attractive old towns, fine beaches, and varied scenery, from marshland and kettle ponds to forest. Also along this stretch are antiques shops and excellent restaurants, several with views of the marsh. The tour covers about 25 miles.

Numbers in the margin correspond with points of interest on the Tours 3 and 4: Hyannis to Orleans map.

Heading east out of Hyannis on Route 28, turn left onto Willow Street. Three miles along you come to Route 6A. Cross 6A onto Mill Lane for a scenic loop (even better on foot); keep left at the intersection of Water Street to go over **Keveney Bridge,** a one-lane wooden bridge over marshy Mill Pond that will make you want to grab a pole and join the others quietly fishing from it. The loop comes back out onto Route 6A, west of where you began. Across the street, on 6A, is **Cummaquid Fine Art** (*see* Shopping, below), a gallery that displays the work of Cape and New England artists.

⓴ Turn left onto 6A for **Yarmouth Port,** with some impressive captains' homes, many now B&Bs. Past North Sandyside Lane on the right is **Hallet's Store,** a country drugstore preserved as it was in 1889, when the current owner's grandfather, Thacher Hallet, opened it. Hallet served not only as druggist but as postmaster and justice of the peace as well. The oak cabinetry has ornate carved detailing; at the all-marble soda fountain with swivel stools, you can order the secret-recipe ice-cream soda, as well as an inexpensive lunch.

As the first real intersection (Summer St.) approaches, try to pull over. The 1886 **Village Pump** is on the right, just before the **Old Yarmouth Inn,** the Cape's oldest inn (1696) and now a restaurant. The black wrought-iron pump, long used for drawing household water, is surrounded by ironwork with cutouts of birds and animals and is topped by a lantern. In front is a stone trough for watering horses. In an old barn across the street is **Parnassus Bookshop** (*see* Shopping, below), great for browsing.

Behind the post office, a bit farther on the right, are the **Botanical Trails of the Historical Society of Old Yarmouth,** 50 acres of woodlands and a pond, accented by blueberries, ladyslippers, Indian pipes, rhododendrons, and holly. Stone markers and arrows mark the trails, and benches are strategically placed for resting and appreciating the view. At the gatehouse, you can pick up maps to the trails and nature books. Just beyond, a right leads to the little **Kelley Chapel,** built in 1873 by a father for a daughter grieving over the death of a child, and moved to this site in 1960. The simple gray-and-white interior is dominated by an iron wood stove and a carved-wood organ. *Off Rte. 6A, tel. 508/362-3021. Admission: 50¢ adults, 25¢ children. Gatehouse open daily 1–4 in summer; trails open anytime.*

Across 6A, set back, is the 1780 **Winslow Crocker House,** an elegantly symmetrical two-story Georgian with 12-over-12 small-pane windows and an elaborate doorway. After Crocker's death, his two sons built a wall dividing the house in half. It was moved here from West Barnstable in 1935 by a Crocker descendant who donated it along with her collection of 17th- to 19th-

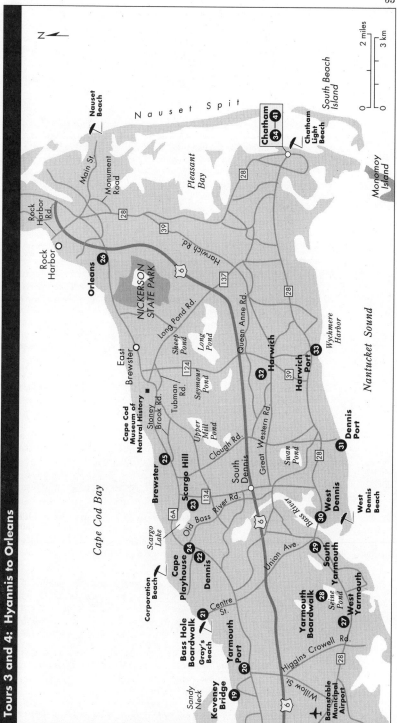

Tours 3 and 4: Hyannis to Orleans

century furniture, to the Society for the Preservation of New England Antiquities, which operates it as a museum. *250 Rte. 6A, tel. 508/227–3956. Admission: $3 adults, $1.50 children, $2.50 senior citizens. Open Tues., Thurs., Sat., Sun. noon–5. Closed mid-Oct.–May.*

Next to the Crocker house is the Swedenborgian **Church of New Jerusalem,** an unusual-looking white church with a tall steeple and stained-glass windows.

Across the street and facing the village green is the **Captain Bangs Hallet House.** A white Greek Revival building with a hitching post and a weeping beech out front, it was built in 1840 for a sea captain in the China trade, then bought by another, who swapped it with a third (this should give you an idea of the proliferation of sea captains hereabouts). In 1988, six 19th-century paintings and 200 pieces of scrimshaw were among the choice items stolen. Remaining are pewter, china, nautical equipment, antique toys and clothing, and more. The kitchen has the original 1740 brick beehive oven and butter churns. *Strawberry La., off Rte. 6A, tel. 508/362–3021. Admission: $1 adults, 25¢ children. Open June, Sun. 2–4; July–Sept., Wed.–Fri. and Sun. 2–4; or by appointment. Closed Oct.–May.*

For a virtually trafficless scenic loop, take a left off Route 6A past the green onto Church Street or Thacher Street, then left again onto Thacher Shore Road. In fall, this route is especially beautiful for its impressive stands of blazing red burning bush. Wooded segments alternate with open views of marsh. At the intersection, take the dirt road on the right (where the Water Street sign is) to get a wide-open view of marshland as it meets the bay. Don't drive in too far, or you may get stuck. Coming out, a right onto Water Street leads to Keveney Bridge, and back to Route 6A.

Turn left off 6A onto Centre Street (east of Church Street) and follow signs to Gray's Beach. At Homer's Dock Road, keep left; signs on the left point to a parking area for walking trails. Adjacent to Gray's Beach, a little crescent of sand with still water ㉑ good for children, is the **Bass Hole Boardwalk,** which extends over a marshy creek; at the end are benches from which you can observe abundant marsh life and, across the creek, the beautiful, sandy shores of Dennis's Chapin Beach.

㉒ Up ahead is **Dennis,** where the back streets, more so than the main route, have a beautifully preserved Colonial charm. The town has a number of conservation areas and nature trails (see the Dennis Chamber of Commerce guide), and many ponds for swimming.

At an intersection of three roads, across from the Dennis Market, take a left off Route 6A onto Nobscusset Road. At the junction of Whig Street, on the left, is the **Josiah Dennis Manse.** The saltbox with add-ons was built in 1736 for Reverend Josiah Dennis, after whom the town was named in gratitude for 36 years of service. Inside, the rooms reflect Reverend Dennis's day. One room has marine artifacts; the keeping room has an antique fireplace and cooking utensils; throughout are toys, china, pewter, and portraits of well-known sea captains. On the grounds is a 1770 one-room schoolhouse—furnished with wood-and-wrought-iron desks and chairs—moved in 1974 from a nearby site. *77 Nobscussett Rd., at the corner of Whig St., tel.*

508/385–2232. Donations accepted. Open July–Labor Day, Tues. and Thurs. 2–4. Closed Labor Day–June.

23 Return to Route 6A; at Old Bass River Road, take a right and follow signs for **Scargo Hill,** the highest spot in the area, at 160 feet. From here the view of wooded Scargo Lake and the village's scattered houses below and of Cape Cod Bay beyond is spectacular—on a clear day, you can see Provincetown. The panoramic view from atop the round tower (up a 38-step spiral staircase) makes sunsets and sunrises equally memorable.

24 Retrace your path to Route 6A and turn right. Just up on the left is the complex built around the **Cape Playhouse,** one of the oldest summer theaters in the country. Californian Raymond Moore—having started a company in Provincetown but finding it too remote—bought an 1820s former Unitarian Meeting House here in 1927 and converted it into a theater. The opening performance was Basil Rathbone in *The Guardsman;* other stars who performed here in the early days, many in their first professional appearances, include Bette Davis, Gregory Peck, and Henry Fonda. Also on the property are the **Cape Cinema,** with a huge ceiling mural by Massachusetts artist Rockwell Kent; the **Cape Playhouse Restaurant** (*see* Dining, below); and an art museum.

The **Cape Museum of Fine Arts,** founded in 1981 to acquire and house a permanent collection of works by Cape-associated artists, already owns more than 500 artworks. Pieces by important Provincetown artists include a 1924 portrait of a Portuguese fisherman's daughter by William Paxton, one of the first artists to summer in Provincetown; a collection of wood-block prints—abstractions of Orpheus—by Varujan Boghosian, associated with Provincetown's Long Point Gallery; and an oil sketch by Karl Knaths, who painted in Provincetown from 1919 until his death in 1971. In 1990 the museum moved to a new building on the grounds. In the off-season, a classic-film series is held in the basement auditorium. *Tel. 508/ 385–4477. Donations accepted. Open Tues.–Sat. 10–5 (Wed. and Thurs. until 8) in-season; Tues.–Fri. noon–5, Sat. 10–5 off-season.*

A left onto Corporation Road, just after the Playhouse complex, leads to **Corporation Beach.** At one time a packet landing owned by a corporation formed of townsfolk, the beautiful crescent of white sand backed by low dunes now serves a decidedly noncorporate use, as a public beach.

Time Out Before leaving Dennis, you might want to stop for a bite at **Cap'n Frosty's** (219 Main St. [Rte. 6A], near the Yarmouth line, tel. 508/385–8548), a favorite local clam shack, with fried seafood, shellfish, and onion rings. For dessert, try homemade ice cream and frozen yogurt at the **Ice Cream Smuggler** (716 Main St., near the Dennis Market, tel. 508/385–5307).

25 The next town is **Brewster,** in the early 1800s the terminus of a packet cargo service from Boston and home to many seafaring families. In 1849, Thoreau wrote that "this town has more mates and masters of vessels than any other town in the country." A large number of mansions built for sea captains remain today, and quite a few have been turned into bed-and-breakfast lodgings.

On the left, past the **Cape Cod Aquarium** (*see* What to See and Do with Children, below), an octagonal windmill on a grassy rise announces the entrance to the unusual **Drummer Boy Museum.** A series of 21 10-foot-high murals—accented by props, costumed figures, and lighting effects—illustrate events in the American Revolution, from the Boston Massacre to Yorktown. Led by well-trained guides, you walk from tableau to tableau on an enthusiastically narrated tour. The gift shop has such items as cranberry glass and pewter miniatures of the Minutemen. *787 Main St. (Rte. 6A), West Brewster, tel. 508/896–3823. Admission: $3.50 adults, $2.95 senior citizens, $2 high school students, $1 younger students. Open mid-May–mid-Oct., daily 9:30–5 (tours hourly). Closed mid-Oct.–mid-May.*

The 1795 **Old Mill** (open July–mid-Sept., weekdays 1–4)—a smock-type mill shingled in weathered pine, with a roof like an upturned boat—was moved here in 1974 and has been restored. The millstones are original. At night the mill is often spotlit and makes quite a sight. Also on the grounds is a one-room house from 1795, the **Harris-Black House,** dominated by a brick hearth and original woodwork.

Farther up on the left is the **Cape Cod Museum of Natural History,** which offers nature and marine exhibits (such as a working beehive and a pond- and sea-life room with live specimens), guided field walks, a natural history library, a book and gift shop, lectures, classes (including stargazing), and self-guided trails through 80 acres of forest, marshland, and ponds, all rich in birds and other wildlife. The exhibit hall upstairs has a wall display of aerial photographs documenting the process by which a barrier beach off Chatham's shore was split in two (*see* Tour 4, below). *Rte. 6A, Brewster, tel. 508/896–3867. Admission: $2.50 adults, $1.50 children 6–14. Open May–mid-Oct., Mon.–Sat. 9:30–4:30, Sun. 12:30–4:30; mid-Oct.–Apr., Tues.–Sat. 9:30–4:30, Sun. 12:30–4:30.*

Just beyond the bend in the road, turn right onto Paine's Creek Road, then left on Setucket Road, to reach the **Brewster Mill,** a restored 19th-century fulling mill—the area once had four— that is now a museum and gristmill. (Stoney Brook Road, just west of the aquarium, leads directly here.) The scene is wonderfully picturesque in true New England fashion: the old weathered-shingle mill, its waterwheel slowly turning, set on a little brook edged with leafy trees. Inside are exhibits, including old mill equipment and looms; if you get there at the right time, you can watch cornmeal being stone-ground (and buy it, too). Out back, across little wooden bridges, is a bench with a pleasant view of the pond and of the sluices leading into the mill area. *Stoney Brook Rd., tel. 508/896-3701. Donations accepted. Open July–Aug., Wed., Fri., Sat. 2–5. Closed Sept.–June.*

Early each spring, Stoney Brook—known as the **Herring Run**— is aboil with millions of alewives, which make their way from Cape Cod Bay by way of Paine's Creek to reach Stoney Brook and the ponds beyond to spawn. Walk across the street from the mill and down a path to the rushing stream spilling over rocks. Farther down the path is an ivy-covered stone wishing well and a wooden bridge with a bench.

Head back toward Paine's Creek Road but instead of turning onto it, keep going straight; you will come out on Route 6A just before the **New England Fire & History Museum.** Set on a re-created 18th-century common, it features vintage fire-fighting apparatus (including the only surviving 1929 Mercedes-Benz fire engine), the late Boston Pops conductor Arthur Fiedler's private collection of fire-fighting memorabilia, an apothecary shop, a diorama of the Chicago Fire of 1871 (complete with smoke and fire), two Civil War uniforms, a historic working forge, and medicinal herb gardens. Guided tours are given, and movies about historic fires and the history of apothecaries are shown. *1439 Main St. (Rte. 6A), West Brewster, tel. 508/896–5711. Admission: $4.50 adults, $2.50 children 5–12. Open mid-May–mid-Oct., weekdays 10–4, weekends noon–4. Closed mid-Oct.–mid-May.*

At the junction of Route 124 is the **Brewster Store** (tel. 508/896–3744), built in 1852. A local landmark, it is a typical New England general store, providing such essentials as the daily papers, sweatshirts, books, toys, and penny candy. It's also a good stop for quick grocery-type refreshments, as the bicycles piled up out front in summer attest.

Near the store is the handsome white **First Parish Church,** with Gothic windows and a capped bell tower. Known as the Church of the Sea Captains, it features pews marked with the names of famous Brewster sea captains. Out back is an old graveyard, where militiamen, clergy, farmers, and captains rest side by side. The church has chowder suppers every Wednesday in July and August.

From here Breakwater Road leads to a former packet landing, and a right onto Route 124, then a left onto Tubman Road, takes you to the **Bassett Wild Animal Farm** (*see* What to See and Do with Children, below).

A few miles up Route 6A on the right is **Nickerson State Park** (*see* Nature Areas, below). These 1,700 acres were part of a vast estate—the largest private acreage on the Cape—belonging to Roland C. Nickerson, son of Samuel Nickerson, a Chatham native who became a multimillionaire and founder of the First National Bank of Chicago. The estate was like a village unto itself. Its gardens provided much of the household's food, supplemented by game from its woods and fish from its ponds. It also had its own electric plant and a nine-hole golf course by the water.

The Nickersons were considered Brewster's "first family." Roland and his wife, Addie, entertained lavishly, at their long private beach or their hunting lodge. Several guest houses made their visitors—who included President Grover Cleveland—feel at home. The style was like that of an English country house, with coachmen dressed in tails and top hats and a bugler announcing carriages entering the front gates. The enormous mansion that Sam built for his son and daughter-in-law in 1886 burned to the ground in 1906, and Roland died two weeks later. The even grander stone mansion that Addie and Sam built in 1908 to replace it is now the conference center at the Ocean Edge resort. In 1934, Addie donated the land for the state park in memory of her son, who died during the 1918 flu epidemic.

26 From the park it's about 2 miles to **Orleans.** Named for Louis-Philippe de Bourbon, duke of Orléans, who reputedly visited the area during his exile from France in the 1790s, it is today the busy commercial center of the Lower Cape. Historically, it has the distinction of being the only spot in the continental

United States to have received enemy fire during either world war. In July 1918, a German submarine fired on commercial barges off the coast; four were sunk, and one shell is reported to have fallen on American soil.

At the junction with Main Street, turn left; Main becomes Rock Harbor Road, a pleasant winding street lined with gray-shingled Cape houses, white picket fences, and neat gardens. At the end is **Rock Harbor,** a former packet landing and site of a War of 1812 skirmish in which the Orleans militia kept a British warship from landing. Now a town landing with a small restaurant and a fish market, it is the base of charter-fishing and party boats in season, as well as of a small commercial fishing fleet. Sunsets over the harbor are memorable.

A right at the junction of Route 6A and Main Street leads east (along what becomes Beach Road) to **Nauset Beach,** a long, wide sweep of sand backed by high dunes.

Time Out | **Nauset Beach Club** (tel. 508/255–8547), on the road to Nauset, is a casual restaurant that serves superb, moderately priced Northern Italian dinners. Entrées include meat dishes such as saltimbocca (scallops of veal layered with spinach, proscuitto, and cheese in garlic-lemon sauce), fish dishes such as swordfish cacciatore and jumbo shrimp in ginger-mango sauce, and pastas, including *penne* with *pancetta* in carbonara sauce. The little place is packed in summer and doesn't take reservations.

Retrace your route, and on Main Street you'll pass Monument Road, on your left. On this street is the **Church of the Holy Spirit,** with a garden of plants that are mentioned in the Bible, including rosemary, flax, and coriander.

At the intersection of Route 28, turn right; at Cove Road is the **French Cable Station Museum,** built in 1890 to house a land extension of the transatlantic cable that originated in Brittany. In World War I, it was an essential link between Army headquarters in Washington and the American Expeditionary Force in France, and was guarded by Marines. In 1959, the station was closed as obsolete; the equipment is still in place. *41 S. Orleans Rd., tel. 508/240–1735. Admission: $1 adults, 50¢ children 7–17. Open July–mid-Sept., Tues.–Sun. 2–4. Closed mid-Sept.–June.*

Tour 4: Route 28, Hyannis to Chatham

There's no getting around it: The part of the Cape everyone hates is Route 28 where it passes through Yarmouth—one motel, strip mall, nightclub, and miniature golf course after another. In 1989, as *Cape Cod Life* magazine put it, "the town [began] to plant 350 trees in hopes that eventually the trees' leaves, like the fig leaf of Biblical lore, will cover the shame of unkempt overdevelopment." But if everyone hates it, why is there always so much traffic here?

This tour takes you into the fray; it is a good way to go if you want to intersperse amusements with your sightseeing, because Route 28 is the main locus of such activities. A sensible option if you don't, is to take speedy Route 6 to the exit nearest the first place you want to visit, then cut across the interior to 28. This route covers about 30 miles. The proliferation of motels, restaurants, and stores thins out somewhat as you go east toward Chatham.

㉗ Heading east out of Hyannis, the first village is **West Yarmouth.** A little past the town line, on the left, is the **Baxter Mill,** by the shore of Mill Pond. Built in 1710, it is the only mill on Cape Cod that is powered by an inside water turbine; the others use either wind or paddle wheels. The mill was converted to the indoor metal turbine in 1860 because of the pond's low water level and the damage done to the wooden paddle wheel by winter freezes; the original metal turbine is displayed on the grounds, and a replica powers the restored mill.

㉘ After about 3 miles, a left onto Winslow Gray Road, then a right onto Meadowbrook Lane, takes you to the **Yarmouth Boardwalk,** a short walk through swamp and marsh to the edge of Swan Pond.

A bit farther on Route 28, on the left, is **Aqua Circus** (*see* What to See and Do with Children, below), with dolphin and other shows.

Time Out Next door to the Aqua Circus is **Jerry's Dairy Freeze** (tel. 508/ 775–9752; open mid-Feb.–mid-Nov.), a roadside place that serves heaping portions of delicious fried clams and onion rings—along with thick frappés, frozen yogurt, and soft ice cream—at very good prices. It stays open until 11 at night in-season.

A right onto Willow Street leads to the 1791 **Judah Baker Windmill,** an octagonal mill with a conical cap. It was moved from South Dennis to West Dennis, then in 1863 to this site on a park with a beach on Bass River. A left off Route 28 onto Long Pond Drive, across from Willow Street, leads to the **Yarmouth Herring Run,** which is active in early spring.

㉙ **South Yarmouth** was once called Friends Village, for its large Quaker population. The 1809 **Friends Meeting House,** still standing and open to the public, has a partition down the center to divide the sexes. A left off Route 28 onto North Main Street will take you there. The nearby cemetery has the usual Quaker markers with no epitaphs, an expression of the Friends' belief that all are equal in God's eyes.

Bass River forms the dividing line between the southern portions of the towns of Yarmouth and Dennis; the area of South Yarmouth just before the bridge is commonly referred to as **Bass River.** Here you'll find charter boats and boat rentals, as well as a river cruise, plus seafood restaurants and markets.

㉚ **West Dennis** (confusingly enough, south of South Dennis) is at the other side of the Bass River Bridge. A right onto School Street leads to the **West Dennis Beach,** one of the best on the south shore. Offshore is an aborted breakwater, begun in 1837 in an effort to protect the mouth of Bass River but abandoned when a sandbar formed on the shore side.

Time Out The 1855 lighthouse that originally watched over the coast here has been converted into part of the aptly named **Lighthouse Inn** (tel. 508/398–2244), a summer resort with a moderately priced restaurant serving three meals a day. Now *you* can watch over the coast, either from behind windows or at café tables outside.

Back on Route 28, a left onto Old Main Street leads to the **Jericho House Museum,** built in 1801 for a sea captain. (The name was given by a subsequent owner, who said the walls seemed to be tumbling down.) The classic Cape, with a bow roof and large central chimney, has been fully restored. Antique furnishings include 1850s portraits, and Chinese and other items brought home from overseas by sea captains. In the barn museum is cranberry-harvesting and woodworking equipment, maritime antiques, and 19th-century sleighs and wagons. Also here is a 150-piece driftwood zoo: a local man collected wood on a beach, then added eyes and beaks to bring out animal shapes. *Old Main St. and Trotting Park Rd., tel. 508/398–6736. Donations accepted. Open July and Aug., Wed. and Fri. 2–4. Closed Sept.–June.*

A left onto Main Street leads to the 1835 **South Parish Congregational Church,** which has the oldest working organ in the United States. The cemetery beside the church has markers dating from 1795; many of them are for early sea captains and say simply "Lost at sea." One stone says only "The Chinese Woman."

③ The last southern village of the Mid-Cape is **Dennisport,** a prime summer resort area, with gray-shingled cottages, summer homes, and condominiums, and lots of white picket fences covered with rambling roses. A right off Route 28 onto Shad Hole Road takes you to the ocean. The Union Wharf Packing Company was located here in the 1850s, and the shore was lined with grocery stores, sailmakers, and ship chandlers. The beach where sea clams were once packed is now packed with sunbathers.

Time Out Farther up Route 28, a right onto Sea Street leads to the **Sundae School Ice Cream Parlor** (corner of Lower County Rd., tel. 508/394–9122; open mid-Apr.–mid-Oct.), which not only has great homemade ice cream but also serves it up at an antique marble soda fountain.

---

③ The next town on Route 28 is **Harwich,** which is made up of seven small villages collectively referred to as the Harwiches. Many cranberry bogs, in use since the 1840s, can be seen as you explore the back roads; in September, bog tours are part of a grand, 10-day Cranberry Harvest Festival (*see* Festivals and Seasonal Events in Chapter 1, Essential Information).

A right off Route 28 just past the town line, onto River Drive, leads to the **Harwich Herring Run,** another active run in spring; the view downriver includes a privately owned windmill silhouetted against the horizon.

Continue on Route 28 to the junction of Route 39, and take that into the heart of the quiet New England village of **Harwich.** Its centerpiece is the **Brooks Academy** (turn left onto Main Street), an 1844 Greek Revival building with fluted pillars that was once a private school and is now the museum of the Harwich Historical Society. Closed for more than a year of renovations after the town hall moved to new quarters, the museum reopened in late 1990 with double the space. Exhibits include old photographs, glass, cranberry-harvesting equipment, deeds and maps, costumes, handmade lace, dollhouses, and tools. On the grounds is a powder house that was used to store gunpowder during the Revolutionary War. Across Main Street from the academy is a cannon used in the same war. *Main St., tel. 508/432–8089. Admission free. Open Mon., Wed., Fri. 11–4.*

In the other direction on Main Street is **Brooks Park,** with a playground, picnic tables, a ballpark, tennis courts, and a bandstand where summer concerts are held. Turn onto Bank Street to get back to Route 28 at **Harwich Port.** A right onto Harbor Road leads to scenic **Wychmere Harbor,** busy with pleasure boats.

Time Out The **Augustus Snow House** (528 Main St. [Rte. 28], tel. 508/430–0528) offers an elegant afternoon tea of finger sandwiches, scones with Devonshire cream, and dessert cakes. It is served in the inn's very Victorian, fireplaced parlors from 1:30 to 4:30 daily year-round (call to confirm or reserve).

For a different kind of dessert, try **Clover Hill Farm** (Rte. 28, corner of Neel Rd., tel. 508/430–0292), with 36 kinds of ice cream, including gourmet flavors like white-chocolate-and-raspberries, plus light ice cream, frozen yogurt, ices, sorbet, fun sundae toppings, and Kahlúa whipped cream. Don't be misled by the name—the place looks like a standard-issue Dairy Queen from the outside.

34 Next to Harwich is **Chatham.** Situated at the bent elbow of the Cape, with water on three sides, it has all the charm of a quiet seaside resort but with relatively little of the commercialism. And it *is* charming: gray-shingled houses with tidy awnings and cheerful flower gardens, an attractive Main Street with crafts and antiques stores alongside homey coffee shops and a five-and-ten. It's a traditional town, with none of Provincetown's flash yet not overly quaint; wealthy yet not ostentatious; casual and fun but refined, and never tacky.

Numbers in the margin correspond with points of interest on the Chatham map.

When you cross the town line via Route 28, begin to watch for **Marion's Pies, Fancy's Farm,** and **Chatham Jelly,** all worth watching for (*see* Farm Stands and Food in Shopping, below). Just before you hit downtown, at the intersection with Queen Anne Road, turn left onto Depot Road for the **Railroad Museum,** in a restored 1887 depot. Exhibits include a 1910 New York Central caboose, old photographs, equipment, and thousands of train models. *No phone. Donations accepted. Open mid-June–mid-Sept., Tues.–Sat. 10–4. Closed mid-Sept.–mid-June.*

Return to the Queen Anne Road junction. For a scenic loop, turn down Queen Anne and skirt Oyster Pond, turning right onto Cedar Street, then left onto Champlain Road. (Samuel de Champlain anchored in Stage Harbor in 1606 and was involved in a skirmish that marked the first blood shed in New England between Europeans and Native Americans.) Half-Cape houses, open fields, and rolling pastures reveal the area's Colonial and agricultural history.

36 As the road winds around, you'll come to the **Old Atwood House and Museums** complex. Built by a sea captain in 1752 and occupied by his descendants until it was sold to the Chatham Historical Society in 1926, the Atwood House features a gambrel roof, variable-width floor planking, fireplaces, an old kitchen with a

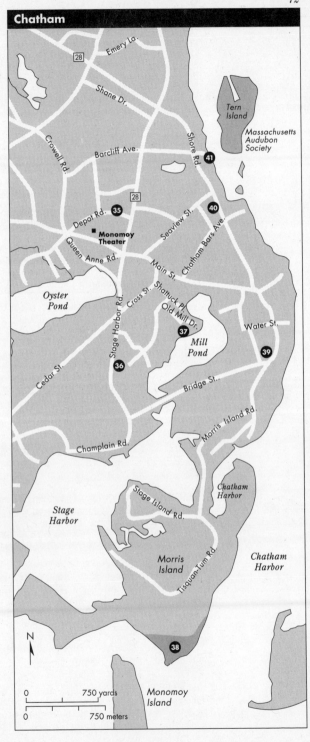

wide hearth and a beehive oven, and a collection of antique dolls and toys. The Joseph C. Lincoln Wing, added in 1949, has the manuscripts and first editions of the Chatham writer. The 1974 Durand Wing houses collections of seashells from around the world (700 in all), threaded Sandwich glass, and Parian ware (unglazed porcelain vases, figurines, and busts). In a remodeled freight shed are a series of murals (1931–1943) by Alice Stallknecht Wight portraying religious scenes in Chatham settings; they have been exhibited at major galleries around the country. On the grounds are picnic tables, an herb garden, and the old turret and lens from the Chatham Light. *347 Stage Harbor Rd., tel. 508/945–2493. Admission: $3 adults, $1 children. Open mid-June–Sept., Mon., Wed., Fri. 2–5. Closed Oct.– mid-June.*

㊲ Turn right onto Cross Street, then right onto Shattuck Place; at the end is the **Old Grist Mill,** moved to the hill here from elsewhere in Chatham. Built in 1797, the extensively renovated mill adjoins **Chase Park,** with a bowling green and picnic tables, on Cross Street. *Donations accepted. Open July and Aug., Wed.–Mon. 9–noon and 1–4:30. Closed Sept.–June.*

Instead of completing the loop, backtrack on Champlain Road and turn onto Bridge Street, which crosses Mill Pond. There's fishing from the bridge, and "bullrakers" ply the pond's muddy bottom with 20-foot rakes in search of shellfish.

㊳ A right onto Morris Island Road and across the dike leads to the headquarters of the **Monomoy National Wildlife Refuge** (*see* Nature Areas, below), on the misleadingly named Morris Island. At the visitor center there (tel. 508/945–0594; open daily 8–5, with gaps) you can pick up pamphlets on **Monomoy Island,** a deserted barrier-beach area–once a fishing village—just south of Morris Island that is a paradise for birdwatchers. Actually two islands, North and South Monomoy, since a 1978 storm divided it, Monomoy was itself separated from the mainland in a 1958 storm. A ¾-mile walking trail around Morris Island gives a good view of the refuge islands and the surrounding waters; there's also an observation platform at the visitor center.

㊴ Returning to the junction of Bridge Street, follow the coast road (go straight) to **Chatham Light.** The view from here—of the harbor, the offshore sandbars, and the ocean beyond—justifies the crowds that gather to share it; when fog shrouds the area, pierced with darting beams from the beacon, there's an appealing dreamlike quality about it.

Coin-operated telescopes allow a close look at the famous "Chatham Break", the result of a fierce 1987 storm that blasted a channel through a barrier beach (now known as North and South Beach) just off the coast. (If you're looking for a crowd-free sandy beach, boats at Chatham Harbor will ferry you across to North Island, actually a sandspit adjoining Orleans's Nauset Beach.) Shorefront property opposite the break suffered severe erosion because of the intense currents generated in the channel, and one house fell into the ocean. The Cape Cod Museum of Natural History in Brewster (*see* Tour 3: Route 6A, Hyannis to Orleans, above) has a display of photos documenting the process of erosion leading up to and following the break.

Go straight on Shore Road, where elegant summer cottages share the view with stately houses of purebred Yankee architecture, including some of the finest bow-roof houses in the country (bow roofs are curved, resembling the inverted bow of a ship). On the left past Main Street, set on a rise overlooking the ocean, is the 1914 **Chatham Bars Inn** (*see* Lodging, below). The last of Chatham's grand old resort hotels, it was recently renovated throughout and is as fresh, elegant, and charming as it ever was.

Time Out Even if you're not staying at the inn, you can experience it in several ways, including breakfast, lunch buffet, and dinner in the dining room (*see* Dining, below); fresh seafood at the casual, oceanfront **Beach House Grill** in summer; English tea by the fire on Saturday, or Sunday jazz brunch in the off-season; or drinks in the clubby bar. Call 508/945–0096 for information.

A bit farther along on the right is the entrance to the **Fish Pier**. The unloading of the boats after Chatham's fishing fleet returns, beginning sometime between noon and 2 PM, is a big local event, drawing crowds who watch it all from an observation deck. From their fishing grounds 10–100 miles offshore, the boats bring in haddock, cod, flounder, and more, which is packed in ice and shipped to New York and Boston.

Main Street, which you passed on Shore Road, takes you to the center of town. On Friday evenings in summer, the place to be is **Kate Gould Park** on Main Street for the Chatham band concert, the town's weekly party (*see* The Arts, below).

North of Chatham, Route 28 winds through wooded upland toward **Pleasant Bay**, to which a number of country roads to the right will take you for a good view of the Nauset spit and the little islands in between.

Tour 5: Route 6, Orleans to Provincetown

Starting at Orleans, this tour explores Eastham and the Outer Cape to the edge of Provincetown (which is covered in Tour 6: Provincetown, below), including the National Seashore. This part of the Cape is markedly different from the rest, much less populous and largely protected from development—an area of high dunes, endless beaches, and arty communities. The tour covers about 30 miles.

Numbers in the margin correspond with points of interest on the Tour 5: Orleans to Provincetown map.

Traveling down-Cape (toward the tip) from Orleans, head east on Route 6. Once in **Eastham**, watch for a sign on the right (1½ miles from the town line) directing you to the **Ft. Hill Area** of the Cape Cod National Seashore. On the approach road is the **Captain Edward Penniman House**, a large yellow, pink, and white house in the French Second Empire style, built in 1868 by a whaling captain. The impressive exterior is noted for its mansard roof, its cupola (which once commanded a dramatic view of bay and sea), and the whalebone entrance gate. To find out when the interior—much in need of attention—is open for guided tours (only by reservation) or browsing through changing exhibits, call the National Seashore at 508/255–3421.

Ahead, the road curves up over Ft. Hill, dead-ending at a viewpoint overlooking a lovely pastoral scene: former farmland traced with stone fences, gently rolling down to Nauset Marsh,

Tour 5: Orleans to Provincetown

ATLANTIC OCEAN

Province Lands Area
52

Pilgrim Lake

Pilgrim Heights Area
51

Head of the Meadow Beach

Highland Light
50

Beach Point

Provincetown
53—66

North Truro

TO BOSTON

Castle Rd.

Truro
49

CAPE

6

COD

Great Pond

Newcomb Hollow Beach

NATIONAL

Chequesset Neck Rd.

Cahoon Hollow Beach

SEASHORE

47

Wellfleet

South Wellfleet

Ocean View Dr.

Great Island
48

Wellfleet Harbor

Marconi Station

45

46

Nauset Light Beach

Wellfleet Bay Wildlife Sanctuary

6

Coast Guard Beach

Doan Rd.

North Eastham

Cape Cod Bay

Salt Pond Visitor Center

44

Nauset

First Encounter Beach

42 **Eastham**

43 **Fort Hill Area**

Samoset Rd.

Nauset Harbor

Rock Harbor

6

Orleans

Nauset Beach

East Brewster

Nickerson State Park

28

Brewster

124

Pleasant Bay

Dennis

6A

6

39

N

Yarmouth

134

39

137

Chatham

South Yarmouth

28

Harwich Port

West Dennis

Wychmere Harbor

0   2 miles

0   3 km

a red-maple swamp, and the moors. Winding through the area are the 1-mile Red Maple Swamp Trail, which begins outside the Penniman house, and the Ft. Hill Trail, also 1 mile, beginning at the parking area; maps are available at trailheads.

Return to Route 6; ½ mile up on the left, at Samoset Road, you'll see the **Eastham Windmill,** a smock mill built in the early 1680s, moved to this site in 1808, and now the centerpiece of a park. This is the only Cape windmill still on a site on which it was in commercial use. *Rte. 6. Donations accepted. Open late June–mid-Sept., Mon.–Sat. 10–5, Sun. 1–5. Closed mid-Sept.–June.*

Opposite the park, next to the post office, is the 1741 **Swift-Daley House,** once the home of Gustavus Swift, founder of the Swift meat-packing company. Inside the full-cape with bow roof you'll find beautiful pumpkin pine woodwork, wide-board floors, a ship's-cabin staircase (which, like the bow roof, was built by ship's carpenters), and fireplaces in every room. The Colonial-era furnishings include an old cannonball rope bed, tools, a melodeon, a stereopticon, and a ceremonial quilt decorated with beads, coins, and so forth. Antique clothing includes gloves, lacework, hankies, baby dresses, and a stunning 1850 wedding dress. *Rte. 6, tel. 508/240–1247. Admission: $1 adults, 50¢ children 6–12. Open July and Aug., weekdays 1:30–4:30. Closed Sept.–June.*

Follow Samoset Road, past marshland, to **First Encounter Beach,** a great spot for watching sunsets. Near the parking lot is a bronze marker commemorating the first encounter between the local Indians and the passengers from the *Mayflower,* led by Captain Myles Standish, who explored the entire area for five weeks before deciding to move on to Plymouth. Also here are the remains of a more recent vessel—a Navy target ship retired after 25 years of battering and now resting on a sandbar about a mile out.

Another ½ mile up Route 6, on the right, is the entrance to the southernmost of the three visitor centers of the **Cape Cod National Seashore.** Established in 1961 by a bill signed by President John F. Kennedy, the 27,700-acre Seashore encompasses and protects 30 miles of superb ocean beaches; great rolling dunes; swamps, marshes, and wetlands; pitch pine and scrub oak forests; all kinds of wildlife; and a number of historic structures. Lacing through these landscapes are self-guided nature trails, as well as biking and horse trails.

All the visitor centers offer programs of guided walks, tours, boat trips, demonstrations, and lectures from late April through October. In summer, evening programs are presented nightly at the Salt Pond Amphitheater in Eastham and most nights at the Province Lands Visitor Center near Provincetown.

44 The **Salt Pond Visitor Center** in Eastham has displays of early Cape Cod artifacts (including antique scrimshaw), a bookstore, and an air-conditioned auditorium for films on the geology of the area, sea rescues, whaling, Thoreau, and Marconi. *Tel. 508/255–3421. Admission free. Open Mar.–June and Sept.–Dec., daily 9–4:30; July and Aug., daily 9–6. Closed Jan. and Feb.*

From the visitor center, hiking trails lead to a red-maple swamp, **Nauset Marsh,** and **Salt Pond,** in which breeding shellfish are suspended from floating "nurseries"; their offspring will later be used to seed the flats. Also here is the Buttonbrush Trail, a nature path for the visually disabled. Roads and bicycle trails lead to **Coast Guard Beach** and **Nauset Light Beach,** which begin an unbroken 40-mile stretch of barrier beach extending to Provincetown—the "Cape Cod Beach" of Thoreau's 1865 classic *Cape Cod.* One can still walk its length, as Thoreau did, though the Atlantic continues to claim more of the Cape's eastern shore every year. To the south, near the end of Nauset spit, is the site of the famous beach cottage of Henry Beston's 1928 book *The Outermost House;* designated as a literary landmark in 1964, the cottage was completely destroyed in the Great Blizzard of February 1978.

A right onto Nauset Road and another onto Doane Road leads to Coast Guard Beach. From there, follow Ocean View Drive for 1 mile along the rolling hills to the much-photographed **Nauset Light,** which tops the bluff where the "Three Sisters" lighthouses once stood. The Three Sisters themselves can be seen in a little landlocked park surrounded by trees, reached by paved walkways off Nauset Light Beach's parking lot.

How the lighthouses got there is a long story, but briefly it is this: In 1838, three brick lighthouses were built 150 feet apart on the bluffs in Eastham, overlooking a particularly dangerous shoals area; in 1892, after the eroding cliff dropped the towers into the ocean, they were replaced with three wood towers. In 1918, two were moved away, and in 1923 the third was; eventually the National Park Service acquired the Three Sisters and brought them together here, where they would be safe, rather than returning them to the eroding coast. The Fresnel lens from the last working lighthouse, called The Beacon, is on display at the Salt Pond Visitor Center. Lectures and guided walks on the lighthouses are conducted throughout the season.

45 A few miles farther on Route 6, just over the Wellfleet line, is the **Wellfleet Bay Wildlife Sanctuary** (*see* Nature Areas, below), 750 acres of moors, marsh, and forest supervised by the Massachusetts Audubon Society.

46 On the right is the **Marconi Station**, the site of the first transatlantic wireless station erected on the U.S. mainland. From here, Italian radio and wireless-telegraphy pioneer Guglielmo Marconi sent the first American wireless message to Europe—from President Theodore Roosevelt to Edward VII of England—on January 18, 1903. The station broadcast news for 15 years. An outdoor shelter contains a model of the original station, of which only fragments remain as a result of cliff erosion (parts of the tower bases are sometimes visible on the beach 100 feet below, where they fell). Inside headquarters is a model of the spark-gap transmitter used at Marconi. Off the parking lot a 1¼-mile (45-minute) trail and boardwalk lead through the Atlantic White Cedar Swamp, one of the most beautiful trails in the Seashore; free maps and guides are available at the trailhead. *South Wellfleet, tel. 508/349-3785. Open year-round, weekdays 9–4:30; Jan. and Feb., also weekends 9–4:30.*

For a scenic loop through a classic Cape landscape, take a left onto LeCount Hollow Road (with scrub and pines on the left, heathland meeting cliffs with ocean below on the right) to **Cahoon Hollow Beach,** a town-managed beach with high dunes; turn left again onto Ocean View Drive, ending at **Newcomb**

Hollow, a scalloped shoreline of golden sand; then backtrack to Cahoon Hollow and take the unmarked right just across from it to return to Route 6 via Great Pond. Head east (right) on 6 and turn off at the sign for Wellfleet Center.

47 Wellfleet was once the center of a large oyster industry and, along with Truro to the north, a Colonial whaling and codfishing port. Less than 2 miles wide, it is one of the more tastefully developed Cape resort towns, with a number of fine restaurants, historic homes, and more than 20 art galleries.

On the way into town, you pass the **First Congregational Church of the United Church of Christ** (Main St., tel. 508/349–6877), a handsome 1850 Greek Revival building. It was originally crowned by a tall spire, but an 1879 northeaster sent the spire flying across the street, and it was replaced by a belfry. The clock is said to be the only town clock in the world to strike on ship's time—for example, one, five, and nine o'clock are "two bells."

The church's interior is lovely, with pale blue walls, a brass chandelier hanging from an enormous gilt ceiling rosette, stained-glass windows in unusual subtle colors, and pews curved to form an amphitheater facing the altar and the 1873, 738-pipe Hook and Hastings tracker-action organ behind it. (Concerts are given on it in July and August on Sundays at 8 PM.) To the right is a Tiffany-style window depicting a clipper ship, with a dedication to the memory of a sea captain and an inscription beginning "They that go down to the sea in ships...."

Farther on the right is a public lot where you can park if you want to wander the town. On Main Street is the **Wellfleet Historical Society Museum,** which exhibits the society's collection of shipwreck material, toys, needlework, navigation equipment, early photographs, Indian artifacts, clothing, and more (along with the **Samuel Rider House** on Gull Pond Road, north of the Wellfleet turnoff on Route 6). *Rider House, tel. 508/349–3876; Museum, tel. 508/349–9157. Admission: $2 adults, free for chidlren 11 and under. Open late June–mid-Sept., Tues.–Sat. 2–5. Closed mid-Sept.–June.*

From Main Street, Bank Street leads to Commercial Street, which has the flavor of the fishing town Wellfleet is; galleries and shops occupy small weathered-shingle houses that look like fishing shacks. For a short walk across **Uncle Tim's Bridge**—with a much-photographed view over marshland and a tidal creek—leading to a small island, park at the small lot on your left (if you haven't used the Main Street lot). At the end of Commercial Street is the **Wellfleet Pier,** busy with fishing boats, sailboats, yachts, charters, and party boats; at the twice-daily low tides you can shellfish for oysters, clams, and quahogs (license required; *see* Shellfishing in Sports, below). Forsaken boats lie picturesquely in the tidal flats, adding some salty flavor.

Continue on the same road (which becomes Chequesset Neck Road) for a pretty 3-mile drive along Cape Cod Bay past Sunset Hill—a great place to catch one. At the end, on the left, is a parking lot and wooded picnic area, from which nature trails **48** lead off to **Great Island,** perfect for the beachcomber and solitude seeker. Actually a peninsula connected by a sand spit, Great Island offers more than 7 miles of trails along the inner marshes and the water, and lots of windswept dunes—a beautiful place. To the right of the Great Island lot, a road leads to another parking area, on **Griffin Island** (not even a peninsula, just an area of Wellfleet), with its own walking trail. Both Great and Griffin islands once actually were islands, but a tidal buildup of sand connected them with the mainland.

49 Return to Route 6 and follow signs for the center of **Truro,** a town of high dunes, estuaries, and rivers fringed by grasses, rolling moors, and houses sheltered in tiny valleys. Truro is a popular retreat of artists and writers. The most prominent painter to have lived here was Edward Hopper, who found the Cape light ideal for his austere brand of realism.

One of the largest towns in terms of area (almost 43 square miles), it is the smallest in population—only about 1,400 year-round. If you thought Wellfleet's downtown was small, wait until you see—or don't see—Truro's. It's a post office, a town hall, a shop or two; you'll know it by the sign that says "Downtown Truro," at a little plaza entrance. There's also a library, a firehouse, a police station, but that's about it.

From the center, Castle Road leads to Corn Hill Road, where a tablet commemorates the finding of a buried cache of corn by Standish and the *Mayflower* crew on **Corn Hill,** above; they took it to Plymouth and used it as seed, returning later to pay the Indians for the corn they'd taken.

Head east again on Route 6, and follow signs for the Cape Cod Light. As you near the lighthouse, you pass the **Truro Historical Museum,** built at the turn of the century as a summer hotel and now a repository of 17th-century firearms, mementos of shipwrecks, early fishing and whaling gear, ship models, a pirate's chest, scrimshaw, and more. One room exhibits wood carvings, paintings, blown glass, and ship models by Courtney Allen, artist and founder of Truro's historical society. An excellent self-guided historic tour of town is available here for 75¢. *Lighthouse Rd., North Truro, tel. 508/487-3397. Admission: $2 adults, free for children under 11, $1.50 senior citizens. Open mid-June–mid-Sept., daily 10–5. Closed mid-Sept.–mid-June.*

50 At the end of the road is **Highland Light,** also called Cape Cod Light, in which Thoreau boarded for a spell in his travels across the Cape's backside (as the Atlantic side of the Outer Cape is called). One of four active lighthouses on the Outer Cape, this one's a beauty, and you can drive right up to it. It is the Cape's oldest lighthouse, and the last to have become automated (in 1986). The first light on this site, powered by 24 whale-oil lamps, began warning ships off Truro's treacherous sandbars in 1798. The dreaded Peaked Hills Bars alone, to the north, have claimed hundreds of ships. The current light, a 66-foot tower built in 1857, is powered by two 1,000-watt bulbs, reflected by a huge Fresnel lens; its beacon can be seen for 20 miles. The lighthouse could fall into the sea within five to 30 years, depending on how quickly the 117-foot cliff on which it stands erodes, and on how successful a local committee is in finding the several million dollars necessary to move the lighthouse back from the cliff.

Back on Route 6 again, still going east, turn right for the **51 Pilgrim Heights Area** of the Cape Cod National Seashore. Off the parking lot is a shelter where lectures on the early history of the region are given in season (call a visitor center for a schedule). A short walking trail leads to the spring where a Pilgrim exploring party stopped to refill their casks, tasting their first New England water. Another path leads to a swamp, and a bike trail leads to Head of the Meadow Beach. You can check out the terrain in advance by looking at the topographical model of the area at the shelter.

Walking through this still-wild area of oak, pitch pine, bayberry, blueberry, beach plum, and azalea gives you a taste of what it was like for these voyagers in search of a new home. "Being thus passed the vast ocean..." wrote William Bradford in *Of Plimoth Plantation*, "they had no friends to welcome them, no inns to entertain them or refresh their weatherbeaten bodies; no houses, or much less towns to repair to, to seek for succour."

From here you can take the coastal Route 6A—past countless ticky-tacky beach shacks and tidier rental cottages that line the bay—straight into **Provincetown,** or follow Route 6 to the Cape Cod National Seashore's **Province Lands Area.**

52

Tour 6: Provincetown

53 This tour explores the 8-square-mile town of **Provincetown**—the Cape's smallest in area, second-smallest after Truro in year-round population—and its neighboring segment of the National Seashore. The town's main street, Commercial Street, is 3 miles from end to end.

Numbers in the margin correspond with points of interest on the Tour 6: Provincetown map.

Near the Provincetown border the massive dunes begin to appear on the right; in places they actually meet the road, turning Route 6 into a sand-swept highway. Scattered among the dunes are primitive cottages, called dune shacks, built from flotsam and other found materials, that have provided atmospheric as well as cheap lodgings to a number of famous artists and writers over the years—among them painter Harry Kemp, Eugene O'Neill, e.e. cummings, Jack Kerouac, and Norman Mailer. These privately leased shacks were designated as eligible for admission into the National Register of Historic Places in 1988, to save them from the National Seashore's onetime plans to demolish them when their occupancy permits expire.

54 Turn right at the traffic light for the **Province Lands Visitor Center.** Inside you'll find literature and small, nature-related gifts, frequent short films (on local geology, the U.S. Life Saving Service, and more), and such exhibits as local fish specimens. You can also pick up information on guided walks, birding trips, lectures, bonfires, and other current programs throughout the seashore, as well as on the Province Lands' own beaches (Race Point and Herring Cove) and walking, biking, and horse trails. Don't miss the wonderful 360-degree view of the dunes and the surrounding ocean from the observation deck. *Tel. 508/487–1256. Open Apr.–June and Sept.–Dec., daily 9–4:30; July and Aug., daily 9–6. Closed Jan.–Mar.*

Beyond the Visitor Center (and the Beech Forest picnic area and trails, across the way) is the small Provincetown airport, where sightseeing flights are available, and beyond that, the beautiful **Race Point Beach** (note that in summer the small parking lot fills up early in the day). Not far from the present Coast Guard Station is the **Old Harbor Station,** a U.S. Life Sav-

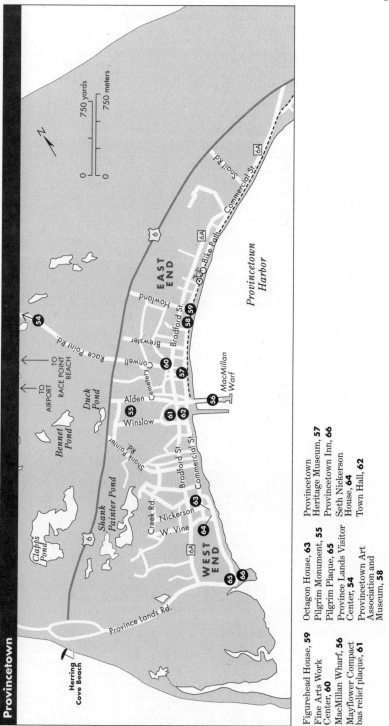

Provincetown

Figurehead House, **59**
Fine Arts Work
Center, **60**
MacMillan Wharf, **56**
Mayflower Compact
bas relief plaque, **61**

Octagon House, **63**
Pilgrim Monument, **55**
Pilgrim Plaque, **65**
Province Lands Visitor
Center, **54**
Provincetown Art
Association and
Museum, **58**

Provincetown
Heritage Museum, **57**
Provincetown Inn, **66**
Seth Nickerson
House, **64**
Town Hall, **62**

ing Service building towed here by barge from Chatham in 1977 to rescue it from an eroding beach. It is reached by a boardwalk across the sand; plaques along the way tell about the lifesaving service and the whales seen offshore. Inside are displays of such equipment as Lyle guns, which shot rescue lines out to ships in distress when the seas were too violent to launch a surf-boat; and breeches buoys, in which passengers were hauled across those lines to safety. *Tel. 508/487–2445. Donations accepted. Open July and Aug., daily 10–4. Closed Sept.–June.*

Leaving Race Point Beach, a right onto Province Lands Road takes you through the heart of the dunes and woods, past **Herring Cove Beach,** and ultimately into the center of Province-town. For this tour, instead return to Route 6 and turn right; take the next two lefts, then a right onto Winslow Street. At the top of the hill, a sharp left leads to the parking lot of the **❺❺ Pilgrim Monument,** commemorating the first landing of the Pilgrims in the New World and their signing of the Mayflower Compact, America's first rules of self-governance, before setting off from Provincetown Harbor to explore the mainland. From atop the 252-foot-high tower (116 steps and 60 ramps) you get a panoramic view—the dunes on one side, the harbor on the other, and the entire bay side of Cape Cod beyond. At the base is a museum of Lower Cape and Provincetown history, with exhibits on whaling, shipwrecks, and scrimshaw; a diorama of the *Mayflower* and another of a glass factory; and more.

The tower was erected of granite shipped in from Maine, to a design modeled on a tower in Siena, Italy; President Theodore Roosevelt laid the cornerstone in 1907, and President Taft attended the 1910 dedication. At Christmas, 5,000 colored lights are hung from the top of the tower, creating a display that can be seen as far away as the Cape Cod Canal. The lights go on the Wednesday before Thanksgiving, accompanied by a museum tour and open house, and they are lit nightly until New Year's. *Tel. 508/487–1310. Admission: $3 adults, $1 children 4–12. Open July–Sept., daily 9–9; Oct.–June, daily 9–5.*

Having looked down upon the town from this great height, it's time to come down and walk around in it. The most central parking lot is at MacMillan Wharf, which is why it fills up so fast, but there are other lots. In season especially, driving from one end of the main street to the other could take all day, so walking is definitely the way to go. Narrated trolley sightseeing tours make the downtown circuit throughout the day in season (*see* Guided Tours, above); the romantically inclined can hire a horse-drawn carriage (*see* Getting Around in Essential Information, above).

Provincetown, here called P-town, is a place of creativity, sometimes startling originality, and infinite diversity. In the busy downtown, Portuguese-American fishermen mix with painters, poets, writers, and in season, whale-watching families, cruise-ship passengers on brief stopovers, and, flamboyant gays and cross-dressers from everywhere who come to enjoy the freedom of a town with a large, visible gay population. In summer, Commercial Street is packed with sightseers and shoppers after the treasures of the many first-rate galleries and crafts shops. At night, raucous music and people spill out of bars, drag shows, and sing-along lounges galore. It's a fun, crazy place, with the extra dimension of the fishing fleet unloading their catch at MacMillan Wharf, in the center of the action.

During the early 1900s, Provincetown became known as Greenwich Village North. Active art schools and inexpensive summer lodgings close to the beaches attracted young rebels and artists, including John Reed, Mabel Dodge, Sinclair Lewis, and Eugene O'Neill. In 1916, O'Neill's play *Bound East for Cardiff* premiered in a tiny wharfside fish house, minimally fitted out as a theater, in the East End. This theater is long since gone, but a model of it and of the old Lewis Wharf on which it stood is on display at the Pilgrim Monument museum.

The Historical Society puts out a series of walking-tour pamphlets, available for less than $1 each at many shops in town, with maps and information on the history of many buildings and the (more or less) famous folk who have occupied them.

The center of town is where the crowds and most of the touristy shops are. The quiet East End is mostly residential, with some top galleries, and the similarly quiet West End has a number of small inns with neat lawns and elaborate gardens. Practically the entire town has been designated part of the new Provincetown Historic District—1,100 buildings spanning many architectural styles, from 18th-century Cape houses to Federals and Victorians.

⑤⑥ MacMillan Wharf is a sensible place to start a tour. One of the remaining five of the 54 wharves that once jutted into the bay, it is the base for whale-watch boats, fishing charters, and party boats. Also here is the **Chamber of Commerce,** which has all kinds of information and schedules of events. A new information column (said to look like a lifeguard stand) in the new park at the foot of the wharf has restroom and parking lot locations, bus schedules, and other information for visitors.

⑤⑦ Head east for two blocks to the **Provincetown Heritage Museum,** on the left. Exhibits include antique fire-fighting equipment, fishing artifacts, art (including donated works by Provincetown-related artists as well as antique prints and watercolors of schooners), wax figures, and a half-scale model of the fishing schooner *Rose Dorothea*, which won the Lipton Cup in 1907. The model was built by a local boat builder and completed in 1989. *356 Commercial St., tel. 508/487–0666. Admission: $2 age 12 and over. Open mid-June–Columbus Day, daily 10–6. Closed Columbus Day–mid-June.*

Time Out | **Gallerani's to Go** (355 Commercial St., tel. 508/487–4418) has soups, sandwiches, pâtés, guacamole, salads, and varied entrées (from pastas to stuffed tenderloin) and desserts as well as espresso and cappuccino, to take away for picnics or just a quick bite. The shop also sells grocery items and newspapers.

Juventino's Portuguese Bakery (338 Commercial St., tel. 508/ 487–2303) puts out fresh Portuguese breads and pastries every day year-round, until 9 or 10 at night in summer.

⑤⑧ Ten more blocks up is the **Provincetown Art Association and Museum,** founded in 1914 to collect and show the works of Provincetown-associated artists. Its 1,500-piece collection is displayed in changing exhibits that combine up-and-comers with established artists of the 20th century. Some of the art is for sale. The museum store has books by or about local artists, authors, and topics, as well as posters, crafts, cards, and gift items. PAAM-sponsored courses (one day and longer) offer the opportunity of studying under such talents as Sal Del Deo and Tony Vevers. *460 Commercial St., tel. 508/487–1750. Admission: $2 adults; $1 children 3–12, senior citizens, and students. Open Nov.–Apr., daily noon–5; Memorial Day–Labor Day, daily noon–5 and 7–10; May, Sept., and Oct., Mon.–Thurs. noon–5, Fri. and Sat. noon–5 and 7–10.*

59 In the next block, at No. 476, is the **Figurehead House,** a yellow mansard-roofed house in the Second Empire style. The name comes from the figurehead of a woman—fished out of the sea during a whaling voyage in the early 19th century—that now adorns the front of this house. Turn up Cook Street and left onto Bradford Street, which runs parallel to Commercial Street and is known locally as Back Street. A right onto Brewster Street will bring you past the former studios of two noted artists: Edwin W. Dickinson, at 46 Pearl Street, and Charles W. Hawthorne, at 48 Pearl. Hawthorne is especially important to Provincetown, because it was his Cape Cod School of Art, established here in 1899, that put the town on its path to becoming a major art colony.

60 At the end of Pearl Street is the **Fine Arts Work Center** (24 Pearl St., tel. 508/487–9960), a nonprofit organization begun in 1968 that sponsors 10 writers and 10 artists from October to May each year with a place to work, a stipend to live on, and access to artists and teachers. The center also has a gallery and sponsors off-season poetry readings and other events. The buildings in the complex around the center, which it owns, were formerly part of Day's Lumber Yard Studios, built above a lumberyard by a patron of the arts to provide poor artists with cheap accommodations.

On Bradford Street you will pass, on your right, Duarte Motors, which is on the site of the former railroad depot. The train ran straight across Bradford and Commercial streets to the wharf, where it picked up passengers from the frequent Boston boats and crates of iced fish from the Commercial Street fish sheds. Train service ended in 1960.

Past Alden Street, in a little park behind the Town Hall, is a **61** **bas-relief plaque** by sculptor Cyrus Dalin, depicting the signing of the Mayflower Compact.

62 The **Town Hall** was used by the Provincetown Art Association as its first exhibit space, and still exhibits local art—from paintings donated to the town over the years. Two of these are scenes of Provincetown by Charles Hawthorne.

Time Out   **Provincetown Fudge Factory** (210 Commercial St., tel. 508/487–2850), across from the post office, makes fudge, peanut-butter cups (with milk, dark, or white chocolate, creamy or chunky), butter crunch, saltwater taffy, and yard-long licorice whips—a must stop for those with a dental death wish.

All the way at the west end of Commercial Street, on the right between Soper and Nickerson streets, is an interesting piece of Provincetown architecture, the self-explanatorily named **63** **Octagon House** (74 Commercial St.), built in 1850 and now a private home.

(64) Across Soper Street from the Octagon House is the oldest building in town, dating to 1746. The small Cape-style **Seth Nickerson House,** currently owned by photographer John Gregory, was built by a ship's carpenter, with pegged, hand-hewn oak beams and wide-board floors. It is furnished in period and open for guided tours. *72 Commercial St., no phone. Admission: $2 adults, 50¢ children. Open June–Oct., daily 10–5. Closed Nov.–May.*

(65) At the bend in the road, the **bronze Pilgrim Plaque,** set into a boulder commemorates the first footfall of the Pilgrims onto Cape soil—Provincetown's equivalent of the Plymouth Rock.

(66) Across the street is the **Provincetown Inn;** inside, a series of 19 murals (painted in the 1930s from old postcards) depicts life in the 19th-century town.

What to See and Do with Children

The main component of children's summer vacations on the Cape is the same as their parents': the beach. Swimming, building sand castles, combing the beach for shells and "neat rocks", and checking out the sea creatures and grasses that wash up have been the stuff of happy memories for generations of children.

Still, there are times when kids crave (and nag for) more modern diversions, and this family-oriented resort area offers enough of these activities to rival Myrtle Beach. Though miniature golf courses, go-cart racetracks, arcades, and the like are ubiquitous, much of the action centers on Route 28 between Yarmouth and Harwich Port. This strip is a monument to commercial overdevelopment and a tangle of traffic in summer, but there's nothing like it when your kids (or you) are in the mood for some tacky fun.

Amusements **Batter's Box** has softball and baseball batting cages and pitching machines, including one with fastballs up to 90 mph. *322 Main St. (Rte. 28), Harwich Port, tel. 508/430–1155. Cost: $1.50 for 10 pitches, $10 for 40 pitches and a video of yourself. Open Apr.–mid-Oct., Mon.–Sat. 11–7, Sun. 11–9. Closed mid-Oct.–Mar.*

Bayberry Hollow Farm (W. Vine St. Ext., Provincetown, tel. 508/487–6584) offers pony rides for children 12 and younger year-round.

Bourne Kart Track has go-carts, minibikes, a roller coaster, children's rides, minigolf, an arcade, and batting cages. *Rte. 28, Monument Beach, 2 mi south of Bourne Bridge, tel. 508/759–2636. Admission: $3 adults, $1 children. Open mid-Mar.–Nov., daily 9 AM–11 PM. Closed Dec.–mid-Mar.*

Bud's Go-Karts, with 20 top-of-the-line go-carts, has been around since 1961. *364 Sisson Rd., off Rte. 28, Harwich Port, tel. 508/432–4964. Cost: $5 for 6 min. Open June–Labor Day, Mon.–Sat. 9 AM–11PM, Sun. 1–11 PM. Closed Labor Day–May.*

Cape Cod Storyland Golf is a 2-acre minigolf course set up as a mini–Cape Cod, with each of the 18 holes a Cape town. The course winds around small ponds and waterfalls, a full-size working gristmill, and reproductions of historic Cape buildings. *70 Center St. (by the railroad depot), Hyannis, tel. 508/778–4339. Admission: $5 adults, $4 children under 13, $3 sen-*

ior citizens; $1 discount in off-season (before mid-June and after mid-Sept.). Open mid-June–mid-Sept., daily 9 AM–11 PM; Mar.–mid-June and mid-Sept.–Oct., daily noon–9. Closed Nov.–Mar.

Heritage Plantation (*see* Tour 1: Route 6A, Sagamore Bridge to Hyannis, above) has a working 1912 carousel for kids, with chariots and hand-carved horses.

Pirate's Cove is the most elaborate of the Cape's many miniature-golf emporiums, with a hill, a high waterfall, and a stream. *728 Main St. (Rte. 28), South Yarmouth, tel. 508/394–6200. Admission: $5 adults, $4 children under 13. Open mid-June–mid-Sept., daily 9 AM–11 PM; Mar.–mid-June and mid-Sept.–Oct., daily 10 or 11 to 6 or 7. Closed Nov.–Mar.*

Ryan Family Amusement centers offer video-game rooms and bowling. *200 Main St., Buzzards Bay, tel. 508/759–9892; Town Hall Sq., Falmouth, tel. 508/540–4877; Capetown Mall, Rte. 132, Hyannis, tel. 508/775–5566; 441 Main St., Hyannis, tel. 508/775–3411; Cape Bowl, Rte. 28, South Yarmouth, tel. 508/394–5644. Open daily; hours vary for each location.*

Trampoline Center has 12 trampolines at ground level over pits (so kids can't fall very far). *296 Rte. 28, West Harwich, tel. 508/432–8717. Cost: $3 for 10 min. Open Apr.–Labor Day, Mon.–Sat. 9 AM–11 PM; Apr.–mid-June, weekends only 9 AM–11 PM. Closed Labor Day–Mar.*

Water Wizz Water Park has a 50-foot-high water slide with tunnels and dips, a river ride, a six-story tube ride, an arcade, and minigolf. *Rtes. 6 and 28, Wareham (near Buzzards Bay, over the bridge), tel. 508/295–3255. Admission: $14. Open mid-June–Labor Day, daily 10–8; Memorial Day–mid-June, weekends only 10–8.*

Arts **Academy of Performing Arts** (Main St., Orleans, tel. 508/255–1963) offers 8- to 13-year-olds two-week sessions of theater, music, and dance classes, with a show at the end of each session.

Harwich Junior Theatre (Division St., Harwich [Box 168, West Harwich 02671], tel. 508/432–2002), a community theater group, presents plays for children and starring children. Write for information on participation in classes and productions.

Mimsy Puppets (tel. 508/432–1279) perform fairy tales and folk tales for children from late June through August at two locations each week (Community Hall, School St., West Dennis, Mon. at 10 AM; First Parish Church, Rte. 6A, Brewster, Thurs. at 10 AM).

Truro Center for the Arts at Castle Hill (Fisher Rd., Truro, tel. 508/349–7511), housed in a converted 19th-century dairy barn, offers summer courses and single classes in art, crafts, writing, and photography for children and adults. Teachers have included notable Provincetown-based artists.

Children's programs are offered by the **Cape Cod Symphony Orchestra,** the **Cape Playhouse,** the **Falmouth Playhouse,** and the **Cape Cod Melody Tent** (*see* The Arts, below).

Camps The Massachusetts Audubon Society offers natural-history day camps for children in grades K–5 in July and August at its **Wellfleet Bay Wildlife Sanctuary** (Box 263, South Wellfleet

02663, tel. 508/349–2615). One-week sessions include classes and excursions (dorm accommodations are available). Reserve as early as possible—the camps are very popular.

The Cape Cod Soccer Camp (265 Washington St., Belmont 02178, tel. 617/484–3808 off-season; Box 747, S. Orleans 02662, tel. 508/896–8194 in season) has one-week summer sessions at its Brewster facility for day campers or live-ins.

The Cape has a number of other day and residential summer camps, some of which teach sailing and water sports or horseback riding. For information, write to the **Cape Cod Association of Children's Camps** (Box 38, Brewster 02631).

Nature **Aqua Circus of Cape Cod** offers dolphin and sea lion shows, a petting zoo, pony rides, wandering roosters and peacocks, a large seashell collection, aquariums, and more. *Rte. 28, West Yarmouth, tel. 508/775–8883. Admission: $7 adults, $4 children 2–9. Open mid-Feb.–June and Sept.–late Nov., daily 9:30–5; July–Aug., daily 9:30–6:30. Closed late Nov.–mid-Feb.*

Bassett Wild Animal Farm has wild and domestic animals, including lions, tigers, and birds, on 20 acres. Hayrides and pony rides are available. *Tubman Rd., between Rtes. 124 and 137, Brewster, tel. 508/896–3224. Admission: $4.75 adults, $3.75 children. Open mid-May–mid-Sept., daily 10–5. Closed mid-Sept.–mid-May.*

Cape Cod Aquarium (formerly Sealand) changed hands in 1989 and is now more educationally oriented, with workshops and lectures. Shows featuring marine mammals, such as sea lions and harbor seals, are given several times daily; exhibits include fish and reptiles. *281 Main St. (Rte. 6A), West Brewster, tel. 508/385–9252 or 800/367–6372. Admission: $7 adults, $4.50 children 5–11, $5 senior citizens. Open June–Oct., daily 9:30–5:30; Nov.–May, Thurs.–Tues. 10–4:30.*

Cape Cod Museum of Natural History (*see* Tour 3: Route 6A, Hyannis to Orleans, above) has a full program of children's activities in summer, including overnights and one-week sessions of art and nature classes.

Green Briar Nature Center in East Sandwich (*see* Tour 1: Route 6A, Sagamore Bridge to Hyannis, above) offers nature walks and slide presentations for children and adults all summer.

National Marine Fisheries Service Aquarium in Woods Hole (*see* Tour 2: Route 6A, Sagamore Bridge to Hyannis, above).

Whale watches (*see* Guided Tours in Essential Information, above).

Miscellaneous **Libraries** usually have a children's librarian with whom you can drop kids off for a few hours. Most offer regular children's story hours or other programs—check them out on a rainy day. Hours are listed in the newspapers each week (*see* The Arts and Nightlife, below).

Tot Drop (64 Enterprise Rd., Hyannis, tel. 508/778–6777) is a baby-sitting service just behind the Cape Cod Mall that lets you drop off your children for a few hours while you shop. The service is available weekdays 9:30–4 (earlier or later by request), and costs $4 per hour for one child, and $2 for each additional child.

Off the Beaten Track

If you're not from an area like New England, traditional pastimes like church suppers, barbecues, and bazaars are off the beaten track. If you're in the mood for a slice of regional Americana, you could give them a try—they're advertised in the papers.

New Alchemy Institute is an experimental farm and research center devoted to finding and demonstrating ecologically safe ideas on food production and heating. It was founded in 1969 by two Woods Hole marine biologists and a writer, on the site of a 12-acre dairy farm, for research in aquaculture, solar power, and organic farming. Today the focus is on gardening, with lectures, a farmer outreach program, and workshops. In addition to 5 acres of gardens, the institute comprises a geodesic-dome greenhouse with six-foot-tall fiberglass, solar "fish ponds" (filled with water, algae, and St. Peter's fish) that store heat for release at night, a composting greenhouse, and the Ark, a larger greenhouse. Children's day programs in gardening and nature study are offered in July and August. The visitor center has exhibits and a shop with books and products geared toward ecologically sound living; a farm stand (open mid-May–Sept., daily 10–6) sells organic produce, herbs, and flowers. *237 Hatchville Rd., East Falmouth, tel. 508/564–6301 or 564–2219. Admission: $3 age 12 and over. Open daily 10–4 for self-guided tours. Guided tours Sat. 1 PM year-round; also Sun. 1 PM mid-June–mid-Sept.*

Cape Cod Potato Chips (Independence Park, Rte. 132, Hyannis, tel. 508/775–3358) offers a free factory tour weekdays 10–5. The all-natural chips are hand-cooked in kettles in small batches, as they were when Steve Bernard began experimenting with them in his own kitchen. The company, started in 1980, was bought in 1985 by Eagle Snacks; Bernard works on new product development.

In front of the **Dennis Police Department** (Rte. 134, South Dennis) is a display of Colonial-era punishment devices: stocks, pillories, and a whipping post.

At the Massachusetts Military Reservation (*see* Tour 2: Route 6A, Sagamore Bridge to Hyannis, above), a tour of **Air National Guard** grounds—including a slide briefing, a film, a look into F-15 fighter planes, and a tour of the museum, with old aircraft engines, missiles, models, and so forth—can be arranged weekdays from 7:30 to 4 by calling the public affairs office (tel. 508/968–4090). An attempt is made to schedule tours around flying activities, so you get to see the Guard in action.

Other of the reservation's tenants give tours as well: **Army National Guard** (tel. 508/968–5975), **Coast Guard** (tel. 508/968–5316), and **PAVE PAWS** (tel. 508/968–3206). It would be possible to see everything in a day, but you would have to reserve a couple days in advance.

Massachusetts Maritime Academy, with a 55-acre campus at Taylors Point on Buzzards Bay, trains future members of the Merchant Marine. Its library has scale models of ships from the 18th century to the present, as well as changing exhibits, and is open to the public at no charge (hours vary widely; call 508/

759–5761, ext. 350). For a 20- to 30-minute tour of the academy's training ship, call 48 hours in advance (ext. 233).

The **Sandwich Fish Hatchery** (Rte. 6A, Sandwich; open daily 9–4) produces 200,000 or so fish each year to stock the state's ponds. Here you'll see some big brook, brown, and rainbow trout at various stages of development—the mesh over the raceways is to keep kingfishers and herons from a free lunch. It's a beautiful spot, led up to by a drive lined with white cedars; you can buy feed for a dime and watch the fish jump for it.

Libraries The **Nickerson Memorial Room** at the Cape Cod Community College (Rte. 132, West Barnstable, tel. 508/362–2131, ext. 445) has the largest collection of information on Cape Cod, including books, records, ships' logs, oral-history tapes, photographs, films, and more. It also has materials on the islands. It is open to the public weekdays 8-4 year-round.

The **Cotuit Library** (Main St., tel. 508/428–8141) has an extensive collection of luxurious leather-bound classics—a donation from a private library—and another of children's books. These may be read on the premises but do not circulate.

Centerville Library (585 Main St., tel. 508/775–1787) has a 42-volume set of transcripts of the Nuremberg Trials.

Hyannis Public Library (401 Main St., tel. 508/775–2280) has a large collection on President John F. Kennedy.

Sturgis Library (Rte. 6A, Barnstable Village, tel. 508/362–6636) has the definitive collection of Cape Cod genealogical material, as well as an excellent maritime history collection, with more than 1,500 charts and maps.

Shopping

Shopping is an important part of a Cape Cod vacation, especially on nonbeach days in summer (and in the rain, when the covered malls and factory outlets are mobbed). Favorite pastimes of many visitors include antiquing and gallery hopping. Throughout the Cape you'll find weavers, candle makers, glassblowers, paper makers, and potters, as well as artists working in metal, enamel, and wood. You'll also find an inordinate number of shops specializing in country crafts, from straw dolls to handmade Christmas-tree ornaments.

Many shops close down for the winter; in season, they tend to stay open late several nights a week, especially in Hyannis and Provincetown. For more on Cape specialties and shop hours, *see* Shopping in Chapter 1, Essential Information.

Shopping Districts

Provincetown has a long history as an art colony and remains an important art center, with many fine galleries and frequent exhibitions of Cape and non-Cape artists. Several artists represented in Provincetown are also shown in prominent New York galleries. Wellfleet has emerged as a vibrant center for art as well. Brochures on galleries in both towns are available by mail (*see* Shopping in Chapter 1, Essential Information).

Provincetown and Wellfleet also attract large numbers of craftsmen, who sell through a number of unique and sophisticated shops. Route 6A, which is the premier area for antiques and antiquarian bookshops, has its share of crafts shops as well, including many focusing on country crafts.

Hyannis's Main Street—the Cape's largest—is lined with bookshops, gift shops, jewelers, clothing stores, summer-wear and T-shirt shops, ice-cream and candy stores, plus minigolf places and fun eating places.

Chatham's pretty Main Street is another main shopping area, with generally more upscale and conservative merchandise than Hyannis. Here you'll find galleries, crafts, and clothing stores, plus a few good antiques shops. Falmouth and Orleans also have a large number of shops of all kinds.

Shopping Malls

Cape Cod Mall (between Rtes. 132 and 28, Hyannis, tel. 508/771–0200), the Cape's largest, has 90 shops, including Jordan Marsh, Filene's, Marshall's, Sears, F. W. Woolworth, restaurants, and a food court. It is open Monday–Saturday 9:30–9:30, Sunday noon–6. Wheelchairs are available at no charge; strollers, for a small fee.

Falmouth Mall (Rte. 28, Falmouth, tel. 508/540–8329) has Bradlees, T. J. Maxx, and 30 other shops, generally open Monday–Saturday 9:30–9:30 and Sunday noon–6.

Mashpee Commons (Mashpee Rotary, junction of Rtes. 28 and 151, Mashpee, tel. 508/477–9838) has more than 50 shops and restaurants in an attractive village square setting. The shops—including The Gap, Peter Malone Ltd. Irish Imports, Puritan Clothing of Cape Cod (traditional wear)—are open Monday–Saturday 10–8, Sunday noon–5. There's also a movie theater.

Village Marketplace I (corner of North and Steven Sts., Hyannis, tel. 508/775–9416) is several buildings connected by brick walkways. Shops include Eastern Mountain Sports, Marshmallow home furnishings, a gourmet grocery, a bookshop, and fine leather, crafts, and women's-wear shops.

Department Stores

These include **K mart** (Rte. 132, Hyannis, tel. 508/771–0012); **F. W. Woolworth** (tel. 508/775–5212), **Jordan Marsh** (tel. 508/771–7111), and **Filene's** (tel. 508/775–3800) in the Cape Cod Mall, and **Sears** in the Cape Cod Mall (tel. 508/771–1700) and the Falmouth Mall (tel. 508/548–9580).

Factory Outlets

Cape Cod Factory Outlet Mall (Factory Outlet Rd., Exit 1 off Rte. 6, Sagamore, tel. 508/888–8417) has a food court and more than 20 outlets, including Corning/Revere, Carter's, Gitano, Bass Shoe, Hanes, Van Heusen, and Toy Liquidators.

Factory Shoe Mart (Rte. 28, Dennisport, tel. 508/398–6000; Rte. 28 at Deer Crossing, Mashpee, tel. 508/477–0017) has all the brand names, such as Penaljo, Nickels, L. A. Gear, 9 West, Evan Picone, Etienne Aigner, and Avia, for men, women, and children.

Victorian Village (Rte. 28, South Yarmouth, no tel.) has eight outlets, including Gitano, Crazy Horse, and American Tourister.

Single-store outlets include **Dansk** (990 Rte. 132, Hyannis, tel. 508/775–3118) and **The Flag Factory Outlet** (404 Main St., Centerville, tel. 508/790–4881), with international, marine, and many other kinds of flags.

Flea Market

The **Wellfleet Drive-In Theatre** (Rte. 6, Eastham–Wellfleet line, tel. 508/349–2520) is the site of a giant flea market (mid-Apr.–June, Sept., and Oct., weekends and Mon. holidays 8–4; July and Aug., Mon. holidays, Wed., Thurs., and weekends 8–4). There's a snack bar and playground.

Farm Stands

Fancy's Farm Stands (199 Main St., East Orleans, tel. 508/255–1949; The Cornfield, Rte. 28, West Chatham, tel. 508/945–1949; 2660 Main St. [Rte. 6A], Brewster, tel. 508/896–8141) sell local and exotic produce, fresh-baked breads and pastries, dried flowers, baskets, hand-dipped candles, frozen prepared gourmet foods, spices and potpourri by the ounce, and more.

Tony Andrews Farm and Produce Stand (398 Old Meeting House Rd., East Falmouth, tel. 508/548–5257) lets you pick your own strawberries (mornings from mid-June), as well as peas, beans, and tomatoes (late June–late Aug.).

Auctions

You'll find an auction going on somewhere on the Cape all year long, from country-barn types to the internationally known Eldred's and Bourne auctions. Though these high-end companies deal in very fine antiques, their auctions always include some lower-priced merchandise (schedules are available by mail).

Eastham Auction House (Holmes Rd., N. Eastham, tel. 508/255–9003) holds auctions the first and last Saturday of each month, the first of household and general antiques, the second of fine antiques and collectibles. The evenings are entertaining, and box lots are always available.

Eldred's (Rte. 6A, Box 796, East Dennis 02641, tel. 508/385–3116) deals in mostly top-quality antiques, such as marine, Oriental, American, and European art; Americana; and estate jewelry. The auctions take place either in a stately sea captain's home, with exhibits previewed in various rooms, or in summer, in a tent on the grounds.

Merlyn Auctions (204 Main St., North Harwich, tel. 508/432–5863) are homey affairs with moderate to inexpensive prices for old and new merchandise.

Richard A. Bourne (Corporation St., Hyannis [Box 141, Hyannis Port 02647], tel. 508/775–0797) has theme auctions, such as art glass, marine art, watches and clocks, fishing and sporting goods, and duck decoys.

Sandwich Auction House (15 Tupper Rd., Sandwich, tel. 508/888–1926) has events every Saturday and emphasizes fun. The specialty is estate sales.

Specialty Stores

Antiques
"Cape Cod Antiques & Arts," a monthly supplement of *The Register* and *The Cape Codder* (Cape Cod Publishing, Box 39, Orleans 02653), is chock-full of information on galleries, upcoming shows, Cape artists, antiques shops, auctions, and so forth. *The Review: Cape Cod's Arts & Antiques Magazine* (Box 34, Centerville 02632, tel. 508/775–7001) is a glossy bimonthly with gallery ads and articles. Both are available at local newsstands.

The **Cape Cod Antiquarian Book Fair** (for information, tel. 508/888–2331) attracts 50 dealers each summer in Sandwich.

B. D. Hutchinson (1274 Long Pond Rd., Brewster, tel. 508/896–6395), a watch- and clockmaker, sells antique and collectible watches, clocks, and music boxes.

Brown Jug (Main St. at Jarves St., Sandwich, tel. 508/888–0940) specializes in antique glass, such as Sandwich glass and Tiffany iridescent glassware, as well as Staffordshire china.

Carriage House Antiques (3425 Rte. 6A, Brewster, tel. 508/896–6570) has museum-quality 18th- and 19-century marine antiques and American furniture, country pine, pottery, china, botanical prints, paintings, antique toy soldiers, and guns.

Eldred Wheeler (866 Main St., Box 90, Osterville 02655, tel. 508/428–9049 or 428–7093; catalogue $4) is well known for handcrafting fine 18th-century furniture reproductions.

Ellipse Antiques (427 Main St. [Rte. 6A], Dennis, tel. 508/385–8626) specializes in "important early glass," such as rare Sandwich glass pieces, and Americana.

Horsefeathers (454 Rte. 6A, East Sandwich, tel. 508/888–5298) sells antique linens, lace, bird cages, baby things, and Victoriana such as valentines.

H. Richard Strand (Town Hall Sq., Sandwich, tel. 508/888–3230), in an 1800 home, displays very fine pre-1840 and Victorian antique furniture, paintings, American glass, and more.

Kingsland Manor (Rte. 6A, West Brewster, tel. 508/385–9741) is like a fairyland, with ivy covering the facade, fountains in the courtyard, and everything "from tin to Tiffany"—including English hunting horns, full-size antique street lamps, garden furniture, jewelry, and chandeliers.

Mark Lawrence (1050 Rte. 6A, Brewster, tel. 508/896–8381) has 18th- and 19th-century furnishings and decorative objects of museum quality, both European and Oriental.

Paul Madden Antiques (146 Old Main St., Sandwich, tel. 508/888–6434 or 888–6886; only by appointment or chance) specializes in Americana, with a selection of choice scrimshaw pieces.

Remembrances of Things Past (376 Commercial St., Provincetown, tel. 508/487–9443) deals with articles from the 1920s to the 1960s, including Bakelite and other jewelry, telephones, photographs of old movie stars, and neon items.

Salt & Chestnut (Rte. 6A at Maple St., West Barnstable, tel. 508/362–6085) has antique and custom-designed weathervanes displayed indoors and in the yard—a fun place to browse.

The Spyglass (618 Main St., Chatham, tel. 508/945–9686) carries telescopes, barometers, writing boxes, sea charts, and other nautical antiques.

Whitman House Gift Shop (Rte. 6, North Truro, tel. 508/487–1740) has Amish quilts and other country items.

Art **Blue Heron Gallery** (Bank St., Wellfleet, tel. 508/349–6724) is one of the Cape's best galleries, with representational contemporary art by regional and nationally recognized artists.

Cape Gallery of Contemporary Art (114 Palmer Ave., Falmouth, tel. 508/548–4121) shows fine traditional paintings, drawings, art glass, and sculptures by Cape and off-Cape artists.

Chandler Gallery (Main St., Wellfleet, tel. 508/349–1620) handles contemporary Cape Cod artists.

Cummaquid Fine Arts (4275 Rte. 6A, Cummaquid, tel. 508/362–2593) has works by Cape Cod and New England artists, plus decorative antiques, beautifully displayed in an old home.

Ellen Harris Gallery (355 Commercial St., Provincetown, tel. 508/487–1414 or 0065) deals in art and crafts, including Native American arts, in all media.

Hell's Kitchen Gallery (439 Commercial St., Provincetown, tel. 508/487–3570) features Provincetown-connected artists, including the photography of Joel Meyerowitz.

Long Point Gallery (492 Commercial St., Provincetown, tel. 508/487–1795) is a collective of well-established artists—including Varujan Boghosian, Robert Motherwell, Paul Resika, Judith Rothschild, and Tony Vevers—founded in 1977.

Origins Gallery (Galleria, 62 Rte. 6A at Rte. 28, Orleans, tel. 508/255–8660) sells tribal and folk art and jewelry from Africa, Asia, and Latin America.

Sweetgrass Gallery (445 Commercial St., Provincetown, tel. 508/487–2352) features very fine Native American art, including intricately beaded moccasins, fetishes, weavings, paintings, furniture, ceremonial items, blankets, pottery, and more.

Wellfleet Collection (Baker Ave., Wellfleet, tel. 508/349–9687), located in a Greek Revival house, deals in folk arts, quilts, baskets, and pottery.

Woods Hole Gallery (14 School St., Woods Hole, tel. 508/548–7594) deals in 19th- and 20th-century New England art.

Books The Cape has a dozen bookshops that sell rare and out-of-print books (at any, ask for the brochure listing them), along with plenty of all-purpose bookstores.

Kings Way Books and Collectibles (774 Rte. 6A, Brewster, tel. 508/896–3639) has out-of-print and rare books, including a large medieval section, plus small antiques, china, glass, silver, coins, linens, and clothing.

Parnassus Book Service (Rte. 6A, Yarmouth Port, tel. 508/362–6420), in an 1840 former general store, has a huge selection of old and new books and is a great place to browse.

Provincetown Art Association and Museum (460 Commercial St., Provincetown, tel. 508/487–1750) has a gift shop with many books on Provincetown artists.

Provincetown Bookshop (246 Commercial St., tel. 508/487–0964) has just about every book ever written on Provincetown, as well as many titles on Cape Cod.

Punkhorn Bookshop (672 Rte. 6A, Brewster, tel. 508/896–2114), an antiquarian- and rare-book seller, specializes in books on the sea and some antique prints and portfolios.

Titcomb's Bookshop (432 Rte. 6A, East Sandwich, tel. 508/888–2331) has used, rare, and new books, including a large collection of Cape-related titles and hundreds on fishing.

Wisdom and Whimsy Unlimited (174 Main St., Sandwich, tel. 508/888–6933) has new books in an antique home.

Yellow Umbrella Books (501 Main St., Chatham, tel. 508/945–

0144) has an excellent selection of new books, many on Cape Cod.

Clothing **Hannah** (47 Main St., Orleans, tel. 508/255–8234; Main St., Wellfleet, tel. 508/349–9884) has high-end women's fashions in unusual styles by such labels as Hannah English, No Saint, Kensington Blue, and shoes by Kenneth Cole and Chinese Laundry.

Howlingbird (91 Palmer Ave., Falmouth, tel. 508/540–3787) carries hand-silkscreened T-shirts and sweatshirts, including some with great architectural images, plus silver and shell jewelry, hand-painted cards, and batik-print summer clothing.

Laguna Sport (1600 Rte. 28, Bell Tower Mall, Centerville, tel. 508/778–5003) has a full complement of wild California and Hawaii surf-type beachwear in fluorescent (and quieter) tones, plus sunglasses, Body Gloves (cold-water surfer wear), beach bags, and more.

Cape Sailboards (661 Main St., Falmouth, tel. 508/540–8800) has similar, plus sail, boogie, and skim boards.

Maxwell & Co. (200 Main St., Falmouth, tel. 508/540–8752) has traditional men's and women's clothing with flair, from European and American designers; handmade Italian shoes and boots; and leather goods and accessories.

Northern Lights Leather (361 Commercial St., Provincetown, tel. 508/487–9376) has high-fashion clothing and accessories of very fine, soft leather. The company runs another shop nearby, which sell all kinds of rope hammocks.

Undercover (377 Commercial St., Provincetown, tel. 508/487–2057) has some of the most interesting young women's shoes and boots on the Cape, plus wild and tame lingerie and jewelry.

Crafts **The Blacks Handweaving Shop** (597 Rte. 6A, West Barnstable, tel. 508/362–3955), in an old barn with the looms upstairs, makes beautiful woven goods in traditional and jacquard weaves.

Chatham Glass Co. (17 Balfour La., Chatham, tel. 508/945–5547) is a glassworks where you can watch glass being blown, and buy it, too—objects including marbles, Christmas ornaments, jewelry, art glass, and antique reproductions.

Impulse (188 Commercial St., Provincetown, tel. 508/487–1154) has wonderful contemporary American crafts, including many kaleidoscopes and jewelry. The Autograph Gallery features photographs, letters, and documents signed by celebrities.

Kemp Pottery (Orleans Cove Gallery, Rte. 6A, Orleans, tel. 508/255–5853; 258 Rte. 6A, West Brewster, tel. 508/385–5782) has stoneware, porcelain, and flame ware, some with Oriental brushwork, some with celadon glaze.

Linda's Originals & the Yankee Craftsman (220 Rte. 6A, West Brewster, tel. 508/385–2285) brings together the work of 500 craftsmen in handcrafted country furnishings and gifts.

Pewter Crafters of Cape Cod (927 Main St. [Rte. 6A], Yarmouth Port, tel. 508/362–3407) handcrafts traditional and contemporary pewter objects from baby's cups to tea services.

Scargo Pottery (off Rte. 6A, Dennis, tel. 508/385–3894) is a 35-year Cape favorite. The setting is a pine forest, and potter Harry Holl's unusual wares—such as his signature castle birdhouses—are displayed outdoors on tree stumps and hanging from branches. Inside is more pottery and the workshop and kiln.

The Spectrum (Rte. 6A, Brewster, tel. 508/385–3322; 342 Main St., Hyannis, tel. 508/771–4554; W. Main St., Wellfleet, tel.

508/349–1962) showcases imaginative American arts and crafts, including pottery, stained glass, art glass, and more.

Sydenstricker Galleries (Rte. 6A, Brewster, tel. 508/385–3272) features glassware handcrafted by a unique process, which you can watch in progress at the studio on the premises.

Tree's Place (Rte. 6A at Rte. 28, Orleans, tel. 508/255–1330), one of the Cape's best and most original shops, has a huge collection of handcrafted kaleidoscopes, plus art glass, hand-painted porcelain and pottery, hand-blown stemware, Russian lacquer boxes, jewelry, imported ceramic tiles, and much more.

Wellfleet Collection (Baker Ave., Wellfleet, tel. 508/349–9687) carries folk art, quilts, baskets, and pottery.

Whippletree (Rte. 6A, West Barnstable, tel. 508/362–3320) is a large barn, beautifully decorated for each season and filled with country gift items and a year-round Christmas section. Offerings include German nutcrackers, from Prussian soldiers to Casanova, plus the title character from *The Nutcracker* ballet.

Gifts **Crystal Pineapple** (1540 Rte. 6A, W. Barnstable, tel. 508/362–3128 or 800/462–4009) has cranberry glass, Tiffany lamps, Lladro figurines, Swarovski crystal, music boxes, scrimshaw, wampum jewelry, kaleidoscopes, and much more.

Home for the Holidays (154 Main St., Sandwich, tel. 508/888–4388) carries superb decorations, gifts, and handcrafted cards for nearly every holiday or special occasion—such as baby gifts, Christmas ornaments and papers, goblin lights for Halloween—as well as elegant glassware and china. Set in an old home, it's a lovely place to browse, with something magical at every turn.

Food **Chatham Jam and Jelly Shop** (10 Vineyard Ave., West Chatham, tel. 508/945–3052) sells preserves, nutty conserves, and ice-cream toppings—cranberry with strawberries and honey, Maine wild blueberry, hot pepper—made on site in small batches.

The Chocolate House Fudge and Gift Shop (11 Cranberry Hwy., Sagamore, tel. 508/888–7065), just over the Sagamore Bridge on the Cape side, sells creamy fudge in 12 flavors, including the unusual spiced cranberry orange nut; hand-dipped chocolates and truffles; and saltwater taffy and penny candy. There's a gift shop with cranberry glass and other Cape items.

The Clambake Celebration (5 Giddiah Hill Rd., Orleans, tel. 508/255-3289 or 800/423–4038) prepares full clambakes, including lobster, clams, mussels, fish, corn, potatoes, and sausage, for you to take away—or they'll air ship year-round. It is all layered in seaweed and ready to steam in a pot.

Marion's Pie Shop (2022 Main St. [Rte. 28], West Chatham, tel. 508/432–9439) sells homemade and home-style fruit breads, pastries, prepared foods (lasagna, Boston baked beans, chowder base), and, of course, pies, both meat and fruit.

Jewelry Also *see* Antiques and Crafts, above.

September Morn (385 Commercial St., Provincetown, tel. 508/487–9092) sells fine estate jewelry, plus art glass and antique Oriental art.

Victorian House Jewelry (121 Rte. 6A, Orleans, tel. 508/240–1299) has sterling silver and marcasite jewelry in designs of the 1920s and 1930s.

Odds and Ends   **Baseball Shop** (26 Main St., Orleans, tel. 508/240–1063) sells everything relating to baseball (and other sports)—cards (new and collectible), hats, shirts, posters, even Christmas ornaments.

Bird Watcher's General Store (37 Rte. 6A, Orleans, tel. 508/255–6974) has everything avian: feeders, notecards, paintings, houses, books, fountains, recordings, calls, ad infinitum.

Christmas Tree Shops (main shop at Exit 1 off Rte. 6, Sagamore, tel. 508/888–7010; others at Bourne, Falmouth, Hyannis, Orleans, West Dennis, West Yarmouth, and Yarmouth Port) sell everything, period: discounted paper goods, candles, furniture, toys, kitchen goods. This is not high-concept shopping, it's pure fun. The newest shop (Rte. 132, Hyannis), a multicolor Victorian-style affair that opened in 1990, is the largest.

Sports and Outdoor Activities

Bicycling

The Dennis Chamber of Commerce (jct. Rtes. 28 and 134, Box 275, South Dennis 02660, tel. 508/398–3568 or 800/243–9920) issues a guidebook with several bike tours and maps. The Wellfleet Chamber (Rte. 6 at Davis Corner, Box 571, 02667, tel. 508/349–2510) puts out a pamphlet, "Bicycling in Wellfleet," with an annotated map. Also, a paperback book on the marked and unmarked bike trails of Cape Cod, **The Cape Cod Bike Book,** is available in Cape bookstores and bike shops; Yarmouth Bicycle and Fitness (63 White's Path, South Yarmouth 02664, tel. 508/394–8941) will send you a copy for $2.50.

The Cape chapter of the **Sierra Club** (tel. 508/563–6706) sponsors bike rides and hikes.

Bike Paths   **Cape Cod Rail Trail,** the paved right-of-way of the old Penn Central Railroad, is the Cape's premier bike path. It is 20 miles long, from Dennis to Eastham, and passes salt marshes, cranberry bogs, ponds, and Nickerson State Park, which has its own path (*see* below). Along the way you can veer off to spend an hour or two on the beach, or stop for lunch. The terrain is easy to moderate. The trail begins in South Dennis (the start is at the parking lot off Rte. 134, south of Rte. 6, near Theophilus Smith Rd.) and ends at the entrance to the Salt Pond Visitor Center. There are parking lots along the route if you want to do only a segment: Across from Pleasant Lake Store (on Pleasant Lake Ave.) in Harwich and at Nickerson State Park in Brewster. The Butterworth Company (476 Main St., Harwich Port 02646, tel. 508/432–8200) sells a guide to the trail for $2.50.

On either side of the **Cape Cod Canal** is an easy straight trail (6½ miles on the south side, almost 8 on the north), offering a view of the bridges and canal traffic. They are accessed from many points along the trails. The **Shining Sea Bikepath** is a nice-and-easy 3½-mile route between Locust Street, Falmouth, and the Woods Hole parking lot. It follows the coast, giving views of Vineyard Sound and dipping into oak and pine woods. Look for a brochure, noting points of interest, at the trailheads.

The Cape Cod National Seashore maintains three bicycle trails (brochure with maps available at visitor centers). **Nauset Trail** is 1⅗ miles, from Salt Pond Visitor Center in Eastham through groves of apple and locust trees to Coast Guard Beach. **Head of the Meadow Trail** is 2 miles of easy cycling between sand dunes and salt marshes from High Head Road, off Route 6A in North Truro, to the Head of the Meadow Beach parking lot. **Province Lands Trail** is a 5¼-mile loop off the Beech Forest parking lot on Race Point Road in Provincetown, with spurs to Herring Cove and Race Point beaches and to Bennett Pond. The paths wind up and down hills amid the Province Lands sand dunes, marshes, woods, and ponds, and offer spectacular views (on a really clear day, you can see the Boston skyline); there's a picnic grove at Pilgrim Spring.

Nickerson State Park (*see* Nature Areas, below) has 3 miles of trails through forest (trail map available at park headquarters).

Fishing

Fishing is one of the Cape's main pastimes (the Cape Cod Chamber's "Sportsman's Guide" gives fishing regulations, surf-fishing access locations, a map of boat-launching facilities, and more). The *Cape Cod Times*'s "CapeWeek" section, published on Friday, has a Fishing Around column that tells the latest in fishing on the Cape—what's being caught, and where.

The Cape Cod Canal is a good place to fish, from the service road on either side, for blues, cod, flounder, mackerel, and black and striped bass (Apr.–Nov.). The Army Corps of Engineers offers a **hotline on Canal fishing** (tel. 508/759–5991).

There are hundreds of freshwater ponds with good fishing; a license for freshwater fishing is available at tackle shops, such as **Eastman's Sport & Tackle** (145 Main St., Falmouth, tel. 508/548–6900), **Riverview Bait & Tackle** (120 Rte. 28, West Dennis, tel. 508/394–1036), and **Truman's** (Rte. 28 at railroad crossing, Hyannis, tel. 508/771–3470), which also rent gear. For absolutely everything fishing-related, including information, equipment, and books, stop in at the fisherman's paradise: the **Goose Hummock Shop** (Rte. 6A, Orleans, tel. 508/255–0455). For rental boats, *see* Boating and Water Sports, below.

Fishing Trips   Charter boats and party boats (per-head fees, rather than the charters' group rates) take you offshore for tuna, mako and blue sharks, swordfish, and marlin; bottom fishing for flounder, tautog, scup, fluke, cod, and pollock.

Deep-sea fishing trips are operated on a walk-on basis from spring through fall by **Cape Mariner Excursions** (Town Pier, Wellfleet, tel. 508/349–6003), **Cap'n Bill & Cee Jay** (MacMillan Pier, Provincetown, tel. 508/487–4330 or 487–2353), *Golden Eagle* (Town Pier, Wychmere Harbor, Harwich Port, tel. 508/945–0167), **Hy-Line** (Ocean St. Dock, Hyannis, tel. 508/778–2600), *Patriot Too* (Falmouth Harbor, tel. 508/548–2626), and *Yankee* (Saquatucket Harbor, Rte. 28, Harwich Port, tel. 508/432–2520). Many of these offer charters as well.

Charter boats are available through **Barnstable Harbor Charter Fleet** (186 Millway, tel. 508/362–3908), **Cape Cod Sportfishing** (Hyannis Harbor, tel. 508/790–3474), **Double Eagle Cruises** (180 Scranton Ave., Falmouth, tel. 508/548–2929),

Patriot Party Boats (227 Clinton Ave., Falmouth, tel. 508/548–2626), and **Rock Harbor Charter Boat Fleet** (Rock Harbor, Orleans, tel. 508/255–9757 or in MA, 800/843–1771).

Golf

The Cape Cod Chamber of Commerce has a "Golf Map of Cape Cod," locating 46 courses on the Cape and Islands. The Cape's mild climate makes golf possible almost year-round, and most of its 20 public courses stay open, though January and February do get nippy (temperatures average in the 30s).

Blue Rock Golf Course (off Highbank Rd., South Yarmouth, tel. 508/398–9295) is a highly regarded, hilly 18-hole course.
Captain's Golf Course (1000 Freeman's Way, Brewster, tel. 508/896–5100), an 18-hole course with plans to add more, was voted among the top 25 public courses in the country by *Golf Digest* in 1990.
New Seabury Country Club (Shore Dr., Mashpee, tel. 508/477–9110) is one of the state's best golf resorts, with one superior 18-hole championship layout and another good 18-hole course.
Ocean Edge Golf Course (1 Villagers Rd., Rte. 6A, Brewster, tel. 508/896–6157), an 18-hole, par-72 course, is the home of the New England PGA Championship. It features Scottish-style pot bunkers, challenging terrain, and one hole over a cranberry bog. Weeklong residential or commuter golf schools are offered in fall.
Tara Hyannis Hotel & Resort (West End Circle, Hyannis, tel. 508/775–7775) has a beautifully landscaped 18-hole course.
Other courses: **Chatham Seaside Links** (the old Chatham Bars Inn course, now town owned; Chatham, tel. 508/945–0096), nine holes, a good beginner's course; and **Cranberry Valley Golf Course** (Oak St., Harwich, tel. 508/432–6300), 18 holes.

Health and Fitness Clubs

Falmouth Nautilus and Fitness Center (133 Main St., East Falmouth, tel. 508/540–6180) has Nautilus, Stairmaster, Lifecycle, and Windracer machines; stationary bikes; free weights; aerobics classes; tanning; and whirlpool.
Falmouth Sports Center (Highfield Dr., Falmouth, tel. 508/548–7433) is a huge facility with three all-weather tennis courts, six indoor tennis courts, three racquetball/handball courts, one squash court, a sauna, and a steam room; Nautilus, Universal, Biocycle, Airdyne, Stairmaster, treadmill, Cybex, and Gravitron machines; and a large free-weights room.
Fitness Club of Cape Cod (55 Attucks Way, Independence Park, off Rte. 132, Hyannis, tel. 508/771–7734) has Nautilus, Universal, Lifecycle, Stairmaster, rowing, and other cardiovascular machines; treadmills; free weights; aerobics classes; five racquetball or wallyball courts; basketball; personal trainers, myotherapy, massage; sauna and whirlpool; day care; and a bar/restaurant with pool table and dart boards.
Mid-Cape Racquet Club (193 White's Path, South Yarmouth, tel. 508/394–3511), the sister club of the Fitness Club in Hyannis, has one outdoor all-weather tennis court and nine indoor courts; two racquetball and two squash courts; indoor and outdoor basketball; free weights; treadmills and Nautilus, Lifecycle, Stairmaster, and rowing machines; personal trainers and racket sports pros; plus whirlpool, steam room, and sauna.

The Norseman Athletic Club (Rte. 6, North Eastham, tel. 508/ 255–6370 or 6371) has five racquetball courts and one squash court, Nautilus machines, free weights, an indoor Olympic-size heated pool, aerobics and self-defense classes, saunas, a steam room, whirlpools, a gym, indoor basketball courts, and six indoor tennis courts.

The Regency Club (Hyatt Regency, Rte. 132, Hyannis, tel. 508/ 775-1153, ext. 535) has Nautilus, Lifecycle, Stairmaster, and Life Rower machines, treadmills, and reclining bike; aerobics, yoga, and Step Reebok classes; a heated indoor pool and whirlpool; and a ladies' steam room and men's steam and sauna rooms.

The Tara Club (Tara Hyannis Hotel & Resort, West End Circle, Hyannis, tel. 508/775–7775) has two outdoor tennis courts; indoor and outdoor pools; aerobics; Nautilus and Cybex machines, Lifecycles, Life Rowers, Stairmasters, and treadmills; sauna, steamrooms, whirlpool, massage, and more.

Willy's Gym (Rte. 6A, Orleans, tel. 508/255–6826) has Nautilus, Nautilus, Body Master, Polaris, and Advanced Physique machines; aerobics and Step Reebok classes; free weights, child care, and a juice bar.

Hiking

The **Cape Cod Museum of Natural History** (*see* Tour 3: Route 6A, Hyannis to Orleans, above), **Cape Cod National Seashore** (*see* Tour 5: Route 6, Orleans to Provincetown, above), and **Nickerson State Park** (*see* Nature Areas, below) offer guided walks and hikes year-round.

The **Cape Cod National Seashore** has nine self-guiding trails through varied terrain (brochures available at visitor centers and at trailheads).

Horseback Riding

Nelson's Riding Stable (Race Point Rd., Provincetown, tel. 508/ 487–0034) is located near the **Province Lands Horse Trails,** three two-hour trails to the beaches through or past dunes, cranberry bogs, forests, and ponds—great at sunset. Other stables: **Deer Meadow Riding Stables** (Rte. 137, East Harwich, tel. 508/432–6580), rides through conservation land; **Haland Stables** (Rte. 28A, West Falmouth, tel. 508/540–2552); **Holly Hill Farm** (Flint St., Marstons Mills, tel. 508/428–2621); **Maushop Stables** (Old Mill Rd., Mashpee, tel. 508/477–1303); **Provincetown Horse and Carriage** (tel. 508/487–1112), dune and beach rides, pony rides.

Ice-Skating

Fall through spring, public skating is available at several town rinks, including the **Falmouth Ice Arena** (Palmer Ave., Falmouth, tel. 508/548–9083), **John Gallo Ice Arena** (231 Sandwich Rd., Bourne, tel. 508/759–8904), **Kennedy Memorial Skating Rink** (Bearses Way, Hyannis, tel. 508/775–0397), and **Tony Kent Arena** (8 Gages Way, South Dennis, tel. 508/760–2400). Some offer roller-skating in summer.

In winter, ponds and shallow flooded cranberry bogs sometimes freeze hard enough for skating; contact the local fire department for advice before venturing onto unfamiliar territory.

Jogging/Running

Aside from the state parks and forests, which have paved trails (*see* Nature Areas, below), the beaches are great places to run, as are the paths alongside the canal.

Lifecourse (Access and Old Bass River Rds., South Dennis) is a 1½-mile jogging trail through woods, with 20 exercise stations along the way.

Many road races are held in season, including the world-class **Falmouth Road Race** (Box 732, Falmouth 02541, tel. 508/540–7000) in August and the **Cape Codder Triathlon** (Box 307, West Barnstable 02668) at Craigville Beach in July. Watch the papers for announcements.

Shellfishing

For shellfishing licenses and information on sites, contact the local town hall.

Skiing

Nickerson State Park has a cross-country skiing trail; the **Cape Cod Rail Trail** and the golf courses also make good trails when there's enough snow.

Tennis and Racquetball

Public tennis courts abound: Falmouth, for example, has more than 20. To locate one near you, call the town recreation department. The busiest times are morning and early evening. Tennis clubs can often find individuals a partner, or a league match to play in. Also *see* Health and Fitness Clubs, above.

Bissell's Tennis Courts (Bradford St. at Herring Cove Beach Rd., Provincetown, tel. 508/487–9512; open Memorial Day–Sept.) has five clay courts and offers lessons.
Chequessett Yacht & Country Club (Chequessett Neck Rd., Wellfleet, tel. 508/349–3704) is a semiprivate club with a nine-hole golf course and five hard-surface tennis courts on the bay. From mid-March to mid-December, the public may use the facility on a space-available basis. Lessons are available.
Manning's Tennis (292 Rte. 28, West Harwich, tel. 508/432–3958) has four championship all-weather tennis courts in a pine grove, and gives lessons.

Nature Areas

Ashumet Holly Reservation (*see* Tour 2: Route 28, Buzzards Bay to Hyannis, above).

Cape Cod National Seashore (*see* Tour 5: Route 6, Orleans to Provincetown, above).

Monomoy National Wildlife Refuge is a 2,097-acre preserve on Monomoy Island, a fragile, 9-mile-long barrier-beach area (actually composed of two islands) south of Chatham (also *see* Tour 4, above). An important stop along the North Atlantic Flyway for migratory waterfowl (peak migration times are May and late July), it provides nesting and resting grounds for 285 species, including large nesting colonies of great black-backed, herring, and laughing gulls and several tern species. North Island has hundreds of barn swallows. White-tailed deer also live on the islands, and harbor seals frequent the shores in winter.

Monomoy is a very quiet, peaceful place of sand and beach grass; of tidal flats, dunes, marshes, freshwater ponds, thickets of bayberry and beach plum and a few pines. Because the refuge harbors several endangered species, visitors' activities are limited; certain areas are fenced off to protect nesting areas of terns and the endangered piping plover. The Audubon Society and others conduct tours of the island (*see* Guided Tours, above); you can also get a boat at Chatham Harbor to taxi you over in season for some lone bird watching. The only structure on Monomoy is the South Island Lighthouse. Built in 1849, the shiny red-orange structure, along with the keeper's house, was refurbished in 1988 and now offers overnight lodgings to the tour groups.

Nickerson State Park (Rte. 6A, Box 787, Brewster 02631, tel. 508/896–3491; map available on-site) is more than 1,700 acres of white pine, hemlock, and spruce forest dotted with eight freshwater kettle ponds (formed by glacial deposits). Ponds are stocked year-round with trout and bass; other recreational opportunities are biking along 8 miles of paved trail, canoeing, sailing, motorboating, picnicking, bird-watching (thrushes, wrens, warblers, woodpeckers, finches, larks, Canada geese, cormorants, great blue herons, loons, hawks, owls, osprey), and ice fishing, ice-skating, and cross-country skiing in winter. Wildlife includes red foxes and white-tailed deer. Tent camping (420 sites) is extremely popular here, and visitor programs are offered.

Scusset Beach Reservation (Scusset Beach Rd., off Rte. 3, Sandwich 02563, tel. 508/888–0859) is 450 acres near the canal, with a beach on the bay. Its pier is a popular fishing spot; other activities include biking, hiking, picnicking, swimming, and camping on its 98 sites.

Shawme Crowell State Forest (Rte. 130, Sandwich, tel. 508/888–0351) is 2,756 acres, ¼-mile from the canal. Activities include camping (280 sites), biking, and hiking.

Wellfleet Bay Wildlife Sanctuary is a 750-acre haven for more than 250 species of birds, which are attracted by the varied habitats found here. Hiking trails lead through woods, past moors and salt marshes that rim Cape Cod Bay. In summer, the Massachusetts Audubon Society refuge sponsors many activities, including walks, hikes, birding, nature classes, day camps for children (*see* What to See and Do with Children, above) and week-long field schools for adults, camping, seabird and marsh cruises, snorkeling, canoe trips, evening slide shows, an evening lecture series under the stars (bring insect repellent), and evening bat watches; a schedule is available on-site, or write for one. *Off Rte. 6 (Box 236), South Wellfleet 02663, tel. 508/ 349–2615. Admission: $3 adults, $2 children (free to Audubon Society members). Open daily 8 AM–dusk.*

Spectator Sports

The **Cape Cod Baseball League** (tel. 508/432–0340) is an invitational league of outstanding college players that boasts Carlton Fisk, Ron Darling, and the late Thurman Munson as alumni. Considered the best summer league in the United States, it is scouted by all the major-league teams. There are 10 teams in the league, which began in 1885. The 44-game season lasts from mid-June to mid-August, and games—played in late afternoon or evening—are free.

Many annual bike races, road races, marathons, triathlons, and golf and tennis tournaments are held on the Cape. Watch the local papers for upcoming events, and also *see* Festivals and Seasonal Events in Chapter 1, Essential Information.

Water Sports

Boating

Cape Cod Boats (Rte. 28 at Bass River Bridge, West Dennis, tel. 508/394–9268) rents powerboats, sailboats, and canoes. **Ryder's Cove Boat Yard** (Rte. 28, North Chatham, tel. 508/945–1064) rents Boston Whalers. *See* also Canoeing and Sailing, below, for outfitters providing other kinds of boats, as well.

Canoeing

Wellfleet Bay Wildlife Sanctuary (*see* Nature Areas, above) offers canoe trips at different levels, as well as kayaking, in season. The **Cape Cod National Seashore** (*see* Tour 5: Route 6, Orleans to Provincetown, above) also conducts canoe trips.

Cape Cod Waterways (16 Main St. [Rte. 28], Dennisport, tel. 508/398–0080) rents canoes, kayaks, and paddleboats for leisurely travel on the Swan River, as well as Windsurfers.

Sailing and Windsurfing

Arey's Pond Boat Yard (off Rte. 28, South Orleans, tel. 508/255–0994) has a sailing school with individual and group lessons.
Cape Sailboards (661–D Main St., Falmouth, and Surfside East Motel, 134 Menauhant Rd., Falmouth, tel. 508/540–8800) rents sailboards and Sunfish and gives lessons.
Cape Water Sports (Rte. 28, Harwich Port, tel. 508/432–7079; six other locations) rents Sunfish, Hobie Cats, sailboards, day sailers, paddleboats, and canoes, and gives instructions.
Flyer's (131A Commercial St., Provincetown, tel. 508/487–0898 or 487–0518) rents sailboards, Sunfish, sailboats (13–22 feet), outboards, and rowboats, and teaches sailing.
Goose Hummock (Rte. 6A, Orleans, tel. 508/255–0455) rents fishing boats, canoes, and Sunfish (along with camping, backpacking, and water sports equipment).
Jack's Boat Rental (Rte. 6, Wellfleet, tel. 508/349–9808) rents paddleboats, Sunfish, Hobie Cats, canoes, boogie boards, and sailboards, and offers sailing and windsurfing lessons.
Monomoy Sail & Cycle (275 Orleans Rd. [Rte. 28], North Chatham, tel. 508/945–0811) rents sailboards and Sunfish and gives lessons.

Windsurfing Unlimited (277A Commercial St., Provincetown, tel. 508/487–9272) rents sailboards, Sunfish, and day sailers, and provides instructions.

Scuba

Water temperatures vary from 50° to 70° in Nantucket Sound, and from 45° to 60° on the ocean side and in Cape Cod Bay. Visibility averages 35–45 feet. Check with a dive shop about conditions in an area you wish to explore. Sign up with a dive boat to explore wrecks, including a steamship and schooners.

Aquarius Diving Center (3239 Cranberry Hwy. [Rtes. 6 and 28], Buzzards Bay, tel. 508/759–3483) provides rentals, instruction, group night dives, and a dive-buddy list.

Cape Cod Divers (269 Barnstable Rd., Hyannis, tel. 508/775–3301 or in MA, 800/DIVING–1; 815 Main St. [Rte. 28], Harwich Port, tel. 508/432–9035; Rte. 28, Falmouth, tel. 508/540–2263; Rte. 6A, Orleans, tel. 508/255–7547) offers scuba trips, charters, equipment rental, and instruction at all levels.

Both offer PADI certification and have information on dive-boat charters and local dive sites.

Surfing

The Outer Cape beaches, including North Beach in Chatham, Nauset Beach in Orleans, Marconi Beach and White Crest Beach in Wellfleet, and Long Nook in Truro, are ideal spots. **Cinnamon Rainbows Surf Co.** (9 Cranberry Hwy., Orleans, tel. 508/255–5832) rents body boards, surfboards, and wet suits.

Swimming

Cape Cod Divers (Rte. 28, Harwich Port, tel. 508/432–9035) opens its indoor, heated pool to the public.

Beaches

Cape Cod has more than 150 ocean and freshwater beaches, with something for just about every taste. Bayside beaches generally have colder water, carried down from Maine and Canada, and gentle waves. Southside beaches, on Nantucket Sound, have rolling surf and are warmed by the Gulf Stream. Open-ocean beaches on the Cape Cod National Seashore are cold and have serious surf. Shell collecting is best on Nantucket Sound beaches, just after high tide.

To avoid the crowds, arrive either early in the morning or later in the afternoon (when the water is warmest, anyway). Parking lots fill up by 10 AM or so. Those beaches not restricted to residents charge (sometimes hefty) parking lot fees; for weekly or seasonal passes, contact the local town hall.

All of the Atlantic Ocean beaches on the National Seashore, though cold, are otherwise superior—wide, long, sandy, dune-backed, with great views. They're also contiguous: from Eastham to Provincetown, you can walk virtually without ever leaving sand. All have lifeguards and rest rooms; none has food. Beginning June 25, parking costs $5 per day, or $15 for a yearly pass good at all National Parks; walk-ins pay $2; senior citizens with

Golden Eagle passports and disabled persons with Golden Access passports (*see* Hints for the Elderly and Hints for the Disabled in Chapter 1, Essential Information) are admitted free.

The National Seashore beaches are **Coast Guard Beach,** backed by low grass and heathland, and **Nauset Light Beach** in Eastham (Coast Guard doesn't have a parking lot; park at the Salt Pond Visitor Center and take the free shuttle to the beach); **Marconi Beach** in South Wellfleet, a narrow but long strand of golden sand backed by high dune cliffs; **Head of the Meadow Beach** in Truro, with steep cliffs and crashing surf; and **Race Point Beach** and **Herring Cove Beach** in Provincetown, with milder surf and slightly warmer temperatures.

Chapin Beach in Dennis is an attractive, dune-backed bay beach with long tidal flats at low tide that allow walking far out, but no lifeguards or services.

Craigville Beach, near Hyannis, is a long, wide strip of beach that is extremely popular, especially with the roving and volleyball-playing young (hence its nickname, "Muscle Beach"). It has lifeguards and a bathhouse, and there are food shops across the road.

Nauset Beach in Orleans is 10 miles of wide, sandy beach with large waves good for bodysurfing or board surfing. There are rest rooms and a food concession.

Old Silver Beach in North Falmouth is a beautiful beach that is especially good for small children because a sandbar keeps it shallow at one end and makes tidal pools with crabs and minnows. There are rest rooms, a snack bar, and showers.

Sandy Neck Beach in West Barnstable, a 6-mile barrier beach between the bay and marshland, is one of the Cape's most beautiful, a wide swath of pebbly sand backed by dunes extending to what looks like forever in both directions. Camping and four-wheel-drive vehicles are allowed on parts of the beach.

Dining

Reviews by Malcolm Wilson

Malcolm Wilson is the longtime restaurant reviewer for the Cape Cod Times.

New England cooking—hearty meat-and-potatoes fare—is the overwhelming cuisine of choice on the Cape, plus, of course, the ubiquitous New England clam chowder and fresh fish and seafood. A number of extraordinary gourmet restaurants coexist with the bastions of tradition, however, along with the occasional purveyor of ethnic cuisines. Portuguese specialties such as kale soup or *linguiça* are found on many menus, thanks to the long history of seafaring Portuguese who have settled on the Cape.

In the off-season especially, many of the Cape's hundreds of restaurants offer "early-bird specials"—low-price dinners in early evening—and Sunday brunches and buffets, often with musical accompaniment. These are advertised in the newspapers.

Category	Cost*
Very Expensive	over $40
Expensive	$25–$40

Moderate	$12–$25
Inexpensive	under $12

per person, excluding drinks, service, and sales tax (5%)

Upper Cape

Very Expensive–Moderate ★ **Regatta of Falmouth-by-the-Sea.** A spectacular view of the Inner Harbor and the Vineyard Sound is matched by the spectacularly creative French and American cuisine, typified by the signature dish, rack of lamb *en chemise:* the lamb is carved from the bone and, surrounded by *chèvre*, spinach, and pine nuts, wrapped in puff pastry, then served with a cabernet sauvignon sauce. The many seafood choices may include Chesapeake Bay soft-shell crab with a three-basil butter sauce and herbed fettuccine or scallop bisque with red-onion confiture. The front room has a full view of the harbor, where the restaurant has docking facilities; the back room is small and intimate, banquette style. *217 Scranton Ave., Falmouth, tel. 508/548–5400. Reservations suggested. Dress: formal to casual (anything goes). AE, MC, V. Dinner only. Closed Oct.–Memorial Day.*

Expensive ★ **Popponesset Inn.** Combine a magnificent ocean view with comfortable dining in the ultimate Cape summer restaurant and you have Poppy, a charming spot that attracts a loyal clientele year after year. Several gray-shingled buildings house a series of bright and airy white-and-blue dining rooms, some open to the sky, others enclosed by glass, but all witness to the varying moods of Nantucket Sound beyond the waving beach grass. The cuisine is traditional New England with a strong emphasis on seafood, such as oysters Rockefeller (spinach, tomato, cheese, and briny, full-bellied oysters) and tournedos of beef cooked with garlic and burgundy and topped with a marvelous béarnaise sauce. *Mall Way, New Seabury, tel. 508/477–1100 or 477–8258. Reservations advised. Jacket preferred. MC, V. Closed Nov.–Mar.; closed Mon. and Tues. before June 20 and after Labor Day; no lunch before June 20 and after Labor Day.*

Expensive–Moderate ★ **Coonamessett Inn.** A classic New England hostelry, this elegant place built in 1796 retains all its old-fashioned charm. The main dining room features paintings by Ralph Cahoon; his signature hot-air balloons are re-created in copper and enamel to form hanging sculptures-cum-planters that add a touch of whimsy to an otherwise subdued and romantic room. The mostly white garden room has a window wall overlooking a leafy pond. The regional American menu focuses on fresh fish and seafood, such as lobster pie: crunchy chunks baked in a ramekin with a light breading and a filling of cream, butter, and sherry. *Jones Rd., Falmouth, tel. 508/548–2300. Reservations recommended. Dress: smart casual to formal. AE, CB, DC, MC, V. Closed Mon. and Jan.–Mar.*

★ **Dan'l Webster Inn.** The Colonial New England patina of this congenial inn, conveyed in the decor and the costumed servers, belies its construction in 1971, on the ruins of the landmark original inn. The glassed-in conservatory has Colonial chandeliers and lush greenery. The regional American and Continental menu emphasizes seafood, such as lobster sautéed with *crimini* and chanterelle mushrooms in Fontina sauce on pasta.

149 Main St., Sandwich, tel. 508/888–3622. Reservations suggested. Dress: smart casual. AE, MC, V.

Domingo's Olde Restaurant. Owner-chef Domingo Pena turned his grandfather's 1841 Greek Revival home into a charming restaurant with two small dining rooms. The ambience is friendly and intimate, with stucco and antique green walls, wide-board pine floors, hanging plants, fresh flowers on glass-top tables, and chandeliers. Domingo, who shops the markets daily for fresh ingredients, describes the cuisine as international, with an emphasis on seafood. Star dishes are bouillabaisse or lobster Americal (wok-sautéed lobster meat, mussels and oysters in the shell, scallops, cognac, garlic, leeks, onions, and mushrooms). *856 Rte. 28A, West Falmouth, tel. 508/540–0575. Reservations recommended. Dress: casual. AE, CB, DC, MC, V. Dinner only.*

Golden Swan. A cozy place with a European country inn flavor— exposed beams, half white plaster and half dark wood walls, wine rack dividers—the Swan serves Continental cuisine. Along with pastas and seafood, veal is a specialty; veal *française*, for example, is medallions sautéed in lemon butter and white wine. The early-bird specials—$7 for complete, delicious meals, served between 5 and 6 PM—are terrific bargains. *323 Main St., Falmouth, tel. 508/540–6580. Reservations suggested. Dress: casual. AE, MC, V. Dinner only.*

Moderate **Amigo's.** This busy strip-mall restaurant, its rough barn-board and plaster walls brightened with Mexican art and Tiffany lamps, serves good traditional Mexican fare—try the *sopa de elote*, a creamy soup of ground corn with nubbles of niblets, tomato, and crunchy onion—as well as "gringo food" and nightly specials such as blackened fish. A children's menu has several offerings for $3. *Tataket Sq., Rte. 28, Falmouth, tel. 508/548–8510. Reservations for 6 or more. Dress: casual. MC, V.*

★ **The Bridge.** Known for good food and a warm welcome, The Bridge has several small dining rooms with recessed lighting and art on the walls. Owner Helen Prete has been cooking Yankee pot roast for 30 years, and the menu doesn't lie when it says "nobody can cook a bottom round like Helen." The eclectic menu also offers *bijoux de la mer*—lobster, scallops, and shrimp with lemon and tarragon on spinach pasta with a smoky mushroom cream sauce—and homemade tortellini *casagrande*, stuffed with chicken and topped with meat sauce. *Rte. 6A, Sagamore, tel. 508/888–8144. Reservations suggested on weekends. Dress: casual. MC, V.*

★ **The Flume.** This clean, plain fish house, decorated only with a few Indian artifacts and crafts (the owner is a Wampanoag chief), offers a small menu of straightforward food guaranteed to satisfy. The chowder is outstanding, perhaps the Cape's best, rich with salt pork, onions, quahogs, butter, and cream. Other specialties are fried smelts and clams, Indian pudding, and, in summer, fresh broiled fish. *Lake Ave. (off Rte. 130), Mashpee, tel. 508/477–1456. Reservations suggested on weekends. Dress: casual. MC, V. Jan. 2–May and Labor Day–Thanksgiving, no lunch weekdays. Closed Thanksgiving–Jan. 1; Labor Day–Thanksgiving and Jan. 2–May, closed Mon. and Tues.; June–Labor Day, closed Tues.*

Michael's at Sandy Neck. The twin-lobster special—in peak season, Michael's sells 3,000 lobsters a week—is the trademark of this relaxed restaurant, with a pubby dining room of exposed beams and white plaster walls, and a glassed-in porch with paper-covered tables you can color on. Fresh swordfish is a specialty, broiled, grilled, or blackened; the liver and onions is impeccable, with crunchy onions and a rich, nutty sauce. Homemade loaves of bread accompany meals. *674 Rte. 6A, East Sandwich, tel. 508/362-4303. Reservations suggested. Dress: casual. MC, V.*

Sagamore Inn. Seek out this diamond in the rough for home-style Italian dishes and seafood served in a family atmosphere. Inside, the look is very old Cape, with captain's chairs, Formica-topped tables, wood booths, cotton curtains, stamped-tin ceilings, and bare varnished floors. The food is top-notch: the fried shrimp are very large and sweet, the chicken cacciatore rich and simple, the eggplant Parmesan flawless, the onion rings tasty enough to merit a special trip. *Rte. 6A, Sagamore, tel. 508/888-9707. No reservations. Dress: casual. AE, MC, V. No lunch Mon. or Wed. Closed Tues. and Dec.-Mar.*

Stir Crazy. Thai, Vietnamese, and Cambodian dishes are served at this little box of a restaurant. The un-ethnic taupe carpeting, off-white paneling, green-and-red paisley curtains, and unflattering neon lighting are offset a bit with posters from the owner's native Cambodia. There are no tame flavors here. The Thai *me-siam* and egg roll is sautéed minced pork, tofu, soybean, coconut milk, and chili on a bed of bean sprouts and rice noodles topped with peanut sauce; the deep-fried finger egg roll appetizer is filled with chopped pork and vegetables and served with a very hot sauce. *100 Main St., Buzzards Bay, tel. 508/759-1781. No reservations. Dress: casual. No credit cards. No lunch Tues. and Sun. Closed Mon.*

Mid-Cape

Very Expensive–Moderate ★

Anthony's Cummaquid Inn. The main dining room is a spacious, genteel place with huge windows that reveal a water view of great beauty. Complemented by an impressive wine list is a traditional New England menu featuring baked stuffed fillet of sole (moist, flaky pieces of sole rolled and stuffed with bread crumbs and lobster and topped with Newburg sauce) and roast beef *au jus*, an oversize piece of exceptionally good meat simply cooked. *Rte. 6A, Yarmouth Port, tel. 508/362-4501. Reservations suggested. Jacket requested. AE, MC, V. Dinner only.*

Expensive

Chanterelle. Set in the King's Way Country Club's luxurious clubhouse is this handsome formal dining room with plush carpeting, wood beams, chandeliers, burgundy swags at windows overlooking the greens, attractive art, and candles and red roses on white-clothed tables. The cuisine is creative American with French sauces, such as rack of lamb with port wine sauce, roasted garlic, wild mushrooms, and sun-dried tomatoes. Fresh swordfish and salmon are featured in summer. The club's café restaurant serves a light menu. *Rte. 6A, Yarmouth Port, tel. 508/362-8195. Reservations required. Jacket suggested. AE, CB, DC, MC, V. Jan.-Apr., often closed Sun. and Mon. (call).*

Cranberry Moose. Past the landscaped courtyard of this 18th-century cottage is a series of attractive dining rooms in different styles, all accented with large floral displays. The new American cuisine emphasizes a clean taste, with light use of cream and butter, as in medallions of duck breast on a bed of wild mushrooms with blackberry sauce. The menu changes often; in summer, it focuses on fish and shellfish, such as salmon poached in a rich lobster-and-salmon stock and served souplike with new potatoes, carrots, cabbage, and thyme. The wine list features more than 125 choices. *43 Main St., Yarmouth Port, tel. 508/362–3501. Reservations requested. Jacket suggested at dinner. AE, CB, DC, MC, V. Jan.–Mar., closed Mon. and Tues.*

★ **The Paddock.** Long the benchmark of consistent quality dining, this formal restaurant is decorated in Victorian style, from the dark, pubby bar to the airy summer-porch area filled with green wicker and large potted plants. The main dining room is a blend of dark beams, frosted-glass dividers, sporting art, upholstered banquettes, and Victorian armchairs. The wine list is extensive and select. The traditional Continental-American menu emphasizes seafood (including two-pound lobsters) and beef, such as steak *au poivre*—pounded with crushed peppercorns, sautéed in shallot butter, and flamed with cognac. *W. Main St. rotary (next to Melody Tent), Hyannis, tel. 508/775–7677. Reservations suggested. Jacket suggested. AE, CB, DC, MC, V. Closed mid-Nov.–Apr.*

Expensive–Moderate **Asa Bearse House.** Set in a graceful old building in the heart of downtown, the restaurant has outdoor seating under the elms, with brick walks and careful landscaping, as well as indoor seating in a wondrous clutter of Victorian bric-a-brac. A conservatory-like room is lit by candles, chandeliers, and the romantic glow of light filtering in from lanterns in the garden; here there's dancing to a jazz quartet many evenings. The Continental and seafood menu, strong on sauces, includes such dishes as tortellini *carbonara*—spinach, tomato, and egg pastas with smoked bacon and green peas studding the sturdy cheese sauce—and chicken and shrimp in Madeira sauce with sun-dried tomatoes and mushrooms. A new raw bar has been added. *415 Main St., Hyannis, tel. 508/771–4131. Reservations suggested. Dress: casual. AE, CB, DC, MC, V.*

Barnstable Tavern & Restaurant. The tavern is a friendly local gathering place, with plank floors and antique signs. The main dining room is a pleasing mix of rustic floorboards, brass accents, an Oriental carpet, and marine and botanical art; another is decorated in paisley and lace. Dinner entrées include "lazy man's lobster" (lobster meat baked with butter and scallop dressing) and grilled chicken breast with raspberry-orange Madeira sauce. The tavern menu features light fare, including appetizers such as Buffalo chicken wings and scallops wrapped in bacon. *3176 Main St. (Rte. 6A), Barnstable Village, tel. 508/362–2355. Reservations suggested in season. Dress: casual. AE, MC, V.*

Captain Howes' Restaurant. The new owners who took over in 1990 describe their cuisine as creative American and Continental, with an emphasis on fresh herbs. Scallops *poireaux* are baked in white wine and cranberry-leek fondue; other specials are Marseilles-style bouillabaisse and homemade pastas. Inside the 1840 gingerbread cottage, beige with brown shutters, are three formal dining rooms reflecting the 19th century, with antique colors (burgundy and old rose), plush chairs, swags and valances, cut-glass chandeliers, damask linens, and antique mirrors and prints. *134 Main St. (Rte. 6A), Yarmouth Port, tel. 508/362–3775. Reservations suggested. Dress: casual. AE, MC, V. Nov.–June, closed Mon. and Tues.*

East Bay Lodge. The casually elegant main dining room, part glassed-in veranda, suggests the 1880 summer house the inn

once was. A highlight of the modified French menu is the lamb
Dijon *bouquettière*, rack of lamb with Dijon mustard, served ta-
bleside French-style; prime rib, steamship round of beef, and
fat spring lamb chops are perennial favorites. Special features
are the Centennial menu (entrées $10 on certain nights), the
high tea by the fire in winter, and a lavish Sunday champagne
brunch buffet year-round. *East Bay Rd., Osterville, tel. 508/
428–6961. Reservations requested. Jacket requested in season.
AE, CB, D, DC, MC, V. No lunch in winter.*

Il Maestro. Behind the brick-and-glass front is regional Italian
cuisine as good as you'll find on the Cape. The specialty is veal,
such as *braciolettine*, rolled veal stuffed with prosciutto and
imported cheeses, sautéed in lemon and wine, with mushroom
marsala sauce. The interior is spare, with dark-green walls,
plaid café curtains, booths and tables, and paintings of Tuscan
villas. *1870 W. Main St., Hyannis, tel. 508/775–1168. Reservations required. Dress: casual. AE, MC, V. Dinner only.*

La Cipollina. This small restaurant (the name means "the little
onion"), begun by the current owner of the Cranberry Moose,
has since 1984 been run by owner-chef Maurice Leduc. The
pleasant interior of the historic building is an amalgam of Colonial and contemporary; one of the intimate dining rooms, with
low ceilings and dark beams, has a glass wall overlooking a
small garden. The menu includes pastas, fish dishes such as
bouillabaisse or scrod in Dijon mustard sauce, and other
French and Northern Italian dishes; a four-course prix-fixe
($20) dinner menu and a prix-fixe ($11) lunch are also available.
*157 Main St. (Rte. 6A), Yarmouth Port, tel. 508/362–4341.
Reservations required. Dress: casual. AE, MC, V. Oct.–Apr.,
closed Mon. and Tues.*

★ **Red Pheasant Inn.** The main dining room is pleasantly intimate
and rustic, with stripped pine floors, exposed beams,
candlelighted tables, Tiffany lamps, and two fireplaces. The
cuisine is American regional, with a French twist in the sauces.
The large menu always features a lamb special—such as medallions in a hearty garlic-and-rosemary sauce of wine and veal
stock—as well as sweetbreads, game, and seafood. The long
wine list is a *Wine Spectator* award winner. *905 Main St. (Rte.
6A), Dennis, tel. 508/385–2133. Reservations strongly suggested. Dress: smart casual. AE, MC, V. Dinner and Sun.
brunch buffet only.*

★ **Regatta of Cotuit.** This sister restaurant to the Regatta in Falmouth is set in an 18th-century landmark stagecoach inn (the
original taproom was restored in 1990 and now serves an inexpensive bar menu). Its nine intimate and romantically lit dining
rooms are perfectly furnished in period, with Venetian mirrors, Chippendale furniture, and Oriental carpeting. The cuisine is American, with grilled foods a specialty as well as sautés
and pâtés of rabbit, veal, or venison. Boneless sliced rack of
lamb with Cabernet sauce is outstanding. *Rte. 28, Cotuit, tel.
508/428–5715. Reservations suggested. Dress: smart casual.
AE, MC, V. Dinner only. May close Jan.–Mar.*

Roadhouse Cafe. This consistently fine downtown restaurant
serves a mix of New England seafood—such as a surprising
scrod Florentine, threads of spinach, nuggets of scallop and bacon, and a creamy sauce with mustard and anisette—and Italian pasta, milk-fed veal, and other dishes. The cioppino is
popular. The interior is cozy and attractive, with Oriental carpets on polished hardwood floors, exposed beams, lots of hanging plants, and a fireplace; there's also a glassed-in porch and,

in season, outdoor dining. *488 South St., Hyannis, tel. 508/775–2386. Reservations suggested. Dress: casual. AE, MC, V.*
Three Thirty One Main. Also called "Penguins Go Pasta"—its logo is a tuxedoed penguin—this sophisticated Northern Italian restaurant focuses on seafood and homemade pastas. The dining room is a two-level affair, the upper section set off by brass railings. On the walls, mirrors alternate with wood paneling and brick; soft lighting and romantic music add to the ambience of this warm and attractive room. A signature dish is veal chops Pasetto, stuffed with prosciutto and Fontina cheese, lightly breaded and panfried, and served with a sauce of shallots, capers, prosciutto, and fresh tomatoes. *331 Main St., Hyannis, tel. 508/775–2023. Reservations recommended for large parties. Dress: smart casual. AE, CB, DC, MC, V. Dinner only.*

Moderate **Cape Playhouse Restaurant.** Under new ownership in 1990, this institution of pre- and post-theater dining (where the chance of rubbing elbows with the performers adds an element of excitement) has acquired new charcoal etchings of theater people and a new attractively priced menu. The simply prepared dishes include broiled and baked fish, chicken pie in puff pastry, and lots of sautés, such as pork tenderloin with apples, mushrooms, and Calvados in heavy cream served over linguine. The front room is bright and airy, surrounded on three sides by small-pane windows and decorated in soft peach and powder blue under a white cathedral ceiling. The back dining room, by the bar, is a crowded, cozy spot prettily decorated with flowered chintz. *Rte. 6A, Dennis, tel. 508/385–8000. Reservations suggested for 6 or more. Dress: casual. AE, MC, V. Usually dinner only (lunch on some matinee days). Closed mid-Jan.–Mar.*
Fiddlebee's. At this casual downtown eating place, three dining levels range around a central well that, on the first floor, opens onto a dance floor. The preparation is rather uneven, but the menu does have something for everyone: blackened chicken breast, Rio Grande Tex-Mex chili (a special), quiche, and basic burgers. *North St., Hyannis, tel. 508/771–6032. No reservations. Dress: casual. AE, MC, V.*
Gina's by the Sea. An intimate little bistro by the bay (perfectly situated for an after-dinner beach walk), Gina's serves some of the tastiest food on the Cape, as the owners of the BMWs and Mercedeses that fill the parking lot seem to agree. The interior has exposed beams, knotty pine walls, a fireplace, and nicely set tables with white cloths, flowers, and candles. The Northern Italian menu is supplemented with seafood specials. Chicken Gismonda is a moist breast of chicken lightly breaded, sautéed in butter, and served on a bed of spinach, garnished with mushrooms sautéed in Madeira sauce—a polished dish. *134 Taunton Ave., Dennis, tel. 508/385–3213. No reservations. Dress: casual. AE, MC, V. Closed Jan.–Mar.; June–Aug., lunch and dinner daily; Apr., May, and Sept.–Dec., dinner only, and closed Mon. and Tues.*
Harry's. A great place for consistently good Cajun food, mesquite-grilled dishes, and Tex-Mex, Harry's offers seating at benches with wrought-iron arms or at tables. New Orleans and Toulouse-Lautrec posters decorate the walls, with plants and art-deco pressed glass as accents. The Cajun potato salad is a memorable alliance of crisp red-skinned potato chunks with mayonnaise, raspberry vinegar, pimiento, and cayenne; hopping John (white rice and black-eyed peas), jambalaya, and

blackened fish are all excellent, as are the substantial sandwiches and side dishes such as apple-orange-raisin chutney. *700 Main St., Hyannis, tel. 508/778–4188. No reservations. Dress: casual. AE, MC, V.*

Inaho. A welcome addition to the ethnic diversity of restaurants on the Cape is this little downtown storefront place with such authentic details as *noren* screens and a sushi bar. Traditional Japanese fare, such as tempura and teriyaki, is served. For beef *shabu-shabu,* a cookpot filled with hot broth is brought to you; you cook the beef in it, then dip it in sauces. *569 Main St., Hyannis Oaks Village, Hyannis, tel. 508/771–9255. No reservations. Dress: casual. AE, MC, V. Dinner only.*

Riverway Lobster House. Owned and run by the same family since 1953, this favorite of locals and tourists alike delivers traditional New England food and hospitality. Lobster is featured in several forms, including baked and stuffed with a crab-and-clam breading. Also on the menu are many other fish and seafood dishes, served panfried, deep-fried, baked, broiled, and Newburg style, along with plenty of choices for landlubbers. Early-bird and children's menus are available. The many dining rooms all have a New England feel, some with barn-board walls. *1338 Rte. 28, South Yarmouth, tel. 508/398–2172. Reservations suggested. Dress: smart casual. AE, CB, D, DC, MC, V.*

Rose's. Rose and Angelo Stocchetti opened the place in 1946; today the family still takes care of business, some in the kitchen, some waiting tables, Rose presiding over all. There are several New England–style dining rooms, as well as a glassed-in white room with a flagstone floor and a wishing well with (fake) birds on branches. Veal is the specialty, as in saltimbocca or scallops sautéed in lemon butter and served on fettuccine. The *calamaretti alla Ronaldo,* squid simmered in a lobster-tomato sauce, and the mussels in cream and wine, both served on linguini, are delicious. *Black Flats Rd., Dennis, tel. 508/385–3003. Reservations suggested on weekends. Dress: casual. MC, V. Dinner only. Closed Feb.–Mar.; also Apr.–May and mid-Oct.–Jan., Mon.*

Scargo Cafe. The setting is a romantic old sea captain's house: one cozy room has a fireplace and exquisite, highly polished golden oak paneling, another has large windows that let in the sun at lunch, a third has nautical prints of whaling ships. The menu mixes simple Italian dishes and pastas, fish (broiled sole topped with cheese and bacon, or blackened swordfish), and several specials. Food is served until midnight in summer. *799 Rte. 6A, Dennis, tel. 508/385–8200. Reservations advised for 5 or more. Dress: casual. AE, CB, D, DC, MC, V.*

★ **Up the Creek.** This comfortable, casual spot with a busy hum about it serves fine food at very good prices with an almost effortless competence. House specialties include chicken Simone (boneless breast stuffed with ham, cheese, and garlic butter and topped with sauce) and seafood strudel—two pastries filled with lobster, shrimp, crab, cheese, and more. The baked stuffed lobster is excellent, as is the wine-laced crab au gratin special. *36 Old Colony Rd., Hyannis, tel. 508/771–7866. Reservations suggested. Dress: casual. AE, CB, DC, MC, V.*

Moderate–
Inexpensive
★

Barbyann's. The success of this place is due to its casual, comfortable interior—exposed-beam ceilings, subdued lighting, and green, pink, and red color scheme—as well as its low-priced, tasty food. The menu mixes fish, steak, teriyaki, Mexican dishes, pizza, burgers, fun appetizers, and sandwiches. The Buffalo fried clams, chicken wings, and serious homemade chili are excellent. Country-style barbecued pork ribs are meaty, darkly charred, and richly smoke-flavored. *120 Airport Rd., Hyannis, tel. 508/775-9795. No reservations. Dress: casual. AE, MC, V.*

Baxter's Fish N' Chips. Right on busy Lewis Bay, the ever-popular Baxter's gets a lot of swimsuit-clad back-in boaters at its picnic tables for possibly the best fried clams on the Cape, as well as other fried, baked, and broiled fresh fish and seafood (plus burgers, chicken, and Cajun steak for landlubbers) and offerings from a raw bar on wheels from June through August. It's a fun place to watch boats at play while you dine. The indoor Baxter's Boat House Club—an airy, open room with sliding glass doors leading to deck tables, paintings of ships, copper lanterns, and a busy bar—has the same menu, plus specials. *Pleasant St., Hyannis, tel. 508/775-4490. No reservations. Dress: casual. No credit cards. Closed Mon. and Oct.–Apr.*

Bob Briggs' Wee Packet. This little restaurant has maintained an enviable reputation for good food and good value since its opening in 1949. The decor is Cape kitsch, with canary-yellow Formica-topped tables, watercolors in driftwood frames, and shells, glass buoys, starfish, lobster claws, and nets everywhere. From the kitchen—open to view and immaculate—comes New England fare with an emphasis on fresh local seafood (such as fish-and-chips, charbroiled swordfish, Cape bay scallops fried or broiled) and a long list of sandwiches. Desserts, made in-house, include blueberry shortcake and bread pudding with lemon sauce. *Depot St., Dennisport, tel. 508/398-2181. No reservations. Dress: casual. No credit cards. Closed late Sept.–Apr.*

Christine's. Lebanese dishes—such as the combination platter, a sampler of lamb shish kebab, stuffed grape leaves, kibbe (ground beef with wheat, pine nuts, and seasonings), *hummus* (pureed chick-peas with garlic, lemon, tahini, and olive oil), and meat or spinach pie—make up half the menu. The rest consists of Italian dishes such as homemade meatballs and sausages, excellent steaks, and baked and fried seafood. The dining room has butterscotch-tartan carpeting, etched glass, Tiffany lamps over low, vinyl-back booths and Formica tables, lots of greenery, and watercolors and lithographs. A small nightclub has entertainment and dancing year-round (*see* Nightlife, below). *Rte. 28, West Dennis, tel. 508/394-7333. No reservations. Dress: smart casual. AE, CB, DC, MC, V.*

Mattakeese Wharf. Extending over the water on pilings, with a view of the warehouses and general helter-skelter of the harbor, this relaxed restaurant features a popular waterside bar and a woody, nautical-looking dining area prettily lit by tiny twinkling lights. Seafoods, pastas, and steaks are served simply. Try the lightly breaded broiled scrod or roast prime rib. *271 Mill Way, Barnstable Harbor, tel. 508/362-4511. Reservations requested. Dress: casual. AE, CB, D, DC, MC, V. Closed Nov.–Apr.*

Sam Diego's. Traditional Mexican dishes are served amid a charming Mexican ambience—ornamental toucans, draped serapes, plants, and polished wood tables—and a crowded good-time bar. An interesting dessert is the crusty deep-fried ice cream, served in a giant goblet. *950 Iyanough Rd. (Rte. 132), Hyannis, tel. 508/771-8816. No reservations. Dress: casual. AE, D, MC, V.*

Starbuck's. The decor is sort of Hard Rock Café but without a theme—from the rafters and on the walls of this "Good Time Eating and Drinking Place" hang flags, a sled, a mannequin, a miniature Fokker D-7, carved pigs, a tuba, and weather vanes. Everything is orchestrated in a glitzy, with-it way, from the marquee lights that trim the striped awnings to the bar, raised like a motionless carousel. The menu is huge and eclectic, including fun Chinese, Japanese, and Mexican dishes and lots of exotic and frozen drinks. *Rte. 132, Hyannis, tel. 508/778–6767. Reservations 1 hr in advance accepted. Dress: casual. AE, CB, D, DC, MC, V.*

Inexpensive
★

Jack's Outback. Jack says he had no place to eat dinner, so he had to build an addition to his breakfast-and-lunch restaurant; local folks sure were glad, too, because now they have a place where they can be insulted at any meal of the day. To say the least, this is a quirky place—the "decor" is a jumble of mismatched stuff—where customers get their own coffee, exchange barbs with staff, and throw tips into a washtub (whereupon the tallier of tabs honks the horns and rings the bell). The food is basic American home cooking, such as pot roast with mashed potatoes and gravy; superb soups; sandwiches, and salads; and simple but exceptional desserts. (Jack's is hidden "out back," down the driveway by La Cipollina.) *161 Main St., Yarmouth Port, tel. 508/362–6690. No reservations. Dress: casual. No credit cards.*

Lower Cape

Very Expensive
★

Chillingsworth. The Cape's best restaurant, this elegant little jewel, lit by candles and decorated in Louis XV furnishings, offers award-winning French and nouvelle cuisine and an outstanding wine cellar. The frequently changing dinner menu is a five-course prix fixe and features such entrées as venison with celery-root puree and fried pumpkin; sweetbreads and foie gras with wild mushrooms and ham julienne, asparagus, and smoky sauce; and peppered striped marlin with lemon basil sauce. Desserts are glorious. *Rte. 6A, Brewster, tel. 508/896–3640. Reservations required at dinner (seatings), suggested at lunch. Dress: casual at lunch, jacket and tie preferred at dinner. AE, MC, V. Memorial Day–Nov., closed Mon.; Nov.–Memorial Day, closed Mon.–Thurs.*

**Very Expensive–
Expensive**
★

Queen Anne Inn. An extensive wine list complements a menu (different each day) that combines the best of Continental and new American. Entrées may include roast Barbary duck breast with wild rice pancakes and raspberry-and-sour-cherry demiglaze, or Norwegian salmon poached in champagne-chive sauce served with smoked-salmon mousse. Appetizers (followed by a sorbet course) and desserts are creative, wonderful, and, like all the kitchen's creations, beautifully presented. The main dining room (off a small room with a fireplace) was recently redecorated in a spare but pretty Early American look: The floor is unpolished stripped wood, antique paintings and prints of ships (along with a flag and old maps) adorn the walls, and curtains are an elegant arrangement of white lace and light blue and white stripes. Soft music and lighting add to the intimacy. *70 Queen Anne Rd., Chatham, tel. 508/945–0394. Reservations required. Jacket and tie suggested. AE, CB, DC, MC, V. Dinner only. Closed Tues. and Thanksgiving–Apr.*

Expensive **Captain Linnell House.** Framed by huge trees, this neoclassic
★ structure with dramatic Ionic columns looks like an antebellum
mansion transported to Cape Cod. Inside is a series of small
dining rooms: one with a Normandy fireplace, exposed beams,
and white plaster; another with a paneled pecan fireplace, oil
lamps, Aubusson rug, and rosette ceiling; another with English rose drapes framing windows overlooking a garden. Wild
mushroom sauté is a striking dish commingling wine, butter,
carrots, celery, tomato, and mushroom with a garnish of wa-
tercress, croutons, and a flaky puff pastry cap. Scrod in parchment is fish, crabmeat, and shrimp with a lime-vermouth
sauce. *137 Skaket Rd., Orleans, tel. 508/255–3400. Reservations required in season. Dress: casual. MC, V. No lunch Sat.*
Chatham Bars Inn. There's no mistaking style, and this grande
dame of Cape Cod hostelries has plenty of that—from the delightful airy lightness of the white-wicker-and-chintz reception
area to the elegant-summerhouse look of the high-ceilinged formal dining room. The latter is a study in white, from the
painted brick walls and woodwork to the ceiling fans, lantern
wall sconces, and crisp linens—set off admirably by the rich
deep green rug and the blue of the ocean seen through the picture windows that wrap the room. (Try for a seat facing the
sea.) The menu—sensibly nouveau New England, not the least
ostentatious—features peerless crab cakes spiced with a generous hand and set in a pool of tomato coulis (purée); an excellent smoked seafood chowder; braised sweetbreads with sea
scallops and lobster cream sauce; and noisettes of lamb niçoise,
a magnificent dish in a dark, dense olive-tomato sauce. From
October through May, Sunday brunch is accompanied by jazz
piano. *Shore Rd., Chatham, tel. 508/945–0096. Reservations
required. Jackets required at night; jacket and tie July–Aug.
AE, CB, DC, MC, V.*
Christian's. Billed as "an elegant Yankee restaurant," Christian's does have a certain panache. The look of the two dining
rooms in the 1818 house is a mix of French country and old Cape
Cod: exposed beams painted Colonial blue, wall sconces with
parchment shades, Vanity Fair prints, Oriental runners on
dark wood floors, lace-covered tables. The cuisine is creative
Continental and American, represented by such dishes as
boneless roast duck with raspberry sauce, chicken with maca-
damia-nut breading and a grain-mustard cream sauce, or superior sautéed sole with lobster and a lemon-butter sauce. The
mahogany-paneled piano bar serves a light menu. *443 Main St.,
Chatham, tel. 508/945–3362. Reservations suggested. Dress:
casual. AE, CB, DC, MC, V. Dinner only. Closed mid-Jan.–
Mar.*
High Brewster. A classic country inn overlooking a pond, the restored sea captain's house offers a glimpse of a more romantic
past: low ceilings, dark exposed beams, richly patinated wide
paneling, small oil paintings in gilt frames, Oriental carpeting
on polished floors. Seasonal four-course prix-fixe menus are offered; a fall menu might include pumpkin-and-sage bisque, tenderloin medallions with chives and cheese glaze, and apple
crisp with maple syrup, walnuts, and apple rum ice cream. In
winter, you can order à la carte from the American regional
menu. *964 Satucket Rd., Brewster, tel. 508/896–3636. Reservations required. Jacket suggested. MC, V. Dinner only. Often
closed Mon.–Wed. mid-Sept.–mid-June (call).*
The Impudent Oyster. A longtime favorite in this part of the

Cape, this restaurant just off Main Street is a big, comfortable room with a high ceiling, exposed beams, large hanging plants, and soft lighting from frosted-glass fixtures. The most popular menu items are grilled veal piccata—medallions with French mustard, rosemary, and lemon-butter sauce—and in summer, bouillabaisse and seafoods *fra diavolo*. *15 Chatham Bars Ave., Chatham, tel. 508/945-3545. Reservations requested in summer. Dress: casual. AE, MC, V. Closed 2 wks in Jan.*

Expensive–
Moderate
Aesop's Tables. Set in an 1800s house built from ships' timbers, Aesop's Tables has since 1965 served consistently outstanding meals. The six dining rooms include a summer porch, a romantic room with a fireplace, the bar (with marble-topped antique tables), and a large room partly decorated in an art-deco style. Everything on the menu, from the breads (including delicious, flinty cornmeal squares and light baking-powder biscuits) to the ice creams, is made in-house. The cuisine is new American, as in pan-roasted lamb chops with a demiglaze of Pommery mustard, rosemary, and garlic. Death by Chocolate, a heavy mousse cake made from imported chocolate, was voted Best Dessert on Cape Cod by *Boston* magazine. *Main St., Wellfleet, tel. 508/349-6450. Reservations suggested. Dress: smart casual. AE, MC, V. Dinner and Sun. brunch only. Closed Columbus Day–Memorial Day.*

Cafe Elizabeth. A Cape captain's house has been converted into a French country inn with a number of intimate dining areas decorated with white lace curtains, hanging pans and baskets, gilt mirrors, art glass, and velvet upholstery. The hallmark dish on the classical French menu is the sampler called La Palette Duchesse: shrimp with a tomato-oregano sauce, veal with wild mushrooms, rack of lamb with tarragon, and filet mignon with béarnaise sauce. Appetizers include homemade gravlax (salmon marinade) with dill and sweet mushroom sauce, and caviar *blini* (small, thin pancakes) with homemade frozen cranberry vodka. Four vegetables accompany entrées. *31 Sea St., Harwich Port, tel. 508/432-1147. Reservations suggested. Dress: casual. CB, DC, MC, V. Dinner only. Closed Nov.–Mar.; also Mon.–Tues. before Memorial Day and after Labor Day.*

Off the Bay Cafe. This is an easygoing storefront restaurant with pressed-tin ceiling, antique brass fixtures, lots of polished woodwork (including golden pine wainscoting), a hunter-green-and-white color scheme softened with floral-print linens, and Cape maps and pictures of seals and birds. The regional American cooking centers on fresh grilled seafood, aged beef, wild game, and pastas. Highlights may include paillard of veal with garlic, shallot, and lemon cream sauce; simple broiled scrod with lemon butter and capers; smoked fish and meats; and rotisseried game birds and duck. An inexpensive light menu is always available. There's a jazz brunch on Sunday. *28 Main St., Orleans, tel. 508/255-5505. Reservations suggested on Sat. Dress: casual. AE, CB, D, DC, MC, V. Oct.–May, closed Mon.–Tues.*

Old Jailhouse Tavern. Tucked away on a rural side road is this 100-year-old house, renovated with a prize-winning architectural design and an all-glass conservatory addition. The chic, hard-edged contemporary interior—a stunning display of brass, etched glass, and the original grouted stone (the stone room was once used as a jail by the sheriff who lived in the house, hence the restaurant's name)—is softened with natural oak and greenery. The cuisine is eclectic, including everything from barbecued chicken and ribs to filet mignon and blackened Delmonico steak. Toast Nelson is a taste bud–popping entrée, crusty French bread smothered with bacon, crunchy onion, crabmeat, shrimp, and scallops, topped with hollandaise sauce and Parmesan cheese. *West Rd., Orleans, tel. 508/255–5245. No reservations. Dress: casual. MC, V.*

Thompson's Clam Bar. A perennial favorite for fresh fish, Thompson's has been renovated extensively over the past few years. The new look is swanky/clubby nautical, with a window wall overlooking the scenic harbor, varnished wood tables, brass marine instruments, hanging green-glass ship's lanterns, a huge mahogany circular bar and mahogany paneling, and a cranberry-glass clerestory. The harborfront patio is a popular spot for watching sunsets over cocktails and selections from the raw bar. Menu highlights are lobster served several ways, a fisherman's platter (an oversize assortment of fried fish and shellfish, onion rings, and shoestring potatoes), and a true shore dinner (chowder, steamers, boiled lobster, corn on the cob, and watermelon, plus sausage); nonfish choices are available, as is a children's menu. The new HarborWatch Room offers a separate Continental menu in more formal surroundings, with a harbor view. *Snow Inn Rd., Harwich Port, tel. 508/432–3595. No reservations. Dress: casual. AE, CB, DC, MC, V. Closed Labor Day–late June.*

★ **Ciro and Sal's.** After 30 years, Sal has left, but Ciro remains, and his stage-set Italian restaurant—raffia-covered Chianti bottles hanging from the rafters, plaster and brick walls, slate flooring, strains of Italian opera—plays out its role with all the confidence of years on the boards. Scampi *alla griglia* is grilled shrimp with lemon, parsley, garlic, butter, leeks, and shallots; veal and pasta dishes are specialties. *4 Kiley Court, Provincetown, tel. 508/487–0049. Reservations required in summer and Sat. night year-round. Dress: casual. MC, V. Christmas–Memorial Day, closed Mon.–Thurs.*

The Mews. The location is super, right on the harbor; the bar extends out over the water. Follow the cobblestone paths down to the glassed-in dining room or the small, intimate Mermaid Bar with mahogany paneling, antiques, gas lamps, and mermaids in etched glass. In season, the emphasis is on fresh seafood and shellfish, such as the popular mixed grill (three kinds of fish, each with its own sauce); other entrées are curried shrimp with kumquats, mesquite-grilled lamb, and steak *au poivre. 59 Commercial St., Provincetown, tel. 508/487–1500. Reservations suggested. Dress: casual. AE, CB, D, DC, MC, V. Closed mid-Nov.–mid-Feb.; also Tues.–Thurs. before late June and after Labor Day.*

★ **Napi's.** A Provincetown institution, Napi's serves original and excellently prepared food in a warm, casual art- and antiques-filled house of natural wood, exposed beams and brickwork, hanging plants, stained-glass windows, and Tiffany lamps. The menu is large and eclectic: Middle Eastern, Moroccan, European, Oriental, vegetarian. Shrimp feta is shrimp flamed with Ouzo and Metaxa, baked in tomato sauce, and topped with feta cheese. Chicken *chambeaux* is boneless chicken in white wine, tarragon, and a mushroom cream reduction. *7 Freeman St., Provincetown, tel. 508/487–1145. Reservations required in summer, recommended off-season. Dress: casual. DC, MC, V. May–Oct., no breakfast or lunch.*

Sal's Place. Everything at this waterfront trattoria is homemade, from the breads and pastas to the *tiramisu* and other desserts. A specialty on the southern Italian menu is shrimp Adriatica, shrimp and calamari with pesto sauce; other specialties are saltimbocca and spinach lasagna. The decor leans to wine basket-bottles and old photos and posters out front; in summer, the dining room overlooking the water is a treat. *99 Commercial St., Provincetown, tel. 508/487–1279. Reservations strongly suggested. Dress: casual. MC, V. Dinner only. Closed Nov.–Apr.; also Mon.–Thurs. before mid-June and after Labor Day.*

Moderate **Chatham Wayside Inn.** Inside this 19th-century inn, past a reception area of fireplace, marbletop tables, and ship portraits, is a dining room of glass and light, with a window wall overlooking the park. Grilled seafood is the star attraction, along with fried fish and baked stuffed lobster with seafood stuffing. Apple-walnut bread pudding with a caramel rum sauce makes a fine end to a traditional American meal. In summer there's dinner cabaret; in the off-season, dining and dancing to piano music (*see* Nightlife, below). The tavern room serves light fare. *512 Main St., Chatham, tel. 508/945–1800. Reservations required for cabaret. Dress: casual. AE, CB, DC, MC, V.*

★ **Land Ho!** Walk in, grab a newspaper from the lending rack, take a seat, and relax—for 20 years Land Ho! has been making folks feel right at home. Decorated in a jumble of quarter boards and business signs, this casual spot serves kale soup that has made *Gourmet* magazine, plus burgers, hearty sandwiches, grilled fish in summer, and very good chicken wings, chowder, and fish-and-chips. *Rte. 6A, Orleans, tel. 508/255–5165. No reservations. Dress: casual. MC, V.*

The Moors. This unique restaurant, constructed of flotsam and jetsam found on Cape beaches, specializes in seafood and Portuguese cuisine, such as kale, *chourico*, and *linguiça* soups; marinated swordfish steaks; and chicken with Madeira. The atmosphere is nautical and informal, and there's entertainment in the lounge (*see* Nightlife, below). *Bradford St. Ext., Provincetown, tel. 508/487–0840. Reservations suggested. Dress: casual. AE, CB, D, DC, MC, V. Closed late Oct.–Mar.*

Lodging

With a tourism-based economy, the Cape naturally abounds in lodging places, including self-contained luxury resorts, grand old oceanfront hotels, chain hotels, mom-and-pop motels, antiques-filled bed-and-breakfasts, cottages, condominiums, and apartments. The Cape Cod Chamber of Commerce's Resort Directory lists hundreds of establishments (also *see* Lodging in Chapter 1, Essential Information).

In summer, lodgings should be booked as far in advance as possible—several months for the most popular cottages and B&Bs. Assistance with last-minute reservations is available in season at the Cape Cod Chamber of Commerce information booths at Bourne, Sagamore, and West Barnstable. Off-season rates are much reduced, and service may be more personalized.

Reservations B&B services include **House Guests Cape Cod and the Islands**
Services (Box 1881, Orleans 02653, tel. 800/666–HOST; $3.95 for directory), with more than 100 properties; **Bed and Breakfast Cape Cod** (Box 341, West Hyannisport 02672, tel. 508/775–2772), with 60; and **Orleans Bed & Breakfast Associates** (Box 1312, Or-

leans 02653, tel. 508/255-3824; send SASE), which specializes in the Lower Cape from Harwich to Truro. **Provincetown Reservations System** (tel. 508/487-2400 or 800/648-0364) makes reservations year-round for accommodations, shows, restaurants, transportation, and more.

Hostels   The homey **HyLand AYH-Hostel** (465 Falmouth Rd., Hyannis 02601, tel. 508/775-2970), on 3 acres of pine woods, offers 50 beds (some private rooms) year-round. **Mid-Cape AYH-Hostel** (Goody Hallet Rd., RR 1, Box 167, Eastham 02642, tel. 508/ 255-2785; open mid-May–mid-Sept.), also on 3 wooded acres, has eight cabins sleeping six to eight each. **Little America AYH-Hostel** (N. Pamet Rd., Box 402, Truro 02666, tel. 508/349-3889; open mid-June–Labor Day), in a former Coast Guard station, has 42 beds.

Camping   The Cape has many private campgrounds (ask the Cape Cod Chamber of Commerce for its listing), as well as camping at state parks and forests. Most popular with nature lovers is **Nickerson State Park** (*see* Nature Areas, above, for more on this and other state facilities); **Bourne Scenic Park** (tel. 508/759-7873) has 472 sites by the Bourne Bridge and offers a saltwater swimming pool. A surprise in this very traditional area is a family nudist campground, **Sandy Terraces** (Box 835-B, Hyannis 02601, tel. 508/428-9209). No camping is permitted on the Cape Cod National Seashore, though a number of private campgrounds serve the area.

Category	Cost*
Very Expensive	over $150
Expensive	$100–$150
Moderate	$70–$100
Inexpensive	under $70

all prices are for a standard double room in high season, excluding 5.7% state tax and 4% local tax

Upper Cape

Expensive   **Admiralty Resort.** Converted in 1989 into an all-suite hotel, this large facility on the highway outside Falmouth offers rooms with a Murphy bed and a sofabed or two queen-size beds. Every unit has cable TV, a wet bar, a minifridge, and a coffee maker and is furnished in pastel Formica and wood, with rose wall-to-wall carpeting. Townhouse suites have cathedral ceilings with skylights; a loft; a living room with queen-size Murphy or king-size bed, sofabed, and table and chairs; and a whirlpool tub. The building down the hill is a bit in disrepair but cheaper. Golf and other packages are available. *51 Teaticket Hwy. (Rte. 28), Falmouth 02540, tel. 508/548-4240, 800/341-5700, or 800/352-7153 in MA. 100 suites. Facilities: outdoor and indoor pools, 2 saunas, restaurant, DJ lounge with dancing. AE, MC, V.*

★   **Coonamessett Inn.** Since 1953, this inn has been providing gracious accommodations and fine dining. One- or two-bedroom suites are located in five buildings ranged around a broad, landscaped lawn that spills down to a scenic wooded pond—a tranquil country setting. Three suites directly overlook the pond. Rooms are casually decorated, with bleached wood or pine paneling, New England antiques or reproductions, upholstered chairs and couches, color TV, and phones. A large collection of art by Ralph Cahoon is displayed throughout the inn. *Jones Rd. and Gifford St., Box 707, Falmouth 02541, tel. 508/548–2300. 24 suites, 1 cottage. Facilities: 2 restaurants, clothing shop. AE, CB, DC, MC, V.*

Quality Inn. Across from a pond, a few miles outside Falmouth center, the inn's three buildings were remodeled in 1989–90. Rooms are large, with plush carpeting, contemporary pastel decor, wood-tone furniture, cable TV/HBO, and phones; suites have minifridges. The large pool area is bright and nicely arranged with patio furniture and greenery. Discount packages are available. *291 Jones Rd., Falmouth 02540, tel. 508/540– 2000 or 800/228–5151. 88 rooms, 5 suites. Facilities: indoor pool, room service, sauna, video game room, restaurant (in season), lounge with entertainment, children under 18 stay free.*

Expensive– Moderate ★
Dan'l Webster Inn. A re-creation of an 18th-century inn that stood on the site, this is a classy, quiet, traditional New England inn with an excellent restaurant. Guest rooms (which are mostly in the main inn; two nearby historic homes have four suites each) have been recently redecorated, with some canopy beds and fine reproduction furnishings. All rooms have phones, cable TV with VCR, and air-conditioning; some suites have fireplaces or whirlpools, and one has a baby grand piano. *149 Main St., Sandwich 02563, tel. 508/888–3622. 38 rooms, 9 suites. Facilities: outdoor pool, membership in local health club, access to private golf club, 24-hr room service, turndown service, gift shop, restaurant, lounge with piano bar and weekend dance bands. AE, CB, DC, MC, V.*

Moderate
Capt. Tom Lawrence House. Set back from the street, just steps from downtown, is this pretty white house with a cupola and green shutters, surrounded by flowers and bushes and a lawn shaded by old maple trees. Built in 1861 for a whaling captain, it is now an intimate B&B. All rooms look fresh and romantic, with antique and painted furniture, French country wallpapers, soft colors, and thick carpeting; the beds, all queen-size canopy or king-size, have firm mattresses, Laura Ashley or Ralph Lauren sheets, and down comforters in winter. *75 Locust St., Falmouth 02540, tel. 508/540–1445. 6 rooms. Facilities: full breakfast, pay phone. MC, V. No smoking.*

★
Mostly Hall. Set in a landscaped park far back from the street and separated from it by tall bushes, trees, and a wrought-iron fence, this inn looks very much like a private estate. The 1849 house itself is imposing, with a wraparound porch and a dramatic cupola (fitted out as a guest den). Accommodations are in large corner rooms, with leafy views through shuttered casement windows, reading areas, antique pieces and reproduction queen-size canopy beds, floral wallpapers, wall-to-wall carpeting, and Oriental accent rugs. First-floor rooms have 13-foot ceilings; most baths are small. *27 Main St., Falmouth 02540, tel. 508/548–3786. 6 rooms. Facilities: full breakfast, bicycles, common phone and TV, lending library, lawn games. No credit cards. No smoking. Closed Jan.–mid-Feb.*

Village Green Inn. In 1986, two former schoolteachers turned this turreted Victorian building into a B&B inn. Guest rooms are spacious and decorated tastefully: antique beds, lovely wallpapers, comforters, dust ruffles, beautiful hardwood floors, elaborate woodwork, and some working fireplaces. The more modern suite has 12 windows, Danish walnut furniture, and a full-size cable TV. The breezy front porch—which faces the Falmouth green—is set with white wicker furniture and hung with colorful potted geraniums. *40 W. Main St., Falmouth 02540, tel. 508/548–5621. 4 rooms, 1 suite. Facilities: full breakfast, afternoon beverages or snacks, common piano and TV. No credit cards. No smoking.*

Moderate– Inexpensive **Earl of Sandwich Motor Manor.** Single-story Tudor-style buildings are ranged in a *U* around a wooded lawn in the back, with areas for croquet and horseshoes as well as lawn chairs. The newer buildings (1981–83) have air-conditioning, unlike the main building (1963); all rooms have phones. The decor is rather somber, with dark exposed beams on white ceilings, dark paneled walls, quarry-tile floors with Oriental throw rugs, olive leatherette wing chairs, and chenille bedspreads, but the rooms are a good size and have large Tudor-style windows and small tiled baths. *378 Rte. 6A, East Sandwich 02537, tel. 508/ 888–1415. 24 rooms. Facilities: minifridges available. AE, MC, V.*

Mid-Cape

Very Expensive ★ **Tara Hyannis Hotel & Resort.** For its beautifully landscaped setting, extensive services and pampering, and superior resort facilities (including a well-equipped health club, an 18-hole golf course, a large indoor pool with a window wall overlooking the gardens, and a popular night spot), it's hard to beat the Tara. The lobby area is elegant, but rooms are decorated a bit boringly in pale colors and standard contemporary hotel style; a revamp is in the works. All rooms have color TV, phone, desk, table and chairs, and a private balcony or patio. Rooms overlooking the golf greens or the courtyard garden have the best views. *West End Circle, Hyannis 02601, tel. 508/775–7775 or 800/843–8272. 216 rooms, 8 suites. Facilities: golf course (fee), 2 putting greens, 2 lighted tennis courts, indoor pool with Roman bath, outdoor pool with grill, health club (fee; see Sports, above), restaurant, lounge, hair salon, gift shop, full children's program, business services, room service until midnight, minifridges (fee). AE, CB, D, DC, MC, V.*

Expensive ★ **Beechwood.** One of the Cape's best B&Bs is set in a yellow and pale green 1853 Queen Anne Victorian trimmed with a touch of gingerbread, wrapped by a wide porch with wicker and tinkling wind chimes, and shaded by big old beech trees. Guest rooms are beautifully decorated with antiques in the unheavy early Victorian style; all have minifridges, and some have fireplaces. Breakfast is served by candlelight and with classical music in the dining room, with pressed-tin ceiling, fireplace, and tables set with lace, flowers, and crystal. *2839 Main St. (Rte. 6A), Barnstable 02630, tel. 508/362–6618. 6 rooms. Facilities: full breakfast, afternoon tea, common phone. AE, MC, V.*

Harbor Village. Set in pine woods by a salt marsh is this community of one- to four-bedroom Cape-style cottages, most with a water view (the ones *on* the marsh are booked far in advance). Each cottage is individually owned (rented out for the summer only), homey, nicely furnished, and clean; each has a fully equipped kitchen, a TV, a fireplace, a barbecue grill, and a deck with patio furniture, and some have phones, microwave ovens, and dishwashers. *Between Sea St. and Scudder Ave.,*

Box 635, Hyannis Port 02647, tel. 508/775–7581. 20 units. Facilities: daily maid service in season. No credit cards. Closed Nov.–Memorial Day.

Simmons Homestead Inn. A rambling 1820 captain's house in a quiet area less than a mile from downtown Hyannis was converted in 1987 into an unusual-looking inn. Each guest room is decorated with an animal theme, such as the Rabbit Room or the wild Jungle Room. The large common rooms feature a mantel-top duck collection and huge Mexican papier-mâché birds. The style of the rooms varies from country to colonial to modern; some have decks, fireplaces, or canopy beds, either antique or fine reproduction. *288 Scudder Ave., Hyannis Port 02647, tel. 508/778–4999. 8 rooms. Facilities: full breakfast, evening wine and cheese, central TV and phone. AE, MC, V as guarantee only. No smoking.*

Inn at Fernbrook. The most striking feature of this easygoing inn is the grounds, originally landscaped by Frederick Law Olmsted, designer of New York's Central Park. Paths wind past duck ponds stocked with Japanese *koi* and blooming with water lilies; a sunken, heart-shaped sweetheart garden of red and pink roses; exotic trees (like Japanese cork and a weeping beech); a windmill; and, of course, a fern-rimmed brook. The house itself, an 1881 Queen Anne Victorian mansion on the National Register of Historic Places, is a beauty, from the turreted exterior to the fine woodwork and furnishings within. Most rooms have garden views; some have bay-windowed sitting areas, canopy beds, pastel Oriental carpets, and working fireplaces. Breakfast is elaborate, formally served, friendly, and delicious. *481 Main St., Centerville 02632, tel. 508/775–4334. 4 rooms, 1 suite, 1 cottage (no kitchen). Facilities: full breakfast, afternoon tea, common phone. AE, MC, V. Smoking restricted.*

Expensive–Moderate   **Capt. Gosnold Village.** An easy walk to the beach and town, this colony of motel rooms and one- to three-bedroom cottages is ideal for families. Children can ride their bikes around the quiet street and compound; the pool is fenced in and is manned by a lifeguard. In many rooms, walls are attractively paneled in knotty pine; floors are carpeted; furnishings are colonial style, simple, and pleasant. All units have TVs and heat; most have decks and deck furniture. Motel rooms have fridges and coffee makers. *Gosnold St., Box 544, Hyannis 02601, tel. 508/775–9111. 8 motel rooms, 12 efficiencies. Facilities: outdoor pool, basketball area, game nets, picnic areas, hibachis, daily maid service. MC, V. Closed Nov.–mid-May.*

Moderate   **Hampton Inn Hotel.** In 1990, Hampton Inns (Holiday Inn's lower-priced division) bought the Iyanough Hills Motor Lodge and put $1 million into renovations, including all-new decor and white-oak-veneer furnishings. All the rooms at this business- and family-oriented cinderblock motel just off the highway now have two double beds or one king-size bed, and either a table and chairs or a desk and chair, a wardrobe, air-conditioning, cable TV with remote, and a phone. The quietest are those on the top floor that face the pond and woods. *1470 Rte. 132, Hyannis 02601, tel. 508/771–4804 or 800/999–4804. 104 rooms (nonsmoking rooms available). Facilities: Continental breakfast, indoor pool, whirlpool, saunas, sun deck, fitness room (stair climber, air rowing machine, stationary bike), children under 18 stay free, senior discounts available. AE, CB, D, DC, MC, V.*

★ **Liberty Hill.** Billed as "an elegant country inn," Liberty Hill lives up to its claim. The 1825 Greek Revival mansion stands on a rise set back from Route 6A, in an attractive setting of trees and flower-edged lawns. Inside, rooms are large, with tall windows and high ceilings, and romantically but unfussily decorated with fine antiques, upholstered chairs, and thick carpets. The Waterford Room has the entire third floor, a king-size bed, an oversize bath, and bay views. *77 Main St. (Rte. 6A), Yarmouth Port 02675, tel. 508/362–3976. 5 rooms. Facilities: full breakfast, afternoon tea, dinner on request (fee), central TV and phone, guest fridge with mixers. AE, MC, V.*

Moderate– **Inn on Sea Street.** This is a charming, relaxed B&B a walk away
Inexpensive from the beach and downtown Hyannis. The 1849 Victorian
★ home has been completely restored and furnished with country antiques and lacy fabrics by the very personable and helpful innkeepers (car buffs will enjoy the antique cars J.B. keeps in the yard and garage). A quirky favorite guest room is a glassed-in sun porch. Delicious breakfasts are served with china, silver, and crystal in a dining room with antiques and lace. *358 Sea St., Hyannis 02601, tel. 508/775–8030. 6 rooms, 3 with shared bath. Facilities: full breakfast, central phone and TV, games. AE, MC, V. Smoking discouraged. Closed Nov.–Mar.*

Lower Cape

Very Expensive **Augustus Snow House.** Luxury is the operative word at this inn, a Princess Anne Victorian with gabled dormers and wraparound veranda, from the whirlpools in some baths to the Gucci amenity baskets. Early evening wine and gourmet hors d'oeuvres are served in silver and crystal, accompanied by candelabra, linen cloths and napkins, and quiet classical music. The rooms are done up in Victorian style, down to reproduction furnishings and wallpapers and authentic period brass bathroom fixtures. All rooms have phones and color TV. An English tea is served to the public in the Victorian drawing rooms. *528 Main St., Harwich Port 02646, tel. 508/430–0528. 5 rooms. Facilities: full breakfast, hors d'oeuvres, turndown service. AE, MC, V.*

★ **Chatham Bars Inn.** The ultimate oceanfront resort in the old style, this Chatham landmark comprises the main building, with its grand-hotel lobby and formal restaurant, and 26 one- to eight-bedroom cottages on 20 beautifully landscaped acres. The entire inn has been renovated to create a casual Cape Cod elegance, though you'll feel free to dress in your best. Some rooms have TVs or ocean-view porches; all have phones and traditional Cape-style furnishings. Service is attentive and extensive. Theme weekends are scheduled in the off-season. Rates include a service charge (no tipping allowed), plus breakfast and dinner in season. *Shore Rd., Chatham 02633, tel. 508/945–0096 or 800/527–4884. 152 rooms. Facilities: private beach, 5 tennis courts, putting green, heated outdoor pool, shuffleboard, launch service to North Beach, children's program (July and Aug.), 2 restaurants, clambakes, lounge with entertainment, bar; 9-hole golf course adjacent. AE, CB, DC, MC, V.*

Ocean Edge. This huge, self-contained resort is more like a town, with 17 "villages" of residential and rental condominiums, as well as a major conference center. The sports facilities are superior, including a world-class golf course; activities such as concerts, tournaments, and clambakes are scheduled throughout the summer. Accommodations range from oversize hotel rooms with sitting areas in the conference center, with direct access to the health club and tennis courts, to luxurious one- to three-bedroom condos in the woods. All are tastefully and recently decorated in modern style, are air-conditioned, and have TVs and phones; condos have washer/dryers and some fireplaces, and hotel rooms have VCRs. The resort is very spread out; you may need your car to get from your condo to the pool. *Rte. 6A, Brewster 02631, tel. 508/896–2781, 800/221–1837, or 800/626–2688 in MA. 125 condominium units, 90 hotel rooms. Facilities: 1,000-foot private beach, championship golf course, golf and tennis schools, driving range and putting greens, heated indoor lap pool and whirlpool, Olympic-size outdoor pool, ponds, 6 all-weather tennis courts, well-equipped fitness room, hot tub, saunas, running courses, 3 restaurants, room service (hotel), concierge, basketball court, bicycle rentals, playground. AE, CB, D, DC, MC, V.*

Wequassett Inn. This tranquil, traditional resort offers first-rate accommodations in 19 Cape-style cottages along a little bay and on 22 acres of woods, plus luxurious dining, attentive service, evening entertainment, and plenty of sunning and sporting opportunities. The recently renovated guest rooms have received design awards; the decor is Early American, with country pine furniture and homey touches such as handmade quilts and duck decoys. Each room has air-conditioning, a minifridge, cable TV/HBO, and a phone; some have fireplaces or wet bars. *Pleasant Bay, Chatham 02633, tel. 508/432–5400, 800/225–7125 in MA, or 800/352–7169. 99 rooms, 4 suites. Failities: 5 all-weather tennis courts, heated outdoor pool, game room, boat tours, beach dropoff, transport to town, restaurant, poolside grill, piano lounge, 15-hr room service, walking path; for extra fee, sailboats, Windsurfers, sailing school (5- to 7-day courses), seaplane rides (sightseeing, islands visits). AE, CB, DC, MC, V. Closed mid-Oct.–mid-May.*

Very Expensive–Expensive **Wychmere Harbor Hotel.** This oceanfront resort offers a wide variety of accommodations in seven weathered-shingle buildings: from small rooms with colonial-style furnishings in the older buildings to large new, contemporary-style rooms with balconies overlooking the ocean or harbor. All rooms have cable TV/HBO and phones; some have air-conditioning. The facilities are first-rate, from the elegant dining rooms to the Olympic-size pool and the 1,000-foot private beach, which is wide, sandy, groomed daily, and adjacent to conservation land. *Snow Inn Rd., Harwich Port 02646, tel. 508/432–1000. 115 rooms, 1 town house with kitchenette. Facilities: afternoon tea (July–Aug.), heated outdoor pool, beach, fishing from jetty, 2 tennis courts and lessons, playground, programs for children, babysitting, putting green, concierge, room service, business services, 2 restaurants, beachfront snack bar, piano bar, dinner dances, charter sailboat. AE, CB, DC, MC, V. Closed Nov.–Memorial Day.*

Expensive **Bradford Inn and Motel.** Just off Main Street are the Bradford's cheery yellow awnings and colorful gardens. Accommodations are in five buildings, ranging from the 1860 main house to the 1978 motel section. Rooms run the gamut from small and basic to luxurious and spacious with fireplaces and canopy beds; all have phones, TVs, minifridges, and air-conditioning. *26 Cross St., Box 750, Chatham 02633, tel. 508/945–1030. 25 rooms. Fa-*

cilities: full breakfast, small heated outdoor pool, fireplaced lounge, library. AE, D, MC, V.

★ **Captain's House Inn.** Finely preserved architectural details, superb taste in decorating, opulent home-baked goods, and an overall feeling of warmth and quiet comfort are just part of what makes this one of the finest small inns anywhere. Each room in the three inn buildings has its own personality. Some are quite large, some have fireplaces; some are lacy and feminine, some refined and elegant. The general style of the inn is colonial Williamsburg; rooms in the Carriage House have a more spare, modern look. The spacious Hiram Harding Room in the Captain's Cottage is spectacular, with 200-year-old handhewn ceiling beams, a wall of raised walnut paneling centered by a large working fireplace, and a rich red Oriental carpet. Teatime provides a good chance to meet fellow guests. *371 Old Harbor Rd., Chatham 02633, tel. 508/945-0127. 14 rooms, 2 suites. Facilities: Continental breakfast, afternoon tea, guest phone. AE, MC, V. No smoking in public areas. Closed mid-Nov.-mid-Feb.*

Holiday Inn. This two-story motor court built in 1969 offers very clean, spacious rooms at the edge of Provincetown. The rooms were refurbished in 1989 and are bright and modern, with pastels and florals; each has two double beds, cable TV/HBO, a phone, and air-conditioning. Second-floor rooms facing the parking lot have a water view, but this side gets noisy. *Shore Rd. (Rte. 6A), Box 392, Provincetown 02657, tel. 508/487-1711 or 800/465-4329, fax 508/487-3929. 78 rooms. Facilities: nonsmoking rooms, large outdoor pool, poolside bar, restaurant (Apr.-Oct.), lounge with dancing or movies, fax service. AE, CB, D, DC, MC, V.*

Queen Anne Inn. A short walk from Chatham center, and perfectly situated for walks and bike rides around scenic Oyster Pond, the Queen Anne has the feel of a European country inn. Built in 1840 (with later additions as a parsonage, the stately gray-shingled building became an inn in 1874 and today offers an intimate gourmet restaurant, tree-fringed tennis courts, and gracious, comfortable accommodations. The decor is simple, with country wallpapers, locally made (and some antique) furniture, white chenille bedspreads, and some fishnet canopies. All rooms have phones; some have air-conditioning, fireplaces, or private balconies looking onto the back lawn, shaded by large old elms. *70 Queen Anne Rd., Chatham 02633, tel. 508/945-0394 or 800/545-4667, fax 508/945-4884. 30 rooms, 1 suite. Facilities: Continental breakfast, 3 Har-Tru tennis courts, bikes, game room, whirlpool room, common TV and VCR, restaurant, boat tours of coast (free) or to Monomoy, Nantucket, or outer beaches (fee). AE, DC, MC, V. Closed Thanksgiving-mid-Apr.*

Sheraton Ocean Park Inn. Located at the entrance to the National Seashore, with a nicely landscaped atrium pool area at its center, this Sheraton offers standard modern-decor rooms with TV, phone, two double beds or one king-size bed, and tiled baths. Rooms have views of the pool or the woods; the outside rooms are a little bigger and brighter and have minifridges. *Rte. 6, Eastham 02642, tel. 508/255-5000 or 800/533-3986. 107 rooms, including suites. Facilities: fitness room with Universal and other equipment, whirlpool, 2 outdoor tennis courts (lighted in summer), saunas, outdoor pool with poolside bar, heated indoor atrium pool, restaurant, lounge with dancing,* *airport and beach shuttles in summer, game arcade, nonsmoking rooms, 16-hr room service. AE, CB, D, DC, MC, V.*

Expensive– Moderate **Hargood House.** An apartment complex on the water, ½ mile from Provincetown center, Hargood House is a great option for longer stays and families. Most of the individually (and sometimes questionably) decorated units have decks and large water-view windows; all have full kitchens and modern baths. The ever-popular No. 8 is like a light, bright beach house: on the water, with three glass walls, cathedral ceilings, private deck, dining table and chairs. Rental is mostly by the week in season; two-night minimum off-season. *439 Commercial St., Provincetown 02657, tel. 508/487–1324. 20 apartments. Facilities: private beach, daily maid service in season, barbecue grills. AE, MC, V.*

★ **Moses Nickerson House.** A love of fine antiques, and warm, thoughtful service characterize this B&B. Guest rooms in the rambling 1839 house feature wide-board pine floors; some have gas-log fireplaces. Each room has an individual look: one with dark woods and leathers and Ralph Lauren fabrics and accessories; another with green and white beach stripes, white walls, and white iron bed; another with a high canopy bed, puffy feather mattress, exquisite 100-year-old white bedspread, and Nantucket hand-hooked rug. Breakfast is served on family china and crystal. *364 Old Harbor Rd., Chatham 02633, tel. 508/945–5859. 7 rooms. Facilities: full breakfast, afternoon wine or tea, complimentary fruit and sherry, turndown service. AE, MC, V. No smoking. Closed Jan.–mid-Feb.*

Provincetown Inn. Located at the tip of Commercial Street, jutting out into the water, the inn is a Provincetown landmark, rather worse for wear. Waterfront rooms are by far the nicest, with wide decks, picture windows looking out to sea, and better furnishings; bay-view rooms overlook the marshes to the dunes; motel rooms are just that. *1 Commercial St., Provincetown 02657, tel. 508/487–9500 or 800/942–5388. 100 rooms. Facilities: full breakfast, big indoor pool, restaurant, coffee shop, bar (all in season only); private beach. MC, V.*

Moderate **Captain's Quarters.** Set back from the highway and surrounded by woods is this single-story motel and small conference center, built between 1982 and 1987. Guest rooms are roomy, with white walls, blond-wood modern motel furniture, and pastel fabrics. All have cable TV/HBO, minifridges, phones, one queen-size or two double beds, and table and chairs; luxury rooms have somewhat nicer fabrics and are newer. *Rte. 6, Box Y, North Eastham 02651, tel. 508/255–5686. 71 rooms, 4 suites. Facilities: Continental breakfast, small outdoor pool, shuttle to beach (July and Aug.), bikes, 2 tennis courts, picnic/barbecue area, volleyball net, basketball hoop, horseshoes. AE, D, DC, MC, V. Closed Dec.–Mar.*

Coachman Motor Lodge. A clean, well-maintained single-story motel just off the highway, the Coachman offers cheerful guest rooms with basic motel-colonial furnishings, including two double beds, a desk, and a sitting area. Each room has a tiled bath, air-conditioning, a phone, and cable TV. *Rte. 28, Harwich Port 02646, tel. 508/432–0707. 27 rooms, 1 efficiency. Facilities: outdoor pool, breakfast restaurant. AE, MC, V. Closed Nov.–Apr.*

Nauset Knoll Motor Lodge. On a low rise overlooking Nauset Beach, two minutes' walk away—the closest accommodation to a National Seashore beach you'll find—this row of adjoining

Cape houses offers basic, ground-level motel rooms. Each is sparsely furnished (Formica and pine, worn carpets, acoustical tile ceilings) but light and bright, with six-foot ocean-view picture windows, tiled baths, and color TV. Book well in advance. *Nauset Beach, East Orleans 02643, tel. 508/255–2364. 12 rooms. Facilities: public phone. MC, V. Closed late Oct.–mid-Apr.*

Moderate–Inexpensive   **Isaiah Clark House.** The 18th-century main house retains much of the flavor of its origins, in variable-width floorboards, old fireplace mantels and moldings, narrow staircases, and the authentically furnished breakfast room, with original keeping-room hearth. The decor is colonial in furnishings and colors, accented with homey antique pieces. Some rooms have canopy beds, fireplaces, or phones; rooms in the main house are air-conditioned. The wooded back yard is perfect for picnicking, lying in the hammock, walking through 5 acres of gardens, fruit trees, and berry patches, or relaxing by the pond. *1187 Rte. 6A, Brewster 02631, tel. 508/896–2223. 7 rooms (all private baths, 4 detached) in main house, 5 rooms (1 private bath, 4 share 2 baths) in cottage. Facilities: full breakfast, afternoon tea, turndown service, bikes, games, beach chairs and towels, airport or train station pickup; common phone, piano, TV, VCR, stereo. AE, MC, V. No smoking in bedrooms.*

The Masthead. Families in particular are welcome at these unpretentious seaside cottages and apartments, some with room for seven—in walking distance of town, but far enough away to escape the frenetic summer pace. No Jacuzzis or Laura Ashley decor here; this is classic Provincetown—funky, friendly, down-to-earth, with cooking facilities and a private deck. The best and most expensive units overlook the water. *31–41 Commercial St., Box 577, Provincetown 02657, tel. 508/487–0523 or 800/395–5095. No charge for children 12 and under. 6 apartments, 4 cottages, 3 efficiencies, 8 rooms. Facilities: private beach, kitchens. AE, MC, V. Moderate.*

★ **Old Sea Pines Inn.** The inn, fronted by a white-columned portico and wraparound veranda overlooking a broad lawn, strongly evokes the feel of a summer estate of an earlier day. The living room is spacious, with an appealing seating area before the fireplace. A sweeping staircase leads to guest rooms decorated with antique-look wallpaper, framed old photographs, and nicely matching antique furnishings. Many rooms are very large; fireplaces are available, including one in the inn's best room, which has a sitting area in an enclosed sun porch. Rooms in a newer building are well but sparely decorated, with bright white modern baths, and have TVs. *2553 Main St. (Rte. 6A), Brewster 02631, tel. 508/896–6114. 19 rooms (5 share 2½ baths), 2 suites. Facilities: full breakfast, afternoon tea Nov.–Mar., pay phone, board games. AE, CB, DC, MC, V. Smoking discouraged.*

Wellfleet Motel & Lodge. Located 1 mile from Marconi Beach and opposite an Audubon sanctuary is this well-maintained and tasteful complex. Rooms in the single-story motel, built in 1964, have attractive knotty-pine paneling. Those in the two-story lodge, built in 1986, are bright and spacious, with white walls, oak furniture, and patios. Each room has a minifridge, a color TV, a phone, air-conditioning, and a coffee maker. *Rte. 6, Box 606, South Wellfleet 02663, tel. 508/349–3535, or 800/852–2900 in MA. 25 motel rooms, 40 lodge rooms. Facilities: heated indoor pool and whirlpool in cedar-lined room, small heated* *outdoor pool, coffee shop (breakfast only), bar, basketball hoop. AE, CB, DC, MC, V. Lodge and facilities closed Thanksgiving–Mar.*

Inexpensive **Handkerchief Shoals Motel.** Located about 2 miles from Harwich Port and 8 miles from downtown Chatham, the single-story property is set back from the highway and surrounded by well-maintained lawn and trees. Rooms are sparse but large and sparkling clean, with sitting and desk areas, tiled baths, and TV, fridge, and microwave—a very good value for the money. *Rte. 28, Box 306, South Harwich 02661, tel. 508/432–2200. 26 units. Facilities: morning coffee, outdoor pool, lawn games, ping-pong. AE, D, MC, V. Closed mid-Oct.–mid-Apr.*

The Arts and Nightlife

Arts and entertainment events are listed in the *Cape Cod Times*'s "CapeWeek" section on Friday, or more extensively in *The Register*'s Thursday "What's Going On Here" section. The *Times*'s "Things to Do Today on Cape Cod" column (daily July–Aug., weekends thereafter) lists sporting, arts, and other events. The twice weekly Tuesday *Cape Codder*'s "Summery" section is also a good source on summer events, and its Friday "Weekend" page lists doings year-round. The bimonthly *Cape Cod Life* magazine includes a calendar of events helpful in planning a trip.

The Arts

Since before the turn of the century, creative people have been drawn to Cape Cod summers, and their legacy and ongoing contribution is a thriving arts scene. Vital art galleries exist in Provincetown and elsewhere (*see* Shopping, above). In addition to the professional theaters, which offer top-name talent in season, almost every town has a community theater that provides quality entertainment—often mixing local players with visiting pros—throughout the year.

The Cape also gets its share of music stars, from pop to classical, along with local groups ranging from barbershop quartets to Bach chorales to early-music or chamber ensembles, often playing at school auditoriums or town halls. Woods Hole, with its strong intellectual community, has several performance groups, including the **Woods Hole Cantata Consort** and the **Chamber Orchestra,** as well as a year-round **Woods Hole Contra Dance** group.

Theater The top summer-stock venues, often featuring star performers, are the Equity **Cape Playhouse** (off Rte. 6A, Dennis, tel. 508/385–3911 or 385–3838) and the **Falmouth Playhouse** (off Rte. 151, North Falmouth, tel. 508/563–5922). Both offer Broadway shows and children's plays.

The **Barnstable Comedy Club** (Village Hall, Rte. 6A, Barnstable, tel. 508/362–6333), the Cape's oldest amateur theater group, gives much-praised performances of musicals and dramas throughout the year.

Monomoy Theater (776 Main St., Chatham, tel. 508/945–1589) presents eight productions—thrillers, musicals, classics, modern drama—by the Ohio University Players from mid-June through August. The 1991 season will be their 34th.

The College Light Opera Company (Highfield Theatre, end of Depot Ave., Falmouth, tel. 508/548–0668), founded in 1969, presents Oberlin students and other college music majors in operettas and musical comedies late June through August. The company includes more than 30 singers and an 18-piece orchestra.

The **Wellfleet Harbor Actors Theatre (W.H.A.T.;** by town pier, tel. 508/349–6835) has attracted a lot of Boston and New York attention, presenting less summer-oriented fare—including satires, farces, black comedies, and dramas—than most Cape theaters in its May–October season.

The **Cape Cod Melody Tent** (*see* Music, below) hosts a Wednesday-morning children's theater series in July and August.

Music **Heritage Plantation** (Grove and Pine Sts., Sandwich, tel. 508/888–3300) sponsors summer jazz and other concerts in its gardens from June to mid-September; bring chairs or blankets. The concerts are free with admission.

The Mews Concert Series in Provincetown (Town Hall, Commercial St., tel. 508/487–0955) presents classical chamber, folk, ethnic, and jazz music throughout the summer.

Popular The Cape's top venue for popular music concerts and comedy is the **Cape Cod Melody Tent** (W. Main St., Box 1979, Hyannis 02601, tel. 508/775–9100; to charge tickets, tel. 800/382–8080), an institution since 1950. Performances are held from July to Labor Day in a 2,300-seat theater-in-the-round under a tent. The 1990 lineup included Ray Charles, the Preservation Hall Jazz Band, Willie Nelson, Starship, and Roseanne Barr.

The **Beach Plum Music Festival**, held in August at the Provincetown Town Hall (260 Commercial St., tel. 508/349–6874; to charge tickets, tel. 800/382–8080), is a series of popular folk and jazz concerts by such performers as Wynton Marsalis and Holly Near.

Classical The 100-member **Cape Cod Symphony Orchestra** (Mattacheese Middle School, Higgins Crowell Rd., West Yarmouth, tel. 508/428–3577), under conductor Royston Nash, gives regular and children's concerts, with guest artists, October–May.

The **Cape & Islands Chamber Music Festival** (Box 72, Yarmouth Port 02675, tel. 508/778–5277) is three weeks of top-caliber performances and master classes at various locations in August.

Band Concerts Traditional New England town band concerts are held weekly each summer in many Cape towns; bring along chairs, blankets, and a picnic supper if you like, and go early to get a good spot. **Chatham's** (Kate Gould Park, off Main St., tel. 508/945–2160), held at 8 PM on Friday, draws up to 6,000 people; as many as 500 fox-trot on the roped-off dance floor, and there are special dances for children and sing-alongs for all.

Other locations (featuring the town band unless otherwise noted): **Buzzards Bay** (Buzzards Bay Park, off Main St., tel. 508/888–6202), different bands, Thursdays at 7. **Dennis** (gazebo, Nathaniel Wixon Middle School, off Rte. 134, South Dennis; Dennis Village Green, junction of Rte. 6A and Old Bass River Rd., tel. 508/398–3568), different bands, alternate Mondays at 7:30; also, Dennisport Village Green (Hall St.), different bands and nights. **Falmouth** (bandshell, Falmouth Inner Harbor, Scranton Ave., tel. 508/548–2416), with the 85-instrument town band, Thursdays at 8. **Harwich** (Brooks Park, tel. 508/432–1600), Tuesdays at 7:30. **Hyannis** (Bismore Park, Ocean St. docks, tel. 508/775–2201), Wednesdays at 7:30. **Sandwich** (bandstand, Henry T. Wing Elementary School, Rte. 130, tel. 508/888–0157), most Thursdays at 7:30. **West Yarmouth** (Mattacheese Middle School, off Higgins Crowell Rd., tel. 508/398–5311), different bands, Mondays at 7:30.

Opera   Two performances a year, in spring and fall, are given at Sandwich High School (Quaker Meetinghouse Rd., East Sandwich) by the touring group from Sarah Caldwell's Boston company, Opera New England. For dates, contact **Opera New England of Cape Cod** (tel. 508/775–3974). (*See* also College Light Opera Company under Theater, above.)

Film   Besides the first-run theaters, the **Cape Museum of Fine Arts Cinema Club** (Cape Playhouse complex, Rte. 6A, Dennis, tel. 508/385–5089) presents classic and avant-garde movies in an intimate setting from fall through spring.

That fast-disappearing American tradition, the drive-in movie, is living still on Cape Cod: at the **Wellfleet Drive-In Theater** (Rte. 6, tel. 508/349–7176 recording, 349–2520 humans), films start at dusk nightly in season, and there's a minigolf course on the property.

Dance   The **Cape Ballet** (Sandwich High School, Quaker Meetinghouse Rd., Sandwich, tel. 508/888–5300), a professional company, performs classical and modern ballet year-round.

Nightlife

Nighttime on Cape Cod can be very special, in many ways. In the less developed areas, the stars are amazingly bright and make beach walks in blackness and silence even more wondrous—more of an experience in the elemental. Also, the power of the lighthouse beacons as they cut through the night sky has a fascination impossible to resist. If you're up *really* late, you might head for Chatham Light to catch a terrific sunrise.

Many daytime activities, such as fishing, take on a completely different aspect at night. Scuba enthusiasts might consider night diving; colors are more vivid by flashlight, a lot of sea life is phosphorescent or bioluminescent, and nocturnal species come out to play. It's important to know the tides and safe locations—ask at a dive shop before setting out.

A number of organizations sponsor outdoor activities at night, including the **Cape Cod Museum of Natural History**'s stargazing sessions (*see* Tour 3, above) and **Wellfleet Bay Sanctuary**'s bat walks (*see* Nature Areas, above). The **Army Corps of Engineers** (tel. 508/759–4431), which maintains the Cape Cod Canal, offers free evening programs in summer, including slide shows about the canal, sing-alongs, and storytelling around campfires at the Bourne Scenic Park and Scusset Beach State Park. The **Salt Pond Visitor Center** in Eastham (Rte. 6, tel. 508/255–3421) also has evening programs, including slide shows and sunset beach walks.

In summer, just walking Main Street in Hyannis or Commercial Street in Provincetown is nightlife in itself. The streets are filled with a fascinating array of people who are from everywhere and into everything, all on vacation and having a great time. All you require to be a part of "the stroll" is an appreciation of life's infinite variety—and maybe an ice-cream cone.

Of course, what you probably turned to this section to find out about is what is more traditionally defined as nightlife, and there's certainly plenty of it on the Cape, though live music has become increasingly scarce, edged out by economic hard times and replaced by DJs and dance music.

Hyannis and Yarmouth have a lot of rowdy dance clubs, bars, and restaurant lounges well patronized by college students on summer vacation. Most of the Upper and Lower Cape is quiet, except for Provincetown (with the added spice of drag shows) and a few places in Chatham. And scattered throughout the Cape are places for dining and dancing in elegant style. In season, many restaurant and hotel lounges have live entertainment nightly; in the off-season, those that remain open cut back to weekends only.

Mixed Menu
The following venues offer mixed programs of entertainment that do not fit into a single category.

Barley Neck Inn restaurant (Main St., East Orleans, tel. 508/255–6830) has a popular, low-key lounge offering live folk, bluegrass, and blues (and Sunday reggae and jazz) year-round.

Christine's (Rte. 28, West Dennis, tel. 508/394–7333; *see* Dining, above) has entertainment nightly in season: Monday jazz groups, Tuesday and Sunday comedy, a Wednesday concert series of bands from the 1950s–1970s (e.g., the Grass Roots), Top 40 bands Thursday–Saturday. Off-season, there's dancing to a DJ, plus special events. The small lounge attracts a 25- to 45-year-old crowd.

Crown & Anchor Complex (247 Commercial St., Provincetown, tel. 508/487–1430) consists of a number of bars under one roof, including a leather bar, a disco, a cabaret of gay and straight comics and drag shows, a pool bar, and a game room with pool tables and video games.

The Laurels, the sophisticated lounge of the Tara Hyannis Hotel & Resort (West End Circle, Hyannis, tel. 508/775–7775), has a daily happy hour with free hors d'oeuvres, plus evening entertainment—including a laser Karaoke show of video sing-alongs and dancing to DJs or live music from big bands to jazz to rock—most nights in season, less frequently in the off-season. The bar has a wide-screen TV for sports events and a window wall overlooking the pool and golf course.

Wayside Inn (Main St., Chatham, tel. 508/945–1800; *see* Dining, above) has dinner cabaret in the main dining room five nights a week (reservations required) and big-name country, blues, and rock bands two nights in season; off-season weekends, there's dining and dancing to piano music, and rock bands later in the evening. The tavern features piano duos and acoustic country, folk, and blues nightly in season, weekends year-round.

Bars and Lounges
Anywhere you find a **Bobby Byrne's Pub** (Rte. 28, Harwich Port, tel. 508/430–1100; Rte. 28, Hyannis, tel. 508/775–1425; Mashpee Commons, Rtes. 28 and 151, tel. 508/477–0600; Rte. 6A, Sandwich, tel. 508/888–6088), you'll find a comfortable pub atmosphere, a jukebox, and a good light menu; open year-round. **Chatham Squire** (487 Main St., Chatham, tel. 508/945–0942), with four separate bars (including a raw bar), is a rollick-

ing year-round local hangout, drawing a young crowd to the bar side and a mixed crowd of locals to the quieter restaurant side. A jukebox and the crowd itself are the only entertainment. **Duck Inn Pub** (447 Main St., Hyannis, tel. 508/775–3000) has a bar and a video jukebox—from rock to Frank Sinatra—year-round. **The Moors** restaurant (Bradford St. Ext., Provincetown, tel. 508/487–0840; *see* Dining, above) has presented Lenny Grandchamp in its lounge for the past 14 years, and the town never tires of him; he plays the piano, sings, does jokes, and leads sing-alongs from about 7, three to six nights a week in season. **Napi's** (7 Freeman St., Provincetown, tel. 508/487–1145; *see* Dining, above) offers easy-listening piano in its upstairs lounge on weekends, nightly in season. **Oliver's** restaurant (Rte. 6A, Yarmouth Port, tel. 508/362–6062) has live guitar music weekends in its tavern year-round. **Wimpy's** restaurant (732 Main St., Osterville, tel. 508/428–6300) has easy-listening piano year-round. **The Woodshed** (Rte. 6A, Brewster, tel. 508/896–7771), the rustic bar at the Brewster Inn, is a good place to soak up local color and listen to the duos or bands that perform popular music most of the year. Also *see* Chatham Bars Inn under Ballroom Dancing, below.

Dance Clubs **Atlantic House** ("A House"; 6 Masonic Pl., Provincetown, tel. 508/487–3821) has a disco with dancing to DJ rock nightly year-round, plus two smaller, predominately male bars also with dancing.

Champions (Rte. 132, Hyannis, next to Starbuck's, tel. 508/790–0100) is a new, year-round sports bar. Part of a chain of 20, it features 18 TVs, along with lots of sports paraphernalia for decor (such as the 2,000 baseball cards laminated onto the bar). There's DJ dancing on a modern dance floor.

Cranberry Bogg's (720 Main St., Hyannis, tel. 508/778–2717) has dancing to taped music or to Top 40 or 1950s and '60s duos and trios year-round in its lounge, and attracts a rowdy over-25 crowd.

Fiddlebee's (North St., Hyannis, tel. 508/771–6032; *see* Dining, above) has dancing to live rock, jazz, and blues.

Governor Bradford (312 Commercial St., Provincetown, tel. 508/487–9618) attracts a young crowd to its basement, where it offers dancing to reggae and other bands in season. Year-round, you can hang out in its old-time bar, with wide-screen TVs usually on the sports channel.

Guido Murphy's (615 Main St., Hyannis, tel. 508/775–7242) is a hopping bar bursting with college kids and young professionals. Entertainment includes singers and dancing to DJ music, as well as Sunday-night comedy and dancing year-round.

Holiday Inn (Shore Rd., Provincetown, tel. 508/487–1711) has dancing to a DJ in season.

Kasbar (Rte. 28, South Yarmouth, tel. 508/760–1616) has dancing to a DJ, Thursday-night male dancers, and occasional reggae and other bands year-round. The large disco has a high-tech sound and laser system.

Mill Hill Club (164 Rte. 28, West Yarmouth, tel. 508/775–2580) has dancing to a DJ nightly and Top-40 bands Thursday–Sunday year-round, plus videos broadcast on large-screen TVs.

Rascals Saloon (261 Rte. 28, West Yarmouth, tel. 508/775–7800) has dancing to a DJ nightly in season.

Pufferbellies (Rte. 28, Hyannis, tel. 508/771–1116) is a huge club (seats 1,500) across from the airport, with three dance floors and two stages, as well as a volleyball court and a pool. The nightly live entertainment includes a guitarist and sing-along at happy hour, dancing to Top-40 and dance bands, a national act (e.g., Steppenwolf or Foghat) once a week, and teen nights on Mondays, when only soft drinks are served.

Starbuck's (Rte. 132, Hyannis, tel. 508/778–6767; *see* Dining, above) has dancing to a Top-40 DJ year-round and attracts a mid-twenties crowd.

Sundancer's (116 Rte. 28, West Dennis, tel. 508/394–1600) has dancing to a DJ year-round and Sunday-afternoon reggae bands in season.

Ballroom Dancing **Chatham Bars Inn** (Shore Rd., Chatham, tel. 508/945–0096) has dancing to big-band or show-music groups in its South Lounge (jacket and tie required) in July and August and to a pianist or other soft music in its dark and clubby cocktail lounge (jacket required) year-round.

Coonamessett Inn (Jones Rd. and Gifford St., Falmouth, tel. 508/548–2300) has dancing to soft piano, Dixieland, or other music in its lounge on weekends year-round, as well as ballroom dancing a few Sunday nights each summer.

East Bay Lodge (East Bay Rd., Osterville, tel. 508/428–6961) has dancing to jazz duos, trios, or quartets on weekends year-round, nightly in season.

Popponesset Inn (Mall Way, New Seabury, tel. 508/477–1100 or 8258; *see* Dining, above) has dancing to bands in its water-view lounge, on a large dance floor, in season.

Rof-Mar Diplomat Club (Popple Bottom Rd., Sandwich, tel. 508/428–8111; reservations required), a function room, has ballroom dinner dances year-round, attracting an over-35 crowd. There's a large dance floor and seating on outdoor porches.

Yarmouth Senior Center (528 Forest Rd., South Yarmouth, tel. 508/362–9538) has dancing to bands on its large dance floor—the largest on Cape Cod—on Saturday nights.

Country and Western **Bud's Country Lounge** (Bearses Way and Rte. 132, Hyannis, tel. 508/771–2505) has pool tables and features country acts year-round.

The Good Times (Rte. 130, Sandwich, tel. 508/888–6655) has dancing to country bands on weekends year-round.

Folk The Cape has three coffeehouses that present a mixture of professional and local folk and blues in a no-smoking, no-alcohol environment, with refreshments available during intermission.

First Encounter Coffee House (Chapel in the Pine, Samoset Rd., Eastham, tel. 508/255–5438 or 225–1710) has since 1974 offered professional folk concerts, held the first and third Saturday of each month (every Saturday in summer; closed May and September).

Liberty Folk Society (Liberty Hall, Main St., Marstons Mills, tel. 508/428–1053) opened in 1989 and holds concerts the first Saturday of each month, featuring mostly local and some professional musicians, to benefit local organizations.

Woods Hole Folk Music Society (Woods Hole Community Hall, Water St., Woods Hole, tel. 508/540–0320), in existence since 1973, offers concerts on the first and third Sundays of the month from October through May.

Irish Music **Cape Cod Irish Village** (512 Main St., West Yarmouth, tel. 508/771–0100) has dancing to two- or three-piece bands performing traditional and popular Irish music year-round. The crowd is mostly couples and over-35s.

Clancy's (8 Upper County Rd., Dennisport, tel. 508/394–6661) has singer/guitarists year-round.

Irish Pub (126 Main St. [Rte. 28], West Harwich, tel. 508/432–8808) has dancing on its large dance floor to bands doing "ballads and blarney"—a mix of Irish, American, and dance music and sing-alongs—in season.

Shamrock Lounge (Mitchells Steak and Rib House, 451 Iyanough Rd. [Rte. 28], Hyannis, tel. 508/775–6700) has duos performing Irish and American songs, sing-alongs, and comedy year-round.

Jazz The Cape Cod Jazz Society operates a 24-hour hotline (tel. 508/394-5277) on jazz events throughout the Cape.

The **Asa Bearse House** restaurant (415 Main St., Hyannis, tel. 508/771–4131; *see* Dining, above) has dancing to a jazz quartet under the stars in a glass-topped atrium year-round.

Gone Tomatoes (junction of Rtes. 28 and 151, Mashpee Commons, tel. 508/477–8100), an Italian restaurant owned by former promoters of the Newport Jazz Festival, has two- or three-piece combos in its café (with a large mahogany bar) year-round.

Bishop's Terrace restaurant (Rte. 28, West Harwich, tel. 508/432–0253) has dancing to a jazz trio (the popular swing-jazz group the Lee Childs Trio) weekends year-round in its small lounge. Set in a converted barn, it has tools hanging on its walls of rustic barn boards.

Dome Restaurant (State Rd., Woods Hole, tel. 508/548–0800) has dancing to a Dixieland jazz band in its lounge, under a geodesic dome, Sundays in July and August; there is easy-listening piano on Friday and Saturday in season.

Wequassett Inn (Pleasant Bay, Chatham, tel. 508/432–5400) has a jazz duo nightly in its lounge in high season (dinner jacket requested).

Oldies **Admiralty Resort** (Rte. 28, Falmouth, tel. 508/548–4240) has dancing to DJ-spun '50s and '60s music in its lounge most nights.
T-Birds (at Dorsie's, 325 Rte. 28, West Yarmouth, tel. 508/771–5898; at King's Ransom, 425 Rte. 28, Dennisport, tel. 508/394–5533) is a '50s and '60s dance emporium, with DJ music year-round. T-Birds Club at Dorsie's has Top-40 duos in its cocktail lounge as well. Waitresses are dressed in period costumes, and the decor helps set the mood. Also *see* Cranberry Bogg's under Dance Clubs, above.

Dinner Theater **Mystery Cafe Cape Cod** (Tara Hyannis Hotel, West End Circle, [Melody Tent rotary], Hyannis, tel. 508/771–1955 or 800/924–4673; reservations required), new in 1990 and held on weekends in season, presents a murder mystery over a 2½-hour four-course dinner and lets diners join in. It's a fully orchestrated theatrical evening laced with plenty of humor; on breaks, actors mingle with the audience in character.

Cruises The *Island Queen* in Falmouth, the *Portuguese Princess* in Provincetown, **Hy-Line** in Hyannis, and **Cape Cod Canal Cruises** in Onset run sunset or moonlight cruises in season (*see* Guided Tours in Essential Information, above). Falmouth's includes dancing under the stars to live music.

Miscellaneous **Boatslip** (166 Commercial St., tel. 508/487–1669) has an extremely popular tea dance on its huge beachfront deck to DJ dance music from 3:30 to 6:30 on summer afternoons (weekends May–Sept.; also weekdays in high season). The crowd is mixed but predominately gay, both male and female, and the place is always packed.
Town House (291 Commercial St., Provincetown, tel. 508/487–0292) has drag shows in its "Backroom Cabaret" most nights in season.
Johnny Yee's Polynesian/Chinese restaurant (228 Rte. 28, West Yarmouth, tel. 508/775–1090) has dinner-show entertainment, including a Hawaiian revue, a comedy show, and a late-night adult comedy show.
Cape Cod Ocean Waves (Yarmouth Senior Center, 528 Forest Rd., South Yarmouth, tel. 508/398–8073) holds square dances about twice a month.

4 Martha's Vineyard

Introduction

Much less developed—by stringently enforced design—than Cape Cod, yet more diverse and cosmopolitan than neighboring Nantucket Island, Martha's Vineyard is an island with a split personality. From Memorial Day through Labor Day it is a vibrant, star-studded place. Edgartown is flooded with seekers of chic who've come to wander the tidy streets lined with boutiques and stately whaling captains' homes. The busy main port, Vineyard Haven, welcomes day-trippers from the ferries and private yachts to browse in its own array of shops. Oak Bluffs has a boardwalk-town air, with less pricey shops, pizza and ice-cream emporiums, and several night spots that cater to the high-spirited, tanned young. Those too long in a city pent find escape on the many bike paths, in nature preserves, and on miles of spectacular white-sand beaches paved with multicolor beach towels. Summer regulars return, including a host of celebrities such as William Styron, Art Buchwald, Walter Cronkite, Jacqueline Onassis, and Carly Simon. Concerts, theater and dance performances, and lecture series draw top talent to the island, while a county agricultural fair, weekly farmer's markets, and fireworks displays viewed from the village green offer earthier pleasures.

This summer persona is the one most people know, but in many ways the Vineyard's other self is even more appealing, for in the off-season the island becomes a place of peace and simple beauty. On drives along country lanes, there's time to linger without deference to a throng of other cars, bicycles, and mopeds. In the many conservation areas, the voices of the summer crowds are gone, leaving only the sounds of birdsong and the crackle of leaves underfoot. The beaches, always lovely, now can be appreciated in solitude, and the water seems to sparkle more under the crisp blue skies.

The locals, too, are at their best now. After struggling to make the most of the short money-making season, they reestablish contact with friends and take up pastimes previously crowded out by work. The result for visitors—besides the extra dose of friendliness they are likely to encounter—is that cultural, educational, and recreational events continue to be offered year-round.

Bartholomew Gosnold charted Martha's Vineyard for the British Crown in 1602 and is credited with naming it, supposedly after his infant daughter and the wild grapes he found growing in profusion. Later, a Massachusetts Bay Colony businessman, Thomas Mayhew, was given a grant to the island, along with Nantucket and the Elizabeth Islands, from King Charles of England. Mayhew's son, Thomas Mayhew, Jr., founded the first European settlement here in 1642, at Edgartown, finding the resident Wampanoag Indians good neighbors. Among other survival skills, they taught the settlers to kill whales on shore; when moved out to sea, this skill would bring the island great prosperity, at least for a while. (Historians estimate a Wampanoag population of 3,000 upon the arrival of Mayhew; today there are fewer than 300. The tribe is now working hard to reclaim and perpetuate its cultural identity, as it has reclaimed ancestral lands in the town of Gay Head.)

Martha's Vineyard

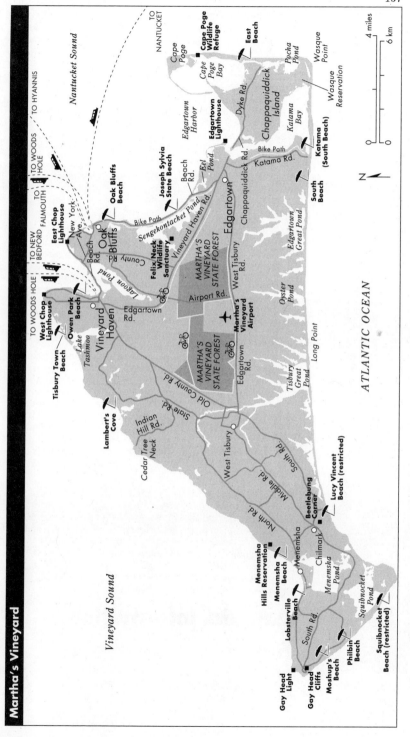

Settled as a community of farmers and fishermen, the island made a decided shift in the early 1800s to whaling as the basis of its economy. Never as influential as Nantucket or New Bedford, Martha's Vineyard still held its own, and many Vineyard whaling masters returned home wealthy men. Especially during the golden age of whaling—around 1830 to 1845—the captains built impressive homes with the profits, and these, along with many graceful houses from earlier centuries, still line the streets of the onetime whaling towns of Vineyard Haven and Edgartown. After the Civil War the industry went into decline, but by that time, a new industry was on the rise, and it has continued to hold sway to this day: tourism.

The story of this development begins in 1835, when the first Methodist Camp Meeting—a two-week gathering of far-flung parishes for group worship and a healthy dose of fun—was held in the then-undeveloped Oak Bluffs area. From the original meeting's nine tents, the number grew to 250 by 1857.

Little by little, permanent platforms were built by returning campers; then the odd cottage popped up, fit into the same space a tent would occupy, ranged around the large central tent of the preachers. By 1880, Wesleyan Grove, as it was called (after Methodism founder John Wesley), was a community of about 500 tiny cottages. Lacy filigree insets began to appear along the facades, becoming more and more ornate as neighbors tried to outdo one another. The style, emerging from Gothic Revival styles imported from Europe, was known as Carpenter Gothic, for the filigree work produced with jigsaws.

Meanwhile, burgeoning numbers of cottagers coming to the island each summer helped convince speculators of its desirability as a resort destination, and in 1867 a separate secular community was laid out alongside the Camp Ground. Steamers from New Bedford, Boston, New York, and elsewhere began bringing in fashionable folk for the bathing and the sea air, for picking berries or playing croquet. Grand hotels sprung up around Oak Bluffs Harbor; a railroad followed, connecting the town with the beach at Katama. The Victorian seaside resort became known as Cottage City; later, the name was changed to Oak Bluffs.

Today, more than 300 of the Camp Ground cottages remain, and just as Edgartown and Vineyard Haven attest to their origins as whaling ports, so Oak Bluffs—with its grassy, open parks, its porch-wrapped beach houses, and its village green and gazebo, where families still gather to hear the town band play—evokes the days of Victorian summer ease. If you close your eyes, the Day-Glo orange bikinis and cones of frozen yogurt seem to fade away, replaced for just a moment by flowing white dresses and parasols languidly held against the sun.

Essential Information

Important Addresses and Numbers

Tourist Information **Martha's Vineyard Chamber of Commerce** is two blocks up from the Vineyard Haven ferry. *Beach Rd., tel. 508/693–0085. Open weekdays 9–5; also Memorial Day–Labor Day, Sat. 10–2.*

Emergencies Dialing 911 will connect you with a **communications center,** where messages are quickly relayed to the hospital, physicians, ambulance services, police, fire departments, or Coast Guard. There's a 24-hour emergency room at **Martha's Vineyard Hospital** (Linton La., Oak Bluffs, tel. 508/693–0410). **Island Medical Services** (261 Main St., Edgartown, tel. 508/627–5181) and **Vineyard Medical Services** (State Rd., Vineyard Haven, tel. 508/693–6933) provide walk-in care; call for days and hours.

Late-Night Pharmacies **Leslie's Drug Store** (Main St., Vineyard Haven, tel. 508/693–1010) is open daily year-round and has pharmacists on 24-hour call for emergencies. The year-round **Oak Bluffs Pharmacy** (Circuit Ave., Oak Bluffs, tel. 508/693–4501) and **Triangle Pharmacy** (245 Vineyard Haven Rd., Edgartown, tel. 508/627–5107) are open daily until 10 PM in July and August.

Cash Machines **Edgartown National Bank** (Cirrus, Cashstream, Yankee 24; 2 S. Water St., 251 Upper Main St., and next to the A&P in Edgartown; 129–131 Circuit Ave., near post office, in Oak Bluffs; tel. 508/627–3343).

Martha's Vineyard National Bank (Cirrus, NYCE, Baybank Xpress 24; opposite steamship ticket office in Vineyard Haven; Oak Bluffs Ave., Oak Bluffs; 19 Lower Main St., Edgartown; Up-Island Cronigs Market, State Rd., West Tisbury; tel. 508/693–9400).

Arriving and Departing by Plane

Airport **Martha's Vineyard Airport** (tel. 508/693–0550) is in West Tisbury, about 5 miles west of Edgartown.

Airlines **Business Express/Delta Connection** (tel. 800/345–3400) has non-stop flights from Boston and Hyannis; **Continental Express** (tel. 800/525–0280), from Boston, Hyannis, and New York; **Express Air** (tel. 800/852–2332) and **Edgartown Air** (tel. 508/627–9631; in Hyannis 508/790–1980; in New Bedford 508/990–3983; in MA 800/637–9631), from New Bedford; **Cape Cod Air** (tel. 508/945–9000 or 800/553–2376 in MA), from Chatham. **Coastal Air Services** (tel. 508/693–5942 on the Vineyard) has charter flights for up to eight people from Groton, Connecticut (tel. 203/448–1001); Nantucket (tel. 508/228–3350); Providence (tel. 401/738–4340); Westerly, Rhode Island (tel. 401/348–9393); and Block Island, Rhode Island (tel. 401/348–2323). All the above provide year-round service.

Service from Nantucket is provided by Business Express/Delta Connection in season and by Continental and Edgartown Air year-round.

Arriving and Departing by Ferry

Car-and-passenger ferries travel to Vineyard Haven from Woods Hole on Cape Cod year-round. In season, passenger ferries from Falmouth and Hyannis on Cape Cod, and from New Bedford, serve Vineyard Haven and Oak Bluffs. Most do not allow payment by credit card for passage on the same day. All provide parking lots for leaving cars overnight (cost: $5–$7 a night).

From Woods Hole The **Steamship Authority** (tel. 508/540–2022; on the Vineyard, 508/693–0367 for information, 508/693–9130 for auto reservations; TDD 508/540–1394) operates the only car ferries, which make the 45-minute trip to Vineyard Haven year-round, and to Oak Bluffs from late May through mid-September. Cost, one-way: $4.25 adults, $2.15 children 5–12; cars, $33 mid-May–mid-Oct., $16.50 rest of year; bicycles, $2.75.

If you plan to take a car to the island in summer or fine week-ends in fall, you *must* reserve as far ahead as possible; spaces are often sold out months in advance. In season, call weekdays from 7 to 9 PM for faster service. Those with reservations must be at the terminal 30 minutes (45 in season) before sailing time. If you're without a reservation, get there very early and be prepared to wait, possibly for hours, for a space to open up. A standby policy guarantees same-day passage from Woods Hole Monday–Thursday in summer to vehicles in the standby line by 3 PM. There is passage from Martha's Vineyard daily if you're in line by 2 PM.

A number of parking lots in Falmouth hold the overflow of cars when the Woods Hole lot is filled; free shuttle buses take passengers to the ferry, about 15 minutes away. Signs along Route 28 direct you to open parking lots, as does a new radio service (AM station 1610) that can be picked up within 5 miles of Falmouth.

Available at the ticket office in Woods Hole is a free reservations phone connecting you with many lodgings and car- and moped-rental firms on the island.

From Hyannis **Hy-Line Cruises** (Ocean St. dock, tel. 508/778–2600, 508/778–2602 for reservations; in Oak Bluffs, tel. 508/693–0112) makes the 1¾-hour run to Oak Bluffs from late May through October. Cost, one-way: $10 adults, $5 children 4–12, $4 bicycles. It's a good idea to reserve a parking space in the lot in high season if you're leaving your car. The "Around the World" cruise, a one-day round-trip from Hyannis with stops at Nantucket and Martha's Vineyard, costs $26 (available mid-June–mid-Sept.).

From Falmouth The *Island Queen* (Falmouth Harbor, tel. 508/548–4800; in Oak Bluffs, tel. 508/548–4800) makes the 40-minute trip to Oak Bluffs from late May through Columbus Day. Cost: round-trip, $8 adults, $4 children under 13, $5 bicycles; one way, $5 adults, $2.25 children under 13, $5 bicycles. Children under 5 sail free Friday–Monday.

Patriot Party Boats (tel. 508/548–2626) offers rides on its daily 4 AM mailboat to Oak Bluffs for $4. If you miss your ferry and want to spend $125, Patriot offers 24-hour boat service.

From New Bedford **Cape Island Express Lines** (tel. 508/997–1688; in Vineyard Haven, tel. 508/693–2088) offers service between Billy Wood's Wharf and Vineyard Haven from mid-May through Columbus Day. The 450-passenger *Schamonchi* makes the 1½-hour trip at least once a day, several times in high season. Cost: round-trip same day, $14 adults, $7 children; one-way, $8 adults, $4.50 children; bicycles, $2 one-way. Senior citizens get a 10% discount.

From Nantucket **Hy-Line** (in Oak Bluffs, tel. 508/693–0112; in Nantucket, 508/228–3949) makes 2¼-hour runs to and from Oak Bluffs three times a day from mid-June to mid-September—the only interisland passenger service. Cost, one-way: $10 adults, $5 children 4–12, $4 bicycles. (To get a car from the Vineyard to Nantucket, you must return to the mainland.)

Arriving and Departing by Private Boat

Harbor facilities are available at **Vineyard Haven** (tel. 508/693–4200), **Oak Bluffs** (tel. 508/693–4355), **Edgartown** (tel. 508/627–4746 or 508/627–4388), and **Menemsha** (tel. 508/645–2846).

Arriving and Departing by Bus and Train

Buses and trains connect with the ferry at Woods Hole—**Amtrak** (tel. 800/USA–RAIL) in summer, **Bonanza Bus Lines** (tel. 800/556–3815, from New York, Providence, and Boston) year-round.

Getting Around

The Martha's Vineyard Transit Authority and Island Transport put out a small pamphlet called "Getting Around on Martha's Vineyard: Public Transportation Guide" that is invaluable if you come without a car. It has trolley and shuttle schedules, routes, and prices, and is available on the trolleys (or tel. 508/627–9663 for information).

By Car In season, the Vineyard gets overrun with cars and the innkeepers will advise you to leave your car home, saying you won't need it. This is true if you are coming over for one to three days and plan to spend most of your time in the three main towns, Oak Bluffs, Vineyard Haven, and Edgartown, which are connected by a shuttle bus. Otherwise, you'll probably want a car. Driving on the island is fairly simple; there are few main roads, and these are all well marked.

Rentals can be booked through the Woods Hole ferry terminal free phone; at the airport desks of **Budget** (tel. 508/693–7322), **Hertz** (tel. 508/627–4727), **National** (tel. 508/693–6454), **All Island** (tel. 508/693–6868), and others; or from companies in the towns, including **Atlantic** (tel. 508/693–0698 in season, 508/693–9191 off-season). **Adventure Rentals** (Beach Rd., Vineyard Haven, tel. 508/693–1959; airport, 508/693–4441) rents cars as well as mopeds, Jeeps, and dune buggies, and offers hourly rates. Cost: $25–$50 per day for a basic model car.

By Four-Wheel-Drive Four-wheel-drive vehicles are allowed on parts of South Beach with $25 annual permits sold on the beach in summer, or anytime at the Dukes County Courthouse (Treasurer's Office, Main St., Edgartown, tel. 508/627–4250); a separate permit is needed to drive on the Wasque nature preserve. Jeeps are a good idea for exploring areas approachable only by dirt roads, but for over-sand travel, even in a Jeep the going can be difficult. In addition to the payment of fees, Wasque requires that vehicles carry certain equipment, such as a shovel; call the rangers (*see* Nature Areas, below) before setting out for the dunes. Also, most rental companies don't allow their Jeeps to be driven over sand, for insurance reasons. Cost: $40–$120 per day (prices fluctuate widely with the season).

By Bus For information on all bus and trolley service, call tel. 508/627–7448 for recorded information; in summer, also 508/693–0058. Late May through mid-October, bus service is provided between Vineyard Haven (pickup on Union Street in front of the steamship wharf), Oak Bluffs (by the Civil War statue), and Edgartown (at the police station on Church St.). The buses operate daily from 8 AM to midnight or so in high season (on the hour and the half hour out of both Vineyard Haven and Edgartown), from 8 to 7 other times (on the hour out of Vineyard Haven, the half hour out of Edgartown); in shoulder seasons, sometimes weekends only. Cost: $1.25–$3 one-way; three-town combination ticket, $4.

Buses from Edgartown to Gay Head—with stops in West Tisbury and Chilmark—run between 9 AM and 5 PM in July and August; at other times, call to confirm. Cost: $1–$3 one-way.

Planned for the 1991 season is an inn and hotel shuttle, originating at the steamship terminal in Vineyard Haven and traveling through Oak Bluffs and Edgartown with stops at 19 hotels; also, minibuses that will make loops in Vineyard Haven and Oak Bluffs, connecting with existing bus loops. For information, call 508/627–9663.

A lift vehicle for the disabled is available year-round (tel. 508/693–4633).

By Trolley
Edgartown
To cut down on traffic from mid-May through mid-September, free trolleys make a continuous circuit of downtown Edgartown, beginning at two free parking lots on the outskirts—at the Triangle, the first right after Four Flags Shopping Mall, and at the Edgartown School on Robinson Road (a right off the West Tisbury Road before Upper Main). It's really worth doing to avoid parking headaches in town, and it's convenient. Trolleys run every 10 minutes from 8 AM to 11:30 PM daily (mid-May–mid-June, 8–7) and can be flagged along the route.

South Beach
Trolley service to South Beach from Edgartown is available mid-June–mid-September for $1.50 one-way. Pickup is at the corner of Main and Church streets every 15 minutes 9–5:30 daily, on the hour in inclement weather, or you can flag a trolley whenever you see one.

By Taxi
Taxis meet all scheduled ferries and flights; in addition, there is a taxi stand by the Flying Horses Carousel in Oak Bluffs. Companies serving the island include **All Island** (tel. 508/693–3705), **Marlene's** (tel. 508/693–0037), and **Up Island** (tel. 508/693–5454).

By Limousine
Muzik's Limousine Service (tel. 508/693–2212) and **Holmes Hole Car Rental & Limo Service** (tel. 508/693–8838) provide limo service on-island or will travel off-island.

By Bicycle
Martha's Vineyard is a great place for bicycling, though Up-Island roads are are hilly, and in season all are often crowded. There are several paved, scenic bike paths (*see* Sports and Outdoor Activities, below).

Rent bikes in Vineyard Haven at **Brickman's** (Main St., tel. 508/693–0047), **Gary's Bike Rental** (Water St., tel. 508/693–0200), and **Martha's Vineyard Scooter and Bike Rental** (Union St., just up from the ferry, tel. 508/693–0782); in Oak Bluffs at **Anderson's** (tel. 508/693–9346), **De Bettencourt's** (tel. 508/693–0011), and **King's Bike & Moped** (tel. 508/693–1887), all on Circuit Avenue Extension near the ferry docks, or at **Sun 'n' Fun** (Lake Ave., tel. 508/693–5457); and in Edgartown at **R.W. Cutler Bike** (1 Main St., tel. 508/627–4052). Cost: $7–$15 per day.

By Moped
Many of the bike-rental shops also rent mopeds; a driver's license is required. **Ride-On Mopeds** (Circuit Ave. Ext., Oak Bluffs, tel. 508/693–2076), on the Hy-Line dock, has rentals by

the hour or the day. Remember that many Vineyard roads are narrow, and watch out for loose gravel and sand. There are many accidents each year.

By Ferry The three-car **On Time** ferry (Dock St., Edgartown, tel. 508/627–9794)—so named because it has no printed schedules and therefore can never be late—makes the five-minute run to Chappaquiddick Island June–mid-October, daily 7 AM–midnight; less frequently off-season. Cost, round-trip: $1 individual, $4 car, $2.50 bicycle, $3.50 moped or motorcycle.

Guided Tours

Orientation The bus companies (tel. 508/693–1555, 508/693–4681, or 508/693–0058) offer two-hour narrated tours of the island, with a stop at the Gay Head cliffs. Buses meet the ferries in season.

Special-Interest See the Vineyard by silent sailplane with **Soaring Adventures of**
Sailplane **America** (Edgartown Airpark, Herring Creek Rd., South Beach, tel. 508/627–3833). Tours, given daily in summer, start at $59.95. It's just you and the pilot—and he'll give you a turn at the controls if you like.

Cruises Day sails, sunset cruises, and overnights to Nantucket or Cuttyhunk on the 54-foot Alden ketch *Laissez Faire* (tel. 508/693–1646) are offered in season out of Vineyard Haven. Cost: $85 full day, $50 half day, $300 overnight. Sunset cruises on the motor tour boat *Skipper* (tel. 508/693–1238), berthed near the *Island Queen* in Oak Bluffs, promise glimpses of celebrities' homes (weather permitting). Cost: $8 adults, $6 children under 13.

Day sails with lunch on the *Shenandoah* (tel. 508/693–1699), a square topsail schooner, are available during only two weeks in the summer (call for schedule) and depart from Coastwise Wharf (south of Steamboat Wharf) in Vineyard Haven. Cost: $75. From mid-June through mid-September the totally wind-powered schooner offers five-night cruises with a maximum of 27 passengers ($600, including hearty Yankee meals). Passengers are ferried to ports, which may include Nantucket, Cuttyhunk, New Bedford, Newport, Block Island, or others.

Ayuthia Charters (tel. 508/693–7245) offers half-day ($50 per person), full-day ($550–$600 for up to 6 persons), and overnight sails to Nantucket or the Elizabeth Islands ($300 per person) on a teakwood sailing yacht, also leaving from Coastwise Wharf in Vineyard Haven from late May through October.

Exploring Martha's Vineyard

Orientation

The island is roughly triangular, with maximum distances of about 20 miles east to west and 10 miles north to south. The west end of the Vineyard, known as Up-Island (from the nautical expression of going "up" in degrees of longitude as you sail west), is more rural and wild than the east end, known as Down-Island (Vineyard Haven, Oak Bluffs, and Edgartown). A fifth of the island is conservation land (11,000 of its 55,000 acres), and more is being acquired all the time by organizations—including the Land Bank, funded by a 2% tax on real estate transactions—that exist in order to preserve as much of the island in its natural state as is possible and practical.

Highlights for First-time Visitors

Dukes County Historical Society museums (*see* Tour 3: Edgartown)
Felix Neck or **Cedar Tree Neck** (*see* Nature Areas)
Gay Head Cliffs (*see* Tour 4: Up-Island)
Menemsha (*see* Tour 4: Up-Island)
Oak Bluffs Camp Ground (*see* Tour 2: Oak Bluffs)
West Tisbury town center (*see* Tour 4: Up-Island)

Tour 1: Vineyard Haven

Numbers in the margin correspond with points of interest on the Vineyard Haven map.

Because most visitors to the island come by ferry and arrive first in Vineyard Haven (the town is officially named Tisbury, but commonly referred to as Vineyard Haven, the name of the port), we begin there. Directly across from the steamship terminal is the **Seaman's Bethel Museum and Chapel** (*bethel* means "house of God" in Hebrew), built in 1892 as a chapel and place of lodging, entertainment, and general comfort for sailors shipwrecked in or just passing through Vineyard Haven on their long schooner voyages. Today it is a museum and chapel, with photographs, scrimshaw, and other exhibits on the island's maritime history. *Union St., tel. 508/693–9317. Donations accepted. Open daily 10–4 (closed some days in off-season).*

A short walk along Water Street, and a right onto Beach Road will take you to the **Martha's Vineyard Chamber of Commerce** for maps and information.

Time Out On Water Street, across from the A&P, you'll pass the **Black Dog Bakery** (tel. 508/693–4786), with fresh breads and pastries, plus Black Dog gift items (*see* Shopping, below).

Just beyond the chamber of commerce is the Federal-style **Jirah Luce House,** built in 1804 and now a museum. Exhibits in eight rooms, including marine artifacts, clothing, and dolls, depict life in 19th-century Tisbury. *Beach Rd., tel. 508/693–5353. Admission: $2 adults, 50¢ children under 16. Open mid-June–mid-Sept., Tues.–Sat. 10–4:30. Closed mid-Sept.–mid-June.*

Main Street, packed with shops and places to eat, is just up the hill from the steamship terminal and runs parallel to the waterfront. Turn right onto Main from Beach Road, then left onto Spring Street. A block up from Main is **William Street,** a quiet, pretty stretch of white picket fences and Greek Revival houses. Many of the houses were the homes of prosperous sea captains, such as the elegant **Captain Richard Luce House,** built in 1833 for a whaling master and still a private home. Now a part of a National Historic District, the street was spared when the Great Fire of 1883 claimed much of the old whaling and fishing town.

Return to Spring Street and turn left for the 1844 **Association Hall.** This neoclassical building houses the town hall as well as

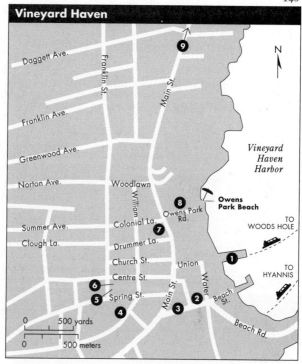

Vineyard Haven

the Katharine Cornell Memorial Theatre, created in part with funds the actress—a longtime summer resident—donated in her will. The walls of the theater, on the hall's second floor, are painted with murals depicting such island scenes as whaling and an Indian gathering; overhead is a blue sky with seagulls. Island artist Stan Murphy painted the murals on the occasion of the town's tercentenary, in 1971. In addition to theatrical performances, concerts and dances are held here.

6 On the hall grounds is the **Centre Street Cemetery,** where pine trees shade grave markers dating as far back as 1817. Some stones are simple gray slate slabs; others are engraved with such motifs as the death's-head, or skull, common on early tombstones. A more recent grave is that of Katharine Cornell.

7 Return to Main Street. The **Old Schoolhouse Museum** here was built in 1829 as the first town school and is now a museum. Exhibits include items brought back from voyages during the whaling days, including Polynesian and Inuit tools, as well as records of 19th-century schoolchildren. Out front is the **Liberty Pole,** erected by the Daughters of the American Revolution in commemoration of three patriotic girls who blew up the town's liberty pole in 1776 to prevent it from being taken for use on a British warship. *110 Main St., tel. 508/693–3860. Donations accepted. Open mid-June–mid-Sept., weekdays 10–2. Closed mid-Sept.–mid-June.*

8 Across the street, just past Colonial Lane, is **Owen Park,** a grassy lawn with benches, swings, and a bandstand where summer band concerts are held (*see* The Arts, below). At the end of the lawn is a public beach with a good view of the boats coming in and out of the harbor.

In the 19th century, this harbor was one of the busiest ports in the world, welcoming thousands of coastwise vessels each year. The headlands on either side—West Chop in Vineyard Haven and East Chop in Oak Bluffs—each came to have a lighthouse at its tip to help bring ships safely into port. Both areas were largely settled in the late-19th to early 20th centuries, when the very rich from Boston and Newport built expansive bluff-top "summer cottages." These houses—built in what is called the Shingle Style, characterized by broad gable ends, dormers, and, of course, natural shingle siding that weathers to gray— were meant to eschew show, though they were sometimes gussied up a bit with a turret or two.

9 Today beautiful, green **West Chop** retains its exclusive air and boasts some of the island's most distinguished residents. A 2-mile drive or bike ride along Main Street, which becomes increasingly residential, will take you there. The 52-foot white and black **West Chop Lighthouse,** on the right, was built in 1881 of brick, to replace an 1817 wood light. It has been moved back twice from the edge of the eroding bluff. Just beyond the lighthouse, on the point, is a scenic overlook with a landscaped area and benches.

If you return to town via Franklin Street you pass the **West Chop Woods,** an 83-acre conservation area with marked walking trails. Across the road is the Mink Meadows Golf Course, and beyond that, the Vineyard Crossing Tennis Courts (*see* Sports and Outdoor Activities, below).

Tour 2: Oak Bluffs

Numbers in the margin correspond with points of interest on the Oak Bluffs map.

Beach Road leads east out of Vineyard Haven across a narrow strip of land between the harbor on the left and Lagoon Pond: a haven for boats passing in storms, a good scalloping area, and the site of the **State Lobster Hatchery** (*see* Off the Beaten Track, below). A left onto Highland Drive, after the drawbridge, takes you past **Crystal Lake** and the wildlife preserve that sur-
10 rounds it. Beyond the lake is **East Chop** and the **East Chop Lighthouse.** Built of cast iron in 1876 to replace an 1828 tower— used as part of a semaphore system between the island and Boston—that burned down, the 40-foot tower stands high atop a bluff from which the views of Nantucket Sound are spectacular.

Keeping to the coast road, you'll come eventually to **Oak Bluffs Harbor.** Once the setting for a number of grand hotels—the
11 1879 **Wesley Hotel** on Lake Avenue is the last of them—the still colorful harbor now specializes in gingerbread-trimmed guest houses and minimalls hawking fast food and souvenirs. This walking tour of town begins where Lake Avenue runs into Oak Bluffs Avenue (which ends at the steamship dock). Here is the
12 building that houses the **Flying Horses,** the nation's oldest carousel and a National Historic Landmark. Handcrafted in 1876, it offers small children entertainment from a Nintendo-less time; those who catch the brass ring ride free. While waiting in line, sample another old-time treat: sinfully sugary cotton can-

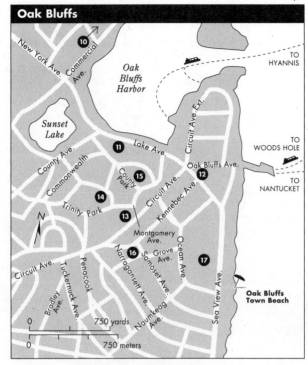

dy. In the waiting area are a number of 20th-century diversions: i.e., ping-ing arcade games. *Oak Bluffs Ave., tel. 508/ 693–9481. Rides cost $1; $8 for a book of 10. Open mid-June– Labor Day, daily 10–10; spring and fall, weekends only; closed in winter.*

Time Out | **Standby Diner** (Oak Bluffs Ave., tel. 508/693–5525), across the street, is light and bright, with lots of small-paned windows and a marble countertop salvaged from an old New Jersey diner by the owner/cook, Jack. Eggs and omelets are served all day, along with lunches and dinners of homemade soups (like pork-and-green-chili stew), burgers and clubs, and $6–$8 blue-plate specials (shepherd's pie, grilled pork chops, steak, fried chicken). Senior citizens get a 10% discount.

Just beyond the Flying Horses is Circuit Avenue, the center of the Oak Bluffs action, with most of the town's shops, bars, and restaurants. Here, on the right, you'll find the entrance to the **13 Oak Bluffs Camp Ground,** a 34-acre warren of streets tightly packed with more than 300 Carpenter Gothic Victorian cottages, gaily painted in pastels with wedding-cake trim. As you wander through this fairy-tale setting, imagine it at night, lit by the warm glow from hundreds of Japanese paper lanterns hung from every cottage porch as far as you can see. This is just what happens each summer on Illumination Night, when the end of the Camp Meeting season—attended these days by some fourth- and fifth-generation cottagers—is marked as it has been for more than a century, with lights, singing, and open houses for families and friends. (Because of overwhelming crowds of onlookers in seasons past, the date is not announced until the week before.)

⓮ As you enter the grounds, before you is the **Tabernacle,** an impressive open-air structure of iron at the center of Trinity Park. On Wednesdays at 8 PM in season, visitors are invited to join in on an old-time community sing. If you know tunes like "The Erie Canal" or just want to listen in (music books are available for a donation), drop by the Tabernacle and take a seat. Also in the park is the **Trinity Methodist Church,** built in 1878.

⓯ **The Cottage Museum,** now in a new home in an 1867 cream-and-orange cottage near the Tabernacle, exhibits cottage furnishings from the early days, including photographs, hooked rugs, quilts, and old Bibles. *1 Trinity Park, tel. 508/693–0525. Donations accepted. Open mid-Sept.–mid-June, Mon.–Sat. 10:30–3:30. Closed mid-Sept.–mid-June.*

Exit the Camp Ground as you entered, but don't leave until you've spotted what's called the Wooden Valentine (25 Washington Ave.); just think purple. At Circuit Avenue, cross the street and turn right. At the junction of the next street, again cross the street and head left. The octagonal building you see is

⓰ the **Union Chapel,** built in 1870 for the Cottage City resort folk who lived outside the Camp Ground's seven-foot-high fence. In summer, concerts are held here. Follow Grove Avenue to Ocean Avenue, a crescent of large Shingle Style cottages, with lots of

⓱ turrets, breezy porches, and pastel facades, circling **Ocean Park.** Band concerts take place at the gazebo here on summer nights, and in August, the park hosts hordes of island families and visitors for a grand fireworks display over the ocean, across Sea View Avenue.

Tour 3: Edgartown

Numbers in the margin correspond with points of interest on the Edgartown map.

The third main town is approached from Oak Bluffs via a scenic 6-mile section of Beach Road. On your left is Nantucket Sound and one of the island's best beach areas; soon the road narrows to an ever-eroding strip separating the Sound from Sengekontacket Pond, on your right. A protected bike path also runs the distance.

Edgartown, a world away from the honky-tonk of Oak Bluffs, is a tidy, polished town of upscale boutiques, elegant 17th- and 18th-century sea captains' houses, well-manicured lawns, and picturesque flower gardens. To orient yourself historically a bit before touring the town, you might want to stop off at a com-

⓲ plex of buildings and lawn exhibits belonging to the **Dukes County Historical Society.** The following service information applies to all the exhibits, which are detailed below. (You pay one fee at the entrance gate to the complex in season.) *Cooke St., corner of School St., tel. 508/627–4441. Admission: mid-June–mid-Sept., $2 adults, 50¢ children under 16; free rest of year. Open mid-June–mid-Sept., Tues.–Sat. 10–4:30; rest of year, Wed.–Fri. 1–4, Sat. 10–4.*

The one property open in summer only is the **Thomas Cooke House,** the society's museum, set in the 1765 home of a customs collector. The house itself is part of the display, including the

Edgartown

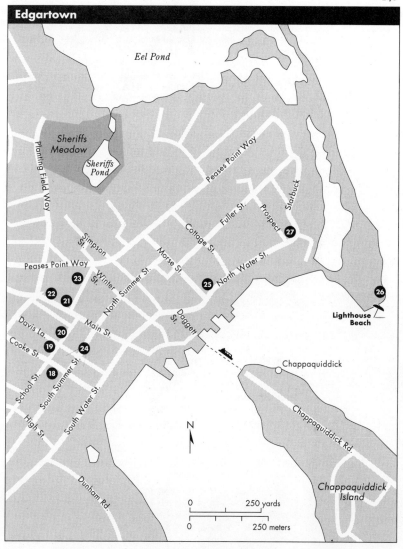

Charlotte Inn, **24**
Dr. Daniel Fisher
House, **22**
Dukes County
Historical Society, **18**

Edgartown
Lighthouse, **26**
86 N. Water St., **25**
Harbor View Hotel, **27**
Old Whaling
Church, **21**
60 Davis Lane, **19**
20 School St., **20**
Vincent House, **23**

low doorways, the wide-board floors, the original raised-panel woodwork with fluted pilasters, and the hearths in the summer and winter kitchens. Docents conduct tours of the 12 rooms, whose exhibits document the island's history through furniture, tools, costumes, portraits, toys, crafts, and various household objects. One room is set up as a 19th-century music room, illustrating the opulence of the golden age of whaling through such period pieces as a two-foot-long inlaid Swiss-movement music box and a pianoforte; another room simulates an early Camp Ground cottage room, with items donated by cottage owners, including clothing, games, furniture, and photographs of the early Camp Meeting days. Upstairs are ship models, whaling paraphernalia, and old customs documents.

The **Francis Foster Museum** houses a small collection of whaling implements, scrimshaw, navigational instruments, and lots of old photographs. One interesting exhibit is a collection of 19th-century miniature photographs of 110 Edgartown whaling masters, grouped by family. In the same building is the **Gale Huntington Library**, with genealogical records, rare island books, and ships' logs from the whaling days, plus some publications for sale.

The **Carriage Shed** displays a number of vehicles, including a whaleboat, a snazzy 1855 fire engine with stars inlaid in wood, and an 1830 hearse, considerably less ornate than the fire engine, and rightly so. The shed also houses some peculiar gravestones that once marked the eternal resting places of some strangely beloved chickens. In the yard outside it are a replica of a 19th-century **brick tryworks,** used to process whale oil from blubber aboard ship; and the 1,008-prism **Fresnel lens** installed in the Gay Head Lighthouse in 1854 and removed when the light was automated in 1952. In summer, the lens lamp is lit briefly on Sunday nights at 8, and the official lighthouse keeper is on hand to talk with aficionados about its operation.

The Historical Society sells an excellent walking-tour book ($2.95) that is full of anecdotes, as well as history, about the people who have lived in the houses along the route over the past three centuries. The following tour takes you along the most interesting streets.

⑲ Leaving the complex, proceed down School Street toward Main Street. On the left, at **60 Davis Lane,** is a handsome white-clap-board Greek Revival with black shutters, surrounded **⑳** bygardens. It was built in 1825 as a private school. At **20 School Street,** on the left, is a white monumental Greek Revival fronted with four big Doric columns; built as a Baptist church in 1839, it is now a private residence.

㉑ At the end of School Street, turn left onto Main Street. On the right, past Church Street, is the **Old Whaling Church,** begun in 1842 as a Methodist church and now the Performing Arts Center. The massive Greek Revival building has a six-column monumental portico, unusual three-sash windows, and a 92-foot clock tower that can be seen for miles.

㉒ Next door is the graceful **Dr. Daniel Fisher House,** with wrap-around roofwalk, small front portico with fluted columns topped by acanthus capitals, and a simple but elegant side portico with thin fluted columns. It was built in 1840 for one of the island's richest men, who was not only a doctor but also the owner of a whale-oil refinery, a spermaceti candle factory, and a gristmill, among other things. The house is now an office building.

In back of the Fisher House is one of the oldest dwellings on the island: the 1672 **Vincent House,** a weathered-shingle farmhouse ㉓ moved to this site in 1977, restored, and now maintained as an architectural museum. Most of the original glass, brick, and hardware remain, and parts of walls have been exposed to reveal such construction methods as wattle and daub. *Main St., tel. 508/627–8017. Donations welcome. Open June–Sept., weekdays 10–3; rest of year by appointment.*

Heading back down Main Street toward the harbor, you might turn right onto South Summer Street for a quick look at the gardens (in season) of the **Charlotte Inn,** one of the island's best ㉔ inns. The main inn, at No. 27, was built in 1865 for a whaling vessel owner and agent; the building across the street, at No. 28, is thought to be from the early 1700s and has an English garden out back.

Back on Main Street, take a right; here you enter the commercial district of Edgartown. Turn left onto North Water Street.

Time Out The **Daggett House** (59 N. Water St., tel. 508/627–4600; days and hours vary), on the right past the intersection of Daggett Street, is an inn, as it has been for most of its life since it was built in 1750. Breakfasts such as walnut French toast or pancakes with blueberry sauce are served in the cellar kitchen, which retains the flavor of the Colonial tavern it once was—or, as the walking-tour book puts it, "a favorite hangout for sailors." Raised-wood paneling surrounds the great hearth; a display cabinet holds antique tools. Small-pane windows look out onto a harbor-front garden.

The upper part of North Water Street is the most photographed strip of architecture in town, for its many very fine captains' houses. There's always some interesting detail you never noticed before—like a widow's walk with a mannequin poised, spyglass in hand, watching for her seafaring husband to return. The 1832 house where this piece of whimsy can be seen ㉕ is at **86 North Water Street,** which the Society for the Preservation of New England Antiquities, maintains as a rental property.

㉖ A right off North Water Street leads to the **Edgartown Lighthouse,** which is surrounded by a sandy public beach. The original light guarding the harbor was built in 1828 on an island made from granite blocks. The island was later connected to the mainland by a bridge. By the time the 1938 hurricane made a new light necessary, sand had filled in the gap between the island and the mainland. The current white-painted cast-iron tower was floated over from Ipswich, Massachusetts, on a barge in 1939.

Returning to North Water Street, a right leads to the gray-shingled Victorian **Harbor View Hotel,** on the left. Built in the ㉗ 1890s and a major player in the Vineyard's early resort days, the very upscale property was totally renovated in 1990, including the addition of such period details as a gazebo off the wraparound veranda and new turrets. This area, called Starbuck's Neck, is a good place to wander about in, with views of ocean, harbor, a little bay, and moorland. Return to town by continuing past the hotel and turning left onto Fuller Street.

Tour 4: Up-Island

Much of what makes the Vineyard special is found here, in the agricultural heart of the island and the largely undeveloped lands along the perimeter, from West Chop in the north to Edgartown in the southeast. Country roads meander through woods and tranquil farmland; dirt side roads lead past crystalline ponds, abandoned cranberry bogs, and conservation lands. In Chilmark, West Tisbury, and Gay Head, nature lovers, writers, artists, and others have established close ongoing summer communities. In winter, the isolation and bitter winds send even many year-round Vineyarders from their Up-Island homes to places in the Down-Island towns.

Numbers in the margin correspond with numbered points of interest on the Up-Island map.

This tour starts from State Road in Vineyard Haven (from Oak Bluffs, take Beach Road west to State Road). Just outside the center of town, on the right just past Sears, is a turnout. Called the Tashmoo Overlook, it is a scenic viewpoint overlooking a meadow leading down to Lake Tashmoo and Vineyard Sound beyond.

Less than a mile past the upper end of Lambert's Cove Road, take a left onto Stoney Hill Road. (From Edgartown, take the Edgartown–Vineyard Haven Road west; after Barnes Road, you'll come to Stoney Hill Road on the left.) Down this woodsy **28** lane is **The Winery at Chicama Vineyards** (tel. 508/693–0309). From 35 acres of trees and rocks, the Mathiesen family— George, a broadcaster from San Francisco; his wife, Cathy; and their six children—have created a vineyard, starting in 1971 with 75 vinifera vines. Today the winery produces 75,000 bottles a year, from chardonnay, cabernet, Riesling, Pinot noir, and other European grapes. Free tours and tastings are given daily Memorial Day–Columbus Day; tastings only for the rest of the year on a limited schedule (call for details). A country-store-type shop selling wines and herbed vinegars, mustards, jellies, and other foods prepared on the premises is open year-round (closed July 4 and Labor Day). A Christmas shop with glassware, gift baskets, wreaths, and more is open mid-November through New Year's Eve.

Down the road a bit is **Thimble Farm** (tel. 508/693–6396), with pick-your-own—or already boxed, if you're not feeling so rural—strawberries and raspberries in season (mid-June–early Oct.; closed Mon.). Also available are cut flowers and melons grown here.

Return to State Road and bear right at the next fork, remaining on State Road. On the right you'll pass the lower entrance to Lambert's Cove Road, an attractive country road flanked by woods and small ponds. Just beyond is Indian Hill Road, also on **29** the right; turning into a dirt road, this leads to the **Mayhew Chapel and Indian Burial Ground.** The small chapel, built in 1829 to replace an earlier one, and a memorial plaque are dedicated to the pastor Thomas Mayhew, Jr., leader of the original colonists, who landed at Edgartown in 1642. Mayhew was an enlightened man, noted for his fair dealings with the local

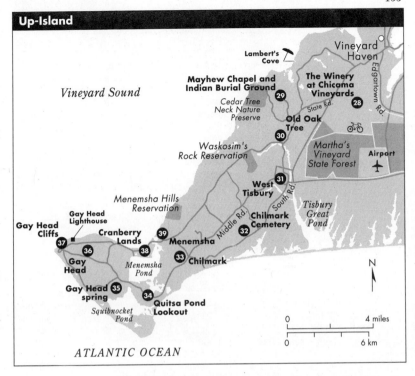

Up-Island

Vineyard Sound

Lambert's Cove

Mayhew Chapel and
Indian Burial Ground **29**

*Cedar Tree
Neck Nature
Preserve*

The Winery
at Chicama
Vineyards **28**

State Rd.

Old Oak
Tree **30**

*Waskosim's
Rock Reservation*

*Martha's
Vineyard
State Forest*

Airport

31
West
Tisbury

*Tisbury
Great
Pond*

*Menemsha Hills
Reservation*

Gay Head **Gay Head
Cliffs** Lighthouse

**Cranberry
Lands**

39
Menemsha

Middle Rd.

Chilmark
Cemetery **32**

37
36
**Gay
Head**

38
*Menemsha
Pond*

33 Chilmark

**Gay Head
spring** **35**

34
**Quitsa Pond
Lookout**

*Squibnocket
Pond*

N

ATLANTIC OCEAN

0   4 miles

0   6 km

Wampanoags. Within a few years, he had converted a number of them to Christianity; called Praying Indians, they established a community here called Christiantown.

Near the chapel is a wildflower garden, and beyond the boulder with the plaque are stones marking Indian grave mounds (the dead are not named, for fear of calling down evil spirits). Behind the chapel is the beginning of a loop trail through the woods (there's a map at the first trail fork), which leads to a lookout tower.

A right just before you rejoin State Road leads to the **Cedar Tree Neck** nature preserve (*see* Nature Areas, below). Back on State Road, turn right. Soon thereafter you'll pass, on the right, **Takemmy Farm** (*see* What to See and Do with Children, below)—keep an eye out for llamas by the fence on the right. At the intersection of North Road is what's fondly known as the **30** **Old Oak Tree**, a massive, ancient oak that is an island landmark.

31 Soon State Road brings you into the center of **West Tisbury**. For centuries a sheep-farming region, the town continues its agricultural tradition with several active horse and produce farms; it also encompasses most of the 4,000-acre **State Forest**. West Tisbury's center looks very much the small New England village, complete with white, steepled church. **Alley's General Store** (State Rd., tel. 508/693-0088), here since 1858, sells everything from hammers and dill pickles to art—the **Gallery at Alley's**, with changing exhibits, is out back.

Time Out Also behind Alley's General Store, next to the gallery, is **Back Alley's** (tel. 508/693-7366), serving gourmet sandwiches and pastries to go year-round.

Past the mansard-roofed town hall is the **Agricultural Hall**, where a county fair, including livestock and produce judging, is held in August (*see* Festivals and Seasonal Events in Chapter 1, Essential Information), and weekly farmer's markets are held in summer (*see* Shopping, below). Across the street is the **Field Gallery** (tel. 508/693–5595), where Tom Maley's large white sculptures, like a colonial horse and rider or a whimsical piper, are displayed on a wide lawn. Inside are changing summer exhibitions of island artists. Just after the First Congregational Church, on the right, is **Music Street,** a street of old sea captains' homes once noted for a preponderance of pianos.

About 2 miles out of West Tisbury center, on the right, is **32 Chilmark Cemetery,** where John Belushi is buried. His tree-shaded grave, near the entrance, is marked by a boulder in which his name is deeply engraved. Visitors often leave tokens of remembrance, such as small candles or shells. Lillian Hellman, a longtime summer resident of the island, is also buried here. Two miles past the cemetery, a dirt road on the left leads to **Lucy Vincent Beach,** perhaps the island's most beautiful.

The crossroads you soon come to is called **Beetlebung Corner,** named for the stand of beetlebung, or black gum, trees on your **33** right). This is the center of **Chilmark,** whose scenic ocean-view roads, rustic woodlands, and lack of crowds has drawn chic summer visitors and, hard on their heels, stratospheric real-estate prices. Everyone meets, eventually, at Beetlebung—in the town hall, the library, the firehouse, a small store, a new deli, or the **Chilmark Community Center,** where everything from auctions to dances to chamber music concerts are held in summer.

Continue on State Road. After a bend, on the right you'll come **34** to the **Quitsa Pond Lookout,** with a good view of the adjoining Menemsha and Nashaquitsa ponds, the woods, and the ocean beyond. Just beyond the Gay Head town line, on the left, is the **35 Gay Head spring;** from an iron pipe gushes pure, fresh water cold enough to slake a cyclist's thirst on the hottest day. Feel free to fill a canteen; locals come from all over the island to fill jugs.

36 Gay Head is an official Native American township: In 1987, after more than a decade of struggle in the courts, the Wampanoag tribe won guardianship of 420 acres of Gay Head land, which are being held in trust by the federal government in perpetuity and constitute the Gay Head Native American Reservation.

At the fork beyond the spring, take a left onto Moshup's Trail, the coastal route, with views of dunes and sea. In this area is the very private 380-acre estate bought by Jacqueline Onassis in the mid-1970s. A stretch of beachfront property belonging to individual Wampanoags but surrounded by her land was for years the cause of much legal dispute. The Wampanoags considered the ground hallowed, as the final resting place of tribal founder Chief Moshup and his wife, Squant, but were unable to reach it except by trespassing on Onassis land. In 1990 a compromise was reached, involving the exchange of another piece of sacred ground for the disputed beachfront, along with a cash settlement.

㊲ Continue to the western tip of the island and the **Gay Head Cliffs,** a National Historic Landmark and part of the Native American reservation land. These dramatically striated walls of red clay are the island's major tourist attraction, as evidenced by the tour bus–filled parking lot. Native American crafts and food shops line the approach to the overlook, from which you can see across the Elizabeth Islands and Noman's Land Island (part wildlife preserve, part military bombing-practice site—with fake bombs) across Vineyard Sound.

Time Out The **Aquinnah** (tel. 508/645–9654), at the end of the row of shops, is an Native American–owned restaurant with a great view—of the 135-foot cliffs over which it is perched, of the long white stretch of beach far below, of the sea and islands, and of the spectacular sunsets over the water. Highlights of the simple menu are fresh fish, and homemade chowder and pies.

Adjacent to the overlook is the **Gay Head Lighthouse** (the largest of the Vineyard's five), precariously stationed atop the rapidly eroding cliffs. In 1798, a wood lighthouse was built here—the island's first—to warn ships away from Devil's Bridge, an area of shoals ¼-mile offshore. The current incarnation, built in 1856 of red brick, carries on with its alternating pattern of red and white flashes. Despite the light, the Vineyard's worst wreck occurred here in January 1884, when the *City of Columbus* sank, taking with it into the icy waters more than 100 passengers and crew. The original Fresnel lens was removed when the lighthouse was automated in 1952, but it is preserved at the Dukes County Historical Society in Edgartown (*see* Tour 3: Edgartown, above).

Head out from the cliffs area by the State Road, which will take you past the "center" of Gay Head. This consists of a combination fire and police station, the town hall, a Tribal Council office, and a public library, formerly the little red schoolhouse (because the town's year-round population is only about 360, Gay Head children attend schools in other towns). A left onto Lobsterville Road and a right onto West Basin Road take you
㊳ along the shore of Menemsha Bight and through the **Cranberry Lands,** an area of cranberry bog gone wild that is a popular nesting site for birds. No humans can nest here, but you can drive by and look. At the end of the road is a terrific view of the
㊴ back of the quiet fishing village of **Menemsha.**

Return to State Road via Lobsterville Road, and at Beetlebung Corner, follow signs to Menemsha. If you think you've seen it before, you probably have: It was used for location shots in the film *Jaws.* The jumble of small fishing and pleasure boats and the drying nets and lobster pots create a picturesque scene not lost on myriad photographers and artists. But this is very much a working village. The catch of the day can be bought from markets along Dutcher's Dock, or from the restaurant Home Port (*see* Dining, below). Along with fishing shacks, you'll find a Texaco station where locals gather for morning coffee, a few crafts and clothing boutiques, good fishing from the jetty, and a public beach to which romantics repair for picnic suppers before watching the miraculous sunsets over the water. Local boat owners sometimes charter themselves out for fishing excursions, trips to Cuttyhunk, or whatever (ask at the Texaco station, or call the harbormaster at 508/645–2846).

Back at Beetlebung, turn left onto **Middle Road** to enjoy pastoral Chilmark at its best, with gently rolling farmland and woodland marked off by low stone fences, as well as ocean views here and there from elevated points. A right at the end of Middle Road brings you back to West Tisbury center, from which roads lead anywhere you want to go on the island.

What to See and Do with Children

Flying Horses Carousel, Oak Bluffs (*see* Tour 2: Oak Bluffs, above).

Children's Theatre in Oak Bluffs (at the high school, Edgartown–Vineyard Haven Rd., tel. 508/693–4060) has performances by and for children daily 9–1 in season.

Vineyard Playhouse (*see* The Arts, below) has children's events—fairy tales, juggling, theater games—Saturday mornings in season.

Windfarm Museum is an unusual introduction to nonpolluting sources of energy, with working windmills, hands-on exhibits, and a lived-in, solar-heated, energy-self-sufficient house. Daily 1½-hour programs on the history and future of energy use end for children with a ride in a donkey cart; they can also pet the farm animals. *Edgartown Rd., 2 mi out of Vineyard Haven, tel. 508/693–3658. Admission: $4 adults, $3 children. Open only for programs: June–Sept., daily at 2:30 PM (sometimes an extra program in high season); Oct., some weekends at 2:30. Closed Nov.–May.*

Storytelling hours for children are offered by all the island's libraries. Call about days and times: **Chilmark** (Beetlebung Corner, tel. 508/645–3360), **Edgartown** (N. Water St., tel. 508/627–4221), **Oak Bluffs** (Circuit Ave., tel. 508/693–9433), **Vineyard Haven** (Upper Main St., tel. 508/693–9721), and **West Tisbury** (Music St., tel. 508/693–3366).

Oak Bluffs has all kinds of attractions for kids, aside from the carousel arcade. **The Locker Room** (Circuit Ave., tel. 508/693–6456; closed in winter) carries T-shirts and caps of all kinds of sports teams; tons of baseball cards from 1910 on for collectors, plus packs of new cards; and lots of goofy candy, like wax lips, "Slime Slurp," and gum that crackles. **South Pole Slush Co.** (Circuit Ave., tel. 508/693–2262) has at least 20 flavors of slush, like canteloupe, tangerine, and piña colada, plus comic books, cool sunglasses, and tons of candy.

Gymnastics and movement day camps for children from age 3½ through high school are available in one-week programs through the U.S. Academy of Gymnastics (Sept.–mid-June, 11 Allen Rd., Norwalk, CT 06851, tel. 203/847–4994; mid-June–Aug., Box 2271, Vineyard Haven 02568, tel. 508/693–5225).

At **Katama Farm** (Katama Rd., toward South Beach, Edgartown, tel. 508/627–9272), a working dairy farm, children can go for a free ride on a wagon pulled by Belgian horses, buy fresh ice cream, watch cows be milked, or pet the wolfhound puppies, goats, or other farm animals that are always around. The farm is open daily year-round; wagon rides are given by appointment on weekends from mid-May to mid-June, daily 2–5 PM from mid-June through September.

At the **Chilmark Community Center** (Beetlebung Corner, tel. 508/645–9484) there are events for children of all ages in summer, including dances, tennis tournaments, concerts, and arts events. It's a great place for kids to meet other kids.

Felix Neck Wildlife Sanctuary (*see* Nature Areas, below) runs the **Fern & Feather Day Camp**, with one- or two-week sessions in which children learn about wildlife, plants, and the stars; camping trips are offered.

From 1 to 5 on Wednesday and Saturday afternoons year-round, kids are invited to visit with the llamas at **Takemmy Farm** (State Rd., North Tisbury, tel. 508/693–2486). Every day year-round, the farm stand sells eggs, as well as natural wool (no colors) from the farm's Columbia sheep; in season, there are vegetables and honey as well.

Off the Beaten Track

The **Nathan Mayhew Seminars** (167 N. William St., Box 1125, Vineyard Haven 02568, tel. 508/693–6603) offer college-level two-day to seven-week courses in humanities, social science, business, and visual and performing arts year-round. The **Henry Beetle Hough Memorial Library,** in the Nathan Mayhew Seminars building, is a research library of more than 10,000 volumes focusing on island studies (same phone; open by appointment year-round). The basis of the collection is the personal library of the Pulitzer Prize–winning journalist who was editor of the *Vineyard Gazette* from 1920 to 1985.

A memorial to Thomas Mayhew, Jr.—called **Place on the Wayside**—was erected on the Edgartown–West Tisbury Road, just east of the airport entrance, on the opposite side. A plaque identifies the spot where Mayhew had his "last worship and interview with them before embarking for England" in 1657, never to return—"no tidings ever coming from the ship or its passengers." (The ship was lost at sea.) According to the Daughters of the American Revolution, who erected the plaque, Wampanoags passing this spot would leave a stone in Mayhew's memory; the stones were later cemented together to form the memorial.

June through August, the **State Lobster Hatchery** (end of Shirley Ave. on Lagoon Pond, Oak Bluffs, tel. 508/693–0060) allows weekday tours of its visitor room, with hatching and rearing tanks and wall displays. The hatchery stocks all of coastal Massachusetts and conducts research on marine life.

Martha's Vineyard Shellfish Group (New York Ave., Oak Bluffs, tel. 508/693–0391) grows seed clams, scallops, and oysters to stock lagoons and beds throughout the country. From spring through fall, tours can be arranged with advance notice.

The **Cape Poge Lighthouse** is far away from just about everything, at the end of the sandspit that constitutes the Cape Poge Wildlife Refuge (*see* Nature Areas, below). This is a location that just does not want a lighthouse. The first was built here in 1802; since then several lights have been swept into the sea or destroyed, despite 10 moves farther inland. In the latest move, in 1987, the present 65-foot-high wood light, which was built in

1922 and casts a light that can be seen for 12 miles, was lifted by helicopter and moved back hundreds of feet. The only access is by four-wheel-drive vehicle (once the Dyke Bridge is repaired) or boat.

Shopping

The Vineyard's long attraction for artists and craftsmen has resulted in an abundance of shops and galleries selling their exceptional wares. A specialty of the island is wampum—black, white, or purple beads made from shells that are fashioned into jewelry—sold at the cliffs and elsewhere. Antique and new scrimshaw jewelry and the ultra-expensive, sometimes scrimshaw-topped pocketbooks called Nantucket lightship baskets can be found at many island shops.

Most Vineyard shops close for the winter, though quite a few in Vineyard Haven remain open; in the off-season, call to make sure a shop is open before making a special trip.

Shopping Districts The three main towns have the largest concentrations of shops. Most of Vineyard Haven's line Main Street. Edgartown's, perhaps the toniest, are clustered together within a few blocks of the dock, on Main, Summer, and Water streets. Primarily fun, casual clothing, and gift shops line Circuit Avenue in Oak Bluffs. At Gay Head Cliffs, you'll find Native American crafts and souvenirs.

Shopping Complexes **Tisbury Marketplace,** on Beach Road between Oak Bluffs and Vineyard Haven, has a dozen specialty shops, including crafts and gift shops, a toy store, and a sporting-goods shop. In Edgartown, the **Colonial Inn Shops** (38 N. Water St.) sell art, crafts, and sports gear; the larger **Nevin Square** (Winter St.) has leather, sports, and other clothing, plus art, antiques, toys, and crafts. **Crispin's Landing** in Vineyard Haven (Main St.) has shops selling leather, pottery, jewelry, and crafts.

Department Store **The Fligors** (27 N. Water St., Edgartown, tel. 508/627–8811) is the closest thing to a department store on the island, with varied offerings, including preppy clothing and a bargain basement.

Food and Flea Markets A **flea market** is held on the grounds of the Chilmark Community Center (Beetlebung Corner, tel. 508/645–9484) Wednesday and Saturday in season until 2:30 or 3 PM. From spring into October, **farmer's markets**—offering fresh flowers, plants, fruits and vegetables, homemade baked goods and jams, honey, and fun—are held at the Agricultural Hall on South Road in West Tisbury Saturday from 9 to noon and at Waban Park in Oak Bluffs on Wednesday from 4 to 6 PM.

Specialty Stores
Antiques
All Things Oriental (Beach Rd., Vineyard Haven, tel. 508/693–0190) has jewelry, porcelains, paintings, and more.
Auntie's Attic (Edgartown, tel. 508/627–9833) sells mostly New England furniture, clothing, lace, quilts, collectibles, and jewelry.
Bramhall & Dunn (Main St., Vineyard Haven, tel. 508/693–6437) carries stripped 19th-century English country pine furniture and objects, garden statuary, crafts, and housewares.
C. W. Morgan Marine Antiques (off State Rd., West Tisbury, tel. 508/693–3622) offers a wide range of nautical items; it is open by appointment only.

Red Barn Emporium (Old County Rd., West Tisbury, tel. 508/
693–0455) displays its country antiques in settings, with the
Granary Gallery's paintings (*see* Art, below) as complements.
Soulagnet Collection (Colonial Inn Shops, Edgartown, tel. 508/
627–7759; Basin Rd., Menemsha, tel. 508/645–3735; Tisbury
Inn, Beach Rd. at Main St., Vineyard Haven, tel. 508/693–
6020) has Americana, from high-end furniture to Fiestaware,
folk art, and clocks.

Art The **Edgartown Art Gallery** (27 S. Summer St., Edgartown, tel.
508/627–5991), in the Charlotte Inn, has 19th- and 20th-centu-
ry oils and watercolors, including English sporting prints, marine art, and works by local artists, plus small English
antiques.
Goff's Gallery & Book Store (State Rd., North Tisbury, tel.
508/693–4484) sells books by Vineyard writers, Clark Goff's
New England–theme prints and notepapers, Heather Goff's
painted pottery (including her signature plates with farm-
scapes, cows, and other Vineyard scenes), and Ingrid Goff's
jewelry—a complete island and family enterprise.
Granary Gallery (Old County Rd., West Tisbury, tel. 508/693–
0455 or 800/343–0471) showcases works by island artists, including folk art textiles and the photographs of Alfred
Eisenstaedt.
Hermine Merel Smith Gallery (Edgartown Rd., West Tisbury,
tel. 508/693–7719) specializes in the work of contemporary
American impressionists.
Spirits Rising (158 Circuit Ave., Oak Bluffs, tel. 508/693–6616)
has "unique and magical" art and crafts, such as Native American jewelry and pottery, crystals, fetishes, local photography,
and hunting knives with deer-horn handles inlaid with turquoise and coral.

Books The **Bunch of Grapes Bookstore** (Main St., Vineyard Haven,
tel. 508/693–2291) and **Bickerton & Ripley Books** (Main St.,
Edgartown, tel. 508/627–8463) carry a wide selection of new
books, including many island-related titles, and sponsor frequent book signings—watch the papers for announcements.
Book Den East (Vineyard Haven Rd., Oak Bluffs, tel. 508/693–
3946) has 20,000 out-of-print, antiquarian, and paperback
books housed in an old barn.

Clothing **Amelia Bloomers** (Main St., Vineyard Haven, tel. 508/693–
9064) specializes in lingerie and also has dance wear, T-shirts,
and more.
Army Barracks (152 Circuit Ave., Oak Bluffs, tel. 508/693–
6846) has army and navy surplus.
Bramhall & Dunn (*see* Antiques, above) in Vineyard Haven carries fine hand-knit sweaters.
Laughing Bear (138 Circuit Ave., Oak Bluffs, tel. 508/693–
9342) has fun children's and women's wear made of Balinese or
Indian batiks and other unusual materials.
Murray's of the Vineyard (Main St., Vineyard Haven, tel. 508/
693–2640) has men and women's fashions, shoes, and accessories, from names such as Ralph Lauren and Liz Claiborne.
Nature Knits (94 Main St., Vineyard Haven, tel. 508/693–7776;
115 Circuit Ave., Oak Bluffs, tel. 508/693–8788) sells natural-
fiber clothing for children, size infant through 14.
Vintage Clothing (Union St., Vineyard Haven, just up from the
ferry, tel. 508/693–7772) has just that, for men and women.

Crafts **Edgartown Scrimshaw** (Main St., tel. 508/627–9439) carries a large collection of scrimshaw, including some antique pieces, as well as Nantucket lightship baskets and jewelry.

Handworks (Nevin Square Shops, Winter St., Edgartown, tel. 508/627–8402) has jewelry, pottery, toys, dollhouses, and more.

Michaela Ltd. Gallery of American Crafts (Towanticut Ave., Oak Bluffs, tel. 508/693–8408) has pottery, blown glass, and jewelry.

Indian & Mexican Crafts (128 Circuit Ave., Oak Bluffs, tel. 508/693–4040) has shells and Indian jewelry in turquoise and silver, plus colorful Colombian *retalbo*, wood-and-ceramic shadow-boxes with doors that open to reveal figures of little people.

Gifts **Black Dog Bakery** (*see* Tour 1: Vineyard Haven, above) sells T-shirts, sweatshirts, beach towels, and many other gift items, all emblazoned with the signature Black Dog logo.

Chilmark Chocolates (State Rd., near Beetlebung Corner, tel. 508/645–3013) sells superior chocolates and buttercrunch that you can sometimes watch being made in the back room.

The Secret Garden (148 Circuit Ave., Oak Bluffs, tel. 508/693–4759), set in a yellow gingerbread cottage, has linens, lace, quilts, baby gifts, wicker furniture, island watercolors, and more.

Tashtego (29 Main St., Edgartown, tel. 508/627–4300) is one of the island's most interesting shops, with small antiques, island crafts, and home furnishings.

At **Vineyard Photo Emporium** (Circuit Ave., Oak Bluffs, tel. 508/693–6435), you can have your picture taken in costume before exotic backdrops; inexpensive sepia prints make fun gifts.

Jewelry **Sioux Eagle Designs** (Crispin's Landing, Main St., Vineyard Haven, tel. 508/693–6537) offers exotic Indian pieces.

Vivian Wolfe & Co. (Main St., Edgartown, tel. 508/627–5822) has antique and estate jewelry.

Sporting Goods Two **Wind's Up!** shops (Tisbury Market Place, Beach Rd., Vineyard Haven, tel. 508/693–4340, year-round; Dock St., Edgartown, tel. 508/627–5886, June–Sept.) sell swimwear, windsurfing and sailing equipment, and other outdoor gear.

Brickman's (Main St., Vineyard Haven, tel. 508/693–0047; Main St., Edgartown, tel. 508/627–4700) sells beach and sports gear, such as camping, fishing, snorkeling equipment and boogie boards; also sportswear and surfer-type clothing.

Sports and Outdoor Activities

Edgartown Recreation Area (Robinson Rd., tel. 508/627–8594) has five tennis courts, a basketball court, a baseball/softball field, a picnic area, and playground equipment. All areas are lighted and available for evening use in the summer. Activities (published in the paper) include tennis instruction and tournaments; softball, soccer, and basketball games; arts and crafts; and rainy-day events. Also see the "Island Recreation" section of *The Vineyard Gazette*'s calendar for announcements of open Frisbee, rugby, and other games.

Bicycling There are paved paths along the coast road from Oak Bluffs to Edgartown, inland from Vineyard Haven to Edgartown, and from Edgartown to South Beach. Any of these connect with scenic paths that weave through the State Forest.

The biggest race of the year is the **Tour of Martha's Vineyard** (tel. 508/693–0085), held on Tivoli Day in September, and beginning and ending in Oak Bluffs. The 60-mile race attracts 7,000 contestants from all over the world. For information on unofficial group rides, call Cycleworks (tel. 508/693–6966).

Cross-country Skiing   **Farm Neck Golf Club** (*see* Golf, below) allows skiing on its "course" when there's enough snow, though the question doesn't come up often.

Fishing   Huge trawlers unload their catch daily at the docks in Vineyard Haven and Menemsha, attesting to the richness of the waters surrounding the island. One of the most popular spots for sport fishermen is **Wasque Point** (*see* Nature Areas, below) on Chappaquiddick. Another is **South Beach** (*see* Beaches, below) and the jetty at the mouth of the **Menemsha Basin.** Striped bass and bluefish are island stars, best caught in spring, early summer, and cool weeks in October.

Join in on the annual **Martha's Vineyard Striped Bass & Bluefish Derby** (Box 2101, Edgartown 02539, tel. 508/693–1881) from mid-September to mid-October, with daily, weekly, and derby prizes in four categories, from boat or shore.

Pick up the current listing of fishing regulations—along with all kinds of other information—at a tackle shop, such as **Larry's Tackle Shop** (25 Dock St., Edgartown, tel. 508/627–5088), **Coop's Bait and Tackle** (147 West Tisbury Rd., Edgartown, tel. 508/627–3909), and **Dick's Bait and Tackle** (New York Ave., Oak Bluffs, tel. 508/693–7669). All rent gear and sell accessories and bait.

A number of party boats leave Oak Bluffs Harbor in season, including the *Skipper* (tel. 508/693–1238). *Moonshark* (tel. 508/693–7235) in Oak Bluffs and **Ruddy Duck Marine** (tel. 508/627–4709) in Edgartown offer fishing charters, as do a number of boats out of Menemsha (call the harbormaster at 508/645–2846).

Golf   **Farm Neck Golf Club** (Farm Neck Rd., Oak Bluffs, tel. 508/693–3057), a semiprivate club on Sengekontacket Pond, has 18 holes in a championship layout, including two holes near water, plus a driving range. The public **Mink Meadows Golf Course** (Franklin St., Vineyard Haven, tel. 508/693–0600), on West Chop, has nine holes.

Health and Fitness Clubs   **Health Club at Tisbury Inn** (Main St., Vineyard Haven, tel. 508/693–7400) has an indoor lap pool, sauna, exercise and cardiovascular equipment, free weights, tanning booths, and aerobics classes. Monthly memberships are available.
Island Health Club (Post Office Sq., Edgartown, tel. 508/627–7760) offers day use of its facilities: Nautilus, Universal, Lifecycle, and Stair Climber machines; treadmills and Concept II rowers; aerobics classes; tanning; personal trainers; massage.

Hiking   The nature preserves and conservation areas (*see* Nature Areas, below) are laced with well-marked, scenic trails through varied terrains and ecological habitats. The miles of uninterrupted beaches are perfect for long walks.

Horseback Riding   **Misty Meadows Horse Farm** (Old County Rd., West Tisbury, tel. 508/693–1870) has a large indoor riding area and offers trail rides and lessons. **Eastover Farms** (across from the airport, off the West Tisbury–Edgartown Rd., West Tisbury, tel. 508/693–3770) offers English and Western riding lessons; it also has indoor and outdoor rings, a hunt course, and beach and other trails. Dawn, sunset, and moonlight rides are available. At either stable, be sure to call ahead to reserve. **Arrowhead Farm** (Indian Hill Rd., West Tisbury, tel. 508/693–8831) offers two- to nine-week horsemanship programs for children 6–14 in summer. The **State Forest** (*see* Nature Areas, below) has horse trails through it.

Ice Skating **Martha's Vineyard Ice Arena** (Edgartown–Vineyard Haven Rd., Oak Bluffs, tel. 508/693–4438) is open from late November through March.

Jogging The **State Forest** (*see* Nature Areas, below) has a 2-mile parcourse—adjacent to the high school—that's free for public use during daylight hours.

Sailing Lessons and rentals are available at the **Harborside Inn** in Edgartown (S. Water St., tel. 508/627–4321; also rents Boston Whalers), and at **Wind's Up!** (Tisbury Market Place, tel. 508/693–4340, and next to Portside Restaurant by Lagoon Pond, tel. 508/693–4252, both on Beach Rd., Vineyard Haven).

Scuba-diving The waters around the Vineyard hold a number of sunken ships, including several schooners and freighters off East Chop. **Leonardo's Scuba Supply** (5 Circuit Ave., Oak Bluffs, tel. 508/693–0288) has scuba and snorkeling information and equipment.

Shellfishing Each town issues shellfish licenses for the waters under its jurisdiction. Contact the town hall of the town in which you wish to fish for a permit, as well as information on good spots and a listing of areas closed because of seeding projects or contamination: **Chilmark** (tel. 508/645–2651), **Edgartown** (tel. 508/627–4033), **Gay Head** (tel. 508/645–9915), **Oak Bluffs** (tel. 508/693–5511), **Vineyard Haven** (tel. 508/693–4200), and **West Tisbury** (tel. 508/693–9659).

Tennis Tennis is very popular on the island, and at all times reservations are strongly recommended. Public courts (reserve court with the attendant the previous day) are on Church Street in Vineyard Haven (clay courts; in season only; fee), in Niantic Park in Oak Bluffs, on Robinson Road in Edgartown, and at the grammar school on Old County Road in West Tisbury (all hard surface; open year-round; fee in season). Courts at the Chilmark Community Center on South Road (tel. 508/645–3061) are available in season.

Farm Neck Tennis Club (County Rd., Oak Bluffs, tel. 508/693–9728; open mid-Apr.–mid-Nov.) is a semiprivate club with four Har-Tru courts. **Island Country Club** (Beach Rd., Oak Bluffs, tel. 508/693–6574; open May–Thanksgiving) has three Har-Tru courts.

Water Sports Martha's Vineyard is an ideal place for windsurfing. With the many bays and inlets there is always a patch of protected water for the neophyte; the oceanside surf provides plenty of action for the expert. Surfing is good at South Beach and Long Point. Coast Guard–licensed captain **Mark Clarke** (tel. 508/693–2838) offers waterskiing lessons and rides at all skill levels on the *M.V. Ski*.

Wind's Up! (*see* Sailing, above) provides windsurfing and sailing lessons and rentals, plus an invaluable brochure on windsurfing, including best locations and safety tips.

Vineyard Boat Rentals (Dockside Marina, Oak Bluffs, tel. 508/693–8476) offers Boston Whalers, Jet Skis, and parasailing.

Beaches

The beaches on the south shore, on the Atlantic Ocean, offer strong surf. Those on the Nantucket or Vineyard soundside tend to be protected and calmer. Inns sometimes make available to guests a parking sticker for town beaches that are otherwise limited to residents; these restricted beaches are often much less crowded than the popular public beaches, and some, such as Lucy Vincent and Lambert's Cove, are the most beautiful. There are, however, miles of superb public beaches on which a couple minutes' walk will get you away from the crowds.

Public **Bend-in-the-Road Beach,** Edgartown's town beach, is a protected area (marked by floats) adjacent to the state beach, beginning at, appropriately enough, the bend in the road. The beach, backed by low, grassy dunes and wild roses, offers calm, shallow waters, some parking, and lifeguards. It can be reached by bike path or shuttle bus.

East Beach, on Chappaquiddick Island, one of the area's best beaches, is part of the Cape Poge Wildlife Refuge and Wasque Reservation (*see* Nature Areas, below). It offers heavy surf, good bird-watching, and relative isolation in a lovely setting, but it is accessible only by boat or four-wheel-drive vehicle.

Joseph A. Sylvia State Beach, between Oak Bluffs and Edgartown, is a mile-long sandy beach with a view of Cape Cod across Nantucket Sound. The calm, warm water makes it popular with families. There's parking along the roadside, and the beach is accessible by bike path or shuttle bus.

Lake Tashmoo Town Beach, at the end of Herring Creek Road in Vineyard Haven, offers swimming in the warm, relatively shallow brackish lake or in the cooler Vineyard Sound, with gentle waves.

Lighthouse Beach, a 10-minute walk from Edgartown center along North Water Street, is a protected, sandy beach good for children. The sailboats and fishing boats in the harbor and the lighthouse make a picturesque setting.

Lobsterville Beach is 2 miles of beautiful sandy barrier beach and dune land on the Vineyard Sound in Gay Head. It is a seagull nesting area and a favorite fishing spot. Though the water tends to be cold, the beach is protected and suitable for children.

Long Point (*see* Nature Areas, below) has a beautiful beach on the Atlantic, as well as freshwater and saltwater ponds for swimming, including the brackish Tisbury Great Pond.

Menemsha Public Beach, adjacent to Dutcher's Dock, is a pebbly beach with gentle surf on Vineyard Sound. Located on the western side of the island, it is a great place to catch the sunset.

Moshup's Beach, in Gay Head, off Moshup's Trail, is a Land Bank property open to the public, offering surf and sand backed by low grasses. There are rest rooms in the cliffs' parking lot. From the lot, signs lead along a boardwalk path, past a scenic overlook, to the beach, a five-minute walk away. Heading to the right along the shore, you can walk eventually to the beach below the cliffs, but PLEASE, *do not climb them!* The cliffs are eroding much too quickly even *without* the added stress of human erosion tactics.

Oak Bluffs Town Beach, by the steamship dock and ending at State Beach, is a crowded, narrow stretch of calm water on Nantucket Sound, with snack joints, lifeguards, and parking.

Owen Park Beach, a small harbor beach off Main Street in Vineyard Haven, is a convenient spot, with a children's play area, lifeguards, and a harbor view.

South Beach (a.k.a. Katama Beach), the island's largest and most popular, is a 3-mile ribbon of sand on the Atlantic, with strong surf and sometimes riptides (check with the lifeguards before swimming). From Edgartown, take the bike path to Katama or catch the trolley. There is limited parking. The beach is a good spot for expert windsurfers and for body surfers, but it is not good for board surfing because the waves break close to shore. Activities such as sand-castle-building contests and nature walks are held on the beach throughout the summer.

Restricted **Lambert's Cove Beach** (West Tisbury), one of the island's prettiest, has fine sand and very clear water. On the Vineyard Sound side, it has calm waters good for children and views of the Elizabeth Islands.

Lucy Vincent Beach (Chilmark), on the south shore, is a very beautiful, wide strand of fine sand and surf overlooked by high clay bluffs. Keep walking to the right for the unofficial nude beach.

Philbin Beach is Gay Head's town beach, adjacent to Moshup's in the direction opposite the cliffs.

Squibnocket Beach (Chilmark), on the south shore, offers a rocky coast, surf, fine sand, and gentle waves.

West Tisbury Town Beach (West Tisbury) is an uncrowded surf beach.

Nature Areas

Several of the island's nature areas offer bird walks, special kids' programs, and a schedule of events (listed in the newspapers year-round; also in the *Best Read Guide*, available free in shops and hotels, in season). All have nature trails. A free map to the islands' conservation lands, including detailed directions, parking information, and usages permitted is available on the island (tel. 508/627–7141).

Cape Poge Wildlife Refuge and Wasque Reservation on Chappaquiddick Island is 489 acres of refuge and 200 adjacent acres of reservation. This wilderness of dunes, woods, salt marshes, ponds, tidal flats, and barrier beach is an important migration stopover or nesting area for many sea and shore birds. There's excellent surfcasting at Wasque (pronounced "WAYCE-qwee")

Point, though the currents are too dangerous for swimming, and a special parking lot with easy access (ask the attendant at the gate for directions to the fishermen's lot). Much of the area is accessible only by four-wheel-drive vehicles with a $50 annual Trustees of Reservations beach permit, available on site or through **Coop's Bait & Tackle** (147 West Tisbury Rd., Edgartown, tel. 508/627–3909). Access is via the Dyke Bridge—infamous as the scene of the 1969 accident in which a young woman was killed in a car driven by Edward M. Kennedy. At press time the bridge was closed, and until funds are found to repair or replace it, the only way to Cape Poge is by boat. (At low tide, you can walk over from South Beach across Katama Bay to Chappy, but it's a long walk.) The beautiful East Beach (*see* Beaches, above) is here, as is Wasque Beach, a sandy surf beach. *Take the Chappy ferry (see Getting Around, above), then follow the main road to the end; from there a ¾-mi dirt road leads to gatehouse. Tel. 508/693–7662. Admission: $4 cars, $2 adults over 15 mid-June–Labor Day; free rest of year. Property open 24 hrs; gatehouse open daily 9–5.*

Cedar Tree Neck, 300 hilly acres of unspoiled woods, offers varied environments, rich wildlife, freshwater ponds, brooks, low stone walls, and wooded trails ending at a stony but secluded North Shore beach (swimming, picnicking, and fishing prohibited). *Indian Hill Rd. (off Vineyard Haven Rd.) to intersection, then left down rough dirt road for 1 mi to parking lot. Tel. 508/693–7233. Admission free. Open daily 8:30–5.*

Felix Neck Wildlife Sanctuary, 3 miles out of Edgartown, has 350 acres, including 6 miles of hiking trails traversing marshland, fields, oak woods, seashore, a pond with a large variety of wildfowl, and a reptile pond. Affiliated with the Massachusetts Audubon Society (members admitted free), it offers a full schedule of events throughout the year, including sunset hikes along the beach, exploration of salt marsh, stargazing, snake or bird walks, snorkeling, and more, all led by trained naturalists. There's also an exhibit center with aquariums, snake cages, and a gift shop. *Off Edgartown–Vineyard Haven Rd., tel. 508/627–4850. Admission: $2 adults, $1 children and senior citizens. Open daily 8–4.*

Long Point, a 580-acre preserve on the south shore, is a wide-open grassland area bounded on the east by Long Pond, a large freshwater pond; on the west by West Tisbury Great Pond, a saltwater pond; and on the south by the Atlantic Ocean. Dense heathland of bayberry, rugosa rose, and goldenrod give way to the beach grass of vast dune, finally ending at ½ mile of South Beach, with swimming, surf fishing, and picnicking. Tisbury Great Pond and Long Cove are ideal spots for duck- and bird-watchers. *In summer, follow unpaved Deep Bottom Rd. (¾ mi west of airport on Edgartown–West Tisbury Rd.) for 2 mi to Long Point parking lot; off-season, watch for signs off Deep Bottom Rd. for alternate parking lot. Tel. 508/693–7233. Admission: $6 per vehicle, $3 adults over age 17 mid-June–mid-Sept.; free rest of year. Open daily 10–6.*

Manuel F. Correllus State Forest. At the center of the island is a 4,000-acre forest of pine and scrub oak laced with hiking trails and circled with a paved bike trail (mopeds are prohibited). Also here is a 2-mile nature trail, a 2-mile parcourse, and horse trails. *Headquarters on Barnes Rd., between Edgartown–*

Vineyard Haven Rd. and Edgartown–West Tisbury Rd., tel. 508/693–2540. Admission free. Open daily sunrise–sunset.

Waskosim's Rock Reservation. Purchased by the Land Bank in 1990, this 145-acre preserve (and hundreds of adjoining acres to which access has been granted by neighbors) is a unique property comprising very diverse habitats, from wetlands to open fields to oak and beetlebung woods. Also on the property are the ruins of an 18th-century homestead. The rock itself—deposited by the retreating glacier and said to resemble the head of a breaching whale—is on a high ridge above the Mill Brook Valley, from which there is a spectacular panorama of 1,000 acres of protected land; in the distance, the Atlantic can sometimes be seen. At press time, a 3-mile walking trail (and map) were being planned. *Access—via rough dirt roads—off Tea La. in Chilmark or off North Rd. in West Tisbury (sign says "Roth Woodlands"), tel. 508/627–7141. Admission free. Open daily sunrise–sunset.*

Dining

The focus of island cuisine is seafood fresh from the surrounding waters, though you will find Mexican, Chinese, and other more exotic cuisines. Dining out here is not the highly developed, gourmet experience it is on Nantucket, but a few establishments do offer sophisticated cooking in equally sophisticated settings.

Note: Only Edgartown and Oak Bluffs allow the sale of liquor. In the "dry" towns, restaurants are glad to provide setups for patrons' bottles.

Box or picnic lunches are provided by **Vineyard Gourmet** (Main St., Vineyard Haven, tel. 508/693–5181), **1940s American Café** in Edgartown (*see* below), and **Savoir Faire** (14 Church St., Edgartown, tel. 508/627–9864).

Highly recommended restaurants in each price category are indicated by a star ★.

Category	Cost*
Very Expensive	over $40
Expensive	$25–$40
Moderate	$12–$25
Inexpensive	under $12

*per person, excluding drinks, service, and 5% tax

Edgartown

Very Expensive **L'étoile.** The Charlotte Inn's restaurant is set in a glass-wrapped summerhouse, with a flagstone floor and a skylight-punctuated peaked roof. An open, airy room with lots of white and lots of greenery—hanging ferns, citrus trees in big clay pots—it has the civilizing influence of liberally placed English antiques (brass lighting fixtures, spotlighted oil paintings in gilt frames, a collection of shining wood mailboxes) and elegant dinner service of bone china, crystal, and silver. The contemporary French menu highlights imaginative native seafood and shellfish as well as game. The four-course dinner menu ($43) includes such entrées as panfried rainbow trout and soft-shell crawfish with bacon-and-bourbon sauce; and grilled veal rib chop with carmelized spring-onion-and-chive butter and a Stilton cheese soufflé. The outdoor patio, a little secret garden with fountain and cascading wisteria, is a good choice on a sunny day for the prix-fixe brunch ($21). The wine list is extensive. *27 S. Summer St., tel. 508/627–5187. Reservations required. Jacket suggested. AE, MC, V. Dinner and Sun. brunch only. Closed Jan.–mid-Feb.; also weekdays mid-Feb.–mid-May and mid-Nov.–Dec.*

Expensive ★ **Andrea's.** Amid unpretentious surroundings in an old house are served excellent classic northern Italian and Continental dishes such as lobster *fra diavolo* (in the shell, with mussels, clams, scallops, and shrimp on a bed of linguine with a spicy marinara sauce) and sirloin Lattenzi (sautéed in cognac with mushroom, truffle, and Madeira sauce; named for the chef). Choose from seats in the glassed-in porch, the main room, two semiprivate rooms, or the rose garden, weather permitting. *Upper Main St., tel. 508/627–5850. Reservations suggested. Dress: smart casual. AE, MC, V. Dinner and Sun. brunch only. Closed mid-Feb.–Mar.; closed Sun.–Tues. Nov.–mid-Feb. and Apr.–May.*

Moderate **1940s American Café.** Their motto is "three squares a day, the old American way." Here you'll find down-to-earth breakfasts; lunches of soups, salads, sandwiches, burgers and dogs, and blue-plate specials such as Yankee pot roast; and reasonably priced American-style dinners, such as fried chicken, broiled or fried fish, and steaks. From a gleaming silver vintage soda fountain come old-time treats such as ice cream sodas and banana splits. The diner look has definitely been taken upscale, with black-and-white-tile floor, marble café tables and black wrought-iron chairs, and there is a beautiful old Wurlitzer cranking out big-band tunes. War-bond and movie posters on the white walls evoke the 1940s. A bakery case offers baked goods to go. *65 Main St., tel. 508/627–7181. No reservations. Dress: casual. MC, V ($25 or more). No dinner Nov.–mid-May.*

Moderate– Inexpensive **Lawry's Seafood Market & Restaurant.** Most of the fish here—served fried, broiled, or baked—comes from the family's own boats. The chowder is very good, as are the Black Diamond steaks. In 1990, Lawry's switched to self-service, cut all entrée prices to under $10, and added a dessert hall—including 16 flavors of ice cream and plenty of sundae fixings. Don't come for atmosphere, unless your taste runs to orange vinyl, rustic wood booths, lots of kids, and a high decibel level. *Upper Main St., tel. 508/627–8857. No reservations. Dress: casual. No credit cards. Closed Nov.–late Apr.*

Menemsha

Very Expensive **Beach Plum Inn and Restaurant.** The owner, a Cordon Bleu–trained chef, and his assistants prepare a limited menu of Continental dishes, served on colorful, hand-painted Italian plates. Dinners are five-course prix fixe ($40) and include such choices as roast boneless duck with a honey curry sauce. Soft music from a white piano, along with two window walls to catch memorable sunsets, makes this a romantic setting for a special evening out. *North Rd., tel. 508/645–9454. Reservations required. Dress: casual. No credit cards. BYOB. Dinner only. Closed mid-Oct.–late May.*

Moderate **Home Port.** Here you'll find very fresh fish and seafood pre-
★ pared in a no-nonsense manner—simply baked, broiled, or fried. The decor, too, is no-nonsense, with plain wood tables and a family atmosphere; window walls overlooking the harbor provide more than enough visual pleasure. The wait for a table is often very long, especially around sunset; take a seat outside and order from the raw bar or the takeout menu, or use the time to wander around the fishing village. *North Rd., tel. 508/645–2679. Reservations required. Dress: casual. MC, V. BYOB. Dinner only. Closed Nov.–Apr.*

Oak Bluffs

Expensive **Oyster Bar.** Subtitled "An American Bistro," the Oyster Bar
★ (named for its 35-foot mahogany raw bar) has a sophisticated art-deco look in white and pink, with a high embossed-tin ceiling, faux-marble and fluted columns, tropical greenery on Ionic-column pedestals, and a line of pink neon along the walls. Though the extensive menu includes pastas, pizzas, hearty soups, and specials, the stars are the 20 or so varieties of fish available each night—including such exotic choices as bonita and mahimahi—cooked any way you like: broiled, sautéed, grilled, steamed, *wasabi*-glazed, blackened, au poivre. Specials may include gumbo filé with duck and shrimp; quail and polenta; or lacquered peppered duck breast with a Pinot noir sauce. *162 Circuit Ave., tel. 508/693–3300. Reservations strongly suggested. Dress: smart casual. AE, DC, MC, V. Dinner only. Closed mid-Oct.–mid-May; Tues. and Wed. in May and Oct.*

Moderate **David's Island House.** New England cuisine featuring fresh seafood is complemented with pastas, barbecued ribs, and such Continental dishes as bouillabaisse and steak au poivre. Pianist David Crohan owns the place and entertains most evenings with dinner music from classical to contemporary. The decor is island casual and New Englandy, with a fun mix of antique tables. The lounge is a civilized spot for drinks, a light menu, and conversation. *Circuit Ave., tel. 508/693–4516. Reservations required for 5 or more. Dress: casual. DC, MC, V. Closed Labor Day–Memorial Day.*

Zapotec. Warm homemade tortilla chips and "serious salsa"—fresh and delicious, with identifiable coriander leaves—accompany authentic and creative regional Mexican dishes at this little place with heart and style. Tag sales supplied the decor, all vaguely Mexican (like the used piñata) or just fun (like the EARTH 1 and EARTH 2 license plates). The outdoor porch, lit by red and green Christmas lights in the shape of chile peppers, is more intimate, even romantic. If you like tequila, try the surprising tequila agave wine. *10 Kennebec Ave., tel. 508/693–6800. No reservations in season. Dress: casual. AE, MC, V. Closed Thanksgiving–Easter; Mon.–Wed. Easter–June and Oct.–Thanksgiving.*

Inexpensive **Giordano's.** Bountiful portions of simply prepared Italian food
★ (pizzas, pastas, cacciatores, cutlets) and fried fish and seafood at excellent prices keep Giordano's—run by the Giordano family since 1930—a family favorite. Several different children's

meals are available for less than $5 (including milk and Jell-O). The ambience suits the clientele: hearty, noisy, and cheerful, with sturdy booths, bright green-topped wood tables, and hanging greenery. Lines often wrap around the corner. *107 Circuit Ave., tel. 508/693-0184. No reservations. Dress: casual. No credit cards. Closed late Sept.-early June.*

Linda Jean's. For quick and easy American classics such as meat loaf, fish-and-chips, and baked chicken, try this homey, diner-style eatery in the middle of the action. It opens at 6 AM for hearty breakfasts. *34 Circuit Ave., tel. 508/693-4093. No reservations. Dress: casual. No credit cards.*

Vineyard Haven

Very Expensive– Expensive **Le Grenier.** At this classic French restaurant, owner/chef Jean Dupon from Lyons offers a menu of more than 20 entrées, such as quail flamed with cognac and grapes, calf brains sautéed with black butter and capers, and poached salmon with cream of leeks. The *feuilleté d'escargot* appetizer is a puff pastry filled with a sauté of escargots, shallots, lemon juice, tarragon, and more, flamed with cognac and combined with garlic butter and heavy cream. Delectable desserts include dark-chocolate mousse cake, crème caramel, and crepes suzette. The look of this second-floor restaurant, entered through a green lattice, is a mix of garret (*grenier* means "loft" or "granary") and garden room. The exposed slats and beams of the slanted ceiling are painted light green, as are the walls; tables are romantically set with green and pink linens, candles in hurricane globes, and flowers in cut-glass vases. In the popular screened porch, painted vine tendrils climb posts to the roof. *Main St., tel. 508/693-4906. Reservations strongly suggested. Dress: casual. AE, MC, V. BYOB. Dinner only. Closed Jan. and Feb.*

Expensive **Black Dog Tavern.** An island landmark, the harborside Black Dog serves basic chowders, pastas, fish, and steak, along with such dishes as grilled tuna with lime, garlic, and jalapeño; and rack of lamb with rosemary, mustard, and garlic. The Black Dog Bakery (on Water St.) provides breads, including little loaves served with dinner, and a large daily selection of desserts. The glassed-in porch, lighted by ship's lanterns, looks onto the harbor; the nautical theme is continued in rustic ship's-planking floors, photographs of sailing ships, and quarterboards. The wait for a table is often long; put your name on the list and walk around the harbor area to pass the time. *Beach Rd. Ext., tel. 508/693-9223. No reservations. Dress: casual. BYOB. AE, MC, V.*

Expensive– Moderate **The Café at the Tisbury Inn.** Regional American dishes—jambalaya, chicken with lime and cilantro, seafood enchiladas—highlight the menu here. Scaled-down portions are available for light eaters. Five or six dessert choices are brought to your table; *try* to say no to the dense "chocolate silk cake" or other decadent offerings from the pastry shop of one of the owners. The dining room is intimate and open, in peach and green. At lunch, dine on soups and sandwiches at tables outside, under a cheery blue awning, in the middle of the downtown action. *Main St., tel. 508/693-3416. Dinner reservations recommended in season. Dress: casual. MC, V. BYOB. Late Sept.-late May, closed Mon. and no lunch Tues. and Wed.*

West Tisbury

Expensive **Lambert's Cove Country Inn.** The country-inn setting (*see*
★ Lodging, below), soft lighting and music, and fine Continental
cuisine make this the coziest, most romantic dining spot on the
island. The daily selection of six or seven entrées may include
cioppino; scallops of veal with a chanterelle Dijon sauce; or filet
mignon with béarnaise sauce. Appetizers are always interesting combinations, such as the goat cheese, strawberries, and
cashew salad; desserts are irresistible. In summer, a lavish
Sunday brunch is served outdoors in the orchard. *Off Lambert's Cove Rd., tel. 508/693–2298. Reservations required.
Dress: smart casual. AE, MC, V. BYOB. Dinner and Sun.
brunch only. Closed Jan. and weekdays in winter.*

Moderate **Roadhouse.** Good barbecued ribs and chicken, chili, and simply
prepared fish and meat dishes, accompanied by warm fresh
whole-wheat rolls, are served at this no-nonsense roadside
place. A beautiful mahogany counter, made by the owner's
boat-builder brother, centers the otherwise simple, bright
room with linoleum floor and shiny pine tables (whose wood, incidentally, once graced Fenway Park). Taped blues or jazz
plays in the background. *State Rd., North Tisbury, tel. 508/
693–9599. Reservations suggested for 6 or more. Dress: casual.
AE, MC, V. BYOB. Closed Nov.–Mar.*

Lodging

You can reserve a room at many island establishments by a toll-
free direct line at the Woods Hole ferry terminal waiting room
year-round. The Chamber of Commerce maintains a listing of
availability in the peak tourist season, from mid-June to mid-
September. During these months, rates are at their highest
and reservations are essential. In the winter, rates go down by
as much as 50%.

Martha's Vineyard and Nantucket Reservations (Box 1322, Lagoon Pond Rd., Vineyard Haven 02568, tel. 508/693–7200), **Accommodations Plus** (RFD 273, Edgartown 02539, tel. 508/627–
8590), and **Dukes County Reservations Service** (Box 1522, Oak
Bluffs 02557, tel. 508/693–6505) book cottages, apartments,
inns, hotels, and B&Bs. **House Guests Cape Cod and the Islands**
(Box 1881, Orleans 02653, tel. 800/666–HOST) books B&Bs
only.

An 85-bed **AYH hostel** (Edgartown Rd., West Tisbury 02575,
tel. 508/693–2665), near a bike path but 7 miles from the nearest beach, is open April–November.

Martha's Vineyard Family Campground (Box 1557, Edgartown
Rd., Vineyard Haven 02568, tel. 508/693–3772), open mid-May–
mid-October, has wooded sites, tent-trailer rentals, bathrooms
and hot showers, a laundromat, and a playground. **Webb's
Camping Area** (Barnes Rd., Oak Bluffs [RFD 2, Box 100, Vineyard Haven 02568], tel. 508/693–0233), on 90 acres, is more
woodsy and private. It is open May–September. Both take
tents and RVs.

For cottages and summer homes, try **Harborside Realty** (Box
1030, 256 Edgartown Rd., Edgartown 02539, tel. 508/627–3721
or 800/537–3721), **Macomber Real Estate** (Box 973, Upper Main

St., Edgartown 02539, tel. 508/627–8030), or **Martha's Vineyard Vacation Rentals** (51 Beach Rd., Box 1207, Vineyard Haven 02568, tel. 508/693–7711 or 800/628–8022).

Category	Cost*
Very Expensive	over $150
Expensive	$100–$150
Moderate	$70–$100
Inexpensive	under $70

all prices are for a standard double room in high season, excluding 5.7% state tax and (Down-Island only) 4% local tax

Chilmark

Expensive–Moderate **Breakfast at Tiasquam.** Set amid acres of peaceful farmland and forest of oak and beech is this B&B, built in 1987 in a contemporary design with 20 skylights, sliding glass doors, and private decks that connect the interior with the natural setting. This is a location for people who want to get away from it all, to bike on country roads, to walk in the woods, or just to lie in the hammocks and read. Lots of comfortable common areas invite mixing. The room decor is spare and soothing, emphasizing fine craftsmanship, as in the woodwork and the baths' hand-thrown ceramic sinks. A few pieces of art adorn the white walls; except for seafoam-green carpeting, earth tones dominate. Breakfast is hearty and varied, served at a handcrafted dining room table. *Off Middle Rd., RR1, Box 296, 02535, tel. 508/645–3685. 8 rooms, 2 with private bath (6 share 3½ baths). Facilities: full breakfast, bikes and car for rent, beach passes. No credit cards. No smoking.*

Edgartown

Very Expensive ★ **Charlotte Inn.** From its original structure, the 1860 home of a whaling company owner, the Charlotte has grown into a five-building complex of meticulously maintained accommodations and an excellent restaurant, L'étoile (*see* Dining, above). Gery Conover, owner for the past 20 years, and his wife, Paula, supervise every detail of the inn, which they have furnished through annual antiquing trips to England. Hallways are hung with original oil paintings and prints; in one, Gery's large collection of antique brass flashlights is displayed in a glass case. Two rooms in the Garden House, with its own fireplaced common room, have porches looking onto a flower-filled English garden. The Summer House has a veranda with wicker chairs and a very large room, No. 14, with a fireplace and a baby grand piano. All guest rooms have down pillows and comforters; some have working fireplaces, TVs, or phones. *27 S. Summer St., 02539, tel. 508/627–4751. 23 rooms (2 with shared bath), 2 suites. Facilities: Continental breakfast, afternoon tea, restaurant, art gallery, pay phone, common TV. AE, MC, V.*

Harbor View Hotel. A $7 million renovation of this full-service hotel was completed in 1990. In the 1891 gray-shingled main building, the historic architecture was maintained, but the entire infrastructure and the room decor is completely new, down to the studs. A gazebo was added to the wraparound veranda (where breakfast or tea may be taken in summer and fall) looking out across landscaped lawns to the harbor, Edgartown Lighthouse, and the ocean beyond. For the 1991 season, all-new landscaping, a new pool area with gardens and fountains, and total renovation of the seven cottages are scheduled. In the Governor Mayhew House, all the spacious rooms have private decks. Town houses have cathedral ceilings, decks, kitchens, and large living areas. All rooms have similar decor—pale-pink carpeting and light walls, painted wicker, pickled-wood armoires, pastel floral drapes tied with silver braided cord—plus phones, air-conditioning, cable TV with remote control and VCR, and a wall safe; suites have fax machines and full stereos. The location is in a residential neighborhood just minutes from town. A beach good for walking stretches ¾ mile from the jetty, from which there's good fishing for blues; children enjoy the sheltered bay. Packages and theme weekends are available. *131 N. Water St., 02539, tel. 508/627–4333 or 800/225–6005. 129 rooms. Facilities: 2 tennis courts, heated outdoor pool, privileges at golf club, pool bar and café, lounge with entertainment, restaurant, concierge, room service, business services, children's program, daily newspaper; boat slips, child care, laundry service, nonsmoking rooms, sails to private beach areas available. AE, DC, MC, V. Closed Jan. and Feb.*

Very Expensive–Expensive **Kelley House.** The less pricey sister property of the Harbor View occupies an entire block at the center of town. For the 1991 season, a total renovation similar to the Harbor View's is scheduled; rooms will have a Laura Ashley country look. The 1742 white-clapboard main house, where the restaurant is, was originally a tavern (a tradition Kelley House's present tavern maintains); the Garden House, surrounded by plantings, has most of the inn rooms. The six large suites in the Chappaquiddick House and the two town houses with full kitchens in the Wheel House have porches (most with harbor views) and living rooms and come with extra amenities, such as turndown service, robes, and fresh flowers. All guest rooms have cable TVs and phones. *23 Kelly St., 02539, tel. 508/627–4394 or 800/225–6005. 60 units. Facilities: restaurant, entertainment, concierge, room service, business services, heated outdoor pool, use of Harbor View's tennis courts, daily newspaper; nonsmoking rooms, child care, laundry service available. AE, DC, MC, V.*

The Victorian Inn. An 1857 whaling captain's home, listed on the National Register of Historic Places, the gingerbread-trimmed Victorian is an easygoing inn furnished with some fine antiques (and a teddy bear in every room). Several of the spacious third-floor rooms, many with comfortable sofas, have balconies with a view of the harbor. Some bathrooms are quite small. In season, breakfast is served in the garden courtyard. *S. Water St., Box 947, 02539, tel. 508/627–4784. 14 rooms. Facilities: full breakfast, central phone. MC, V.*

Expensive–Moderate **Daggett House.** The flower-bordered lawn that separates the main house from the harbor makes a great retreat after a day of exploring town, a minute away. The breakfast room of the 1750 house preserves much of the tavern it once was, including a secret stairway (it is now a private entrance to an upstairs guest room, but the innkeeper may let you peek in if the room is unoccupied). This and two other buildings are decorated with fine wallpapers, antiques, and reproductions. *59 N. Water St., Box 1333, 02539, tel. 508/627–4600. 22 rooms, 4 suites (2 with kitchen). Facilities: full breakfast, common TV and phones; laundry service, box lunches available. MC, V.*

Gay Head

Very Expensive
★ **Outermost Inn.** In 1990, Hugh and Jeanne Taylor converted the home they built 20 years ago by the Gay Head Cliffs into a bed-and-breakfast. Their design takes full advantage of the superb location: standing alone on acres of moorland, the house is wrapped with windows revealing breathtaking views of sea and sky in three directions. The romantic Lighthouse Suite has a separate entrance and French doors leading onto a private deck with a great view of the Gay Head Lighthouse, adjacent to the property. The decor is simple, with white walls and polished light-wood floors; each room has a phone, and one has a Jacuzzi. The beach is a 10-minute walk away. Hugh has sailed area waters since childhood and charters out his 33-foot sailboat to guests for excursions to remote beaches or other destinations. *Lighthouse Rd., RR 1, Box 171, 02535, tel. 508/645–3511. 7 rooms. Facilities: Continental breakfast, afternoon setups and hors d'oeuvres; beach passes, TVs, box lunches, dinners, sailboat charters available. MC, V. No smoking in guest rooms.*

Menemsha

Very Expensive **Beach Plum Inn and Cottages.** The main draws of this 10-acre retreat are the woodland setting, the panoramic view of the ocean and the Menemsha harbor, and the romantic gourmet restaurant offering spectacular sunsets. Cottages (one with Jacuzzi) are decorated in casual beach style. Inn rooms—some with private decks offering great views—have modern furnishings and small new baths; some are air-conditioned. Rates include breakfast and afternoon cocktails and hors d'oeuvres served on the sweeping lawn. *North Rd., 02552, tel. 508/645–9454. 5 inn rooms, 3 cottages. Facilities: full breakfast, restaurant, tennis court, pond for fishing, passes to Chilmark beaches, twice-daily maid service. AE, MC, V. Closed mid-Oct.–mid-May.*

Expensive–Moderate **Menemsha Inn and Cottages.** For 40 years *Life* photographer Alfred Eisenstaedt has returned to his cottage on the hill here for the panoramic view of Vineyard Sound and Cuttyhunk beyond the trees below. The rustic, colonial pine-furnished cottages, with plaster and wood-paneled walls, are nicely spaced on 10 acres; some are more private than others, and the extent of the water view varies. The decor of inn rooms—the building was new in 1989—and Carriage House suites is white walls, blond-wood trim, plush blue or sea green carpeting, and Appalachian light pine reproduction furniture. All rooms and suites have private decks, some with water and sunset views; suites have sitting areas, desks, minifridges, and big tiled baths. *North Rd., Box 38, 02552, tel. 508/645–2521. 9 rooms, 6 suites, 12 cottages. Facilities: Continental breakfast (inn only), all-weather tennis court, passes to Chilmark beaches, common phones. No credit cards. Closed Thanksgiving–Apr.*

Oak Bluffs

Expensive **Oak House.** The wraparound veranda of this pastel-front, 1872
★ Victorian looks across a busy street to a wide strand of beach.
Several rooms have private terraces, and some have TVs; if
you're bothered by noise, ask for a room at the back. The decor
centers on well-preserved woods—some rooms have oak wainscoting from top to bottom—choice antique furniture, and nau-
tical-theme accessories. An afternoon tea with fancy tea cakes
baked by the innkeeper, Betsi, a former pastry chef, is served
in a glassed-in sun porch, with lots of white wicker and plants.
*Sea View Ave., Box 299, 02557, tel. 508/693–4187. 8 rooms, 2
suites. Facilities: Continental breakfast, afternoon tea. Closed
mid-Oct.–Apr 1. MC, V.*

Expensive– **Admiral Benbow Inn.** Located on a busy highway between
Moderate Vineyard Haven and Oak Bluffs harbor, the Benbow is a small,
homey B&B. The house, built for a minister at the turn of the
century, features elaborate woodwork, a comfortable hodge-
podge of antique furnishings, and a Victorian parlor with a
stunning carved-wood-and-tile fireplace. *520 New York Ave.,
Box 2488, 02557, tel. 508/693–6825. 7 rooms. Facilities: full
breakfast, afternoon tea, common TV, pay phone. No smoking. AE, MC, V.*

Inn at Dockside. Right on the street opposite Oak Bluffs harbor, this new inn was built in 1989 in the Victorian style, with
pastel front and gingerbread-trimmed wraparound porches on
its three floors. Though a bit short on personality, the inn is
long on amenities for its price range: Rooms have individual
air-conditioning and heat, color cable TV/HBO, reproduction
Victorian furniture, and wall-to-wall carpeting. *Circuit Ave.
Ext., Box 1206, 02557, tel. 508/693–2966 or 800/245–5979 in
MA. 19 rooms, 3 efficiencies. Facilities: Continental breakfast,
central refrigerator and phones, auto and moped rental discounts, bicycles, gas grills, picnic tables; nonsmoking rooms
available. AE, MC, V. Closed Nov.–Apr.*

Sea Spray Inn. In 1989, artist and art restorer Rayeanne King
converted her summer house into a year-round B&B that feels
like a summer house. It is a quiet spot, situated on a drive circling an open, grassy park; beyond the park, and just a minute's
walk from the inn, is a sandy ocean beach. The decor is simple
and restful, highlighted by cheerful splashes of color, including
painted furniture and floors. In the Honeymoon Suite (one
room), an iron-and-brass bed is positioned for viewing the sunrise through bay windows draped in lacy curtains; the new, cedar-lined bath includes an extra-large shower. *2 Nashawena
Park, Box 2125, 02557, tel. 508/693–9388. 6 rooms (2 with
shared bath). Facilities: Continental breakfast, common TV,
phone, refrigerator, barbecue grill. MC, V. No smoking.*

Moderate **Martha's Vineyard Surfside Motel.** Right in the thick of things
(it gets noisy in summer) are these two buildings, the newest
built in 1989. Rooms are spacious, bright (corner rooms more
so), and well maintained, each with typical motel furnishings,
carpeting, table and chairs, individual air-conditioning and
heat, color TV, and phone; deluxe rooms have minifridges, remote control, and water views. *Oak Bluffs Ave., Box 2507,
02557, tel. 508/693–2500 or 800/537–3007 outside MA. 40
rooms. Facilities: room service. AE, D, MC, V.*

Inexpensive **Attleboro House.** This mom-and-pop guest house across from bustling Oak Bluffs harbor is a big 1874 gingerbread Victorian with wraparound verandas on two floors. It offers small, simple rooms, some with sinks, powder-blue walls, lacy white curtains, and a few antiques; singles have three-quarter beds. Linen exchange but no chambermaid service is provided during a stay. The shared baths are rustic and old but clean. *11 Lake Ave., Box 1564, 02557, tel. 508/693–4346. 9 rooms share 3½ baths. Facilities: Continental breakfast, common TV and phone. No credit cards. Closed Oct.–mid-May.*

Vineyard Haven

Very Expensive **Thorncroft Inn.** Set on 3½ acres of woods about a mile from the ★ ferry, the main inn, a 1918 Craftsman bungalow, has been renovated from top to bottom. Fine Colonial and richly carved Renaissance Revival antiques are combined with tasteful reproductions to create an environment that is somewhat formal but not fussy. In addition to the bungalow, the inn comprises three other buildings, two closer to town. All rooms have air-conditioning, phones, and wiring for computers. Deluxe rooms have cable TV and minifridge; some have working fireplaces, Jacuzzis, or canopy beds. Gourmet breakfasts are served at seatings and are conducive to meeting and chatting with other guests. *278 Main St., Box 1022, 02568, tel. 508/693–3333 or 800/332–1236. 17 rooms, 2 suites. Facilities: full breakfast, afternoon tea, turndown service, newspaper; picnic lunches and 5-course dinners available. No smoking. AE, MC, V.*

Expensive **Captain Dexter House.** Set in an 1843 sea captain's house at the edge of the shopping district, this B&B has an intimate, historic feeling about it. The small guest rooms are beautifully appointed, with period-style wallpapers, velvet wing chairs, and 18th-century antiques and reproductions, including several four-poster canopy beds with lace or fishnet canopies and hand-sewn quilts. The Captain Harding Room is larger, with original wood floor and Oriental carpet, fireplace, bay windows, canopy bed, sofa, desk, and large, bright bath. *100 Main St., Box 2457, 02568, tel. 508/693–6564. 7 rooms, 1 suite. Facilities: Continental breakfast, afternoon tea; common refrigerator, TV, phone. AE, MC, V.*

Moderate **Tisbury Inn.** No fuss, no frills—the Tisbury Inn offers location (in the middle of the shops of Main Street), tiled bathrooms with tub showers, firm beds, and some amenities. Rooms have cable TV/HBO. *Main St., Box 428, 02568, tel. 508/693–2200 or 800/332–4112. 27 rooms, 2 suites. Facilities: Continental breakfast, health club, indoor pool, sauna, restaurant, pay phone. AE, MC, V.*

West Tisbury

Expensive **Lambert's Cove Country Inn.** This special place is what a country inn should be. The 1790 farmhouse is secluded and peaceful, ★ approached by a road through pine woods and set amid an apple orchard. A profusion of wisteria and gardens make this a perfect place for strolling. The inn is elegant with rich woodwork and large floral displays, yet it makes you feel snugly at home with good beds, electric blankets, and unpretentious furnishings in the good-size guest rooms. It has lots of common areas, including a gentleman's library, well-used fireplaces, and a lovely English garden. Its restaurant serves a popular Sunday brunch. Add to that your access to the lovely, private Lambert's Cove Beach, and you have a surefire winner. (A car is a necessity here.) *Lambert's Cove Rd., West Tisbury (Box 422, RFD, Vineyard Haven 02568), tel. 508/693–2298. 15 rooms. Facilities: Continental breakfast, tennis court in woods. Closed Jan. AE, MC, V.*

Apartments and Houses

Mattakesett. This large community of three- or four-bedroom homes and condominiums, each unit privately owned and rented out for the summer, is within walking distance of South Beach. Each house is individually decorated by its owner— some are superior and some just average (ask about furnishings when you're reserving)—but all are spacious, sleep eight, and have phone, full kitchen with dishwasher, and washer/ dryer (cable TV available); many have decks with or without bay and ocean views, and some have whirlpools or wood-burning stoves. The staff provides plenty of service, and the full children's program, pool, and barbecue grills add to the definite family atmosphere of the place; some units are more removed from the action. Most of the time there's a one-week minimum; it's best to book by January 15. *Katama Rd., tel. 508/ 627–4432 (to reserve in the off-season, Mattakesett Properties, c/o Stanmar Corp., Boston Post Rd., Sudbury, MA 01776, tel. 508/443–1733). 82–92 units (depending on availability). Facilities: private tennis club with 6 Har-Tru and 2 all-weather courts, outdoor pool, swimming lessons, bicycles, aerobics classes, children's program, ferry auto reservations (high season). No credit cards. Closed Columbus Day–Memorial Day. Very Expensive.*

The Arts and Nightlife

A calendar of events is published every Thursday in the *Martha's Vineyard Times* and every Friday in the *Vineyard Gazette*. Also see the *Best Read Guide*, free at shops and hotels.

The Arts

Throughout the year, lectures, classic films, concerts, plays, and other events are held at the **Old Whaling Church** in Edgartown; watch the papers.

Theater The **Vineyard Playhouse** (10 Church St., Vineyard Haven, tel. 508/693–6450) offers a summer season (late June–mid-Sept.) of five plays, a mix of drama, classics, and comedies, performed by a mostly Equity troupe on the newly air-conditioned main stage; a community-theater Shakespeare production for two weeks at the natural amphitheater at Tashmoo Overlook on State Road in Vineyard Haven (bring a pillow); children's programs (*see* What to See and Do with Children, above) and late-night cabaret (*see* Nightlife, below), also in season; and a full winter schedule of community-theater productions. Theater classes (individual classes or four- to six-week sessions) and art exhibitions are held throughout the year. One performance of each show is interpreted in American sign language.

Music A summer music program is held at the **Tabernacle** in Oak Bluffs. Past highlights have included jazz trumpeter Wynton Marsalis, singer Emmy Lou Harris, Bavarian folk dancers, and a Gilbert and Sullivan show. For a schedule, see the local papers or contact the Camp Meeting Association (Box 1176, Oak Bluffs 02557, tel. 508/693-0525). The Tabernacle is also the scene of a popular Wednesday-night community sing (*see* Tour 2: Oak Bluffs in Exploring, above).

The **Boston Chamber Music Society** (tel. 617/536-6868) gives three performances—called the Vineyard Concerts—at the Old Whaling Church in Edgartown in July and August.

Chilmark Chamber Players (tel. 508/645-9606) perform eight summer concerts and three in winter at the Chilmark Community Center and the Union Chapel in Oak Bluffs.

A free **organ recital** is given at Federated Church (S. Summer St., Edgartown) every Friday at 12:10.

The Sunday night (8 PM) **Vineyard Haven Town Band concerts** take place on alternate weeks in summer at Owen Park in Vineyard Haven and at the gazebo on Beach Road in Oak Bluffs.

Dance **The Yard**—a colony of dancers and choreographers, formed in 1973—gives several performances throughout the summer at its 100-seat Barn Theater in a wooded setting (off Middle Rd., Chilmark, tel. 508/645-9663). Artists are selected each year from auditions that are held in New York. Dance classes are available to visitors. Some shows are followed by artists' receptions; children's pieces are sometimes offered.

Film A 24-hour hot line with schedules for all movie theaters on the Vineyard is 508/627-3788. The island has three first-run movie theaters: **Capawock** (Main St., Vineyard Haven), and Oak Bluffs' **Island Theater** (Circuit Ave.) and **The Strand** (Oak Bluffs Ave. Ext.). At least one stays open year-round. Films are shown at other locations from time to time; see newspaper listings.

Nightlife

Dances and other events for different age groups are held throughout the summer at the **Chilmark Community Center**; watch for announcements in the papers.

Coffeehouses **Wintertide Coffeehouse** (Box 1836, Vineyard Haven 02568), begun in 1980, takes place from January to March on Saturday nights; the location varies from year to year (watch the papers for announcements). Tables are set with cloths, candles, and flowers; entertainment is provided by islanders as well as off-islanders.

Cabaret The **Vineyard Playhouse** (*see* The Arts, above) has musical or comedy cabaret Wednesday–Saturday from 10:45 to midnight.

The **Seafood Shanty** restaurant (Dock St., Edgartown, tel. 508/627-8622) has performances of jazz standards, contemporary songs, and musical comedy by college students Monday–Saturday nights in season. There is no cover charge.

Bars and Lounges The **Ritz Café** (Circuit Ave., Oak Bluffs, tel. 508/693-9851) has live blues and jazz on weekends in season; the rest of the year it's a popular bar with a pool table and a jukebox.

At **David's Island House** restaurant (*see* Dining, above), owner and renowned pianist David Crohan entertains patrons with popular and classical music in season; a light menu is served in the lounge.

Dance Clubs Two major clubs offer a mix of live rock and reggae and deejay-spun dance music. **Hot Tin Roof** (at the airport, tel. 508/693–0320; open May–late Sept.), once owned by Carly Simon, is larger and has a bit more live music than the **Atlantic Connection** (124 Circuit Ave., Oak Bluffs, tel. 508/693–7129; open year-round), which features fancy light and sound systems and a glitter ball. Hot Tin Roof also has comedy nights. The Atlantic Connection offers theme parties (M*A*S*H, summer beach parties).

5 Nantucket

Introduction

At the height of its prosperity, in the early to mid-19th century, the little island of Nantucket was the foremost whaling port in the world. In the bustling harbor, ships set off for or returned from the whaling waters of the Pacific while coastal merchant vessels put in for trade or outfitting. Along the wharves, a profusion of sail lofts, ropewalks, ship's chandleries, cooperages, and other shops stood cheek by jowl. Barrels of whale oil were loaded from the ships onto wagons, then wheeled along the cobblestone streets to refineries and candle factories. On the strong sea breezes the smoke and smells of booming industry were carried through the town as its inhabitants eagerly took care of business.

The boom years didn't last long, but before they ended, some of the hard-won profits had gone into the building of grand homes that remain as eloquent testimony to Nantucket's glory days. The wharves still teem with shops of merchants and craftsmen who tend to the needs of incoming ships, though today those vessels are filled with tourists whose needs tend more toward T-shirts and chic handbags than to ropes and barrels.

Thanks in no small part to the island's isolation, 30 miles out in the open Atlantic (the name Nantucket is a corruption of the Indian word *Nanticut*, meaning "faraway land"), and to its frequently depressed economy, Nantucket has managed to retain much of its 17th- to 19th-century character. Indeed, the town — with its streets lit by old-fashioned street lamps and its hundreds of beautifully preserved houses — hardly seems changed since whaling days. But this remarkable preservation also owes much to the foresight and diligence of people working to ensure that what makes Nantucket special can be enjoyed by generations to come. In 1955, legislation to designate the island an official National Historic District was begun. Now any outwardly visible alterations to a structure—even the installation of air conditioners or a change in the color of paint—must conform to a rigid code.

The code's success is obvious in the restful harmony of the buildings, most covered in weathered gray shingles, sometimes with a facade of clapboard painted white or gray (in early Nantucket a clapboard facade was a sign of wealth, because it would need painting; these practical people saw no need for more than one showy side). In town, which is more strictly regulated than the outskirts, virtually nothing jars. You'll find no neon, stoplights, billboards, or fast-food franchises. In spring and summer, when the neat gardens are in bloom and the gray shingles are blanketed with cascading pink roses, it all seems picture perfect.

The desire to protect Nantucket from change extends to the land as well. When the tourism boom began, in the 1960s, it became imperative that something be done to preserve the breezy, wide-open terrain of the island—the miles of clean, white-sand beaches, and the heath-covered moors—that is as much a part of its charm as the historic town. A third of the 12-by 3-mile island is now protected from development, thanks to the ongoing efforts of several public and private organizations and the generosity of Nantucketers, who have donated thousands of acres to the cause. The Nantucket Conservation Foun-

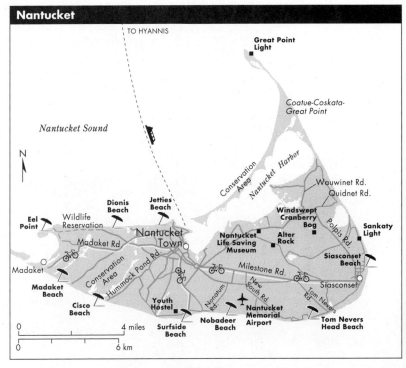

Nantucket

TO HYANNIS

Great Point Light

Nantucket Sound

Coatue-Coskata-Great Point

N

Conservation Area

Nantucket Harbor

Wauwinet Rd.
Quidnet Rd.

Dionis Beach

Jetties Beach

Windswept Cranberry Bog

Sankaty Light

Eel Point

Wildlife Reservation

Nantucket Town

Nantucket Life Saving Museum

Alter Rock

Polpis Rd.

Madaket Rd.

Siasconset Beach

Madaket

Conservation Area

Hummock Pond Rd.

Milestone Rd.

Siasconset

New South Rd.

Tom Nevers Rd.

Madaket Beach

Cisco Beach

Youth Hostel

Nonantum Rd.

Nantucket Memorial Airport

Tom Nevers Head Beach

Surfside Beach

Nobadeer Beach

0   4 miles

0   6 km

dation (*see* Tour 2 in Exploring Nantucket, below), established in 1963, has acquired through purchase or gift more than 7,800 acres, including working cranberry bogs and vast tracts of moorland. A land bank, funded by a 2% tax on Nantucket real estate transactions, was instituted in 1984 and has since acquired over 1,000 acres. Most of these areas are open to the public and marked with signs on the roadside.

The first settlers came to the island to get away from repressive religious authorities on the mainland—having themselves fled to the New World to escape persecution in England, the Puritans of the Massachusetts Bay Colony proceeded to persecute Quakers and those who were friendly with them. In 1659, Thomas Mayhew, who had obtained Nantucket through royal grant and a deal with the resident Wampanoag tribe, sold most of the island to nine shareholders for £30 and two beaver-skin hats. These shareholders then sold half shares to people whose skills the new settlement would need. The names of these families—Macy, Coffin, Starbuck, Coleman, Swain, Gardner, Folger, and others—are inescapable in Nantucket, where three centuries later many descendants still live.

The first year, Thomas Macy and his family, along with Edward Starbuck and the 12-year-old Isaac Coleman, spent fall and winter at Madaket, managing with the assistance of the local natives. The following year, 1660, Tristram Coffin and others arrived, establishing a community—later named Sherburne—at Capaum Harbor, on the north shore. When storms closed the harbor early in the 18th century, the center of activity was moved to the present Nantucket Town. Relations with the Wampanoags seem to have been cordial, and many of the tribe would become expert whalemen. Numbering about 3,000 when the settlers arrived, the native population was greatly reduced by a 1763 plague; the last full-blooded Wampanoag on the island died in 1855.

The settlers first tried their hand at farming, though their crops never thrived in the sandy soil. In 1690 they sent for a Yarmouth whaleman to teach them to catch right whales from small boats just offshore, and this kept them happy until 1712. In that year a ship was blown farther out to sea and managed to capture a sperm whale, whose oil was much more highly prized; thus began the whaling era on Nantucket.

In the 18th century, whaling voyages never lasted much longer than a year; by the 19th century the usual hunting grounds had been so overhunted that ships had to travel to the Pacific to find their quarry and could be gone for five years. (Some Nantucket captains have South Sea islands named for them, including Gardner, Starbuck, Swain, and Mitchell.) The life of a whaler was hard, and many never returned home. An account by Owen Chase, first mate of the Nantucket whaling ship *Essex*, of "the mysterious and mortal attack" of a sperm whale, which in 1820 ended in the loss of the ship and most of the crew, fascinated a young sailor named Herman Melville and formed the basis of his 1851 novel, *Moby-Dick*.

The fortunes of Nantucket's whaling industry rose and fell with the tides of three wars and ceased altogether in the 1860s— a result of diminished whale populations, the replacement of whale oil by cheaper kerosene, and the emergence of a sandbar that prevented the large whaling ships from entering Nantucket harbor. By the next decade tourism was being pursued, and hotels began springing up at Surfside, on the south shore. Developments at Siasconset (called 'Sconset), to the east, followed, and in the 1920s the area was a fashionable resort for theater folk. The tourist trade waxed and waned until the 1960s and has since become the island's main industry.

Like the original settlers, most people who visit Nantucket today come to escape—from cities, from stress and hurry, and in some ways from the 20th century. Nantucket has a bit of nightlife, including two raucous year-round dance clubs, but that's not at all what the island is about. It's about people who don't know you but who smile and wave anyway as you pass— you'll surprise yourself and find you're doing it, too, before long. It's about small gray-shingled cottages covered with pink roses in summer, about daffodil-lined roads in spring. It's about the moors, swept with brisk salt breezes and scented with bayberry, wild roses, and cranberries. Perhaps most of all, it's about rediscovering a quiet place within yourself and within the world, getting back in touch with the elemental and taking it home with you when you go.

Essential Information

Important Addresses and Numbers

Tourist Information
The **Chamber of Commerce** (Pacific Club Bldg., Main St., tel. 508/228-1700) is open weekdays 9–5. The **Nantucket Informa-**

tion **Bureau** (25 Federal St., tel. 508/228–0925) is open daily 9–6 in summer, Monday–Saturday 10–3 during the rest of the year.

Emergencies Dial 911 for **police or fire emergency.** The **Nantucket Cottage Hospital** (S. Prospect St., tel. 508/228–1200) has a 24-hour emergency room.

Late-night **Island Pharmacy** (Finast Plaza, Sparks Ave., tel. 508/228–
Pharmacies 6400) is open weekdays until 9 and weekends until 10 from mid-June to September; the rest of the year, until 8 nightly. **Congdon's** (47 Main St., tel. 508/228–0020) is open nightly until 10 from mid-June to mid-September; **Nantucket Pharmacy** (45 Main St., tel. 508/228–0180), until 10 nightly from Memorial Day to Labor Day or Columbus Day.

Helpline Dial 508/228–7227 for information on island health services, activities, and transportation. In summer the line is open Monday–Saturday 9–6, Sunday 10–4; in winter, Monday–Saturday 10–3.

Cash Machines Machines connected with the Express 24, Cirrus, and NYCE networks are at the **airport** (lobby), **Steamship Authority terminal** (Steamboat Wharf), **Nantucket Bank** (2 Orange St. or 104 Pleasant St., tel. 508/228–0580), **A&P** (Straight Wharf, tel. 508/228–9756), and **Finast** (Lower Pleasant St., tel. 508/228–2178).

Arriving and Departing by Plane

Airport and **Nantucket Memorial Airport** (tel. 508/325–5300) is about 3½
Airlines miles southeast of town via Old South Road.

Nonstop service from Boston, New York, and from Newark is provided year-round through **Continental Express** (tel. 800/525–0280). **Delta Connection/Business Express** (tel. 800/345–3400) has daily nonstop flights from Boston year-round and from New York from April through Labor Day; on weekends from June through August, it may offer nonstop service from Washington, DC, and direct from Philadelphia (the return flight makes a stop in Hyannis).

Nantucket Airlines (tel. 508/228–6234; in Hyannis, 508/790–0300; elsewhere in MA, 800/635–8787) provides service from Hyannis; **Edgartown Air** (tel. 508/627–9631 or in MA, 800/637–9631) and **Express Air** (tel. 508/999–3231 or 800/852–2332), from New Bedford; **Cape Cod Air** (tel. 508/945–9000; in MA, 800/553–2376) from Chatham; and **Coastal Air Services** (tel. 203/448–1001; on Nantucket, 508/228–3350) from Groton, Connecticut. All services are year-round.

For interisland plane service between Martha's Vineyard and Nantucket, *see* Arriving and Departing by Plane in Chapter 4, Martha's Vineyard.

Arriving and Departing by Ferry

From Hyannis The **Steamship Authority** (tel. 508/540–2022; on Nantucket, 508/228–3274, TDD 508/540–1394) runs car-and-passenger ferries to the island from Hyannis year-round. If you plan to take a car to the island in summer or on fine weekends in fall, you *must* reserve as far ahead as possible; spaces are often sold out months in advance (*see also* Getting Around, below). No reservations are taken for passengers. No credit cards are accepted for same-day passage. The trip takes 2¼ hours. The one-way fare for pedestrians is $9.50 adults, $4.75 children 5–12; for cars the fare is $78 from mid-May to mid-October, $47 the rest of year; bicycles, $4.50.

Hy-Line (tel. 508/228–3949; in Hyannis, 508/778–2600) carries passengers from Hyannis from mid-May through October. The trip takes 1¾ to two hours. The one-way cost is $10 adults, $5 children 3–12, $4 bicycles. Its ship MV *Great Point* offers a first-class section with a private lounge, rest rooms, uphol-stered seats, carpeting, a bar, and a restaurant ($18 one-way, adult or child).

From Martha's Vineyard   **Hy-Line** (tel. 508/228–3949; on Martha's Vineyard, 508/693–0112) ferries run between Oak Bluffs and Nantucket from mid-June to mid-September. The trip takes 2½ hours. The one-way cost is $10 adults, $5 children 3–12, $4 bicycles.

Arriving and Departing by Private Boat

Harbor facilities are available in town year-round at the **Boat Basin** (tel. 508/228–1333), with shower and laundry facilities, electric power, and, in summer, concierge service.

Madaket Marine (tel. 508/228–9086) has moorings year-round and slips in the off-season for small boats in Hither Creek.

Getting Around

One of the attractions of a Nantucket vacation is escape from the fast lane. Most visitors find themselves walking a lot more than they're used to and taking advantage of the island's miles of scenic bike paths. Even so, in high season the main streets are clogged with traffic (and the parking spaces filled), and res-idents beg you to leave your car at home.

If your visit will be short and spent mostly in town and on the beaches, taxis and beach shuttles can supplement foot power adequately. If, on the other hand, your focus will be on the less accessible areas, such as the farther-out beaches and nature preserves; or if you'll be staying a week or longer, a car may make life simpler. Renting a car on the island for a day is cheap-er and less troublesome than bringing one over on the ferry (but do reserve).

Some of the island's most beautiful and least touristed areas are accessible only by over-sand, four-wheel-drive vehicles. The town-owned portions of Cliffside, Dionis, and Jetties beaches are open to vehicles from mid-September through May. Coatue–Coskata–Great Point (*see* Tour 2 in Exploring Nantucket, below) is open to Jeeps but requires licenses.

By Car   Cars and Jeeps are available at the airport desks of **Avis** (tel. 508/228–1211), **Budget** (tel. 508/228–5666), **Hertz** (tel. 508/228–9421), **National** (tel. 508/228–0300), **Nantucket Windmill** (tel. 508/228–1227 or 800/448–1227), and, across from the airport, at **Nantucket Jeep Rental** (3 Square Rigger Rd., tel. 508/228–1618). Cost varies with the season; in high season, you will pay $35–$50 a day for cars, $80–$140 for Jeeps (reserve ahead for Jeeps; they disappear quickly).

By Bus   From mid-June to Labor Day, **Barrett's Tours** (20 Federal St., tel. 508/228–0174), across from the Information Bureau (*see* Important Addresses and Numbers, above), runs shuttles to 'Sconset ($3.50 one-way), Surfside ($2.50 one-way), and Jetties ($1 one-way) beaches several times daily.

By Taxi   Taxis are usually available outside the airport or at a stand at the foot of Main Street as you come up from the ferry. The many year-round taxi "companies," several with just one or two cabs, include **A-1 Taxi** (tel. 508/228–3330 or 508/228–4084), **All Points Taxi** (tel. 508/228–5779), **Atlantic Cab** (tel. 508/228–1112), and **John's Taxi** (tel. 508/228–4084). Rates are flat fees, based on one person carrying two bags: $3 within town (1½-mile radius), $5 to the airport, $9 to 'Sconset, $10 to Wauwinet.

By Bicycle and **Moped**   Mountain bikes are best if you plan to explore the dirt roads (*see* also Bicycling in Sports and Outdoor Activities, below). To drive a moped you must have a driver's license and helmet; you may not use the vehicle within the town historic district between 10 PM and 7 AM, and you may never drive it on the bike paths. Moped accidents happen often on the narrow or dirt roads—be extremely careful of loose gravel.

Rentals are available on Steamboat Wharf from **Young's Bicycle Shop** (tel. 508/228–1151), which also rents cars and Jeeps in season, and from **Nantucket Bike Shop** (tel. 508/228–1999, Easter–Columbus Day). Both provide excellent touring maps. Rental costs are $12–$16 per day for a bicycle, $30–$40 per day for a moped.

By Horse-drawn **Carriage**   **Spring Rose Carriage** (tel. 508/228–3039) sometimes offers carriage rides in season, but availability is unpredictable. Call if you're interested.

Guided Tours

Orientation   **Barrett's Tours** (20 Federal St., tel. 508/228–0174) and **Nantucket Island Tours** (Straight Wharf, tel. 508/228–0334) give 1¼- to 1½-hour narrated bus tours of the island from spring through fall; buses meet the ferries.

Native Scenic Rides (tel. 508/257–6557 Apr.–Dec.) offers a lively 1¾-hour van tour narrated by sixth-generation Nantucketer Gail Johnson, who knows all the inside stories.

The Grey Lady (Gaslight Theatre, N. Union St., tel. 508/228–4435) is a documentary film that gives an overview of the island and its history. It is shown several times daily in summer.

Special-interest *Cruises*   Boats of all kinds leave from Straight Wharf for harbor sails throughout the summer; many are available for charter as well. The 43-foot sailing yacht *Fair Tide* (Slip 18, tel. 508/228–4844) also does Sunday-brunch sails. The 31-foot Friendship sloop *Endeavor* (Slip 15, tel. 508/228–5585) also offers sails to Coatue, where you are rowed ashore to spend a private morning beachcombing. The motorized tour boat *Anna W II* (Slip 12, tel. 508/228–1444) offers picnic, sunset, and moonlight cruises.

Fishing   **Jeep Excursions Ltd.** (1 Old North Wharf, tel. 508/228–3728) offers fishing trips to Great Point, complete with gear; also available are picnicking and swimming excursions and general tours.

History **Roger Young's historic walking tours** (tel. 508/228–1062 in season) of the town center are entertaining and leisurely.

Anita Stackpole Dougan (tel. 508/228–1861), a 12th-generation Nantucketer, and her husband, Edward, lead 1½-hour walking tours of town focusing on the people who have lived in the historic homes seen along the walk.

Nature **The Maria Mitchell Association** (Vestal St., tel. 508/228–9198) organizes wildflower and bird walks from May to mid-October.

Whale-watching **Nantucket Whalewatch** (Hy-Line dock, Straight Wharf; tel. 508/283–0313 or 800/942–5464; in MA, 800/322–0013) runs excursions Tuesday–Thursday July–September led by naturalists conducting research.

Exploring Nantucket

Orientation

The 12- by 3-mile island of Nantucket has one town, also called Nantucket; the village of 'Sconset, with a number of services, on the east coast; the village of Madaket, on the west, with a harbor, good sunsets, a restaurant, and blue fishing off the point; and a number of residential areas with no commercial or tourist facilities. Although major roads will take you to most of these areas, exploring them must often be done on dirt roads. Bike paths lead east to 'Sconset, south to Surfside Beach, and west to Madaket.

Nantucket town has a small commercial area of a few square blocks leading up from the waterfront; beyond it, quiet residential roads fan out. As you wander you may notice a small round plaque by some doorways. Issued by the Nantucket Historical Association, the plaques certify that the house dates from the 17th century (silver), 1700–1775 (red bronze), 1776–1812 (brass), 1813–1846 (green), or 1847–1900 (black). Unfortunately, all the plaques seem to turn a coppery green with age.

Highlights for First-time Visitors

Altar Rock (*see* Tour 2)
Eel Point (*see* Beaches in Sports and Outdoor Activities, below)
First Congregational Church, for the view (*see* Tour 1)
Museum of Nantucket History (*see* Tour 1)
Siasconset (*see* Tour 2)
"Three Bricks" (*see* Tour 1)
Whaling Museum (*see* Tour 1)

Tour 1: Nantucket Town

Numbers in the margin correspond with numbered points of interest on the Nantucket Town map.

1 The geologic and historical overview given by the **Museum of Nantucket History** helps put into perspective the sights you will see when touring the island. The brick building in which the museum is set was built by Thomas Macy after the Great Fire of 1846—which destroyed the wharves and 400 buildings, about a third of all those in the town—as a warehouse for the supplies needed to outfit whaling ships. It has been restored to

Nantucket Town

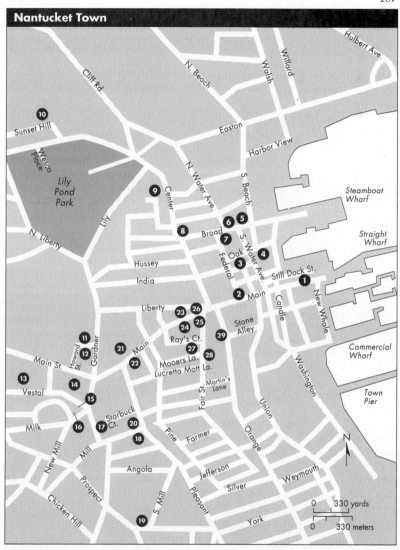

Atheneum, **3**

Charles G. Coffin House, **24**

Dreamland Theatre, **4**

1800 House, **18**

Fire Hose Cart House, **11**

First Congregational Church, **9**

Greater Light, **12**

Hadwen House, **22**

Henry Coffin House, **23**

Hinchman House, **16**

Jared Coffin House, **8**

John Wendell Barrett House, **25**

Maria Mitchell Science Library, **15**

Mitchell House, **14**

Moors' End, **20**

Museum of Nantucket History, **1**

Nantucket Historical Association Research Center, **6**

Nantucket Information Bureau, **7**

Old Gaol, **13**

Old Mill, **19**

Oldest House, **10**

Pacific Club/Chamber of Commerce, **2**

Pacific National Bank, **26**

Quaker Meeting House/Fair Street Museum, **27**

St. Paul's Episcopal Church, **28**

Starbuck refinery and candleworks, **17**

Three Bricks, **21**

Unitarian Universalist Church, **29**

Whaling Museum, **5**

be accurate historically, down to period doors, hatchways, and hoists. Inside, audio and visual displays include an early hand-pumper (fire-fighting vehicle), ship models, photographs, and a 13-foot diorama showing the shops, ships, and activities of the bustling waterfront before the fire. Live demonstrations of such early island crafts as candle making are sometimes given; temporary exhibits are mounted on the second floor. *Straight Wharf, tel. 508/228–3889. Admission free. Open in season, daily 10–5, 7–10; otherwise, daily 11–3. Closed mid-Oct.–mid-Apr. The museum is run by the Nantucket Historical Association (tel. 508/228–1894), which oversees 13 properties. A Visitor's Pass allowing a single visit to all 13 is available at any of the sites for $6 adults, $2.50 children 5–14.*

② Walking up Main Street, you'll come to the redbrick **Pacific Club** building, still housing the elite club of Pacific whaling masters for which it is named. Understandably, since the last whaling ship was seen here in 1870, the club now admits whalers' *descendants*, who gather for the odd cribbage game or a swapping of tales. The building began in 1772 as the counting house of William Rotch, owner of the ships *Dartmouth, Beaver,* and *Eleanor,* which hosted a famous tea party in Boston. Upstairs is the office of the **Chamber of Commerce** (*see* Important Addresses and Numbers in Essential Information, above), where you might want to stop for maps and other information.

From here you get the most photographed view of Main Street. The cobblestone square has a harmonious symmetry; at the foot it is anchored by the Pacific Club, and at the head, by the Pacific National Bank, another redbrick building. The only broad thoroughfare in town, Main Street was widened after the Great Fire leveled all its buildings, except those made of brick, to safeguard against flames hopping from one side of the street to the other in another fire. The cobblestones—brought to the island as ballast in returning ships—were laid to prevent the wheels of carts heavily laden with whale oil from sinking into the dirt on their passage from the waterfront to the factories.

At the center of Lower Main is an old horse trough, today overflowing with flowers. From here the street gently rises; at the bank it narrows to its pre-fire width and leaves the commercial district for an area of mansions that escaped the blaze. The simple shop buildings that replaced those lost are a pleasing hodge-podge of sizes, colors, and styles. Elm trees—thousands of which were planted in the 1850s by Henry and Charles Coffin—once formed a canopy over Main Street, but Dutch elm disease took most of them not long ago.

Turning down Federal Street, you'll come to a huge white Greek Revival building with an odd windowless facade and **③** fluted Ionic columns. This is the **Atheneum** (Lower India St., tel. 508/228–1110), Nantucket's town library, built in 1846 to replace a structure lost to the fire. The opening ceremonies featured a dedication by Ralph Waldo Emerson, who—along with Daniel Webster, Henry David Thoreau, John James Audubon, and other important men of the day—later delivered lectures in the library's second-floor Great Hall.

A right turn onto Oak Street brings you to South Water Street. **④** Across the way is the **Dreamland Theatre,** a good illustration of early Nantucketers' penchant for multiple use of dwellings as well as for moving houses around. Trees, and therefore lumber, were so scarce that Herman Melville joked in *Moby-Dick* "that pieces of wood in Nantucket are carried about like bits of the true cross in Rome." Currently a summer movie theater, the Dreamland was built on Main Street as a Quaker meeting house; became a straw factory, then an entertainment hall; was moved to Brant Point as part of the grand Nantucket Hotel in the late 19th century; and was floated across the harbor by barge about 1905 and installed in its present location.

From Oak Street, turn left on South Water; at the end is the ❺ **Whaling Museum,** set in an 1846 factory built for refining spermaceti and making candles. (Spermaceti candles, incidentally, which you'll see for sale at various shops, give off a clean, steady light and only a slight fragrance, which is why they became such popular replacements for smelly tallow candles.) This wonderful museum immerses you in Nantucket's whaling past. Exhibits include a fully rigged whaleboat, harpoons and other implements, portraits of sea captains, a large scrimshaw collection, a full-size try works (used to process whale oil aboard ship), the skeleton of a 43-foot finback whale, replicas of cooper and blacksmith shops, and the original 16-foot-high glass prism from the Sankaty Light. The knowledgeable and enthusiastic staff give a 20- to 30-minute introductory talk peppered with tales of a whaling man's life at sea. Don't miss the museum's gift shop next door (*see* Specialty Stores in Shopping, below). *Broad St., tel. 508/228–1736. Admission: $3 adults, $1 children; or NHA Visitor's Pass. Open July–Aug., daily 10–5; Sept.–Oct. and mid-Apr.–June, daily 11–3. Closed Nov.–mid-Apr.*

❻ On the other side of the museum is the **Nantucket Historical Association Research Center,** with an extensive collection of manuscripts, books, photographs, ships' logs and charts, genealogical records, and audiovisual materials on Nantucket maritime and other history—open only to those doing research. In 1990 the Peter Foulger Museum, which shared the building with the center, was dissolved to give the center more space. *Broad St., tel. 508/228–1655. Research permit: $5 (2 days). Open weekdays 10–5. Closed Labor Day–Memorial Day except by appointment.*

Time Out   Across the street from the Research Center is the **Juice Bar** (12 Broad St., tel. 508/228–5799), with homemade ice cream, waffle cones, lots of toppings, baked goods, and always a long line.

❼ Just around the corner on Federal Street is the **Nantucket Information Bureau** (*see* Tourist Information in Essential Information, above), with public phones, rest rooms, and a bulletin board posting events.

Most of the Greek Revival houses you will see as you continue up Broad Street were replacements for buildings lost in the ❽ Great Fire. Pause to admire the **Jared Coffin House,** which has operated as an inn since the mid-19th century. Coffin, a wealthy merchant, built this Georgian brick house with Ionic portico, parapet, hip roof, and cupola—then the only three-story structure on the island—for his wife, who wanted to live closer to town. They moved here in 1845 from their home on Pleasant Street, but (so the story goes) nothing would please the woman, and within two years they had left the island altogether for Boston.

❾ A right onto Centre Street takes you past the **First Congregational Church** (also known as the Old North Church), the largest on the island. Its tower—whose steeple is capped with a weathervane depicting a whale catch—rises 120 feet, providing the best view of Nantucket to be had. On a clear day the reward for climbing the 92 steps (many landings break the climb) is a panorama encompassing Great Point, Sankaty Light, Muskeget and Tuckernuck islands, moors, ponds, beaches, and the winding streets and rooftops of town. Peek in at the church's interior, with its old box pews, a chandelier seven feet in diameter, and a trompe-l'oeil ceiling done by an Italian painter in 1850 and since restored. The organ, installed in 1904, has 914 wood and metal pipes. (Organ aficionados may want to have a look at the 1831 Appleton organ—one of only four extant—at the United Methodist Church, next to the Pacific National Bank on Main Street.) The Old North Vestry in the rear, the oldest house of worship on the island, was built in 1725 about a mile north of its present site. The main church was begun in 1834. *62 Centre St., no tel. Admission: $1.50 adults, 50¢ children. Open mid-June–Sept., Mon.–Sat. 10–4, also Wed. and Thurs. 6–8 PM. Closed Oct.–mid-June.*

❿ A short walk along Centre Street (past lovely Lily Street) and West Chester Street leads to the **Oldest House**, also called the Jethro Coffin House, built as a wedding gift for Jethro and Mary Gardner Coffin. The 1686 saltbox—the oldest house on the island—was severely damaged by lightning in 1987; the roof blew off, the chimney was destroyed, floorboards exploded, and the foundation was badly shaken. After almost $1 million in painstaking restoration, the house reopened in 1990. Its most striking feature is the massive central brick chimney with brick horseshoe adornment; other highlights are the enormous hearths and diamond-pane leaded-glass windows. Cutaway panels show 17th-century construction techniques. *Sunset Hill, tel. 508/228–1894. Admission: $1 adults, 50¢ children 5–14; or NHA Visitor's Pass. Open in season, daily 10–5; off-season, daily 11–3. Closed mid-Oct.–late May.*

Return to West Chester Street and follow Wesco Place to the **Lily Pond park,** a five-acre conservation area a few minutes from town. Its grassy lawn and wetlands (there is a trail, but it's muddy) foster abundant wildlife, including birds, ducks, and deer.

⓫ Follow West Chester Street to North Liberty Street and walk for about 10 minutes in this quiet area to reach the **Fire Hose Cart House.** Built in 1886 as one of several neighborhood fire stations—Nantucketers had learned their lesson—the house displays a collection of fire-fighting equipment used a century ago. *8 Gardner St., tel. 508/228–1894. Admission free. Open in season, daily 10–5; off-season, daily 11–3. Closed mid-Oct.–mid-June.*

⓬ Just across Howard Street is **Greater Light,** an example of the summer homes of the artists who flocked to Nantucket in its early resort days. In the 1930s two unusual Quaker sisters from Philadelphia—an actress and an artist—converted a barn into what looks like the lavish set for an old movie. The exotic decor includes Italian furniture, Native American artifacts and textiles, a wrought-iron balcony, bas reliefs, and a coat of arms. The sisters also remodeled the house next door, called Lesser Light, for their parents. *8 Howard St., tel. 508/228–9591. Ad-*

mission: $1.50 adults, 50¢ children 5–14; or NHA Visitor's Pass. Open daily 10–5. Closed mid-Oct.–mid-June.

Continue on Howard Street to Main Street, turn right, then **⓭** left on Bloom; a sign on the right points the way to the **Old Gaol,** an 1805 jailhouse in use until 1933. Shingles mask the building's construction of massive square timbers; walls, ceilings, and floors are bolted with iron. The furnishings consist of rough plank bunks and open privies, but you needn't feel too much sympathy for the prisoners: Most of them were allowed out at night to sleep in their own beds. *15R Vestal St., tel. 508/ 228–1894. Admission free. Open June–mid-Oct., daily 10–5.*

⓮ Back at the beginning of Vestal Street is the **Mitchell House,** birthplace of astronomer and Vassar professor Maria (pronounced Mah-RYE-ah) Mitchell, who in 1847, at age 29, discovered a comet while surveying the sky from the top of the Pacific National Bank. (Her family had moved to quarters over the bank, where her father—also an astronomer—worked.) The restored 1790 house, an excellent example of the architecture of the period, contains family possessions and Maria Mitchell memorabilia, including the telescope with which she spotted the comet. The kitchen, of authentic wide-board construction, retains the antique utensils, iron pump, and sink of the time. Tours of the house, the roof walk, and the wildflower gardens are available; the adjacent observatory is used by researchers and is not open to the public. *1 Vestal St., tel. 508/228–2896. Admission: $3 adults, $1 children. Open mid-June–Aug., Tues.–Sat. 10–4.*

⓯ Across the street is the **Maria Mitchell Science Library,** which has natural-history books and periodicals, including field-identification guides and gardening books. *Tel. 508/228–9198. Open Tues.–Sat. 10–4.*

⓰ The **Hinchman House**—a natural-science museum, with specimens of local birds, shells, insects, and plants—is located at the corner of Vestal and Milk streets. *7 Milk St., tel. 508/228–0898. Admission: $3 adults, $1 children. Open mid-June–Aug., Tues.–Sat. 10–4.*

The three previous properties—as well as the **Loines Observatory** (Milk St. Ext., tel. 508/228–9198), which offers Wednesday-night stargazing from 9 to 10 and evening astronomy lectures for adults and children in July and August; and an aquarium (*see* What to See and Do with Children, below)—are administered by the Maria Mitchell Association, established in 1902 by Vassar students and Maria's family. A combination admission ticket to all sites is $4.

One of 10 children of Quaker parents, Mitchell attained many firsts in her day—first woman astronomy professor in the United States and first woman to discover a comet—and world fame to boot. It is not surprising that a Nantucket woman would do so, given the history of women on the island. During the whaling days men would be gone for up to five years at a time; the women learned to keep the town going. They became leaders in every arena, from religion to business. Mary Coffin Starbuck helped establish Quakerism on the island and was a celebrated preacher. Lucretia Coffin Mott was a powerful advocate of the antislavery and women's-rights movements. During the post–Civil War depression, Centre Street near Main

Street became known as Petticoat Row, a reflection of the large number of women shopkeepers.

Cross Gardner Street and walk down New Dollar Lane; on your **(17)** left, down a long driveway, are the remains of the **Starbuck refinery and candle works,** now used as apartments and garages.

(18) A left onto Mill Street leads to the **1800 House** museum, typical of a Nantucket home—one not enriched by whaling money—of that time. Once the residence of the high sheriff, the house features locally made furniture and other household goods, a six-flue chimney with beehive oven, and a backyard pump. *10 Mill St., tel. 508/228–1894. Admission: $1.50 adults, 50¢ children 5–14; or NHA Visitor's Pass. Open late May–mid-Oct., daily 10–5.*

Make a right onto Pleasant Street and another onto South Mill **(19)** Street for the **Old Mill,** a 1746 Dutch-style octagonal windmill built with lumber from shipwrecks. Several such windmills sat on hills in Nantucket in the 1700s, but only this one remains. The Douglas-fir pivot pole used to turn the cap and sails into the wind is a replacement of the originial pole, a ship's foremast. The mill is worked with wood gears and wind power (when the wind is strong enough) to grind corn into meal that is sold here. *South Mill St., tel. 508/228–1894. Admission: $1 adults, 50¢ children 5–14; or NHA Visitor's Pass. Open late May–mid-Oct., daily 10–5.*

From here, return to town via Pleasant Street. At No. 19 is **(20)** **Moors' End,** the handsome Federal brick house where Jared Coffin lived before building what is now the Jared Coffin House. It is a private home, but insiders tell of vast murals of the whaling era on the walls, and of scrawled notes about shipwreck sightings in the cupola. Behind high brick walls is a lavish garden.

Turn right on Main Street for the mansions of the golden age of **(21)** whaling. At Nos. 93–97 are the well-known **Three Bricks,** identical redbrick mansions with columned, Greek Revival porches at their front entrances. Similar in design to the Jared Coffin House but with only two stories, they were built between 1836 and 1838 by whaling merchant Joseph Starbuck for his three sons. One, the Middle Brick, still belongs to a Starbuck descendant.

The two white, porticoed Greek Revival mansions across the street—referred to as the Two Greeks—were built in 1845 and 1846 by factory owner William Hadwen for himself and for the niece he and his wife had adopted. (Hadwen's wife, incidentally, was a sister of the three Starbuck brothers; another sister **(22)** lived at 100 Main Street.) Number 96, called the **Hadwen House,** is now a museum. A guided tour points out the grand circular staircase, fine plasterwork, carved Italian-marble fireplace mantels, and other architectural details. Regency, Empire, and Victorian furnishings are accented with portraits, needlework, silver doorknobs, and other 19th-century decorative objects. Behind the house are period gardens. *96 Main St., tel. 508/228–1894. Admission: $1.50 adults, 50¢ children 5–14; or NHA Visitor's Pass. Open late May–mid-Oct., daily 10–5; 11–3. Closed mid-Oct.–late May.*

Farther along Main Street, facing each other, are two more at- **(23)** tractive brick houses built for brothers, the **Henry Coffin** **(24)** **House** (at No. 75) and the **Charles G. Coffin House** (No. 78).

Wealthy shipping agents and whale-oil merchants, the Coffins used for these 1830s houses the same mason who later built the Three Bricks.

㉕ The last of the grand Main Street homes is the **John Wendell Barrett House,** on the right at No. 72. Legend has it that Lydia Mitchell Barrett stood on the steps and refused to move when, during the Great Fire, men tried to evacuate her so they could blow up the house to stop the spread of the fire; luckily, a shift in the wind settled the showdown.

㉖ Across the street is the 1818 **Pacific National Bank.** Like the Pacific Club it faces, the bank is a monument to the far-flung voyages of the Nantucket whaling ships it financed. Inside, above old-style teller cages, are murals of street and port scenes from the whaling days. Near the bank, at 62 Main Street, is Murray's Toggery, the site of R. H. Macy's first retail store.

㉗ A right on Fair Street will bring you to the **Quaker Meeting House,** built around 1838 as a Friends school and now a Quaker place of worship in summer. A small room of quiet simplicity—white-and-gray walls, windows with 12-over-12 antique glass, and unadorned wood benches—it is in keeping with these peaceful people, who believe that the divine spirit is within each person and that one does not require an intermediary to worship God.

Attached to the meeting house is an unattractive 1904 concrete building that houses the **Fair Street Museum.** Downstairs, a series of paintings by Rodney Charman—commissioned by a private foundation in 1986—chronicles the history of Nantucket. Upstairs are paintings by early Nantucketers. *1 Fair St., tel. 508/228–5205. Admission: $1. Open in season, daily 10–5; limited days and hours other times. Closed early Dec.–mid-Apr.*

㉘ Across the street is the 1901 **St. Paul's Episcopal Church,** a massive granite structure adorned at the front and back by beautiful Tiffany windows. The interior is cool and white, with dark exposed beams. You might take a minute to wander down one of the pretty side streets, such as Lucretia Mott Lane or Mooers Lane.

Continue along Fair Street to Martin's Lane and make a left onto Orange Street. On the left, past the only **row houses** ever built on the island (1831), is the 1809 **Unitarian Universalist Church,** also known as South Church, with the gold-domed spire that soars above the town as the First Congregational Church's slender white steeple does. Also like First Congregational, South Church features a trompe-l'oeil ceiling painting, this one a false, intricately detailed dome, executed in 1840 by another European painter. Here, however, illusion is taken to greater lengths: the curved chancel and paneled walls you see are creations in paint. The 1831 mahogany-cased Goodrich organ in the loft is played at services and concerts. In the octagonal belfry of the tower, which houses the town clock, there is a bell cast in Portugal that has been ringing out the noon hour since it was hung in 1815.

Across the street is **Stone Alley,** a byway that's as pleasant a way of returning to town as any. A left onto Union Street brings you back to the foot of Main Street; on the wall of the last building on the left on Union Street, notice the sign listing distances from Nantucket to various points of the globe (it's 14,650 miles to Tahiti, for instance).

Tour 2: Town—'Sconset—Polpis Loop

Siasconset is reached by road or by a mostly level 7-mile bike path and makes a lovely day trip; off-season there's not a lot to see in the village, but the ride still has its attractions. From town, take Orange Street to the rotary, where Milestone Road and its bike path begin.

Time Out The **Nantucket Bake Shop** (79 Orange St., tel. 508/228–2797; in season) is a great place to stop to fill a knapsack with Portuguese breads and pastries.

About 5½ miles east of the rotary (white stone mile-markers on your left tick out the distance to 'Sconset), signs on the left point to the **Milestone Bog,** more than 200 acres of working cranberry bog surrounded by conservation land. Cultivated since 1857, the bog was the world's largest contiguous natural cranberry bog until it was subdivided after 1959. The land was donated to the Nantucket Conservation Foundation in 1968; a contractor works the bog and harvests the crops, which are sold mostly to Ocean Spray. (For a map of the foundation's properties, as well as walking-tour maps, visit NCF headquarters at 118 Cliff Rd., tel. 508/228–2884, weekdays 9–5.)

The harvest begins in late September and continues for six weeks, during which time harvesters work every day from sun-up to sunset in the flooded bog. The sight of the bright red berries floating on the surface while the moors turn the rich colors of autumn is not to be missed. At other times the color of the dry bog may be green, rust-red, or, in June and early July, the pale pink of cranberry blossoms, but always the bog and the moors always have a quiet beauty that's worth the effort to get there.

Another ½ mile on Milestone Road brings you to an intersection that marks the center of **'Sconset,** a charming village of pretty streets with tiny rose-covered cottages and driveways of crushed white shells. A community of cod and halibut fishermen from the 17th century, Siasconset was already becoming a summer resort as early as the 1870s, when people from Nantucket town would come here as a getaway. In 1884 the narrow-gauge railway—built three years earlier to take spiffily clad folk from the New Bedford steamers to the beach at Surfside for hot-air balloon rides, concerts, or fireworks—came to 'Sconset, bringing ever more off-islanders. These included Broadway actors and actresses on holiday during the theaters' summer recess; attracted by the village's beauty, remoteness, sandy ocean beach, and cheap lodgings (the converted one-room fishing shacks and cottages were built to look like them), they spread the word, and by 1900 'Sconset had become a thriving actors' colony.

Today the village is almost entirely a summer community—it is said that 200 or so families live here year-round, but you would never know it. At the central square are a post office, a liquor store, a bookstore, a market, a restaurant, and a box-lunch place. The town is so small that you really can't make a wrong turn no matter what route you take, but here's a suggestion.

Head back the way you came and turn left onto Morey Lane, where you'll find an English hedge tunnel. At Ocean Avenue, the shore road, turn left. Pochick Avenue, a side street to the left, is one of three in this area (with Evelyn and Lily streets) on which a development of rental cottages in the fishing-shack style was built in the 1890s. These lanes remain much as they were a century ago.

Back on Ocean Avenue, just past Magnolia Avenue, is the **Summer House,** an upscale inn of cottages, with an outdoor pool, a poolside bar, and a restaurant, all open to the public (*see* Sports and Outdoor Activities, Dining, and Lodging, below). Walk on and you'll return to the square; here, turn onto Gulley Road for 'Sconset Beach (or Codfish Park Beach), signaled by a children's swing set. Head back up Gulley to return to town.

At Center Street turn right for the **'Sconset Pump,** a preserved well marked with a plaque proclaiming it was "dug in 1776." Take a left onto New Street here, where you'll pass an art gallery on the right. Past Park Lane, on the opposite side, is the much-photographed entryway of the **Chanticleer** restaurant (*see* Dining, below), spectacular in summer when the greenery-covered trellis frames the blooming rose garden, in the center of which is a flower-bedecked carousel horse. Across from it is the **Siasconset Casino,** built in 1899 during the actors'-colony heyday as a venue for summer-theater productions. Though some theater is still seen here, the Casino is more frequently used as a summer tennis club and cinema.

Also on the left, past Chapel Street, is the **'Sconset Union Chapel,** the village's only church, which on summer Sundays holds a Roman Catholic mass at 8:45 AM and Protestant services at 10:30. Retracing your steps on New Street, turn right onto Center Street, turn left at the end, and right onto Broadway for more cottages, then continue to bear right.

At Baxter Road turn right to head out of 'Sconset by a different route. On the left you'll pass the Scottish-looking golf course of the very private **Sankaty Head Golf Club.** Across from it is red-and-white-striped **Sankaty Light,** one of three Coast Guard–operated lighthouses on Nantucket. Situated on a 90-foot-high bluff that has lost as much as 200 feet of shoreline in the past 75 years, Sankaty is in danger of being lost, as Great Point Light was in 1984, to further erosion. In early 1990 the Army Corps of Engineers recommended moving Sankaty Light away from the shore by as much as 300 feet within five to 15 years.

A fragile piece of land, Nantucket loses more of its shoreline every year, especially at Sankaty and on the south shore, where no shoals break the ocean waves as they do on the north shore. In 1990 oceanfront houses at Cisco were condemned after a winter storm eroded the bluff.

Baxter Road eventually meets Polpis Road, alongside which hundreds of thousands of naturalized daffodils bloom in spring. A million Dutch bulbs donated by an island resident were planted along Nantucket's main roads in 1974, and more have been planted every year since. A bike path is planned for the Polpis Road in the near future.

On the right you'll pass **Sesachacha Pond** (pronounced Seh-SAH-kah-cha or, more often here, where long words seem to be too much trouble, just SAH-kah-cha). At the intersection of

Quidnet Road, take either a right (which will bring you to an Audubon wildlife area a mile down the road, with a walking path around the pond and a good view of Sankaty Light high above) or a left, remaining on Polpis Road. The entrance to the 205-acre **Windswept Cranberry Bog** (part working bog, part conservation land), with a parking area, is a bit farther on the left. (A map of the bog, as well as the 30-page, $4 *Handbook for Visitors to the Windswept Cranberry Bog*, is available from the Nantucket Conservation Foundation; *see* above.)

Continuing on Polpis, a right onto Wauwinet Road leads (after about 2 miles) to the gateway of **Coatue–Coskata–Great Point,** an unpopulated spit of sand comprising three cooperatively managed wildlife refuges. The area may be entered only by four-wheel-drive vehicle, for which a permit is necessary; annual permits cost $40 (or $10 a day for a rental vehicle) and are issued June–October at the gatehouse at Wauwinet, tel. 508/228–0006). In the off-season, you can buy a sticker on the property from a ranger patroling the area). You can also enter on foot, but be aware that Great Point is a 5-mile walk from the entrance on soft, deep sand; Jeepless people often hitchhike here.

Coatue is open for many kinds of recreation—shellfishing for bay scallops, softshell clams, quahogs, and mussels (license required); surf casting for bluefish and striped bass (spring through fall); picnicking; or just enjoying the crowdless expanse. Its beaches, dunes, salt marshes, and stands of oak and cedar attract marsh hawks, oystercatchers, terns, herring gulls, and many other bird species.

Because of frequent dangerous currents and riptides and the lack of lifeguards, swimming is strongly discouraged, especially within 200 yards of the 70-foot stone tower that is the **Great Point Light.** A 1986 re-creation of the lighthouse on that spot that was destroyed by a storm in 1984, the new light was built to withstand 20-foot waves and winds of up to 240 miles an hour.

Continue on Polpis for about 1½ miles, past large areas of open moorland technically called lowland heath, which is very rare in the United States. On the left, opposite Quaise Road, is an unmarked dirt track that leads to **Altar Rock,** a high spot in the midst of moor and bog land from which the view is spectacular. The entire area, of which the Milestone Bog is a part, is laced with trails leading in many directions, so if you want to find your way back to Polpis Road, watch how you come . . . or leave a trail of crumbs.

About ½ mile farther along on Polpis Road, to the right, is the **Nantucket Life Saving Museum,** housed in a re-creation of an 1874 Life Saving Service station. It honors the men who valiantly lived by the service's motto: "You have to go out, but you don't have to come back." Exhibits include original rescue equipment and boats, and photos and accounts of daring rescues. *Polpis Rd., tel. 508/228–1885. Admission: $1. Open mid-June–mid-Oct., Tues.–Sun. 10–5.*

After another 3 miles, Polpis meets the Milestone Road just before the rotary, where Orange Street leads back into Nantucket town.

What to See and Do with Children

The Atheneum (*see* Tour 1, above) has a story hour in its children's wing Wednesday morning at 10 and a children's film Saturday at 10.

Maria Mitchell Association (tel. 508/228–9198) offers nature classes in summer for children ages 5–12.

Maria Mitchell Aquarium displays local marine life in salt- and freshwater tanks. Family shell- and plant-collecting trips are given weekly in season. *29 Washington St., near Commercial Wharf, tel. 508/228–5387. Admission: $1. Open mid-June–Aug., Tues.–Sat. 10–4.*

Actors Theatre of Nantucket (*see* The Arts and Nightlife, below) offers storytelling, music, and more for children in July and August.

Nantucket Island School of Design and the Arts (*see* The Arts and Nightlife, below) offers a year-round program of classes, lectures, and slide shows for children.

J.J. Clammp's is an 18-hole minigolf course set in gardens. There is also motorboating on two ponds. *Nobadeer Farm and Sun Island Rds., off Milestone Rd., tel. 508/228–8977. Admission: 10 AM–6 PM, $5 adults, $4 children; 6 PM–midnight, $6 adults, $5 children. Open July–Aug., daily 10 AM–midnight; June and Sept., daily 10–6.*

Off the Beaten Track

At **Bartlett's Ocean View Farm & Greenhouses,** a 100-acre farm run by eighth-generation Bartletts, visitors are welcome to tour the high-tech facilities, which include computerized greenhouses. A farm stand is open in season; in June you can pick your own strawberries. *Bartlett's Farm Rd., off Hummock Pond Rd., tel. 508/228–9403. Admission free. Open in season, daily 9–5; off-season, Mon.–Sat. 9–5, Sun. 11–5.*

Miacomet Pond. A right turn off Surfside Road onto Miacomet Road (which begins paved but turns to dirt) leads to a freshwater pond surrounded by grass and heath and separated from the ocean by a narrow strip of sand. The pond—in whose reedy fringes swans and snapping turtles are sometimes seen, along with the resident ducks—is a peaceful setting for a picnic or quiet time.

Nantucket Vineyard. Five varieties of vinifera grapes grow at this vineyard and winery 2½ miles south of town. Tastings of red, white, and blush wines are available year-round, as are bottles for purchase. *3 Bartlett Farm Rd., tel. 508/228–9235. Admission free. Open Mon.–Sat. 10–6 (call first in winter).*

Shopping

The island specialty is Nantucket lightship baskets, woven of oak or cane, with woven covers adorned with scrimshaw or rosewood. First made in the 19th century by crew members passing time between chores on a lightship that stood off Sankaty Head, the baskets are now used as chic purses by those who can afford the hefty price tags (from $400 to well over $1,000).

Miniature versions of the baskets are made by plaiting fine threads of gold or silver wire. Some have working hinges and latches; some are decorated with plain or painted scrimshaw or small gems. Prices start at around $300 for gold versions.

Another specialty is sailors' valentines, glass shadow-boxes containing intricate designs made of hundreds of tiny colored shells. Like scrimshaw, the valentines were a way of passing time for whalers on those long, long voyages.

A signature island product is a pair of all-cotton pants called Nantucket Reds, which fade to pink with washing; they're sold only at Murray's Toggery Shop (*see* Clothing, below).

The majority of Nantucket's shops are seasonal, opening sometime after April and closing between Labor Day and November, though an active core stays open longer. Shops below are open year-round unless otherwise specified.

Shopping Districts Nantucket town's commercial district—bounded approximately by the waterfront and Main, Broad, and Centre streets—contains virtually all of the island's shops.

Nantucket Commons (Pleasant St., across from Finast) is a complex of shops about 2 miles from Main Street via Old South Road, past the rotary. Here you'll find a department store, a garden café, a hair salon, a travel agency, and other stores.

Old South Wharf, built in 1770, hosts crafts, clothing, and antiques stores; a ship's chandlery; and art galleries in small, connected "shanties." There is a bank of phones at the end of the wharf.

Straight Wharf, where the Hy-Line ferry docks, is lined with T-shirt and other tourist-oriented shops, a gallery, a museum, and restaurants. Phones and rest rooms are at the end of the wharf; boats for sails and charters line up alongside.

Department Stores **The Mercantile** (Nantucket Commons, tel. 508/228–8739) is the island's only department store, with clothing, toys, household goods, and a one-hour photo lab.

Food Market Monday through Saturday in season, colorful farm stands are set up on Main Street to sell local produce and flowers.

Auctions Antiques auctions are held by **Rafael Osona** (tel. 508/228–3942) from May through October in the American Legion Hall at 21 Washington Street. For a schedule, write to Box 2607, Nantucket 02584.

Specialty Stores The brochure "Antiquing in Nantucket," profiling more than
Antiques 20 antiques shops and locating them on a map, is available at many of the following shops. (*See also* Art and Crafts, below.)

Forager House Collection specializes in folk art and Americana, including whirligigs, wood engravings, vintage postcards, Nantucket baskets, and antique maps and charts. *The Courtyard, 22 Broad St., tel. 508/228–5977. Open May–Dec.*

Nina Hellman Antiques carries scrimshaw, ship models, nautical instruments, and other marine antiques plus folk art and Nantucket memorabilia. *48 Centre St., tel. 508/228–4677. Open May–Dec.*

19 Petticoat Row (19 Centre St., tel. 508/228–5900) carries French and English country china, needlework, lace, linens, pottery, and furniture.

Tonkin of Nantucket (33 Main St., tel. 508/228–9697) has two floors of fine English antiques, including furniture, china, art, silver, marine and scientific instruments, and Staffordshire miniatures; plus new sailors' valentines for $45–$85.

Art **Janis Aldridge** has beautifully framed antique engravings, including architectural and botanical prints, plus home furnishings. *7 Centre St., tel. 508/228–6673. Open May–Nov.*

Main Street Gallery has changing exhibits of paintings, sculptures, and graphics. *50 Main St., tel. 508/228–2252. Open late June–early Sept.*

Paul La Paglia (38 Centre St., tel. 508/228–8760) has antique prints, including Nantucket and whaling scenes, botanicals, and game fish, in a lower price range than Janis Aldridge.

Sailor's Valentine Gallery (38–40 Centre St., tel. 508/228–2011) has folk art in one building and contemporary art and exquisite sailor's valentines next door.

Sherburne Gallery (48 Main St., tel. 508/228–6246) carries fine contemporary American art, most of it representational.

William Welch Gallery exhibits this watercolorist's signature Nantucket scenes, as well as the Nantucket oil paintings of Jack Brown. *Easy St., tel. 508/228–0687. Open Apr.–Dec.*

Books **Mitchell's Book Corner** (54 Main St., tel. 508/228–1080) has a room full of books on Nantucket, plus the usual bookstore fare.

Nantucket Bookworks (25 Broad St., tel. 508/228–4000) carries hardcover and paperback books and unusual gift items.

Clothing **Cordillera Imports** (18 Broad St., tel. 508/228–6140) sells clothing, jewelry, accessories, and crafts from Latin America.

Murray's Toggery Shop (62 Main St., tel. 508/228–0437) is a provider of traditional clothing (much of it designer-label) and footwear for men, women, and children. An outlet store at 7 New Street (tel. 508/228–3584) offers discounts of up to 50%.

The Peanut Gallery (31 Centre St., tel. 508/228–2010) has a discriminating collection of children's clothing.

Vanity Fair has fashions in exotic prints from India and Indonesia, plus jewelry and accessories. *42–44 Centre St., tel. 508/ 228–4263 or 508/228–4384. Open May–mid-Oct.*

Zero Main has stylishly classic women's clothing, shoes, and accessories. *0 Main St., tel. 508/228–4401. Open Apr.–Dec.*

Crafts **Artisans' Cooperative** sells Amish, Appalachian, and other American crafts, such as quilts, jewelry (including miniature lightship baskets), and sweaters. *58 Main St., tel. 508/228– 4631. Open May–mid-Jan.*

Four Winds Craft Guild (6 Straight Wharf, tel. 508/228–9623) carries a large selection of antique and new scrimshaw and lightship baskets, as well as ship models, duck decoys, and a kit for making your own lightship basket.

Nantucket Accent (11 S. Water St., tel. 508/228–1913 or for catalog, 800/323–9276) features Claire Murray's Nantucket-theme hand-hooked rugs, plus knitting and needlework supplies.

The Spectrum sells distinctive art glass, wood boxes, jewelry, kaleidoscopes, and more. *26 Main St., tel. 508/228–4606. Open mid-Apr.–Dec.*

Basketmakers include **Chin's** (29 Centre St., tel. 508/228–4922), **Nantucket Basket Works** (14 Dave St., tel. 508/228–2518), and **Sayle's** (112 Washington St., tel. 508/228–9876).

Gifts **Museum Shop** has a fascinating collection of island-related books, antique whaling tools, spermaceti candles, reproduction furniture, and toys. *Broad St., next to the Whaling Museum, tel. 508/228–5785. Open May–mid-Dec.*

Seven Seas Gifts stocks every kind of fun gift item you can think of, including an exhaustive paper-doll collection, shells, rocks and minerals, T-shirts, and Nantucket jigsaw puzzles. *46 Centre St., tel. 508/228–0958. Open Apr.–Dec.*

Jewelry **Avanti** carries antique and estate jewelry. *4 Federal St., tel. 508/228–5833. Open May–Dec.*

The Golden Basket (44 Main St., tel. 508/228–4344) and its affiliated shop, **Golden Nugget** (Straight Wharf, tel. 508/228–1019), sell miniature lightship baskets and other fine jewelry.

Sports and Outdoor Activities

Bicycling The **Madaket Bike Path,** reached via Cliff Road, is a hilly but beautiful 6-mile route to the western tip of the island. There are picnic tables by Long Pond along the way. The 7-mile **'Sconset Bike Path** starts at the rotary east of town and parallels Milestone Road, ending at 'Sconset. It is mostly level, with some gentle hills (*see* Tour 2 in Exploring Nantucket, above). The easy 3-mile **Surfside Bike Path,** which begins on the Surfside Road (from Main Street take Pleasant Street, then turn right onto Atlantic Avenue), leads to the island's premier ocean beach.

Nantucket Cycling Club (tel. 508/228–2904 or 508/228–8480) holds open races year round, including a triathlon in June and a biathlon in September.

Boating **Club Nautico** (Old South Wharf, tel. 508/228–9865 or 508/228–1333) rents powerboats: bow-riders, center consoles, and cuddy cabins. (*See* also Sailing, below.)

Fishing Bluefish and bass are the main island catches. The bluefishing is best at Great Point. **Barry Thurston's Fishing Tackle** (Harbor Sq., tel. 508/228–9595) and **Bill Fisher Tackle** (14 New La., tel. 508/228–2261) rent equipment and have lots of information on good fishing spots and more.

Leaving out of Straight Wharf in season are several fishing-charter boats, including the *Herbert T* (Slip 14, tel. 508/228–5622). **Captain Gibby Nickerson's** (Slip 16, tel. 508/228–9224) also offers charters. For guided surf-casting by four-wheel-drive, including gear, contact **Whitney Mitchell** (tel. 508/228–2331) or **Beach Excursions** (tel. 508/228–3728).

Golf   **Miacomet Golf Club** (off Somerset Rd., tel. 508/228–9764) and **Siasconset Golf Club** (Milestone Rd., tel. 508/257–6596) are nine-hole public courses.

Health and Fitness Clubs   **Nantucket Health & Fitness Center** (45 Surfside Rd., tel. 508/228–3945) offers aerobics classes; Nautilus, Lifecycle, Stairmaster, Ayrdyne, and rowing machines; free weights; and whirlpool and steam rooms.

Racquetball and Squash   **Nantucket Racquet Club** (10 Young's Way, near the airport, tel. 508/228–0155) has one racquetball and one squash court.

Sailing   The following offer rentals and instructions: **Harbor Sail Livery** (Washington St. Ext., tel. 508/228–1757), which rents O'Day 17's and Sunfish; **Indian Summer Sports** (Jetties Beach, tel. 508/228–9401; Steamboat Wharf, tel. 508/228–3632); **Force 5 Watersports** (Jetties Beach, tel. 508/228–5358; Madaket Rd., tel. 508/228–3322; 37 Main St., tel. 508/228–0700), which rents Sunfish; and **Nantucket Sail** (Petrel Landing, tel. 508/228–4897), which also rents outboards.

Shellfishing   The **shellfish warden** (38 Washington St., tel. 508/228–7260) issues permits for digging for littleneck and cherrystone clams, quahogs, and mussels.

Swimming   Besides the beaches (*see* Beaches, below) and many ponds, the **Summer House** in 'Sconset (tel. 508/257–9976) offers its pool, on the bluff above the ocean beach, to the public in season. Year-round, the **Nantucket Community School's** new indoor pool—just short of Olympic size—is open for lap swimming most days (Atlantic Ave., tel. 508/228–7280, ext. 179, or 228–7257).

Tennis   There are outdoor **town courts** at Jetties Beach; sign up for one hour (usually the limit) of court time, or for lessons or tennis clinics, at the Park and Recreation Commission building there. *Tel. 508/228–3028 or for lessons and clinics, 228–7213. Open mid-June–Labor Day.*

Nantucket Tennis Club has four red-clay courts and offers lessons. *12 Westmoor La., tel. 508/228–3611. Open mid-June–Columbus Day.*

Sea Cliff Tennis Club has nine fast-dry clay courts and offers lessons. *N. Beach St., tel. 228–0030 or 228–4734. Open mid-May–mid-Oct.*

Siasconset Casino is a private club with seven clay courts and one poor hard court; infrequently the club has openings at its courts at 1 or 2 PM; call ahead to check. *New St., tel. 508/257–6661. Open mid-June–mid-Sept.*

Water Sports   Surfing is good on the south coast, windsurfing in the protected areas in the north coast around Dionis Beach. **Harbor Sail Livery** (*see* Sailing, above) rents Windsurfers. **Indian Summer Sports** (*see* Sailing, above) rents Windsurfers, surfboards, body boards, kayaks, Sunfish, and Hobie Cats, and it provides wetsuits and instruction. **Force 5 Watersports** (*see* Sailing, above) rents Windsurfers, surfboards, boogie boards, Sunfish, and other water gear, and offers Windsurfer and sailing lessons.

The Sunken Ship sporting-goods store (Broad and S. Water Sts., tel. 508/228–9226) offers complete dive-shop services, including lessons, equipment rentals, and charters; it also rents water skis, tennis racquets, fishing poles, and other gear.

Beaches

The water around Nantucket is warm from mid-June to sometime into October. The south and east shores have strong surf; those on the north and west side are calmer and warmer. Some beaches are accessible by bike path (*see* Bicycling, above), others by shuttle bus (*see* Getting Around in Essential Information, above), and others by foot or four-wheel-drive only.

Children's A calm area by the harbor, Children's Beach is an easy walk from town (along South Beach Street from Steamboat Wharf) and is good for small children. It offers a grassy park with benches, a playground, lifeguards, food service, and rest rooms.

Cisco For this less-crowded but beautiful beach, from the top of Main Street turn onto Milk Street, which turns into Hummock Pond Road; at the end—a 4-mile ride—is a surf beach with lifeguards.

Dionis To get to this north-shore beach, take the Madaket bike path to Eel Point Road and look for the white rock pointing to Dionis Beach—about 3 miles from town. The narrow strip of beach at the entrance turns into a wider, more private strand with high dunes and fewer children. The beach has a rocky bottom and calm, rolling waters, lifeguards, and rest rooms.

Eel Point Accessible only by foot or four-wheel-drive, Eel Point—an unspoiled conservation area covered in places with goldenrod, wild grapes, roses, bayberries, and other scrub plants—is arguably the island's most beautiful and interesting beach. A spit of land with harbor on one side and shoal-protected ocean on the other, the area is a nesting place for gulls. It also attracts great numbers of other birds, who perch on small islands formed by a sandbar that extends out 100 yards or more. The water is clear, calm, and shallow, and the surf fishing is good.

Take a right off the Madaket bike path onto Eel Point Road; Jeeps can make the trip, but cars will have to be left along the dirt road about ½ mile before the beach, 6 miles from town. (For the Maria Mitchell Association book on Eel Point, stop by the association's office or send $4.50 to 2 Vestal St., Nantucket 02554.)

Jetties A short bike ride (or shuttle-bus ride) from town, Jetties is the most popular beach for families because of its calm surf, lifeguards, bathhouse, rest rooms, and snack bar. It's a lively scene, especially with Windsurfer rentals on the beach.

Madaket Known for great sunsets, this surf beach is reached by the Madaket bike path and offers lifeguards and rest rooms.

Nobadeer This south-shore surf beach, which abuts the eastern end of Surfside, is the party beach for college kids, so expect blasting boom boxes. There are no services. Turn left off Surfside Road at Nonantum Avenue, a rough dirt road; the beach is about ½ mile down.

'Sconset (Codfish Park) Follow the 'Sconset bike path to the village, then take your first right to this calm golden-sand beach with lifeguard and playground. Shuttle-bus service is available.

Surfside Three miles from town by the Surfside bike path or by shuttle bus, this is the premier surf beach, with lifeguards, rest rooms, a snack bar, and a wide strand of sand. It attracts college students as well as families.

Dining

Dining in Nantucket's restaurants is one of the island's greatest—and most expensive—pleasures. Most establishments are in town. If you're on a budget, you might try two drugstore soda fountains with cheap and good soups and sandwiches: **David's** (Congdon's Pharmacy, 47 Main St., tel. 508/228–4549) and **Nantucket Pharmacy** (45 Main St., tel. 508/228–0180). The annual *Nantucket Restaurant Guide*, available at The Hub newsstand (29 Main St., tel. 508/228–4187) and elsewhere, includes menus from 25 or so restaurants and maps locating them.

There are no restaurants or grocery stores to speak of outside town and 'Sconset, aside from Madaket's newly rebuilt **Westender** (Madaket Rd., tel. 508/228–5197), which offers a fish-based menu (including a clambake and a raw bar) and harbor views. The following places put up box lunches in season: **Provisions** (Straight Wharf, tel. 508/228–3258), **Something Natural** (50 Cliff Rd., tel. 508/228–0504), and **Claudette's** ('Sconset center, tel. 508/257–6622).

Category	Cost*
Very Expensive	over $40
Expensive	$30–$40
Moderate	$20–$30
Inexpensive	under $20

per person, excluding drinks, service, and 5% tax

Reviews by Malcolm Wilson

Very Expensive

Chanticleer. Within a rose-covered cottage in 'Sconset is what many consider the island's finest restaurant. For two decades owner-chef Jean-Charles Berruet has created sumptuous classic-French fare using fresh local ingredients and herbs. Characteristic dishes include sautéed boneless loin of lamb with port-and-tarragon sauce, grilled sea bass with roasted peppers and aïoli, and escargot-filled ravioli in garlic broth. Desserts may include a puff-pastry apple tart with Calvados custard or a chocolate-mousse cake with warm orange sabayon. A five-course prix-fixe menu ($50) is offered at dinner (à la carte also available). The main dining room is formal, with a low ceiling, pearl-gray and faux-marble walls, flickering candle-bulb sconces, a fireplace, and a view of the gardens through small-pane windows. The upstairs dining room is smaller and more casual, in pale pink and blue. Lunch in the rose garden is the closest thing to heaven. The wine cellar is legendary, with more than 900 selections from California and France. *9 New St., Siasconset, tel. 508/257–6231. Reservations required well in advance for lunch and dinner. Jacket required at dinner. AE, MC, V. Closed Wed. and Columbus Day–Mother's Day.*
Club Car. The name comes from the railway car—one of those that ran from Steamboat Wharf to 'Sconset years ago—in

which the piano bar is housed. The dining room, though rather noisy, is pleasantly decorated with hanging plants, cane-back chairs, soft-glow lighting, and linen and silver. The Continental menu, which often features seafood, changes with the season and includes game in fall. Cream of chanterelle soup is tangy with onion and herbs; veal sweetbreads may be served with lemon zest and Grand Marnier or braised in butter with veal stock, wine, and herbs. *1 Main St., tel. 508/228–1101. Reservations advised. Jacket advised. AE, CB, DC, MC, V. No lunch. Closed Tues. early Dec.–mid-May and Wed. May–June and Sept.–Oct.*

Topper's. Far from town at the exclusive Wauwinet resort (complimentary jitney service is provided), Topper's serves New American cuisine dishes, such as sautéed lobster with citrus, wild mushrooms, and roasted peppers in a Chardonnay beurre blanc; and medallions of beef with sun-dried tomato and Gorgonzola butter, served with marinated deep-fried onions. The interior, a sophisticated yet relaxed setting, reflects the quality of workmanship that is apparent throughout the inn: hand-decorated floors, fine wood paneling, lovely oil paintings. The outdoor patio overlooking the water is a pleasant place for lunch or drinks, especially at sunset. *Wauwinet Rd., tel. 508/228–8768. Reservations required. Jacket advised at dinner. AE, DC, MC, V. Closed Nov.–Mar.*

Very Expensive–Expensive

DeMarco. A chic, formal restaurant in a refurbished old home in the historic district, DeMarco serves excellent Northern Italian cuisine "with a healthy flair," including homemade pasta and local vegetables and fish. Among the many imaginative dishes produced here are roast medallions of lamb with portabella mushrooms, leeks, and *pancetta* (cured ham or bacon); grilled swordfish with tomatoes, lemon, olive oil, and basil; and fettuccine with lobster, served with arugula and lobster-butter sauce. The overall look is refined rustic: Downstairs there's dark wood, brick walls, and lacy white curtains, while the upstairs is more spacious and brighter, with white walls. *9 India St., tel. 508/228–1836. Reservations required. Dress: smart casual. AE, MC, V. No lunch. Closed late-Sept.–late-May; some weekdays in June and Sept.*

Summer House. A prime location—a bluff looking out to sea in 'Sconset—as well as fine food attract a stylish clientele to this bastion of easygoing classiness. The bar/lounge is an informal area with piano music nightly in season. The dining room carries on the '30s and '40s beach look, with white painted furniture, rose and light-green linens, lots of flowers and hanging plants, and paintings of Nantucket scenes. The menu centers on fresh fish, such as seared swordfish with a pecan-nutmeg crust; nonfish entrées include beef with truffle-and-port sauce. Appetizers may include smoked scallops, bluefish, and salmon with wasabi *crème fraîche.* Frozen drinks and light lunches (pâté; steamed mussels; salad bar with tabouli, chèvre, and grilled mushrooms) are served poolside. *Ocean Ave., Siasconset, tel. 508/257–9976. Reservations advised. Dress: casual. AE, MC, V. No lunch in indoor dining room. Closed Nov.–Apr.; Mon. and Tues. May–mid-June and Labor Day–Oct.*

Expensive

★ **American Seasons.** A few blocks from town, chef-proprietors Everett and Stuart Reid have created an exemplary provincial American menu with such main dishes as duckling with maple-cranberry sauce and a pilaf of wild rice and pecans; grilled calf's liver with smoked bacon and applejack-onion jam; and New York sirloin with bourbon gravy and straw potatoes. The creative cuisine is not matched by the interior, which lacks intimacy despite the low ceiling, Colonial wall sconces, white linens, and long white candles in hurricane globes. *80 Centre St., tel. 508/228-7111. Reservations advised. Dress: smart casual. AE, MC, V. No lunch. Sun. brunch served Sept.-Dec. Closed Jan.-Mar.*

★ **Boarding House.** The changing menu of New American dishes at this consistently fine restaurant may include swordfish with toasted pecans and a shallot-and-parsley béarnaise sauce; roast rack of lamb with shoestring potatoes; and excellent soups, such as lobster-and-leek bisque. A limited menu of such appetizers as rolled veal bundle with pancetta and sage is available in the bar, an airy room with marble-top tables; in good weather lunch is served at café tables outside, amid the bustle of town. The dining room is intimate, with low ceilings, soft lighting, muted music, salmon-colored upholstery and napkins, and white linen tablecloths. Exposed beams and pipes and brick or plaster wall surfaces add a pleasant rustic touch. *12 Federal St., tel. 508/228-9622. Reservations required in season. Jacket advised. AE, CB, DC, MC, V. Closed mid-Jan.-mid-Feb.*

Company of the Cauldron. The dark-red, small-pane windows at the entrance of this romantic spot are framed with climbing ivy. Inside, a profusion of flowers and antique decorative items—hanging copper pans, ship paintings and models, a Colonial chandelier, pie-plate sconces and pierced-tin lanterns with candles—completes the mood. A single four-course prix-fixe menu is offered at two seatings each evening. An example: medallions of duck breast in rich gravy, sliced peach cooked with mango-chutney stock, snow peas, nutty wild rice, diced green and red sweet peppers, and dessert of pound cake in raspberry *coulis* (purée). Service is unhurried but impeccable. *7 India St., tel. 508/228-4016. Reservations advised. Dress: smart casual. MC, V. No lunch. Closed Mon. and Columbus Day-Memorial Day.*

India House. This downtown inn, built as a private home in 1803, has two small dining rooms that reflect their origins, with low beamed ceilings, hardwood floors, and small-pane windows with white café curtains. In the blue room, walls are covered half in wainscoting and half in Colonial-print wallpaper, with period paintings and petit-point lacework. The pink room has the original wide-board floors and fireplace. The cuisine is nouvelle American, with seafood well represented in dishes like grilled swordfish with a zesty papaya salsa, and poached salmon with fennel aïoli. There's also outdoor dining in summer from a lighter and less expensive menu. The popular Sunday brunch includes such temptations as pumpkin pancakes and poached eggs with smoked salmon and caviar. *37 India St., tel. 508/228-9043. Reservations advised. Dress: smart casual. MC, V. No lunch. Closed Nov.-Memorial Day.*

Le Languedoc. This delightful place in a refurbished building in the historic district consists of a formal upstairs dining room decorated in Pierre Deux fabrics and English pine for a French-country effect, and a bistro-style café downstairs and on the garden terrace. Examples of the dining room's innovative American and Continental cuisine are roast rack of lamb with honey, mustard, and beluga; soft-shell crabs Parisian, with white wine, shallots, vermouth, tomatoes, and lemon-risotto cakes; and game. Mainstays of the lower-price café menu are seasonal soups, Caesar salad, smoked-chicken sandwiches, and simply cooked fish. *24 Broad St., tel. 508/228–2552. Reservations advised for dining room. Jacket advised in dining room. AE, MC, V. No lunch July–Aug. Closed Jan.–mid-Apr.; Mon. mid-Apr.–June and Oct.–Dec.*

21 Federal Street. The epitome of sophisticated island dining, this is a place to be seen, as well as to enjoy some of the best new and traditional American cuisine served north of Manhattan. An informal dining room extends into the dark-paneled bar. Beyond are two other dining rooms, with gray wainscoting, black-suede banquettes, and damask-covered tables; a curving staircase leads to a similar second floor. Lunch and a 5-to-7 PM raw bar are served on the patio. Entrées include roast tenderloin of pork with coriander and fresh tomatillos, and grilled leg and rack of lamb with roasted garlic. The only complaint ever heard about 21 is that service can be less than friendly. *21 Federal St., tel. 508/228–2121. Reservations required. Dress: smart casual. AE, MC, V. Closed mid-Jan.–mid-Apr.*

Moderate–Expensive

Bounty. Bounty has a sparse, cool look, with bare-wood floors, lemon-yellow walls, and green-and-white valances on the windows. Soft music, watercolors and abstracts, a few plants, and a fireplace add touches of warmth. The basically American menu centers on fresh seafood, including chowder made of clams, corn, and leeks, and scrod Alforno (browned cod fillets baked with Parmesan cheese and topped with herb dressing. Among the nonfish dishes are grilled marinated leg of lamb with mint-and-garlic sauce. *20 Broad St., tel. 508/228–8505. Reservations required. Dress: casual. AE, MC, V. Closed Jan.–Apr.*

Jared's. The formal restaurant of the Jared Coffin House is the island's most elegant dining room, with a high ceiling, salmon-colored pale-green table linens and swag drapes, Federal-period antique furnishings, and chandeliers with frosted-glass globes. The American fare is equally elegant, typified by such dishes as grilled breast of duck with honey-plum glaze, served with duck confit and wild-rice pancakes; and chicken breast stuffed with rock shrimp and baked in pastry, served with a mustard-dill cream sauce. A menu of $25 prix-fixe meals is offered. Service is impressive and pleasant, and the wine list is large. *29 Broad St., tel. 508/228–2400. Reservations advised. Jacket advised. AE, DC, MC, V. No lunch; no dinner Jan.–Apr. (breakfast year-round).*

Sconset Cafe. In 'Sconset center one of the finest cooks on the island serves an imaginative American cuisine in a beach-café setting: white ceiling, walls, and ceiling fans; chintz tablecloths; and rotating displays of Nantucket art. Inexpensive lunch offerings include sandwiches and salads, such as the popular *fajitas* chicken salad: a crisp flour tortilla shell filled with marinated chicken breast, lettuce, tomato, scallions, guacamole, sour cream, and salsa, topped with lime vinaigrette. Save room for the homemade desserts. The evening menu, which changes daily, features more elaborate dinners, such as confit of duck with sun-dried Bing cherries. *Post Office Sq., Siasconset, tel. 508/257-4008. No reservations. Dress: casual. No credit cards. BYOB (liquor store next door). Closed mid-Sept.-mid-May.*

Woodbox. The three small dining rooms on the first floor of this inn a few blocks from town reflect their 1709 origins, with seasoned variable-width plank floors, exposed beams, and braided rugs. One room at the back looks like the kitchen it was in the inn's early days, with walls of aged brick and extra-wide "king's boards," antique kitchen implements, and Colonial-style furniture. Yankee, contemporary American, and Continental dishes—chowder, scampi with sun-dried-tomato-and-basil sauce, beef Wellington with cabernet sauce—and wonderful popovers are served on English china and silverplate. *29 Fair St., tel. 508/228-0587. Reservations advised. Jacket advised. No credit cards. Breakfast and dinner only. Closed Mon. and Oct.-May.*

Moderate

★ **Beach Plum Cafe and Bakery.** A casual place well outside town, with polished-wood floors and softly hued local artworks on white walls, this restaurant offers early breakfasts (from 7 AM), great lunch sandwiches (such as smoked turkey and fresh cranberry on French bread), and a dinner menu that is an eclectic mix of cuisines. Choices may include a Thai stir-fry of chicken with crunchy peapods, bean sprouts, red peppers, and ginger sauce; or simply cooked bay scallops. The bakery sells take-out sandwiches, breads, and desserts. *11 West Creek Rd., tel. 508/228-8893. Reservations required for 8 or more. Dress: casual. MC, V. Closed Tues.*

The Hearth at the Harbor House. After a major face-lift in 1989, the restaurant has a new outdoor patio and an attractive dining room with a chessboard-design parquet floor, oversize steel-and-copper chandeliers, antique-red walls, and red-and-green-plaid taffeta-look upholstered chairs. The New England fare is simply prepared—surf-and-turf combinations (filet mignon, lamb chop, and baked stuffed shrimp, for example) are popular, as are charbroiled swordfish and baked flounder stuffed with crabmeat and moistened with parsley butter. A Sunday brunch buffet is also offered. The four-course early-bird special helps beat the high cost of eating. *S. Beach St., tel. 508/228-1500. Reservations advised; required for Sun. brunch. Dress: casual. AE, CB, DC, MC, V. No lunch. No breakfast Oct.-May.*

The Tap Room. The downstairs tavern restaurant of the Jared Coffin House is a dark, woody, cozy room decorated with ship prints and whale models. The dinner menu features hearty meat and fish dishes, such as prime rib, fried clams, and baked stuffed fillet of sole; at lunch choose from a light menu or more substantial dishes like fried or broiled fish, eaten on the outdoor patio, weather permitting. *29 Broad St., tel. 508/228-2400. No reservations. Dress: casual. AE, DC, MC, V.*

Inexpensive

Atlantic Cafe. This casual, sometimes noisy place at the center of town offers an active bar and a fun menu, with large portions at a good price. Finger foods include zucchini sticks that are golden and crispy on the outside, moist on the inside, sprinkled with grated cheese, and served with a hot sauce. Entrées are a mix of simply prepared fish, chicken, burgers, Mexican items, and more. At the front of the restaurant, with exposed beams and hanging plants, are tables topped with floral cloths and glass; at the back are booths. *S. Water St., tel. 508/228–0570. No reservations. Dress: casual. AE, CB, DC, MC, V.*

★ **The Brotherhood of Thieves.** Long lines are a fixture outside this English-style pub restaurant. Inside, lit by flickering candles, is a dark room with low ceilings, exposed brick and beams, and a fireplace that is especially welcoming on cold or rainy evenings. When the place gets busy, strangers are seated together at long tables; a section at the back has more intimate seating. A convivial atmosphere prevails—thanks partly to the live folk music at night and to the hundreds of alcoholic beverages on the menu. Dine happily on good chowder and soups, fried fish and seafood, burgers, jumbo sandwiches, and shoestring fries (long curls with the skins on). *23 Broad St., no tel. No reservations. Dress: casual. No credit cards.*

Downy Flake. Folks line up outside this no-frills diner in the center of town for the down-home cooking: soups and sandwiches, thick grilled ham steaks, and daily specials (like flaky, moist fish-and-chips). Worth a trip are the hot biscuits. Breads and doughnuts are available to take out. *S. Water St., tel. 508/228–4533. No reservations. Dress: casual. No credit cards. Breakfast and lunch only. Closed Wed.*

★ **Quaker House.** This storefront restaurant—two small, prettily decorated rooms whose small-pane windows framed in lace look out onto Centre Street—is one of the best bargains on the island. Prix-fixe four-course dinners feature such entrées as Bombay chicken (a curry with apple, raisins, and coconut), swordfish with béarnaise sauce, and beef and pasta dishes. The owners take pride in the quality of their ingredients. At breakfast try the baked-apple pancake, huge and sweet, with cinnamony apples and powdered sugar. *5 Chestnut St., tel. 508/228–9152. No reservations. Dress: casual. MC, V. Breakfast and dinner only. Closed Columbus Day–Memorial Day.*

Rose & Crown. A fun, lively place, the Rose & Crown is a barnlike room with beam ceiling, walls hung with old signs and musical instruments, a big bar, and a dance floor (there's live music many afternoons and evenings). Choose from appetizers such as cheddar fries, Buffalo chicken wings, and popcorn shrimp; for main courses, there are fish-and-chips, burgers, and more adventurous offerings such as crab-and-shrimp croissants, chicken quesadillas, and chicken teriyaki. *23 S. Water St., tel. 508/228–2595. No reservations. Dress: casual. AE, MC, V. Closed Nov.–mid-Apr.*

Lodging

Other than cottages (which are scattered throughout the island) and a few inns and hotels, all of Nantucket's lodging places are in town. Those in the center are convenient, but houses are close together and right on the street; in season there may be street noise until midnight. Inns a five- or 10-minute walk from the center, as on Cliff Road or Fair Street, are quieter. 'Sconset is quieter still and has the rose-covered cottages and less crowded beach, but those looking for action will be frustrated by the 7-mile commute to town.

In the off-season, places that remain open drop their prices dramatically, often by 50%. The **Nantucket Information Bureau** (*see* Important Addresses and Numbers in Essential Information, above) maintains a list of room availability in season for last-minute bookings.

Nantucket Accommodations (Box 217, Nantucket 02554, tel. 508/228–9559) and **Martha's Vineyard and Nantucket Reservations** (Box 1322, Lagoon Pond Rd., Vineyard Haven 02568, tel. 508/693–7200) book inns, hotels, bed-and-breakfasts, and cottages. **House Guests Cape Cod and the Islands** (Box 1881, Orleans 02653, tel. 508/896–7053 or 800/666–4678) books B&Bs only. **Heaven Can Wait** (Box 622, Siasconset 02564, tel. 508/257–4000) plans island honeymoons. The Chamber of Commerce and the Information Bureau will provide a list of realtors who handle rental cottages. No camping is allowed on Nantucket.

The **Star of the Sea AYH-Hostel,** a 72-bed facility in a former life-saving station, is a 3-mile ride on a bike path from town, at Surfside Beach. Reserve one month in advance. *Surfside, Nantucket 02554, tel. 508/228–0433. Open May–Columbus Day.*

Category	Cost*
Very Expensive	over $200
Expensive	$150–$200
Moderate	$90–$150
Inexpensive	under $90

*all prices are for a standard double room in high season, excluding 5.7% state tax and 4% local tax

Very Expensive

Cliffside Beach Club. Although the cedar-shingle exterior, landscaped with climbing roses and hydrangeas, and the pavilion on the private sandy beach reflect the club's 1920s origins, the interiors have been redesigned in summery contemporary style, with white walls, fine woodwork, white or natural wood furniture, cathedral ceilings, and local art. All rooms have refrigerators, cable TV/HBO, and phones; some have air conditioning, kitchenettes, fireplaces, wet bars, or private decks. Two big new town-house suites have full kitchens and decks overlooking dunes, moors, and Nantucket Sound. A complimentary Continental breakfast is served; town is about a mile away. *Jefferson Ave., Box 449, Nantucket 02554, tel. 508/228–0618. 19 rooms, 8 apartments, 1 cottage. Facilities: restaurant; piano bar; beach; playground; exercise room with Nautilus, Stairmaster, treadmill; day sails available. AE. Closed mid-Oct.–late May.*

Summer House. Here, across from 'Sconset Beach and clustered around a flower-filled yard, are the rose-covered cottages we associate with Nantucket summers. Each one- or two-bedroom cottage is furnished in a blend of unfussy, breezy beach style and romantic English country—white walls, white lace and eyelet curtains and spreads, Laura Ashley floral accents, and stripped English-pine antique furnishings. Some cottages have fireplaces or kitchens; all have new marble baths with whirlpools. A complimentary Continental breakfast is served. *Ocean Ave., Box 313, Siasconset 02564, tel. 508/257–9976. 8 cottages. Facilities: 2 restaurants, piano bar, poolside bar, oceanfront outdoor pool, volleyball; tennis nearby. AE, MC, V. Closed mid-Oct.–mid-May.*

★ **Wauwinet.** An exquisite location, impeccable furnishings, and extensive services and amenities make this perhaps Nantucket's most luxurious accommodations. A sweeping lawn with white chaise longues leads to a pebbly private harbor beach. A minute's walk through dunes gives you a view of miles of sandy Atlantic Ocean beach stretching in relative isolation—there is little else here, at the gateway to Coatue. Jitney service to and from town 8 miles away and airport and ferry pickup make the location convenient for those without cars. This historic 19th-century hotel was given a $3 million renovation in 1988. Each guest room—individually decorated in country/beach style, with pine antiques—has a phone, air-conditioning, and color TV with VCR; the most expensive have spectacular views of the sunset over the water. A complimentary Continental breakfast is served. *Wauwinet Rd., Box 2580, Nantucket 02584, tel. 508/228–0145 or 800/426–8718, fax 508/228–6712. 29 rooms, 5 cottages. Facilities: restaurant, bar, room service, 2 Har-Tru tennis courts, Windsurfer and Sunfish rentals and lessons, harbor sails, croquet, turndown service, concierge, videocassette library, business services, massage. AE, DC, MC, V. Closed Dec.–Mar.*

Expensive–Very Expensive

Wharf Cottages. These weathered-shingle cottages sit on a wharf in Nantucket harbor, with yachts tied up just steps away. Each has a telephone, cable TV with VCR, a fully equipped kitchen, and a modern nautical decor that includes white walls, navy-blue rugs, and light-wood floors and furniture. Studios have a queen-size sleep-sofa, armoire, kitchen, and table and chairs; other cottages have one to three bedrooms. There's a three-night minimum in season, and monthly and seasonal rates are available. *New Whale St., Box 1139, Nantucket 02554, tel. 508/228–4620; for reservations, tel. 508/228–5500 or 800/475–2637. 40 cottages. Facilities: daily linen exchange, maid service (extra charge), children's program Memorial Day–Labor Day. AE, CB, DC, MC, V.*

White Elephant. Like the Wauwinet, the White Elephant is known for its location—in this case, on Nantucket harbor—and its complete services: The concierge staff will take care of just about anything for you. The hotel consists of the main building, several gray-shingled cottages, and The Breakers, offering the most luxurious accommodations. Between 1989 and 1990 the entire property was renovated, and all the furnishings are fresh and new. All rooms have phones and cable TV with VCR; some have air-conditioning and harbor views. In The Breakers' top-price waterside rooms, French doors open onto the lawn or on a private deck overlooking the harbor, with a great view. A Continental breakfast is served. *Easton St., Box 359, Nantucket 02554, tel. 508/228–2500; for reservations, tel. 508/228–5500 or 800/475–2637. 48 rooms, 22 1- to 3-bedroom cottages. Facilities: restaurant, lounge with entertainment, room service until 10 PM, poolside food service, concierge, heated outdoor pool, croquet court, putting green, reduced rate at local* *health and tennis clubs, minifridges, business services (meeting rooms, audiovisual equipment, fax), boat slips available, children's program Memorial Day–Labor Day. AE, CB, DC, MC, V.*

Expensive

★ **Harbor House.** This family-oriented complex is owned by the same people who own the Wharf Cottages and the White Elephant (*see* above), and, like its more upscale sibling, it has been extensively renovated and prides itself on service. The 1886 main inn and several cottages are set on a nicely landscaped quadrangle steps from the town center. Standard rooms are done in English-country style, with bright floral fabrics; town houses have a more traditional look, with upscale pine and pastels. The town-house rooms are generally larger; some have whirlpools, cathedral ceilings, and pull-out couches. All rooms have phones and TVs with VCR; some have decks. The Garden Cottage has its own garden, an elegant entrance hall decorated with antiques, and pressed-tin ceilings, but rooms in this cottage are smaller than others at Harbor House. *S. Beach St., Box 1048, Nantucket 02554, tel. 508/228–1500; for reservations, tel. 508/228–5500 or 800/475–2637. 11 rooms. Facilities: restaurant, lounge with entertainment, poolside bar, room service until 10 PM, concierge, heated outdoor pool, putting green, business services, reduced rate at local health and tennis clubs, children's program Memorial Day–Labor Day. AE, DC, MC, V.*

Seven Sea Street. This inn on a quiet side street in the center of town was built in 1987. Though the all-new furnishings are in the colonial style and colors, the place has a cool Scandinavian look. The building is done in tongue-in-groove light pine and red oak, with exposed-beam ceilings, white walls with pine trim, and highly polished wide-board floors. Each room is furnished with a braided rug, a queen-size pencil-post bed with fishnet canopy and quilt, a rocking chair, a modern bath with large fiberglass stall shower and brass fittings, a phone, cable TV, refrigerator, and desk area. A complimentary Continental breakfast is served. *7 Sea St., Nantucket 02554, tel. 508/228–3577. 8 rooms. No smoking. Facilities: group-size Jacuzzi. AE, MC, V.*

Moderate–Expensive

★ **Jared Coffin House.** This complex of six buildings is a longtime favorite of many visitors to Nantucket for its dependability and class. The main building, a three-story brick mansion built in 1845 by a wealthy shipowner and topped by a cupola, has a historic tone that the others don't. The public and guest rooms are furnished with period antiques (the other buildings, with reproductions), Oriental carpets, and lace curtains; the second-floor corner rooms are the most comfortable, with more windows and sitting areas. The Harrison Gray House, an 1842 Greek Revival mansion across the street, offers larger guest rooms with large baths and some sofas, as well as less street noise. All rooms have phones and, except in the main house, color TV; some have minifridges. Small, inexpensive single rooms are available. *29 Broad St., Nantucket 02554, tel. 508/228–2405. 58 rooms. Facilities: restaurant, tavern, outdoor café, concierge. AE, DC, MC, V.*

Moderate

Centerboard Guest House. The look of this inn, a few blocks from the center of town, is different from any other. The white walls (some with murals of moors and sky in soft pastels), blond-wood floors, white or natural wood furniture, and natural woodwork with a light wash of mauve tint create a cool, spare, dreamy atmosphere. There is yet more white, in the lacy linens and puffy comforters on the feather beds. Touches of color are added by small stained-glass lamps, antique quilts, and fresh flowers. The first-floor suite is a stunner, with 11-foot ceilings, a large Victorian living room with working fireplace and wet bar, parquet floors, exquisite furnishings and decor, and a green-marble bath with Jacuzzi. The small studio apartment has a private entrance. Each room has a TV with VCR access (you rent tapes in town), a phone, and a minifridge. A complimentary Continental breakfast is served. *8 Chester St., Box 456, Nantucket 02554, tel. 508/228–9696. 5 rooms, 1 suite, 1 studio. AE, MC, V.*

Century House. This 1833 house, a few blocks from the town center, was built to serve guests, and it continues to do so with warm and casual style. All the wallpapers and fabrics are in the Laura Ashley light-floral style. Simple, homey furnishings stand on spatter-painted wide-board floors. A breakfast buffet highlighted by homemade granola is served in the country kitchen or on the large wraparound veranda. In the afternoon guests gather for tea or cocktails; setups and snacks are provided. The innkeepers also rent two cottages, one in 'Sconset across from the beach and one on Nantucket harbor. A complimentary Continental breakfast is served. *10 Cliff Rd., Nantucket 02554, tel. 508/228–0530. 10 rooms, 8 with private bath. Facilities: common TV. No credit cards.*

Parker Guest House. Clean and cheerful, with new beds, a minifridge, color cable TV, and a coffee maker in every room, this guest house is at the low end of the moderate price scale but smack in the center of town. This makes it convenient, though it may be noisy at night. The decor is simple, with pine paneling and furnishings and country curtains. In the first-floor rooms' quirky bathrooms, fixtures are tucked in wherever they fit. *4 E. Chestnut St., Nantucket 02554, tel. 508/228–4625 or 800/248–4625. 7 rooms, 5 with private bath. No smoking. AE, MC, V.*

★ **76 Main Street.** Built in 1883 by a sea captain, just above the bustle of the shops, this B&B carefully blends antiques and reproductions, Oriental rugs, handmade quilts, and lots of fine woods. The Victorian entrance hall is of cherry and is dominated by a long, elaborately carved staircase. Room No. 3, originally the dining room, also has wonderful woodwork, a carved-wood armoire, and twin canopy four-posters; spacious No. 1, once the front parlor, has three large windows, a high ceiling, massive redwood pocket doors, and a canopy bed with eyelet spread and canopy. Both are on the first floor. The motel-like rooms in the 1955 annex out back have low ceilings and are a bit dark but are large and good for families: they have color TV and a refrigerator. A complimentary Continental breakfast is served. *76 Main St., Nantucket 02554, tel. 508/228–2533. 18 rooms. No smoking. Facilities: common refrigerator. AE, MC, V.*

★ **Ten Lyon Street Inn.** A five-minute walk from the town center, this mostly new house has been rebuilt with historical architectural touches such as variable-width plank floors, salvaged Colonial mantels on the nonworking fireplaces, and hefty ceiling beams of antiqued red oak. The white walls and blond woodwork provide a clean stage for exquisite antique Oriental rugs in deep, rich colors; choice antiques, such as Room No. 1's French tester bed draped in white mosquito netting; and English floral fabrics. Bathrooms are white and bright; several have separate shower and antique tubs and all have antique porcelain pedestal sinks and brass fixtures. A complimentary health-conscious Continental breakfast is served. *10 Lyon St., Nantucket 02554, tel. 508/228–5040. 7 rooms. AE, MC, V. Closed mid-Dec.–Apr.*

Wade Cottages. On a bluff overlooking the ocean, this complex of guest rooms, apartments, and cottages in 'Sconset couldn't be better located for beach lovers. The buildings, most from the 1800s and furnished in casual, somewhat worn beach style, are arranged around a central lawn with a great ocean view; the prize catch is a newer cottage nearer the water. Most inn rooms and cottages have sea views. Inn rooms include Continental breakfast. *Shell St., Siasconset 02564, tel. 508/257–6308 or 257–6383; off-season, 212/989–6423. 8 rooms, 3 with private bath; 5 apartments; 3 cottages. Facilities: ping-pong, badminton, common refrigerator, laundry, beach. No credit cards. Closed mid-Oct.–late May.*

Woodbox. The inn comprises the 1709 main building, an annex, and a house a few doors down. Accommodations include one- and two-bedroom suites, each with sitting area and fireplace, and some double rooms; minifridges are available. The two-bedroom suite and double room over the restaurant are exquisitely done, with superb antique pieces. The other buildings are less formally furnished, but antiques are sprinkled throughout. *29 Fair St., Nantucket 02554, tel. 508/228–0587. 9 units. Facilities: restaurant. No credit cards. Closed Oct.–May.*

Moderate–Inexpensive

Carlisle House Inn. A block or two from the center of town is this 1765 Colonial. A deluxe first-floor guest room has an original wall of pine paneling and with working fireplace, an Oriental carpet, a canopy bed, a marble-top dresser and side table, a TV, and a small bath. Most rooms have a casual, Grandma's-house feel, with wicker chairs, iron-and-brass or other antique beds, working fireplaces (five rooms), pumpkin-pine floors, country curtains and stenciled walls, and a claw-foot tub here and there. A complimentary Continental breakfast is served in a bright, glassed-in sunporch. Small single rooms are available. *26 N. Water St., Nantucket 02554, tel. 508/228–0720. 14 rooms, 8 with private bath (6 rooms share 2 baths). AE.*

★ **Corner House.** Accommodations at this B&B a block or two from the town center range from tiny, rustic third-floor rooms (with equally tiny baths) in the main house, built around 1790, to large rooms with cathedral ceilings in a new building nearby. Some rooms have sitting areas, TVs, or refrigerators; all have antique brass or canopy beds, down pillows and comforters, and firm new mattresses and box springs. The many common areas include the main house's original keeping room, where guests gather for tea, and a large living room with fireplace;

both feature richly detailed Colonial woodwork. A complimentary Continental breakfast is served. *49 Centre St., Nantucket 02554, tel. 508/228–1530. 14 rooms, 1 suite. Smoking discouraged. Facilities: common TV, fax. AE, MC, V. Closed 2–3 wks in Jan.*

Martin's Guest House. This casual and homey B&B in an 1803 house off the main drag offers mostly spacious rooms with country curtains, four-poster beds or canopies, and fresh flowers. Room No. 21, on the second floor, has a queen-size bed, a sofa, and a private porch overlooking the backyard. The large, comfortable living room with a fireplace invites lingering. A complimentary Continental breakfast is served. *61 Centre St., Nantucket 02554, tel. 508/228–0678. 13 rooms, 9 with private bath (4 rooms share 1 bath). Facilities: common TV, piano. AE, MC, V.*

Quaker House. An 1847 storefront in the center of town houses a restaurant downstairs (*see* Dining, above) and inn rooms on the second and third floors. Rooms have queen-size beds with fabric-covered headboards, French-style wallpapers, and window swags. Each room has some antique pieces; small rooms have air-conditioning. An attic room (with tree) is different and, with its steeply sloped ceiling, fun for those under 6 feet 2. Rooms at the front get street light and noise. The bathrooms were built in 1987–88, and some are tiny indeed. *5 Chestnut St., Nantucket 02554, tel. 508/228–0400. 8 rooms. No smoking. Facilities: restaurant. MC, V. Closed Columbus Day–Memorial Day.*

Inexpensive

★ **Chestnut House.** At this centrally located guest house, the innkeepers' hand-hooked rugs and paintings, along with their son's Tiffany-style lamps, are everywhere, creating homey guest rooms. All rooms have minifridges; each suite has a sitting room with sofa, desk, TV, and sherry. The cottage sleeps four (queen-size bed and sofa-bed) and has a full kitchen and bath—a convenient option for a family here in the center of town. Morning coffee is served. *3 Chestnut St., Nantucket 02554, tel. 508/228–0049. 3 rooms, 3 suites, 1 cottage. Facilities: common TV. MC, V.*

Hawthorn House. Not only did innkeeper Mitch Carl continue the family business when he opened his guest house; he opened his inn just down the street from his folks' place, the Chestnut House (*see* above). Mitch and his wife, Diane, have filled their 1850 house with art, hooked rugs, and stained glass. The small rooms are decorated with antiques and pretty wallpapers. A dark but conveniently located cottage sleeps two. Morning coffee is served. *2 Chestnut St., Nantucket 02554, tel. 508/228–1468. 7 rooms, 5 with private bath; 1 cottage. Facilities: common TV, refrigerators. MC, V.*

Nesbitt Inn. This family-run guest house in the center of town offers comfortable, shared-bath rooms (including cheap singles) in Victorian style, with lace curtains, some marble-top and brass antiques, and a sink in each room. The beds are not as firm as they should be, and the location (next door to a popular bar-restaurant) means it gets noisy (ask for a room on the opposite side, which is quieter), but the Nesbitt is still a good buy. A complimentary Continental breakfast is served. *21 Broad St., Nantucket 02554, tel. 508/228–0156 or 228–2446. 10 doubles*

and 3 singles share 3 baths. Pets allowed. Facilities: swing set.
MC, V.

The Arts and Nightlife

The "Complete Dining & Entertainment Guide" in the free *Nantucket Map & Legend*, published weekly from May through October, is the best source for information on events; the guide can be found all over Nantucket. Also see *Yesterday's Island*, a free paper available on the ferries, and the weekly newspaper sections "What's Up" in the *Nantucket Beacon* and "Nightlife" in the *Inquirer and Mirror*.

All venues listed below are located in Nantucket town, unless otherwise indicated.

The Arts

Nantucket: Closed for the Season is a slide show on Nantucket, created by one of the island's best photographers, Cary Hazlegrove. *Methodist Church, Centre St., tel. 508/228–3783. Shows given June–Sept.*

Nantucket Arts Council (tel. 508/228–2227) sponsors a series of classical and other performances at the Methodist Church on Centre Street from September through June.

Nantucket Island School of Design and the Arts (Wauwinet Rd., tel. 508/228–9248; for schedule, write to Box 1848, Nantucket 02554) offers a year-round program of classes, lectures, and slide shows for adults and children.

Theater The **Actors Theatre of Nantucket** (Folger Hotel, 89 Easton St., tel. 508/228–6325) presents seven plays each season, from May through October, plus a guest-artist series and children's matinees.

Theatre Workshop of Nantucket (Little Theatre, Bennett Hall, 62 Centre St., tel. 508/228–4305), a community theater since 1956, offers plays and musicals year-round.

Music **Nantucket Chamber Music Center** (Coffin School, Winter St., tel. 508/228–3352) offers year-round choral and instrumental concerts as well as instruction.

In July and August, **Nantucket Musical Arts Society** (Box 897, Nantucket 02554, tel. 508/228–3735) holds Tuesday-evening concerts featuring internationally acclaimed musicians (past participants include Virgil Thomson and Ned Rorem) at the First Congregational Church (62 Centre St.), and free informal "Meet the Artists" gatherings the previous evening at the Little Gallery on Straight Wharf.

Also in July and August, **Noonday Concerts** on an 1831 Goodrich organ are given Thursdays at noon at the Unitarian Church (11 Orange St., tel. 508/228–0738 or 228–5466).

Band concerts (tel. 508/228–1700) are held on Sundays in July and August at 7 PM in Harbor Square.

Film **Dreamland Theatre** (19 S. Water St., tel. 508/228–5356) and **Gaslight** (N. Union St., tel. 508/228–4435) are the island's two first-run theaters. The **Siasconset Casino** (New St., 'Sconset, tel. 508/257–6661) shows first-run films in season—bring a pillow to make sitting on the metal folding chairs more comfortable.

Nightlife

Except for two dance clubs, Nantucket's evening entertainment takes place in restaurants and restaurant lounges.

Tavern Restaurants **The Brotherhood of Thieves** (*see* Dining, above) has live folk music year-round. The well-stocked bar offers an interesting selection of beers and ales, plus dozens of cordials and liqueurs.

The Tap Room (*see* Dining, above) has live easy-listening piano or guitar, and sometimes Irish folk music, year-round.

Piano Lounges **The Hearth at the Harbor House** (*see* Dining, above) has dancing to live music year-round and to Top 40 tunes by a piano-and-vocal duo in season. The crowd is upscale middle-age.

The Regatta at the White Elephant (*see* Lodging, above) has a formal lounge with pianist playing show tunes from mid-May to mid-September. Proper dress is required.

Windsong (27 Macy's La., at the airport, tel. 508/228–6900), the Nantucket Inn's seafood restaurant, has easy-listening and jazz piano. Free transportation from town is provided.

Dance Clubs The island's two dance clubs, open daily year-round, are **The Box** (or Chicken Box; 6 Dave St., off Lower Orange St., tel. 508/228–9717) and **The Muse** (44 Atlantic Ave., tel. 508/228–6873 or 508/228–8801). All ages dance to rock, reggae, and other music, live or recorded, or enjoy the comedy nights.

The **Rose & Crown** (*see* Dining, above) is a friendly, noisy restaurant with a big bar and a small dance floor; the entertainment is a mix of live and deejay-spun rock and other music, plus comedy acts. *23 S. Water St., tel. 508/228–2595. Open mid-Apr.–Oct.*

Index

Personal Itinerary

Departure   *Date*

Time

Transportation

Arrival   *Date*   *Time*

Departure   *Date*   *Time*

Transportation

Accommodations

Arrival   *Date*   *Time*

Departure   *Date*   *Time*

Transportation

Accommodations

Arrival   *Date*   *Time*

Departure   *Date*   *Time*

Transportation

Accommodations

Personal Itinerary

Arrival *Date*   *Time*

Departure *Date*   *Time*

Transportation

Accommodations

Arrival *Date*   *Time*

Departure *Date*   *Time*

Transportation

Accommodations

Arrival *Date*   *Time*

Departure *Date*   *Time*

Transportation

Accommodations

Arrival *Date*   *Time*

Departure *Date*   *Time*

Transportation

Accommodations

Personal Itinerary

Arrival *Date*   *Time*

Departure *Date*   *Time*

Transportation

Accommodations

Arrival *Date*   *Time*

Departure *Date*   *Time*

Transportation

Accommodations

Arrival *Date*   *Time*

Departure *Date*   *Time*

Transportation

Accommodations

Arrival *Date*   *Time*

Departure *Date*   *Time*

Transportation

Accommodations

Addresses

Name	Name
Address	Address
Telephone	Telephone
Name	Name
Address	Address
Telephone	Telephone
Name	Name
Address	Address
Telephone	Telephone
Name	Name
Address	Address
Telephone	Telephone
Name	Name
Address	Address
Telephone	Telephone
Name	Name
Address	Address
Telephone	Telephone
Name	Name
Address	Address
Telephone	Telephone
Name	Name
Address	Address
Telephone	Telephone

Fodor's Travel Guides

U.S. Guides

Alaska
Arizona
Boston
California
Cape Cod
The Carolinas & the
  Georgia Coast
The Chesapeake
  Region
Chicago
Colorado
Disney World & the
  Orlando Area

Florida
Hawaii
Las Vegas
Los Angeles
Maui
Miami & the
  Keys
New England
New Mexico
New Orleans
New York City
New York City
  (Pocket Guide)

Pacific North Coast
Philadelphia & the
  Pennsylvania
  Dutch Country
Puerto Rico
  (Pocket Guide)
The Rockies
San Diego
San Francisco
San Francisco
  (Pocket Guide)
The South
Texas

USA
The Upper Great
  Lakes Region
Vacations in
  New York State
Vacations on the
  Jersey Shore
Virgin Islands
Virginia & Maryland
Waikiki
Washington, D.C.

Foreign Guides

Acapulco
Amsterdam
Australia
Austria
The Bahamas
The Bahamas
  (Pocket Guide)
Baja & the Pacific
  Coast Resorts
Barbados
Belgium &
  Luxembourg
Bermuda
Brazil
Budget Europe
Canada
Canada's Atlantic
  Provinces
Cancun, Cozumel,
  Yucatan Peninsula
Caribbean

Central America
China
Eastern Europe
Egypt
Europe
Europe's Great Cities
France
Germany
Great Britain
Greece
The Himalayan
  Countries
Holland
Hong Kong
India
Ireland
Israel
Italy
Italy 's Great Cities
Jamaica
Japan

Kenya, Tanzania,
  Seychelles
Korea
Lisbon
London
London Companion
London
  (Pocket Guide)
Madrid & Barcelona
Mexico
Mexico City
Montreal &
  Quebec City
Morocco
Munich
New Zealand
Paris
Paris (Pocket Guide)
Portugal
Rio de Janeiro
Rome

Saint Martin/
  Sint Maarten
Scandinavia
Scandinavian Cities
Scotland
Singapore
South America
South Pacific
Southeast Asia
Soviet Union
Spain
Sweden
Switzerland
Sydney
Thailand
Tokyo
Toronto
Turkey
Vienna & the
  Danube Valley
Yugoslavia

Wall Street Journal Guides to Business Travel

Europe   International Cities   The Pacific Rim   USA & Canada

Special-Interest Guides

Cruises and Ports
  of Call
Healthy Escapes

Fodor's Flashmaps
  New York
Fodor's Flashmaps
  Washington, D.C.

Shopping in Europe
Skiing in North
  America

Smart Shopper's
  Guide to London
Sunday in New York
Touring Europe